The Essentials of Teaching Children to Read

What Every Teacher Needs to Know

D. Ray Reutzel
Utah State University

Robert B. Cooter, Jr.
The University of Memphis

PEARSON

Merrill
Prentice Hall

Upper Saddle River, New Jersey
Columbus, Ohio

Library of Congress Cataloging in Publication Data

Reutzel, D. Ray (Douglas Ray)
   The essentials of teaching children to read : what every teacher needs to know / D. Ray
Reutzel, Robert B. Cooter, Jr.
    p. cm.
   Abridged version of: Teaching children to read. 4th ed. c2004.
   Includes bibliographical references and index.
   ISBN 0-13-118665-5
    1. Reading (Elementary) 2. Reading (Elementary)—Language experiences approach 3.
Language arts (Elementary) I. Cooter, Robert B. II. Reutzel, D. Ray (Douglas Ray),
1953- Teaching children to read. III. Title

LB1573.R48 2005
372.4—dc22

2004044622

Vice President and Executive Publisher: Jeffery W. Johnston
Editor: Linda Ashe Montgomery
Editorial Assistant: Laura Weaver
Development Editor: Dawne Brooks
Production Editor: Mary M. Irvin
Production Coordination: Lea Baranowski, Carlisle Publishers Services
Design Coordinator: Diane C. Lorenzo
Cover Designer: Ali Mohrman
Cover Images: Susan Sturgill
Production Manager: Pamela D. Bennett
Director of Marketing: Ann Castel Davis
Marketing Manager: Darcy Betts Prybella
Marketing Coordinator: Tyra Poole

Photo Credits: Scott Cunningham/Merrill, pp. 9, 24, 54, 77, 89; KS Studios/Merrill, p. 18; Anthony Magnacca/Merrill, p. 43; provided by D. Ray Reutzel, p. 113; Todd Yarrington/Merrill, p. 5.

This book was set in Souvenir by Carlisle Communications, Ltd. It was printed and bound by Courier Kendallville, Inc. The cover was printed by Coral Graphic Services, Inc.

Pearson Education Ltd.
Pearson Education Singapore Pte. Ltd.
Pearson Education Canada, Ltd.
Pearson Education—Japan

Pearson Education Australia Pty. Limited
Pearson Education North Asia Ltd.
Pearson Educación de Mexico, S.A. de C.V.
Pearson Education Malaysia Pte. Ltd.

10 9 8 7 6 5 4 3 2 1
ISBN: 0-13-118665-5

About the Authors

D. Ray Reutzel

Utah State University

D. Ray Reutzel is the Emma Eccles Jones Endowed Chair and Distinguished Professor of Early Childhood Education and Director of the *Emma Eccles Jones Center for Early Childhood Education* at Utah State University. He works regularly with teachers and children in local public schools and in the Edith Bowen Laboratory School on the Utah State University campus. He is a former provost and vice president for academic affairs at Southern Utah University, associate dean of teacher education in the David O. McKay School of Education, and former chair of the Department of Elementary Education at Brigham Young University. While at BYU, he was the recipient of the 1992 Karl G. Maeser Distinguished Research Professor Award. Several years ago, he took a leave from his university faculty position to return to full-time, first-grade classroom teaching in Sage Creek Elementary School to pilot *comprehensive balanced reading* practices. He has taught kindergarten and the first, third, and sixth grade.

Dr. Reutzel is the author of more than 130 articles, books, book chapters, and monographs. He has published in *Reading Research Quarterly, Journal of Reading Behavior, Journal of Literacy Research, Journal of Educational Research, Reading Psychology, Reading and Writing Quarterly, Reading Research and Instruction, Language Arts, Journal of Reading, The Reading Teacher,* and *Instructor,* among others. He is the past editor of *Reading Research and Instruction* and coauthor of the best-selling college textbook *Teaching Children to Read: Putting the Pieces Together* (4th ed.) and *Strategies for Reading Assessment and Instruction: Helping Every Child Succeed* (2003), published by Merrill/Prentice Hall. He is or has been a reviewer for the *Reading Teacher, Reading Research Quarterly, Reading Psychology,* and *Reading Research and Instruction* and a past reviewer for *Journal of Reading Behavior, Journal of Literacy Research,* and *Elementary School Journal.* He is also an author of Scholastic Incorporated's Literacy Place 1996 and 2000 School Reading Program. He received the **A.B. Herr Award for Outstanding Research and Published Contributions to Reading Education** from the College Reading Association in 1999. He was recently appointed with his colleague, Judith P. Mitchell, editor of the International Reading Association's elementary section journal *The Reading Teacher.*

Robert B. Cooter, Jr.

The University of Memphis

Dr. Robert Cooter is Professor of Reading & Urban Literacy Education and Chair of the Department of Instruction and Curriculum Leadership at The University of Memphis. His primary research focus is urban literacy issues in grades PK–12. Dr. Cooter has taught grades 1, 3, 4, 7, 11, and 12 in the public schools and has also served as a Title I reading specialist.

Professor Cooter formerly served as the first "Reading Czar" (or Associate Superintendent for Reading/Language Arts) for the Dallas Independent School District (TX). He engineered the district's highly acclaimed *Dallas Reading Plan,* a collaborative project supported by Dallas area business and community enterprises involving the training of approximately 3,000 teachers in "comprehensive literacy instruction." In March of 1998, Dr. Cooter was recognized as a "Texas State Champion for Reading" by then-Governor George W. Bush and Texas First Lady Laura Bush as a result of the many successes of the Dallas Reading Plan initiative.

In addition to coauthoring the best-selling text *Teaching Children to Read: Putting the Pieces Together* with D. Ray Reutzel, currently used at over 200 universities to prepare elementary teachers, Cooter has also authored or coauthored six other professional books. These include *The Flynt/Cooter Reading Inventory for the Classroom* (Merrill/Prentice-Hall, 2004), *Strategies for Reading Assessment and Instruction: Helping Every Child Succeed* (Merrill/Prentice-Hall, 2003), and *The Flynt/Cooter English-Español Reading Inventory* (Merrill/Prentice-Hall, 1999). Cooter recently served as contributing editor to *Perspectives on Rescuing Urban Literacy Education: Spies, Saboteurs, & Saints* (Lawrence Erlbaum Associates, 2004).

Professor Cooter is currently working on a new book tentatively titled *Urban Literacy Instruction: Helping City Kids Succeed as Readers* (Merrill/Prentice Hall). He has published well over 50 articles on reading research and instruction in such journals as *The Reading Teacher, Journal of Reading, Language Arts*, and the *Journal of Educational Research*. He currently contributes a regular column on Urban Literacy Issues for *The Reading Teacher*, a professional journal of the International Reading Association.

A native of Nashville, Tennessee, Dr. Cooter now lives in Memphis with his wife, Dr. Kathleen Spencer Cooter, a popular education consultant and Special Education professor at The University of Memphis. He enjoys vacationing with his wife on their houseboat, christened *Our Last Child*; performing Southern folktales for children of all ages; listening to good blues; and dining on catfish and cheese grits. Bob is the proud father of five children and three stepchildren, has nine grandchildren (so far), and is owned by a hound dog of unknown breed and questionable utility.

Preface

The Essentials of Teaching Children to Read is a concise, yet comprehensive, compilation of the best documented scientifically based reading research (SBRR) on the five key areas of reading development: phonological and phonemic awareness, phonics instruction, reading comprehension, reading fluency, and vocabulary development. This book is primarily designed to be a tool for practicing teachers and a resource for improving daily reading instruction. In these pages, the reader will discover the essentials of proven classroom strategies backed up in large measure by direct experience and research conducted by the authors themselves in classrooms around the country—urban, rural, and suburban. In other words, we have walked in the shoes of reading teachers.

HOW IS *THE ESSENTIALS OF TEACHING CHILDREN TO READ* ORGANIZED?

Teachers accustomed to lengthy texts on reading instruction in college courses will be pleasantly surprised. *The Essentials of Teaching Children to Read* is a "lite" text designed for real-world teachers dealing with the demands of real-world classrooms. At every turn, we have constructed a book that respects your time by providing only the critical information for improving reading instruction and nothing more. We begin with the fundamentals of organizing our thinking about comprehensive reading instruction, followed by specifics on scientifically based reading research (SBRR) in the five critical areas of reading instruction, then show you how to organize for instruction. We also include summaries along the way on national standards in reading instruction as described by the most influential organizations across America so that we are all "speaking the same language." The following is a brief description of the chapters contained in *The Essentials of Teaching Children to Read*.

- **Introduction: A Nation Refocusing Its Attention on Reading—** The book begins with an introductory narrative describing the current scene in America and the need for a comprehensive approach to reading instruction. We summarize the rationale and need for the No Child Left Behind Act of 2001 and the Reading First legislation that made progress possible. We argue for, among other things, scientifically-based instructional approaches based on clear data from the classroom as well as consistency and high quality in delivery so that no child is left behind. In sum, we believe in insuring that every classroom should be as good as our best.
- **Chapter 1: *Theoretical Roots of Reading Instruction*—**We believe that there is nothing so practical as a good theory. Here we "cut to the chase" on theories of how children learn to read and the implications for teachers, support personnel and, yes, families. This chapter helps you to become grounded in the essential principles of learning and how they relate to daily decision making about the "just right" strategies for your students.
- **Chapter 2: *Phonemic Awareness and Phonics Instruction*—** With Chapter 2, we begin a careful study of the "Big Five" in reading instruction

with a summary of scientifically based reading research (SBRR) in two key areas that lead to automaticity in decoding. This chapter begins with a look at research on early reading development and the seminal work titled *The Report of the National Reading Panel* as well as other key research findings. This is must-know information for all reading teachers. Next comes a presentation of the scope and sequence of benchmark skills to be learned in phonemic awareness, the alphabetic principle, and phonics. As with all later chapters, we equip the reader with "nuts and bolts" explanations of research-proven strategies to teach each and every benchmark skill on the pathway to literacy.

- **Chapter 3: *Increasing Vocabulary and Word Knowledge***— Reading is a language-sharing activity that is heavily dependent on vocabulary knowledge. A child can become quite accomplished at decoding words using phonics and other strategies; however, if the words she translates to language are not meaningfully *known* then true reading cannot occur. In this chapter, we first discuss what research tells us about how vocabulary is learned through language interactions, the types of vocabulary we acquire, the words we should teach, and the basic principles of effective language instruction. As you might suppose at this point, we close the chapter with the most effective strategies for teaching vocabulary in your classroom, including ways we meet the needs of English Language Learners (ELL).

- **Chapter 4: *Improving Reading Comprehension***—Comprehension is the essence of reading. Understanding the author's message is our goal, yet many of our students struggle with higher-order comprehension as they move into the upper elementary grades and beyond. Using SBRR as our springboard, we move quickly into relevant theory and an analysis of common comprehension difficulties. Next, we summarize an extremely practical model called the *gradual release of responsibility* for coaching students into higher levels of comprehension and conclude with a large number of strategies to assist your students in becoming accomplished "comprehenders."

- **Chapter 5: *Developing Reading Fluency***—Many students learn to read fairly well in the early grades but sometimes struggle with fluency (the ability to read text smoothly and at a reasonable rate). In this chapter, we combine research and practice by introducing a comprehensive approach refined as part of the Dallas Reading Plan initiative in Texas known as *The Fluency Formula*.

- **Chapter 6: *Materials and Programs for Literacy Instruction: Basals and Beyond***—Basal reading programs have been a staple of reading instruction for many decades. In this chapter, we describe the common components of basal programs and their strengths and limitations. We also probe further by discussing commercial reading programs and their significance on the national stage. We also discuss ways commercial programs assist teachers with students who have special needs and ways to help teachers work effectively with students whose first language is not English.

- **Chapter 7: *Assessing Literacy Learning***—It is critical that teachers hone their skills—quickly and efficiently—in assessing the reading development of all students in their classrooms. This information helps teachers plan appropriate instruction, monitor student progress, and report student learning to families and stakeholders. In this chapter on comprehensive reading assessment, we present seven key principles governing classroom reading assessment and how to get started. Next, we propose ways of assessing each of the five areas of reading development. Then, to help you form small groups for instruction based on common student needs, we share ways of profiling each student's reading development as well as methods for forming dynamic instructional clusters. Finally, consistent with the Reading First legislation, we discuss four purposes of reading assessment and commercial tools available for carrying them out. These include *Screening Assessments*, *Outcome Assessments* (e.g., Dynamic Indicators of Basic Early Literacy Skills or *DIBELS*, Texas Primary Reading Inventory), *Diagnostic Assessments* (e.g., Peabody Picture Vocabulary Test, Woodcock Reading Mastery Tests), and *Progress-Monitoring Assessments*.

- **Appendices**—Last but not least, we include in the Appendices additional tools to help you plan scientifically based reading instruction. These include *Standards for the English Language Arts* published jointly by the National Council for Teachers of English and the International Reading Association, Internet links to the various *State Standards* from around the nation, and a complete References section to help you in delving further into areas of interest.

DISCOVER THE COMPANION WEBSITE ACCOMPANYING THIS BOOK

The Prentice Hall Companion Website: A Virtual Learning Environment

Technology is a constantly growing and changing aspect of our field that is creating a need for content and resources. To address this emerging need, Prentice Hall has developed an online learning environment for students and professors alike—Companion Websites—to support our textbooks.

In creating a Companion Website, our goal is to build on and enhance what the textbook already offers. For this reason, the content for each user-friendly website is organized by chapter and provides the professor and student with a variety of meaningful resources.

For the Professor

Every Companion Website integrates **Syllabus Manager™**, an online syllabus creation and management utility.

- **Syllabus Manager™** provides you, the instructor, with an easy, step-by-step process to create and revise syllabi, with direct links into Companion Website and other online content without having to learn HTML.
- Students may logon to your syllabus during any study session. All they need to know is the web address for the Companion Website and the password you've assigned to your syllabus.
- After you have created a syllabus using **Syllabus Manager™**, students may enter the syllabus for their course section from any point in the Companion Website.
- Clicking on a date, the student is shown the list of activities for the assignment. The activities for each assignment are linked directly to actual content, saving time for students.
- Adding assignments consists of clicking on the desired due date, then filling in the details of the assignment—name of the assignment, instructions, and whether or not it is a one-time or repeating assignment.

- In addition, links to other activities can be created easily. If the activity is online, a URL can be entered in the space provided, and it will be linked automatically in the final syllabus.
- Your completed syllabus is hosted on our servers, allowing convenient updates from any computer on the Internet. Changes you make to your syllabus are immediately available to your students at their next logon.

Common Companion Website features for students include:

For the Student

- **Chapter Objectives**—Outline key concepts from the text.
- **Interactive Self-quizzes**—Complete with hints and automatic grading that provide immediate feedback for students.

    After students submit their answers for the interactive self-quizzes, the Companion Website **Results Reporter** computes a percentage grade, provides a graphic representation of how many questions were answered correctly and incorrectly, and gives a question-by-question analysis of the quiz. Students are given the option to send their quiz to up to four email addresses (professor, teaching assistant, study partner, etc.).
- **Web Destinations**—Links to www sites that relate to chapter content.
- **Message Board**—Virtual bulletin board to post or respond to questions or comments from a national audience.

To take advantage of the many available resources, please visit *The Essentials of Teaching Children to Read* Companion Website at

www.prenhall.com/reutzel

ACKNOWLEDGMENTS

Special thanks to our wives and children. And to the many teachers, administrators, and colleagues who have contributed so selflessly to our work and to children throughout the nation.

Thank you for choosing *The Essentials of Teaching Children to Read* as a new addition to your professional library. Please feel free to contact us if we may be of further assistance!

D. Ray Reutzel
Utah State University
E-mail: rreutzel@coe.usu.edu

Robert B. Cooter, Jr.
The University of Memphis
E-mail: rcooter@memphis.edu

EDUCATOR LEARNING CENTER: AN INVALUABLE ONLINE RESOURCE

Merrill Education and the Association for Supervision and Curriculum Development (ASCD) invite you to take advantage of a new on-line resource, one that provides access to the top research and proven strategies associated with ASCD and Merrill—the Educator Learning Center. At www.EducatorLearningCenter.com you will find resources that will enhance your students' understanding of course topics and of current educational issues, in addition to being invaluable for further research.

HOW THE EDUCATOR LEARNING CENTER WILL HELP YOUR STUDENTS BECOME BETTER TEACHERS

With the combined resources of Merrill Education and ASCD, you and your students will find a wealth of tools and materials to better prepare them for the classroom.

Research

- More than 600 articles from the ASCD journal *Educational Leadership* discuss everyday issues faced by practicing teachers.
- A direct link on the site to Research Navigator™ gives students access to many of the leading education journals as well as extensive content detailing the research process.
- Excerpts from Merrill Education texts give your students insights on important topics of instructional methods, diverse populations, assessment, classroom management, technology, and refining classroom practice.

Classroom Practice

- Hundreds of lesson plans and teaching strategies are categorized by content area and age range.
- Case studies and classroom video footage provide virtual field experience for student reflection.
- Computer simulations and other electronic tools keep your students abreast of today's classrooms and current technologies.

LOOK INTO THE VALUE OF EDUCATOR LEARNING CENTER YOURSELF

A four-month subscription to Educator Learning Center is $25 but is FREE when used in conjunction with this text. To obtain free pass codes for your students, simply contact your Merrill/Prentice Hall sales representative, and your representative will give you a special ISBN to give to your bookstore when ordering your textbooks. To preview the value of this website to you and your students, please go to www. EducatorLearningCenter.com and click on "Demo."

Brief Contents

Contents

Chapter 3   Increasing Vocabulary and Word Knowledge   60

Chapter 4   Improving Reading Comprehension   94

Chapter 5   Developing Reading Fluency   136

Chapter 6   Materials and Programs for Literacy Instruction: Basals and Beyond   160

Chapter 7   Assessing Literacy Learning   202

Introduction

A Nation Refocusing Its Attention on Reading

READING IN SOCIETY

Concern over the widening achievement gap for America's schoolchildren has resulted in an unprecedented national focus on research-based methods to improve reading instruction (National Assessment of Educational Progress [NAEP], 2000; Neuman, 2001; Rayner, Foorman, Perfetti, Pesetsky, & Seidenberg, 2001, 2002). At no time since the 1950s, when it was said that "*Johnny can't read*" (Flesch, 1955), has so much political attention and funding been focused nationally on reading research, teacher development, and reading instructional practices.

Literacy demands on our society have increased exponentially as we progressed from the Industrial Age to the Information Age (Bronfenbrenner, McClelland, Wethington, Moen, & Ceci, 1996). The U.S. Bureau of Labor, in a report issued to the nation's governors, indicated that 85% of employment in the twenty-first century would require skilled or professional levels of training—all of which require the ability to read and read well (U.S. Bureau of Labor, 1995).

Despite the increasing needs for a literate workforce, American students have made no discernable progress in reading achievement. In fact, the National Assessment of Educational Progress (NAEP) (U.S. Department of Education; 2000) has registered no appreciable gains in fourth-grade reading achievement in decades. To make matters worse, reading achievement has continued to decline drastically for children of poverty in both urban and rural areas (Cooter, 2004; NAEP, 2000). In his presidential initiative called "America's Reading Challenge" (U.S. Department of Education, 1997), former President Clinton declared,

> Forty percent of all children are now reading below basic levels on national reading assessments. Children who cannot read early and well are hampered at the very start of their lives. This will be truer as we move into the twenty-first century. To participate in America's high-skill workplaces, to cruise—much less use—the Internet, all children need to read better than ever before.

The High Price of Reading Failure

The cost of reading failure to our society and to individuals is very high. For many years, researchers have found a high correlation between poor early reading and later failure in school (Juel, 1988; Torgesen, Wagner, Rashotte, Alexander, & Conroy, 1997). Evidence is also mounting that reading achievement is strongly linked to adolescent/young adult substance abuse as well as criminal behavior (National Institute of Child Health and Human Development, 2000b). Further, there is a clear link between poor reading performance in early elementary years and later incarceration (Downing, 1990; Newman, 1996; Pray, 1983). Cooter and Cooter (2004) summed up the problem thus:

> In many city centers fewer than half of third grade children can read on grade level. The reading problem seems to cascade downhill after that into a rather bleak abyss littered with the relics of high dropout rates and limited life options. While one cannot generalize about causal factors for such diverse populations, poor reading development seems to be the traveling companion of poverty, inadequate language development, high mobility of students, and inadequate teacher preparation. (p. 41)

Now as never before, teachers need to understand how children can be taught to read successfully. Fortunately, the reading crisis is being addressed through landmark federal legislation.

Mobilizing a Nation: Reading First and the No Child Left Behind Act of 2001

On January 23, 2001, President George W. Bush made education his number one domestic priority (U.S. Department of Education, 2000; p. 1) when he sent his No Child Left Behind plan for comprehensive education reform to Congress. The president expressed concern that "too many of our neediest children are being left behind," despite nearly $200 billion being spent since the passage of the Elementary and Secondary Education Act of 1965 (ESEA).

Following the events of September 11, 2001, President Bush and a bipartisan coalition in Congress succeeded in the passage of the **No Child Left Behind Act of 2001** (NCLB Act), also known as House Resolution (H.R. 1.) Intended to close the achievement gap between disadvantaged and minority students and their peers, H.R. 1 has four key provisions: stronger accountability for positive results, expanded flexibility and local control, wide-ranging options for parents, and an emphasis on teaching methods that have been proven to work. It is the fourth element, *focusing on teaching methods that have been proven to work*, that is the focus of this book.

Improving Teacher Expertise: Reading First Grants

H.R. 1 asks the states to ensure that there is a *highly qualified teacher* in every public school classroom by 2005 (U.S. Department of Education, 2004). Highly qualified teachers, according to the law, hold at least a bachelor's degree and state teacher certification and have passed a rigorous state test on subject knowledge and teaching skills.

Under the provisions for **Reading First** grants, the funding segment of the legislation, states now receive funding to assist in teacher development for a 6-year period. Targeted assistance grants are awarded based on evidence of significant increases in the percentage of grade 3 students reading at the proficient level and for the improved reading skills of students in grades 1 to 3.

Adequate Yearly Progress

States receiving grants under H.R. 1 are expected to develop annual **adequate yearly progress** objectives. Data are analyzed by student groups based on poverty levels, race and ethnicity, disability, and limited-English-proficiency populations. The national goal is for *all* students to achieve proficiency in reading and mathematics within 12 years. A benchmarking system based on the biennial participation of states in their versions of the National Assessment of Educational Progress will be used to ensure the rigor of state-level performance objectives over time.

The "Big Five" Focus Areas of Reading First

In 1997, a landmark review of scientifically based reading research was begun under the auspices of the U.S. Congress. The National Institute of Child Health and Human Development, in consultation with the secretary of education, was asked to convene a panel to assess the status of research-based knowledge on the various approaches to teaching children to read. The National Reading Panel, comprised of leading reading researchers, representatives from higher education, reading teachers, educational administrators, and parents, was assembled and, in April 2000, issued their findings.

Five important areas of reading acquisition were identified by the National Reading Panel (2000) as having substantial scientific research about which they could report findings. The **"big five,"** as we like to refer to them, are the instructional areas of *phonemic awareness, phonics, fluency, vocabulary,* and *comprehension.* Up to 20% of Reading First funding may be used to train teachers in these areas. These five areas, drawn from the National Reading Panel Report (2000), are the main focal points for this book and may be described as follows:

- **Phonemic awareness.** Phonemic awareness refers to the understanding that *spoken* words are made up of individual speech sounds (Burns, Griffin, & Snow, 1999; Pikulski & Templeton, 1997). For example, *no* and *she* each have two speech sounds, or **phonemes.**
- **Phonics.** This involves instruction that emphasizes how spellings are related to speech sounds in systematic and predictable ways (Burns et al., 1999; Reutzel & Cooter, 2003). Research confirms that systematic and explicit phonics instruction is more effective than nonsystematic instruction or programs that ignore phonics (National Reading Panel, 2000).
- **Fluency.** Reading fluency involves the ability to read text smoothly and at a reasonable rate and is the "bridge" between word recognition and comprehension (Rasinski & Padak, 2004). Typically, fluent readers demonstrate (a) accuracy of decoding, or *automaticity;* (b) appropriate use of pitch, juncture, and stress (*prosodic features*) in one's voice; and (c) an acceptable reading speed, or *rate.* Fluency is a necessary and important part of successful reading instruction (Kuhn & Stahl, 2000).
- **Vocabulary.** There are essentially four types of vocabulary: listening, speaking, reading, and writing (Reutzel & Cooter, 2004). When students encounter a word in print and can decode it, if it is in their listening and speaking vocabularies, then they can understand the author's meaning. Thus, having a strong vocabulary is essential to reading success (National Reading Panel, 2000).
- **Comprehension.** Understanding the author's message is the essence of reading. Comprehension is purposeful and active and is enhanced by instruction (Armbruster, Lehr, & Osborn, 2001). Comprehending text is critical in academic and lifelong learning. Many of our students struggle with all but the most basic types of comprehension, thus necessitating a redoubling of our efforts in this important area of reading instruction using research-proven practices.

COMPREHENSIVE READING INSTRUCTION IS A RESEARCH-BASED SOLUTION

Scientific research is the foundation of successful reading instruction. It informs our choices as teachers and helps ensure that all children receive instruction based on evidence rather than intuition alone. We advocate a form of research-based teaching known as comprehensive reading instruction.

Comprehensive reading programs provide a framework for teaching students skills in reading and writing based on their individual needs and within the context of appropriately leveled reading materials of interest to the learner. Comprehensive reading programs often use basal readers, "decodable text," and other, more traditional programmed reading materials; but they also include daily encounters with fiction and nonfiction trade books. In comprehensive reading classrooms, one typically sees oral reading by teachers and children alike, direct skill instruction and practice in guided oral reading (Fountas & Pinnell, 1996; National Reading Panel, 2000), and "process" writing and spelling instruction.

The Politics of Comprehensive Reading Instruction

Comprehensive reading instruction has taken root in many states and gained prominence as a political issue. During the 1998 Texas gubernatorial campaign, for instance, comprehensive reading instruction was a major plank in the election platform of then-Governor George W. Bush. The same was so in recent elections in many other states, including California. On the national proscenium, U.S. Secretary of Education Rod Paige pushed to the forefront initiatives that support comprehensive reading programs involving "scripted" materials (i.e, those that literally tell teachers word for word what should be said during instruction). *We advocate comprehensive reading programs that go well beyond the scripting of instruction and call for the unfettered influence of highly educated and skilled teachers in the reading classroom.*

Becoming a highly skilled and successful reading teacher happens gradually over time. Professional development is a transitioning process, one that takes years, not months. The transition begins by understanding the research behind quality reading instruction.

"EVERY CLASSROOM AS GOOD AS OUR BEST": THE KEY TO IMPROVING READING INSTRUCTION

Commercial Reading Programs Are Necessary But Not Sufficient

Reading rescue efforts of the past have failed largely for two reasons (Cooter, 2003): an overreliance on commercial reading programs as the *only* solution to reading woes and anemic efforts at teacher development or *capacity building*. To attack reading problems quickly and economically, some school district leaders purchase commercial reading programs—a predictable response that has some merit.

Commercial, research-based reading programs can be very useful in helping new or inexperienced teachers provide consistent instruction. They can also help school districts stabilize instruction for highly mobile students and provide systemwide consistency in delivering good reading instruction. However, even though they play an important and necessary role in reading instruction, they are not sufficient in meeting the needs of all students. *Many average and below-average students fail to respond to commercial programs and need alternative learning strategies delivered by a well-trained teacher.*

Teacher Capacity Building: You Win on Talent!

The most effective way to ensure that solid reading instruction is available to all students is through **teacher capacity building** (Cooter, 2003). Teachers, as with professionals in business, medicine, and the sciences, require high-quality, ongoing professional development to remain on the cutting edge of effectiveness. As Baskin (2004) remarked, "You win on talent!" meaning that all school districts must invest in their *talent*—teachers. Without this essential piece of the reading rescue puzzle, school districts cannot hope to break through the performance glass ceiling they experience.

Research on the Benefits of Teacher Capacity Building

Improving the quality of teachers in the classroom "does more to assist students who are educationally at-risk than any other policy-controllable issue" (Denson, 2001, p. 34), including smaller pupil-to-teacher ratios or adopted materials (Darling-Hammond, 1999). *Teacher capacity building* has been found to be the most productive investment for schools and far exceeds the results of teacher experience or class size (Greenwald, Hedges, & Laine, 1996).

Plecki (2000) examined ways researchers have used productivity and human capital theory to measure return on investments in teacher capacity building. Educational productivity analysis is sometimes used by school districts searching for professional development interventions that are cost effective (Denson, 2001). What have research studies using educational productivity analysis revealed concerning the benefits of teacher capacity building?

Effects of Teacher Training on Student Achievement

We find strong research evidence of the positive impact of teacher capacity building on student achievement. For example, in 1992 and 1996, Connecticut students registered huge gains in reading and mathematics on the National Assessment of Educational Progress. State officials credited the development of 4-week institutes with follow-up coaching for teachers at all grade levels as being the primary factor (Darling-Hammond, 1999). Newman (2001) found that teachers who were offered high-quality professional development followed through in using more interactive teaching methods, leading to higher achievement gains on the *Iowa Test of Basic Skills*. Similarly, in a comparative analysis of highly successful schools with lower-achieving schools, researchers (Mosenthal, Lipson, Mekkelsen, Russ, & Sortino, 2001) found that the lower-achieving schools had limited professional development and lacked common vision.

Complex problems often require complex solutions. While it is not difficult to conclude after reviewing evidence-based research that high-quality teacher capacity building helps children become better readers, obtaining consistent results over time is neither quick nor simple.

The Essentials of Teaching Children to Read: What Every Teacher Needs to Know

The Essentials of Teaching Children to Read: What Every Teacher Needs to Know is a handbook containing the very best research-proven practices for teachers of reading at all levels. We intend it to be used primarily in high-quality teacher development (i.e., capacity-building) programs whose intent is to realize the goals set forth in the No Child Left Behind legislation, but it is also appropriate for teachers interested in deepening their knowledge and expertise independently or with a group of colleagues.

As noted earlier, this book focuses on teaching and assessment practices related to the "big five" areas identified for Reading First projects: phonemic awareness, phonics, fluency, vocabulary, and comprehension.

The first chapter provides fundamental information on the theories that lie at the very root of successful reading instruction. This will help you select methods and materials for teaching reading with confidence and integrity.

Theoretical Roots of Reading Instruction

Focus Questions

When you are finished studying this chapter, you should be able to answer these questions:

1. What can be said about the need for reading in our society today and in the future?

2. Why do teachers need to study and understand the reading process?

3. How do theories of the reading process relate to instructional practices?

4. Which of the instructional practices for teaching reading do you believe are most effective and why?

5. What is comprehensive reading instruction?

Key Concepts

Bottom-Up Reading
  Theories
Automaticity
Subskills Reading
  Instruction
Top-Down Reading
  Theories
Whole-Word Method
Sight-Word Approach
Interactive Reading
  Theories

Skills-Based Reading
  Instruction
Transactional Reading
  Theories
Efferent Stance
Aesthetic Stance
Comprehensive Literacy
  Instruction

Fundamental knowledge for every teacher of literacy includes understanding theories of the reading process and the variety of instructional models that spring from these theories. Throughout the history of reading instruction, a debate has and continues to rage around (a) whether reading instruction should focus on helping learners recode symbols into sounds and put sounds together to make words or b) whether reading instruction should focus on helping learners extract or construct meaning from the print as a primary emphasis of instruction. New and experienced teachers are less likely to be persuaded to believe that extreme positions on either side of the reading debate are realistic when contextualized in the elementary classroom. In this chapter, we describe the nature of the debates around reading instruction and the need for understanding theory and reading instructional models.

Children learn to read from many people, but most children learn to read from teachers who know and use effective reading instructional practices in classrooms.

Visit Chapter 1 of our Companion Website at www.prenhall.com/reutzel to look into the chapter objectives, standards and principles, and pertinent Web links associated with theoretical roots of reading instruction.

Standards Note
Standard 2.11: The reading professional will know relevant reading research from general education and how it has influenced literacy education. As you read this chapter, record in a personal study notebook how each reading theory connects to research on how to teach young children to read and write.

THE NEED FOR UNDERSTANDING HOW CHILDREN LEARN TO READ

On several occasions, we have been asked by exasperated teachers just what we would do if we had to teach 30 youngsters to read. As former classroom teachers, our responses to such a question usually lead to a discussion of the role and importance of teachers, teacher knowledge, and teacher skills. Recently, the National Education Association's Task Force on Reading 2000 report declared, "It is not the method that makes the difference, it is the teacher!" (2000, p. 7). Teacher knowledge and competence form the foundation for effective reading instruction. Teachers of young children must come to know and understand (1) reading theories, (2) best practices in reading instruction, (3) the structure and elements of language, and (4) how children develop into successful readers and writers.

Young children learn to read from people who know and use effective instructional practices. Despite what many publishers claim, the overwhelming evidence shows that teachers make the difference in children's reading achievement, not published and/or purchased reading programs! Evidence has been mounting for years that adopting a new published reading program is not the answer to the problems of providing effective reading instruction. In fact, published reading programs typically have very limited effects on students' reading achievement. In the 1985 *Becoming a Nation of Readers Report,* it was concluded that adopting a new core reading program influences students' reading achievement scores by only 3%, whereas the competence of the teacher influences student reading achievement scores by 15%—five times more than programs.

To clarify the contrast between knowledgeable teachers and reliance on published reading programs, we turn to a metaphor about carpenters and their tools. It is a well-accepted fact that a skilled, master carpenter can produce excellent quality work with access to only marginally adequate hand tools. Admittedly, access to better tools makes such carpenters more efficient as well as effective. However, an unskilled, novice carpenter is likewise incapable of turning out quality craftsmanship even when he or she has access to the finest and newest power tools and technology. In the end, it is the knowledge and skill of the carpenter that makes the difference in the quality of the product, not the tools. So it is with teaching children to read. It is the touch of the master teacher's hand that makes the real difference—not the program.

You may recall a television commercial advertising a specific brand of picante sauce in which the cowpokes seated around the campfire requested a new bottle of picante sauce from the cook. They were disappointed when it was not their usual brand and remarked disparagingly, "This stuff's made in New York City!" Well, a similar response is often heard about published reading programs—this program is made in New York City. Reading programs developed in New York City cannot appropriately anticipate the needs of students and teachers in the far reaches of Mississippi, Montana, or Minnesota. Although many published programs promise success for all children, they typically deliver success only for some without the thoughtful use and adaptation of a competent classroom teacher.

Knowledgeable teachers produce excellent results regardless of the programs found in the classroom. On the other hand, we recognize that the best of all possible worlds puts a highly knowledgeable and skilled teacher with a rich array of reading materials, programs, and resources in every classroom so that all children can enjoy optimal conditions for learning to read.

THEORIES OF THE READING PROCESS

Unfortunately, the mere mention of the word *theory* causes some teachers to go into near apoplexy, dismissing complex explanations of the reading process as *impractical*. In defense of the practicality of reading theories, Moffett and Wagner (1976) asserted that nothing is so practical as a good theory. All teachers have in-the-head theories to guide their reading instructional decisions (DeFord, 1985; Gove, 1983). On the other hand, we have also found that few teachers can clearly or explicitly articulate the theories from which they make decisions about reading instruction.

Theories of the reading process offer explanations about how children become proficient readers. By definition, a theory is "a system of ideas, often stated as a principle, to explain or to lead to a new understanding" (Harris & Hodges, 1981, p. 329). The reading process is defined as "what happens when a person processes text to obtain meaning" (Harris & Hodges, 1995, p. 212). Thus, theories of the reading process offer, through the articulation of a system of ideas, new understandings about what happens when a person processes text to obtain meaning.

Reading theories are alternative explanations of the complex process of learning to read. Theories are neither proven nor unproven. They are neither true nor false. They are neither right nor wrong. They can be viewed, however, as more or less complete. This means that some reading theories do a better job of explaining the complex nature of the reading process than do others. Also, theories of the reading process have led researchers and teachers to propose a variety of successful instructional practices for helping children develop into successful, flexible, and strategic readers.

Before leaving this section, stop and list two reasons why knowing reading theories will help you know how to help children learn to read more effectively. This can

Standards Note
Standard 1.5: The reading professional will perceive reading as the process of constructing meaning through the interaction of the reader's existing knowledge, the information suggested by the written language, and the context of the reading situation. As you read this chapter, notice how each of the four reading theories and the accompanying reading instructional approaches address the issues of constructing meaning, readers' prior knowledge, and the context of the reading situation in how young children learn to read and write.

Focus on several ways theory can be practical.

Developing a belief system about how students learn to read and write begins with putting theories into practice.

List two reasons why knowing reading theories helps teachers know how to help children more effectively.

help you establish a purpose for learning about the upcoming four types of reading theories and the instructional practices developed by teachers and researchers in response to these reading theories.

In the sections that follow, we describe four reading theories: (a) bottom-up, (b) top-down, (c) interactive, and (d) transactional. We show how these theories have influenced the production of curriculum materials and reading programs and influence teachers' choices about effective teaching practices. We believe by making the link between *theory* and *practice* more explicit, we can help all teachers, novice and expert alike, come to realize that all reading instructional choices are derived from personally held *theories* about the reading process. We also believe that in making these connections explicit, teachers can discover that no single theory of the reading process in and of itself provides a complete explanation. Teachers who know how theory and practice relate are better able to see and understand connections between various explanations of the process of learning to read and the multitude of potential instructional choices for teaching children to read.

Bottom-Up Theories of the Reading Process

Notice some weaknesses associated with two of the earliest models representing the bottom-up theoretical position.

Bottom-up theories hypothesize that learning to read progresses from children learning the *parts* of language (letters) to understanding *whole* text (meaning). Much like solving a jigsaw puzzle, bottom-up models of the reading process say that the reading puzzle is solved by beginning with an examination of each piece of the puzzle and then putting pieces together to make a picture. Two bottom-up theories of the reading process remain popular even today: *One Second of Reading* by Gough (1972) and *A Theory of Automatic Information Processing* by LaBerge and Samuels (1974).

Gough's (1972) *One Second of Reading* model described reading as a sequential or *serial* mental process. Readers, according to Gough, begin by translating the parts of written language (letters) into speech sounds, then piece the sounds together to form individual words, then piece the words together to arrive at an understanding of the author's written message.

Bottom-up reading theories *suggest that children learn to read by learning the parts of language (letters) and progressing to the whole text (meaning).*

In their reading model, LaBerge and Samuels (1974) describe a concept called automatic information processing or **automaticity.** This popular model of the reading process hypothesizes that the human mind functions much like a computer and that visual input (letters and words) is sequentially entered into the mind of the reader. Almost without exception, humans have the ability to perform more than one task at a time (computer specialists sometimes call this "multitasking"). Because each computer (and by comparison the human mind) has a limited capacity available for multitasking, attention must be shifted from one job to another. If one job requires a large portion of the available computer's attention capacity, then capacity for another job is limited. The term "automaticity" implies that readers, like computers, have a limited ability to shift attention between the processes of decoding (sounding out words) and comprehending (thinking about the meaning of the author's message in the text). If readers are too bogged down in decoding the text, they will not be able to focus on the job of comprehending the author's message.

The term ***automaticity*** *suggests that readers have limited attention capacity that can be shifted rapidly between the parallel processes of decoding and comprehension.*

An example of automaticity in action can be seen in the common skill of learning to ride a bike. Novice bike riders focus so intently on balancing, turning the handlebars, and pedaling that they sometimes fail to attend to other important tasks like direction and potential dangers. Similarly, a reader who is a poor decoder focuses so much of his attention on phonics and other sounding out strategies that he has little brainpower left for comprehending. When this happens, the reading act, like an overloaded computer, "crashes." In contrast, children who are accomplished bike riders

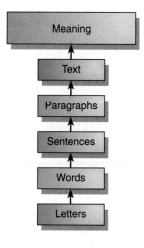

Figure 1.1 Bottom-up theories of the reading process

can ride without hands, carry on a conversation with a friend, dodge a pothole in the road, and chew gum at the same time. Like the accomplished bike rider, fluent readers can rapidly focus on the author's message because decoding no longer demands the lion's share of their attention capacity. In summary, the LaBerge and Samuels (1974) model predicts that if reading can occur automatically, without too much focus on the decoding process, then improved comprehension will be the result. A bottom-up theory of the reading process is represented in Figure 1.1. Important features of this reading theory are summarized in the left-hand column of Figure 1.3 (see p. 9).

Teachers who believe that bottom-up theories fully explain how children become readers often teach subskills first: they begin instruction by introducing letter names and letter sounds, progress to pronouncing whole words, then show students ways of connecting word meanings to comprehend texts. Although bottom-up theories of the reading process explain the decoding part of the reading process rather well, there is certainly more to reading than decoding. To become readers, students *must* compare their knowledge and background experiences to the text in order to understand the author's message. Truly, the whole purpose of reading is comprehension.

The Relationship of Bottom-Up Reading Theories to Phonics-First Reading Instruction

Subskills, also called "phonics-first" reading instruction, may be thought of as a pyramid with sound/symbol relationships (the parts of language) at its base and comprehension (constructing the meaning) as the capstone (Weaver, 1988, 1994). Chall (1979, 1983), a strong proponent of the phonics-first instructional model, characterized decoding as the first stage of learning to read:

> The essential aspect of *Stage One* is learning the arbitrary set of letters and associating these with the corresponding parts of spoken words [phonics]. . . . The qualitative change that occurs at the end of this stage is the insight gained about the nature of the spelling system of the particular alphabetic language used. (Chall, 1979, p. 39)

Phonics-first teachers, whether they realize it or not, base their instruction on bottom-up theories of the reading process (see Figure 1.2). Why? Because they typically focus instruction on teaching children letter-sound relationships during the earliest stages of reading instruction. Although comprehension is also important in a

Phonics is the foundation of reading in the subskills model with comprehension as the capstone.

Figure 1.2   Subskills or
phonics-first reading instruction

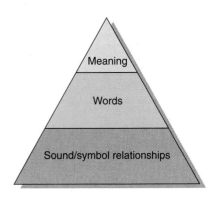

phonics-first instructional approach, this approach assumes that efficient decoding leads directly to comprehension.

As you might expect, phonics-first teachers assume the primary cause some readers struggle is the inability to decode. Therefore, they believe that children must be taught phonics first via the letters of the alphabet and the sounds these letters represent *before* beginning to read books independently. Flesch (1955, 1979), among others, cautioned that allowing children to attempt to read words or books without knowing the 26 letters and the 44 speech sounds they represent could lead to reading failure and frustration. Thus, letter names and letter sounds become the basic building blocks of reading within a subskills or phonics-first instructional approach.

The use of supplemental phonics programs, along with the exclusive use of phonically controlled (decodable) readers, often characterizes the components of a sub-skills or phonics-first instructional approach. *Decodable books* are usually made up of words that follow phonic generalizations or patterns children have been taught, such as short vowel word families like *can, man, fan.* The rationale for having children read decodable books is well illustrated in the *Becoming a Nation of Readers* report statement: "The important point is that a high proportion of the words in the earliest selections children read should conform to the phonics they have already been taught" (Anderson, Hiebert, Scott, & Wilkinson, 1985, p. 47). This argument has recently surfaced again in calls for the production and use of "decodable texts," or phonics readers, in states like California and Texas (Allington, 1997, 2002).

As you examine Figure 1.3, notice the clear connection of bottom-up theories of the reading process to phonics-first instruction. Phonics-first teachers begin reading instruction by teaching each of the parts of language (letters) as a prerequisite to reading words, sentences, and stories. Notice how beginning reading passages (decodable texts) use words that are phonically regular and follow specific phonic generalizations. Finally, notice in phonics first instruction it is assumed that *if* a child masters decoding, *then* comprehension will automatically follow in this instructional model.

Top-Down Theories of the Reading Process

Top-down theories of the reading process are rooted in Gestalt psychology, a school of thought that became popular in America in the early 1960s. To gain insight into Gestalt psychology, consider the classic example shown of Rubin's vase in Figure 1.4.

Gestalt psychology asserted that learners respond to physical stimuli such as images, letters, or drawings. This means that learners *act* on what they see using their

Instruction using a subskills model begins with the letters of the alphabet and the sounds these letters represent.

Subskills models *assume the primary cause of reading difficulty to be the inability to decode.*

Top-down reading theories *place primary emphasis on the role of a reader's prior knowledge rather than on the print on the page.*

Figure 1.3 Connecting bottom-up and subskills and phonics-first reading instructional practices

Bottom-Up Theories of the Reading Process

• During reading and learning to read, language is processed from the parts to the whole, as in building a structure from blocks one at a time.
• Learning to read is based on stimulus-response chains posited by behaviorists.
• Learning to read is accomplished by reducing the skill of reading to its smallest parts to be mastered one at a time.
• Repetition in reading is focused on practicing the parts of the complex skill of reading to a level of overlearning or automaticity.
• Language stimuli for reading are carefully controlled to represent consistently identified language rules or patterns to be learned.
• Mastery of the smallest parts of reading is assumed to lead to competent understanding and performance of the whole act of reading.
• Automatic decoding of the smallest parts of language is a prerequisite to reading and comprehending connected texts or books.
• Correctness is expected; mistakes are to be corrected.
• Pronouncing words provides access to one's speaking vocabulary to enable comprehension.
• Comprehending words provides access to new vocabulary words and comprehension of text.

Subskills or Phonics-First Reading Instructional Practices

• Reading instruction is begun by learning the 26 letters and the 44 sounds.
• Instruction proceeds to demonstrate the association(s) between the 26 letters and the 44 sounds.
• Blending the sounds represented by the letters in a word from left to right in temporal sequence or "sounding out" phonically regular words is taught.
• A limited number of high-frequency sight words are taught.
• Texts composed of carefully controlled words that are either known sight words or are phonically regular words are introduced to children for reading practice.
• More phonic patterns, rules, and generalizations are taught and learned.
• Texts are controlled to include new words as application for the patterns, rules, or generalizations learned.
• Control over text is gradually released, allowing phonically irregular words.
• Comprehending text is a direct outgrowth from the ability to pronounce words.

Figure 1.4   The Rubin vase

own knowledge and experiences. As you viewed the Rubin vase in Figure 1.4, what did you see? Did you see the vase? Or did you see two people facing each other? How did you decide to attend to one or the other interpretation of the picture? Did you notice that the picture did not change but that your perception of the picture did? Did you see the vase first because it was named "Rubin's vase"? What if it had been named "Rubin's *faces*"? Perhaps you would have noticed the faces first and the vase second.

According to Gestalt psychology, what is seen, such as pictures, words, or letters, is processed from the whole image to its parts (Otto, 1982). First, the whole of a picture is perceived (see Figure 1.4). After determining the nature of the image, one perceives the parts (i.e., shape, contours, identity). Once you decided the picture in Figure 1.4 was a vase, you perceived the base, the top, and the shape of the vase. However, had you seen the other interpretation of the picture, two people facing each other, then you would have noticed the neck, the chin, the nose, and the heads of two people.

Because you already knew this was a picture of a vase, your perceptions of the picture were affected by that perception. Gestalt psychologists explain that learners *actively* organize and interpret visual stimuli rather than *passively* taking in the visual image without interpretation. Because the *whole* of a stimulus, such as a picture, influences the perception of its *parts,* Gestaltists were often heard to say, "the whole is greater than the sum of its parts."

Since learning to read involves visual stimuli, it is conceivable, according to the Gestalt school of thought, that reading begins with a visual check of the "whole" first (text, sentences), and then proceeds to identification of the smaller parts (words, letters, and letter features). Reading goes beyond the visual (e.g., cognitive, affective, and linguistic factors). For example, when one reads, the words do not have meaning; rather, the reader brings personal meaning to the text from background experiences and collected knowledge.

Gestalt psychological thought led to the development of *top-down* theories of the reading process. In top-down theories, the knowledge and experiences the reader brings to the print influence, shape, and direct comprehension rather than the print on the page. Reading begins with the reader's knowledge, not the print. Top-down theories of the reading process suggest that reading is a meaning-construction process first and foremost, not merely a process of carefully attending to visual clues in print. A top-down theory of the reading process is represented in Figure 1.5.

Gestaltist psychology does not view the reading act as passive. Readers are seen as actively responding to the stimuli presented in print and texts.

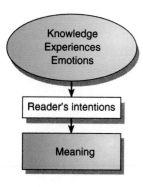

Figure 1.5 Top-down theories of the reading process

To understand at a practical level how reading can be influenced by a reader's background knowledge and experience, read a few lines from the well-known poem "Jabberwocky" by Lewis Carroll (1872):

'Twas brillig, and the slithy toves
Did gyre and gimble in the wabe;
All mimsy were the borogoves,
And the mome raths outgrabe.
Beware the Jabberwock, my son!
The jaws that bite, the claws that catch!
Beware the Jubjub bird, and shun
The frumious Bandersnatch!

It is obvious that you cannot read or understand this poem by simply pronouncing the words on the page or by attending more carefully to the visual stimuli (words, letters) displayed on the page. As readers, we use our knowledge about the animal kingdom—jaws, claws, and birds—to deduce that the Jabberwock is some kind of creature. We also use our experience with grammar and language to determine that the Jabberwock is a thing, not an action or a description. In spite of the intuitive appeal of top-down reading theories, it is clear that at some point in the reading process all readers *must* attend to the print in order to know which aspects of their knowledge and background experiences to retrieve and apply to understand the author's message.

It is clear that readers cannot "read" text without attending to the details of the print. Consequently, there can be no purely "Top-down" models of the reading process in any real application.

The Relationship of Top-Down Reading Theories to Whole-Word Reading Instruction

In the mid-1880s, a German researcher at the University of Leipzig named James M. Cattell published a paper titled "The Time Taken Up in Cerebral Operations," in which he found that adult readers could recognize words as rapidly as letters. Students were shown letters and words with a device called a *tachistoscope*—a piece of equipment that used a tiny shutter as found in many cameras to expose words and letters to a viewer at various speeds and for varying amounts of time. From these early experiments, coupled with results of research in the mid-1920s and early 1930s showing that many children were failing first grade because they were not learning to read successfully, a new approach to teaching reading called the **whole-word method** was born in the late 1930s.

It was thought that children could be taught to recognize whole words by sight, without any analysis of letters or sounds. Learning to read words not only would be more interesting and motivating for young children, but, as was shown in Cattell's

Nineteenth-century research found that adult readers could recognize short words as quickly as they could recognize individual letters.

*The **whole-word or sight-word approach** to teaching reading operates on the belief that children can recognize and learn to read frequently used words by sight rather than by analyzing letters or sounds.*

Children were taught to recognize on sight the most "highly frequent" words in the language during the whole-word reading movement.

research, could be done without the dull, boring, and needless trek through learning letter names and letter sounds.

As a part of the **whole-word** or **sight-word approach** to teaching reading, researchers undertook studies of "word frequency" (i.e., how often words appear in most writing) in printed texts. Lists of the most frequent words in the English language were developed. The most frequent words in English were taught first to young children. Words like *the, and, a,* and *look* were taught using word lists displayed on walls and in little reading books. Children practiced reading these words until they were memorized. Some of the most famous of these early reading books were known as the *New Basic Readers* or the *Dick and Jane* readers, originally published in 1941.

Once children learned to recognize the frequent words by sight, teachers were to teach children to "discover" how the sounds and letters within known words worked. In doing so, children could then figure out unknown words. So, once a whole word was recognized, the parts of the word could be studied to determine how the parts contributed to the whole (see Figure 1.6). Can you see how these instructional practices relate to top-down theories of the reading process?

A more recent variation on the whole-word instructional approach was an approach to teaching reading called *whole language* (Heymsfeld, 1989). With *whole language,* teachers and researchers believed that students would learn to read as naturally as they had learned to speak. The central unit of meaning, the sentence, was thought to be the smallest unit of meaning for teaching children to read in whole language approaches. Children were immersed in print-rich classrooms where they would hear stories read aloud, and they would repeatedly read the same story or poem, typically within the pages of a "big book" or on large chart paper, again and again with the assistance of the teacher. All this was to proceed without invasive, meaningless drills and skills and the use of decodable texts often associated with phonics-first instruction (K. S. Goodman, 1986; Rayner, Foorman, Perfetti, Pesetsky, & Seidenberg, 2002). Notice how top-down theories of the reading process influenced whole language reading instruction by examining the information in Figure 1.7.

Figure 1.6 Whole-word, sight-word, or holistic reading instruction

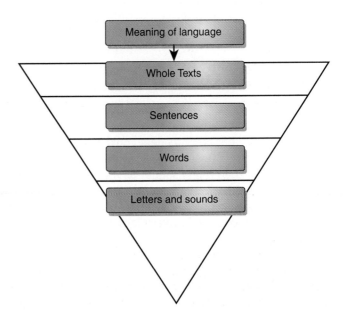

Figure 1.7 Connecting top-down theories of the reading process and whole-word reading instructional practices

Top-Down Theories of the Reading Process
- During reading and learning to read, language is processed from the whole to the parts, as in taking a completed jigsaw puzzle apart.
- Learning to read is based on "the whole is greater than the sum of its parts," as asserted by Gestalt psychology.
- Learning to read is accomplished naturally and holistically through immersion in print-rich and language-rich environments.
- Repetition in reading is focused on practicing phrases, sentences, or stories again and again until the text elements are internalized.
- Language stimuli in beginning reading materials are not controlled but represent naturally occurring patterns of language such as "run, run as fast as you can. . . ." in the "Gingerbread Man" story.
- Learning how to read stories, sentences, or phrases is assumed to lead to a perception of the parts and their relationship to the whole text and meaning.
- Repeated readings of authentic books of interest with help or independently are assumed to lead to an ability to read fluently with comprehension.
- Mistakes or miscues are seen as positive indicators of students' willingness to take risks.
- Having a large oral language base gives students access to printed language.
- Comprehending texts provides access to new vocabulary words and increased insights into how the sound-symbol system works for decoding unknown words.

Whole-Word, Sight-Word, or Holistic Reading Instruction
- Reading instruction begins by engaging children in an abundance of stories and books read aloud to and with children.
- Instruction proceeds to demonstrate during the reading of various sizes and types of books how good readers sound when they read.
- Guessing the identity of a word based on the pictures, the meaning of the text, or the first letter clue (minimal cues) is encouraged so as to leave large amounts of attention capacity available for meaning or comprehending.
- Children are encouraged to learn many words by sight without further decoding or analysis. Using letter sounds to unlock unknown words is seen as the strategy of last resort.
- Children are taught to read with patterned books and authentic children's literature stories to optimize the chance that children will have something to read of worth and something that will make sense. Controlling the language too strictly is viewed as having a detrimental effect on the comprehensibility of the language.
- Children practice reading a story again and again to internalize the language, structure, and meaning of stories. Analyzing story language too closely (sound-to-letter blending) is viewed as unnecessary to produce skilled, fluent readers.
- Control over the reading of the stories or books is gradually released from the teacher model to the children.
- Decoding ability is the product of language insights gained as children construct the meanings of a variety of texts and text patterns.

Do you see the connection between first comprehending the whole, whether it was a word, a sentence, or a text, and then interpreting the parts of the whole?

Before continuing this discussion of reading theories and reading instruction, we want to alert you to the fact that as a teacher you will probably experience these extreme theories of the reading process—bottom-up and top-down and their attendant instructional practices (phonics first and whole word/whole language) at least once during your career as a teacher. These extreme views have and continue to provoke heated debates, "reading wars," and political mandates. Whether it was the adoption of phonics-first reading instruction in the 1960s, 1970s, and 1980s or the turn to whole language from the 1980s into the 1990s, these extreme instructional approaches are never likely to be as effective as approaches in which these extremes are combined (Rayner et al., 2002). Attempts to combine these theoretical extremes have resulted in *interactive theories* of the reading process.

Interactive Theories of the Reading Process: Resolving the Weaknesses and Combining the Strengths of Bottom-Up and Top-Down Reading Theories

As theorists came to better understand the reading process, it became clear that neither top-down nor bottom-up theories adequately explained the complexity of the reading process. As a consequence, **interactive reading theories** were created that combined the strengths of both top-down and bottom-up explanations of reading while minimizing weaknesses associated with either theory alone (see Figure 1.8).

Interactive theories of the reading process explain that readers apply what knowledge is needed to understand a text while simultaneously decoding print. Put another way, readers must process an array of information sources from the print (e.g., context, clues, sentences, and sounding out unknown words) and draw upon their background knowledge to understand the author's message.

Interactive processing of print requires that readers take on what some reading experts call active and passive roles (Vacca, Vacca, & Gove, 1995). For example, if a reader possesses a great deal of prior knowledge or experience about spiders and the text is about spiders, then the reader will be more likely to use her knowledge about spiders and not need to focus as much attention on the print. This kind of reader involvement is considered *active processing*. On the other hand, if readers

Extreme bottom-up or top-down models of the reading process exclude elements of the reading process necessary for children to learn to read.

Interactive theories *of reading place an equal emphasis on the print or text and the reader's prior knowledge.*

Interactive theories of reading are drawn from cognitive psychology and represent a combination of bottom-up and top-down theories.

Figure 1.8 Interactive theories of the reading process

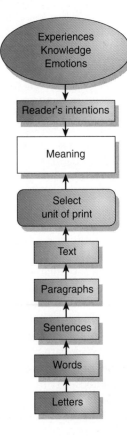

know very little about spiders, then they may take on a more *passive print processing* role—relying more heavily on the information on the printed page to understand the author's message.

To better demonstrate active and passive print processing, consider the following two examples. Many of us will have little or no trouble reading the first passage below about Cody's birthday surprise because we possess a good bit of prior knowledge of and experience with birthday parties. We are able to *actively* process the text and predict ahead of the print to move the reading process forward.

CODY'S BIG DAY

Today was Cody's birthday. He was 5 years old, big enough to go to kindergarten this fall. His mother had planned a sledding party up the canyon on the gently sloping foothills of the rugged mountains above. The sun shone brightly that day, and all the children had fun riding their sleds down the slopes. After the sledding party, Cody and his friends played games and opened presents. To top off the party, the boys and girls ate pizza, ice cream, and cake. That night Cody went to bed as happy as any little boy could be.

Now, read the next passage about syntactical structures in language. Because only a few people, such as linguists, for know much about this topic, readers cannot predict ahead of the print and must depend more heavily on the print to understand the author's message. In this situation readers construct meaning *passively* by relying on the print to direct their selection of prior knowledge or experiences—if indeed the readers are able to understand the author's message at all. In some cases, an author may assume too much prior knowledge, leaving too many gaps in necessary information for readers to construct meaning at all.

SYNTACTICAL STRUCTURES

. . . we must be careful not to exaggerate the extent to which a behavioral reinterpretation of intuition about form will clarify the situation. Thus suppose we found some behavioral test corresponding to the analysis of "John finished eating". . . . Or, to choose a more interesting case, suppose that we manage to develop some operational account of synonymy and significance. (Chomsky, 1975, p. 102)

Interactive theories of reading suggest that readers use what is necessary, either text information or background knowledge, to achieve the goal of making sense of text. Teachers who subscribe to interactive models of the reading process will probably adopt a *skills-based instructional approach* for teaching children to read.

Readers must integrate an array of information sources from the text and from their background to construct a valid interpretation of the author's message.

The Relationship of Interactive Theories of the Reading Process to Skills-Based Reading Instruction

Skills-based reading instruction includes three important instructional components: comprehension, vocabulary, and decoding. These components are important because skill-based teachers believe that children need to be given instruction that helps them activate and use their background knowledge, vocabulary, and experiences

*The **skills model** is composed of three major skill areas: comprehension, vocabulary, and decoding.*

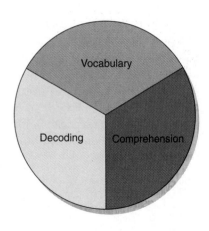

Figure 1.9   Skills-based reading instruction

to construct meaning or comprehend text along with applying decoding skills/strategies to figure out the pronunciation of unknown words.

Children are taught to use their background knowledge and remember new vocabulary words the teacher has just introduced, before reading a new story or text. After students finish reading and discussing a story, three separate skill lessons are taught—one each on comprehension, vocabulary, and decoding (see Figure 1.9, Weaver, 1988).

Notice that in skills-based reading instruction, decoding knowledge is not shown as the foundation of the reading instructional process as it was in the subskills or phonics-first instructional model, but rather as an equal part of the reading instructional process. This is because students are taught the skills of decoding text and text comprehension simultaneously. Children do not learn to decode and then learn to comprehend. Rather, in skills-based reading instruction, children are expected to integrate their knowledge of decoding and their background knowledge, vocabulary, and experiences as needed to construct the meaning from text.

Skills-based reading instruction has been one of the most commonly used approaches for providing reading instruction in schools. The reason for the popularity of skills-based reading instruction is related to the fact that the basal reader (i.e., reading textbooks) *teacher's editions* typically provide teachers with a carefully prescribed "script" to follow. Prior to reading a story, teachers are helped to activate students' background knowledge through discussion and preteaching new vocabulary words. After reading a story, teachers are provided with skill or strategy lessons on vocabulary, comprehension, and decoding skills that children need to learn at each level of development.

In many basal reader teachers' editions, the reading skills to be taught are found in a *scope and sequence chart*. The scope and sequence of reading skills is typically organized around three major components of reading instruction—decoding, comprehension, and vocabulary. Skills-based reading instruction treats the teaching of comprehension as a set of separate skills to be taught, such as predicting outcomes, getting the main idea, summarizing, understanding cause/effect, and so forth. The same can be said of the teaching of vocabulary and decoding skills. Each skill is to be learned one at a time and applied in a reading selection.

Several assumptions are associated with skills-based reading instruction. First, reading ability is achieved by learning a skill + a skill + a skill. Second, skills-based reading instruction is designed so that each of the language-cueing components—

After students read a story, three skill lessons are typically taught—one each on comprehension, vocabulary, and decoding.

The skills model treats comprehension as a set of discrete skills.

decoding, context, and meaning—is taught simultaneously with the other two categories of reading instruction. Third, each skill is usually taught in a self-contained lesson and must later be applied by the reader in a reading selection. Finally, readers must independently integrate the use of all the skills taught in the three reading components of decoding, vocabulary, and comprehension.

In Figure 1.10, the connection between interactive theories and skills-based reading instruction is summarized. It is important to understand that interactive theories emphasize a blending of the elements of print (bottom-up) and the reader's knowledge and experiences (top-down). As such, interactive theories or explanations of the reading process influence skills-based teachers' instructional practices. Skills-based teachers place emphasis on developing reading skills by helping students use their prior knowledge, vocabulary, and experiences to comprehend text.

Texts for reading instruction are developed that (presumably) match students' backgrounds, speaking vocabulary, and world knowledge levels. The validity of this claim can be questionable in urban schools, since so many children come to our schools as English language learners. There is also an attempt to control text difficulty based on the number of words, size of words, and the length of sentences. Familiar and unfamiliar words are taught from a vocabulary list before reading each passage. Next, a *purpose* (reason) for reading the selection is discussed, such as "Let's read to find out why Charlotte the spider is trying to help her friend, the pig." Comprehension is checked after reading each selection, typically through a question and answer session with the students. The most notable practice in skills-based reading instruction is that after reading a story in the basal reader, three skill lessons are taught: (a) decoding, (b) vocabulary, and (c) comprehension. By examining interactive reading theories as shown in Figure 1.9, one can see the theory that equal emphasis on using background knowledge and the features of the print leads to skills-based reading instruction.

Since interactive theories of reading emphasize a balanced emphasis on text and prior knowledge and skills instruction, notice how these influence the teaching of decoding, vocabulary, and comprehension skills.

Transactional Theories of the Reading Process

Transactional theories of the reading process are an *elaboration of interactive theories*. **Transactional reading theories** include all of the elements found in interactive, but also factor in how a reader's knowledge and experiences can influence the way an author's message is understood. As with some of the recent cognition theories that take into consideration students' intentions when they read and how that can affect understanding (Kirshner & Whitson, 1997), transactional theories explain that reading comprehension can be altered by influences within the reader. Figure 1.11 shows how transactional theories contain the full interactive model, but it is embedded within the social and situational context of the reading event.

Transactional theories of the reading process originated with the early work of Dewey and Bentley (1949) and show us that the reader, the text, and the social or situational setting are linked during the reading event. You may think of the reading transaction in many ways, but perhaps it is best understood by using the metaphor of a real estate transaction.

Let us say two individuals meet in an attorney's office for the purpose of purchasing and selling a home. The seller cannot be present for the event, so she gives her real estate agent power of attorney to complete the transaction in her behalf. Each person brings the documents, papers, checks, and such necessary to complete the transaction. When the transaction is completed, neither individual's circumstance

Transactional theories of the reading process are an elaboration of interactive theories.

Transactional theories of the reading process suggest that there is an interdependency between individuals and their environment.

Figure 1.10   Connecting interactive reading theories and skills-based reading instructional practices

Interactive Theories of the Reading

• During reading and learning to read, language is processed by balancing the features of the print with the reader's prior knowledge, culture, and background experiences.
• Learning to read is thought to be the *construction of meaning* through emphasizing information gained from the print and from the reader's prior knowledge.
• Learning to read is accomplished by placing a balanced emphasis on mastering three skill areas: decoding, vocabulary, and comprehension.
• Language stimuli for reading practice are carefully controlled to represent words that are familiar to the child's background and used frequently in the language.
• Mastery of the skill areas of reading, decoding, vocabulary, and comprehension is assumed to lead to competent understanding and performance of the whole act of reading.
• A balanced emphasis on isolated lessons in each of the three skill areas of decoding, vocabulary, and comprehension is assumed to be integrated by each learner.
• Integration of the three skill areas is assumed to enable skilled, independent reading.
• Correctness is expected, although varying interpretations for meaning based on background knowledge are accepted.

Skills Reading Instructional Approach

• Reading instruction focuses on three skill areas in isolated lessons: decoding, vocabulary, and comprehension.
• Instruction begins in all three areas:
  - Decoding: Learning the 26 letters and 44 sounds.
  - Vocabulary: Learning high-frequency sight words in lists, e.g., *the, and, me, look*, etc.
  - Comprehension: Listening to stories read aloud for the main idea, sequence, or details.
• Instruction continues in the three skill areas in connection with the introduction of simple stories in books called "pre-primers."
  - Decoding: Letter-sound associations learned along with some blending and the sounds letters represent in selected sight words.
  - Vocabulary: New high-frequency sight word lists are learned along with attention to new conceptual knowledge focused around word meaning categories.
  - Comprehension: Simple comprehension skills related to short stories in the teacher's edition focus on main ideas and noting details.
• Instruction progresses to the use of a student's anthology of stories (some use controlled text, some use literature-based stories) and instruction in the three skill areas continues throughout the elementary years.
  - Decoding: Prefixes, suffixes, context clues, etc.
  - Vocabulary: Unfamiliar words, multiple meaning words, word categories, synonyms, antonyms, etc.
  - Comprehension: Sequencing, literary devices, following directions, etc.

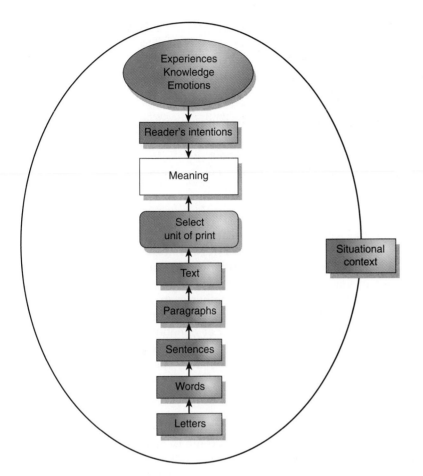

Figure 1.11   Transactional theories of the reading process

is the same as before. One is hopefully wealthier, or at least free from a mortgage obligation; the other is the proud owner of a piece of real estate. Furthermore, our real estate transaction is likely to occur in specific situations or places, such as a title company, attorney's office, or mortgage company—one would not expect to conduct a real estate transaction in a swimming pool or a bakery.

A reading transaction can be compared to this real estate transaction. Two people have agreed to come together to share a reading event. The author or writer cannot be present at the event, so she sends her representative—the text. The reader brings her life experiences, language background, and reading skills to make sense of the writer's text. On successful completion of the reading transaction, neither the reader nor the text is quite the same as before the event. The text delivered by the writer has been interpreted, reconstructed, and stored in the mind of the reader in a unique, personalized manner. In a way, the text is no longer an exact duplicate of the text sent by the author. The reader's knowledge structures and experiences have also been changed in the transaction. She is now the proud owner of a new piece of knowledge or experience because of the reading transaction. As a result, both the text and the reader's knowledge structures have been changed during the reading event.

Reading transactions also occur in specific social or situational settings. For example, in a kitchen the texts to be encountered are typically such texts as lists, food ads, coupons, directions, or recipes. This specific situation, the kitchen, causes the reader to adopt a particular purpose and use appropriate strategies for reading kitchen-related texts.

Rosenblatt (1978) described reading as a carefully orchestrated relationship between reader and text in a social situation. Situational conditions, such as *time, location, mood, pressures, reasons, intents,* and *purposes* influence a reader's *stance* for selection of reading strategies when reading a specific text. Rosenblatt described two stances or purposes for reading—*efferent* and *aesthetic.*

Transactional theories of the reading process are well represented in Rosenblatt's transactional theory of the literary work.

Efferent Stance

*When readers focus their attention on information to be remembered and used from reading a text, they are taking an **efferent stance.***

When readers focus their attention on information to be gathered, retrieved, or remembered from reading a text, they take an **efferent stance.** For example, reading the driver's license manual in preparation for an upcoming driving examination exemplifies an efferent stance toward a text. Reading a novel for the purpose of writing a book report to summarize the plot is another example of taking an efferent stance toward a text. Also, when readers assume an efferent stance toward reading a novel as an assignment in school, the focus of attention is on remembering or gleaning information from the text to pass a test rather than reading for recreation. Obviously, then, there is a need to account for another type of *transactional stance* or motivation for reading a text—an aesthetic stance.

Aesthetic Stance

*Think of a time when you took an **aesthetic stance.** Can you recall the book and the emotions evoked as you read?*

Think of a time when you took an **aesthetic stance** to read a text. Can you recall the book and the emotions felt as you read? When reading aesthetically, the learner draws on past experiences, connects these experiences to the text, savors the beauty of the literary art form, and becomes a participant in the unfolding events of the text. For example, when a teacher reads Wilson Rawls's (1961) story *Where the Red Fern Grows,* a feeling of reverence and sensitivity grows with the reading of the story. The teacher's voice may break a little bit toward the end of a read-aloud session, which deepens the emotions for the children. The listeners wonder how love could sacrifice itself so tenderly, so completely, and yet so sadly that a red fern would grow. When the teacher closes the book, there is silence in the room, and many eyes are filled with tears. This is the silence of reverent reflection—a silence in which readers ponder the significance of the experience they have had through reading.

Transactional theories hold that the social and situational context for reading influences the kinds of reading tasks to be completed. Context, or reasons for reading, influence the types of texts to be read, the purposes of the reader, and the strategies selected by to the reader (see Figure 1.11).

The Relationship of Transactional Theories of the Reading Process to Comprehensive Literacy Instruction

Transactional theories seem to best align with approaches to teaching known as **comprehensive literacy instruction.** The elements associated with comprehensive reading instruction have been carefully defined in several recently published and nationally disseminated reading research reports. Several of these reports are listed here:

Transactional reading theories are best related to comprehensive literacy instruction.

- *Preventing Reading Difficulties in Young Children* (Snow, Burns, & Griffin, 1998)
- *Starting Out Right: A Guide for Promoting Children's Reading Success* (Burns, Griffin, & Snow, 1999)
- *Report of the National Reading Panel* (National Reading Panel, 2000)
- *Put Reading First: The Research Building Blocks for Teaching Children to Read* (Armbruster, Lehr, & Osborn, 2001)
- *Every Child a Reader* (California Reading Task Force, 1995)

It is important to note that comprehensive reading instruction is firmly grounded in scientifically researched elements of effective reading instruction. Recommended teaching practices include, but are not limited to, the following (Reutzel & Cooter, 2003):

Explicit, Direct, Systematic Instruction of
- Comprehension
- Phonemic Awareness
- Phonics
- Vocabulary
- Fluency

Comprehension Instruction
- Story Structure
- Self-Monitoring
- Prediction
- Clarifying
- Making Inferences
- Summarizing
- Activating Background Knowledge
- Text Structures
- Questioning (Self, Author, Differing Types)
- Imagery

Early Reading Instruction
- Oral Language Development
- Concepts of Print
- Letter Recognition and Production
- Phonemic Awareness
- Phonics
- Common Spelling Patterns
- High-Frequency Sight Words

English-as-a-Second-Language and Bilingual Instruction
- If resources are available, teach reading in the first language

Book Reading and Literature Study
- Use discussion groups (i.e., book clubs, literature circles)
- Read a variety of text types and genres
- Provide time and practice reading books
- Provide an independent reading program
- Establish a print-rich classroom
- Promote out-of-school reading programs

Quality Reading Instruction for All Grades
- Teach strategy lessons
- Design consistent, focused, and cohesive instruction
- Teach the purposes of reading and writing
- Read aloud to students
- Use guided reading, especially for younger children
- Give students oral feedback on decoding, meaning, and fluency of their reading

Writing Instruction
- Provide time for writing extended texts
- Teach children grammar, handwriting, spelling, and conventions
- Publish children's writing

Best practices for teaching reading cited in the national reading research reports are shown in Figure 1.12.

The success of comprehensive reading instruction is dependent on the teacher's knowledge of these research-based practices *and* the ability to use them *effectively* with all children. Some teachers and researchers summarize the use of best reading

Comprehensive literacy instruction focuses on helping children learn to read using essential components of instruction within a framework of reading and writing TO, WITH, and BY children.

Figure 1.12   Best practices associated with comprehensive literacy instruction
Based on *The Foundations of Literacy* by D. Holdaway, Copyright © 1979 by D. Holdaway. Reprinted by permission of Scholastic Australia Pty Limited.

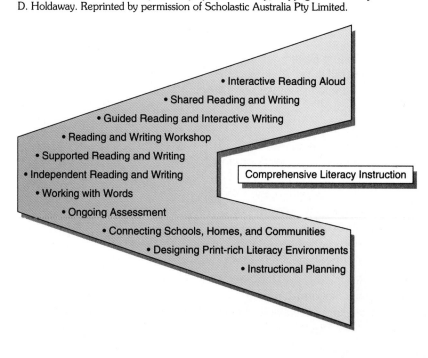

- Interactive Reading Aloud
- Shared Reading and Writing
- Guided Reading and Interactive Writing
- Reading and Writing Workshop
- Supported Reading and Writing
- Independent Reading and Writing
- Working with Words
- Ongoing Assessment
- Connecting Schools, Homes, and Communities
- Designing Print-rich Literacy Environments
- Instructional Planning

Comprehensive Literacy Instruction

instructional practices using three prepositions—TO, WITH, and BY. Comprehensive reading instruction involves teachers and children in daily reading of texts where the teacher reads TO children, works WITH children individually and in groups, and provides time and proper conditions for reading practice BY children (Fountas & Pinnell, 1996; Mooney, 1990). A comprehensive reading program begins with a careful and ongoing assessment of each child's reading development. This assessment helps the teacher know where to begin to meet the diverse needs of each learner.

In comprehensive reading classrooms, teachers read aloud *to* and interact *with* children about books regularly, knowing that this helps them see, understand, and develop appropriate reading skills. The classroom environment is rich with print from the everyday lives and learning of the children. Learning activities are designed to provide stimulating opportunities for children to read and write for differing purposes and for children to experience a variety of text types and in a variety of purposes. Favorite storybooks are read and reread in a structured setting that supports children as they make sense of print with expert help and guidance from a skilled teacher.

Early in the process, children's attempts to make sense of print are often assisted with sensitive demonstrations and intentional, explicit skill or strategy instruction while reading a text in a whole class setting or in small reading groups. Direct, explicit, and systematic instruction is provided in the areas of phonemic awareness, concepts of print, letter identification, phonics, vocabulary, comprehension, and fluency. Reading skills are practiced and applied daily while reading a variety of texts.

Teachers who subscribe to comprehensive literacy instruction use a variety of reading materials, such as decodable texts, pattern texts, leveled texts, stories, and information books. Children are taught to use reading skills and strategies in books carefully selected to present children with just the right amount of reading challenge. Guided reading instruction provides teachers with a structure with which to guide, teach, model, and assist children in developing and applying essential skills. Finally, children are provided with abundant reading materials and time to read personally selected, challenging, and varied reading materials.

Similar practices in writing are incorporated into comprehensive literacy programs. Teachers demonstrate and reveal to children the many ways in which writing can be used (Calkins, 1994; Graves, 1983): to tell the stories of our own lives, to organize and record ideas, to manage our time (or the time of others). Children are also helped to understand the form, features, and functions of the various writing styles. This is done via demonstrations of writing strategies during carefully planned writing activities. Children are shown how to use strategy/skill lessons in grammar, handwriting, punctuation, and spelling to improve their own writing. Children are given time to write each day. They are encouraged to keep notebooks, lists, and journals.

In summary, teachers implementing the elements of comprehensive reading instruction put transactional reading theory into practice by teaching reading and writing skills using a diversity of text types, for a variety of purposes, and in a variety of social and situational settings found in school and out. For example, comprehensive literacy teachers may design a science laboratory learning center complete with information books, materials for conducting experiments, lab manuals, directions, a computer for on-line research, experimenter's notebooks, and so on. In this example, children learn to perform various reading and writing tasks, for the purposes scientists use literacy, in a specific place or situation in which the literacy occurs in a real-world context.

The connection between transactional theories of the reading process and comprehensive reading instruction is shown in Figure 1.13.

Think of two ways in which transactional theories of the reading process connect with comprehensive literacy instruction.

Comprehensive literacy instruction attends to all the components of effective literacy instruction as well as the context in which reading instruction takes place.

Figure 1.13 Connecting transactional theories of the reading process and comprehensive reading instructional practices.

Transactional Theories of the Reading Process

• During reading and learning to read, readers process language by constructing meaning using the print and their own experiences and knowledge as conditioned by their intentions, purposes, and the situational context.

• Learning to read is thought to be an event where a reader's response to a text is conditioned by sound-symbol, grammatical, and meaning cues appropriate to the print, the people, the physical environment, the cultural expectations of the situation, and each individual's experiences, knowledge, skills, and strategies for processing text.

• Reading materials should include a variety of types of books and levels to meet the needs of all children.

• Children approximate the demonstrations of fluent reading and writing with significant guidance from a competent, well-prepared teacher.

• Teachers and children carefully study reading materials to understand text structure, language patterns, challenges, tricky words, and other print features that may influence the ability to successfully process the print.

• Mistakes are expected in learning to read and are viewed as "risk taking" and indicators of progress among young children.

• Teacher demonstrations and modeling of fluent reading and writing are integral for children to learn how to construct meaning from print that is appropriate to the text and the situational context.

Comprehensive Reading Instructional Practices

• Instruction focuses on teaching children oral language, phonemic awareness, letter recognition and production, concepts about print, phonics, spelling, writing conventions, vocabulary, text comprehension, and fluency using a variety of text types and levels of challenge.

• Instruction in processing the print uses a whole-to-part-to-whole approach.

• Because instruction focuses on the end goal of constructing meaning, instructional activities are based on best practices substantiated in scientifically based reading research such as interactive read-aloud, shared reading, guided reading, independent reading, shared writing, interactive writing, guided writing, and independent writing.

• A print-rich, active, and well-organized classroom is considered to be an integral part of comprehensive reading instruction.

• Because oral language is considered the basis of all language learning, talking, discussing, and interacting about texts is integral to comprehensive reading instruction.

• Reading information trade books in science, social studies, math, art, etc., is a part of integrating comprehensive reading instruction with other curricular areas of study.

• Children receive guidance and opportunity on a regular basis to choose books and write for personal and authentic reasons.

• Classrooms are busy language-learning workshops filled with literacy tools, books, and print and lively interactions around these resources in a variety of learning centers and situations.

Transactional reading theories suggest that children learn to actively construct meaning from encounters with texts using their own experiences, along with information available on the printed page. Children are assisted in their learning by competent teachers providing explicit instruction on essential reading and writing skills. Teachers provide real stories and poems to be read; design learning centers and practice areas where children can try out their literacy skills in a variety of real-world situations; present exemplary models of reading and writing behaviors; offer sensitive and helpful guidance about how to apply reading skills and strategies; and create a learning environment and specific classroom situations that provide children with motivation to read and write.

Summary

A cursory survey of reading habits among the American population today revealed significant problems for teachers, children, families, and schools. Increasing numbers of young children are not learning to read on grade level by third grade. Recent reports suggest that the achievement gap rather than narrowing is widening. Although not all indicators are negative, today's teachers need to understand that now, more than ever, the ability to read is necessary to survive and prosper in a rapidly progressing technological and information-oriented society and economy. The goal of producing minimally competent readers simply is not sufficient for today's schools.

For teachers to achieve the objectives associated with high-quality comprehensive reading instruction, they must study children and understand how they learn to understand and process printed language. They must also clearly comprehend the way language is used by humans to communicate and learn. What is more, they must have a working knowledge of dominant reading theories and how these theories connect to or drive instructional decisions and classroom instructional practices.

Check your understanding of chapter concepts by using the self assessment for Chapter 1 on our Companion Website at www.prenhall.com/ reutzel.

Concept Applications

In the Classroom

1. Conduct a poll in your college classes about the numbers of trade books (excluding college textbooks) read by each person in the last year. Then find out how much time each person spends reading narrative versus information texts. What proportion of the time is spent reading for information purposes?

2. After reading this chapter, write a brief description of how your current beliefs about teaching reading and writing have been changed. Then, as you read the remainder of the book, keep a log of information you learn that may cause you to further rethink your initial beliefs about reading instructional practices.

3. List the major assumptions and characteristics of the bottom-up, top-down, interactive, and transactional models of the reading process and summarize each in writing.

4. List the major assumptions and characteristics of the four approaches to reading instruction—subskills or phonics first, whole word, sight word or holistic, skills based, and comprehensive reading instruction—and summarize each in writing.

5. List three major connections between theories of the reading process and instructional practices used to teach reading in classrooms.

In the Field

1. Visit a kindergarten or first-grade classroom. Describe in detail how children are being engaged in learning to read and write. You may also be able to gather some writing samples to photocopy and return to the children. Make a list of the types of books you saw them reading. Which of the major models of the reading process best explains what you saw? Why?

2. Ask a teacher to tell you about his or her reading instructional beliefs. Visit the teacher's classroom, and determine if these beliefs are reflected in his or her classroom instruction. Describe what you saw and how it related to one of the four reading instructional approaches.

3. Visit children in several grade levels. Interview them using questions based on the *Burke Reading Interview* (Burke, 1987). Ask them the following:
   a. What is reading?
   b. Who do you think is a good reader in your class? Why?
   c. What would you do to teach someone how to read?
   d. How did you learn to read?
   e. What might you do to become a better reader?

   Record the responses for the different grade levels and compare. How do children's understandings of reading differ from grade to grade? Discuss your findings with a peer in your class. Did the two of you notice similar differences?

Recommended Readings

Armbruster, B. B., Lehr, F., & Osborn, J. (2001). *Put reading first: The research building blocks for teaching children to read.* Washington, DC: The Partnership for Reading—NIL, NICHHD, and U.S. Department of Education.

Birdshaw, D., Burns, S. Carlisle, J. F., Duke, N. K., Garcia, G. E., Hoffman, J.V., et al. (2001). *Teaching every child to read: Frequently asked questions.* Ann Arbor, MI: Center for the Improvement of Early Reading Achievement.

Blair, S. M., & Williams, K. A. (1999). *Balanced reading instruction: Achieving success with every child.* Newark, DE: International Reading Association.

Burns, M.S., Griffin, P., & Snow, C. E. (1999). *Starting out right: A guide to promoting children's reading success.* Washington, DC: National Academy Press.

Cooter, R. B. (Ed.). (2004). *Perspectives on rescuing urban literacy education: Spies, saboteurs, & saints.* Mahwah, NJ: Erlbaum.

Fielding, L., Kerr, N., & Rosier, P. (1998). *The 90% reading goal.* Kennewick, WA: National Reading Foundation.

Fitzgerald, J. (1999). What is this thing called "balance"? *The Reading Teacher, 53*(2), 100–115.

Gambrell, L. B., Morrow, L. M., Neuman, S. B., & Pressley, M. (1999). *Best practices in literacy instruction.* New York: Guilford Press.

Pressley, M. (2002b). *Reading instruction that works: The case for balanced teaching* (2nd ed.). New York: Guilford Press.

Rayner, K., Foorman, B. R., Perfetti, C. A., Pesetsky, D., & Seidenberg, M. S. (2001). How psychological science informs the teaching of reading. *Psychological Science in the Public Interest, 1*(2), 31–74.

Rayner, K., Foorman, B. R., Perfetti, C. A., Pesetsky, D., & Seidenberg, M. S. (2002, March). How should reading be taught? *Scientific American,* 85–91.

Reutzel, D. R., & Cooter, R. B. (2003b). *Strategies for reading assessment and instruction: Helping every child succeed* (2nd ed.). Upper Saddle River, NJ: Merrill/Prentice Hall.

Routman, R. (2003). *Reading essentials: The specifics you need to teach reading well.* Portsmouth, NH: Heinemann.

chapter 2

Phonemic Awareness and Phonics Instruction

Focus Questions

When you are finished studying this chapter, you should be able to answer these questions:

1. Does instruction in *phonemic awareness* help children succeed in reading?

2. How is phonemic awareness (PA) developed in children? Why is PA such an important skill to be acquired?

3. What is the *alphabetic principle*?

4. Does phonics instruction improve reading achievement?

5. What is the value of teaching onsets and rimes?

6. What is meant by *structural analysis* of words?

Key Concepts

National Reading Panel
Phonemic Awareness
Phonemes
Phonological Awareness
Graphemes
Alphabetic Principle

Phonics
Onset
Rime
Morphemes
Structural Analysis
Early Literacy Milestone
Skills

In 1950s America, children loved to discover a "secret decoder ring" inside their Cracker Jack box. It was fun to think about encrypting messages for others to discover and, even more thrilling, *decoding* secret communiqués from neighborhood friends. Without the secret decoder ring, though, you were locked out of all communications.

Teaching children to translate written symbols into words is foundational to reading. After many years of debate as to how this decoding process can best be developed, several new research reports were issued that brought a good bit of clarity to the field of reading education. At the heart of these studies were findings related to two specific areas: phonemic awareness and phonics. In this chapter, we summarize these findings and describe in some detail the specific skills that must be learned by young readers—what we refer to sometimes as the "what" of teaching.

Visit Chapter 2 of our Companion Website at www.prenhall.com/ reutzel to look into the chapter objectives, standards and principles, and pertinent Web links associated with phonemic awareness and phonics instruction.

RESEARCH ON EARLY READING

Every once in a while, research in reading instruction comes along that is much like a flash of lightning illuminating the teaching and learning landscape. If it is taken to heart and put into practice, its influence can be profound. Important research on beginning reading by Marilyn Jager Adams (1990a, 1990b) came onto the scene in the 1990s and began a kind of chain reaction in the field. Based on a review of nearly 100 years of reading research, Adams concluded that the two best predictors of beginning reading success are *alphabet knowledge* and *phonemic awareness* (i.e., the understanding that spoken words are made up of individual speech sounds). These findings contributed to a major swing in the reading education pendulum toward "evidenced-based" solutions to current reading issues. The next major research report to come forward with Adams-like impact was one issued by the National Reading Panel.

Report of the National Reading Panel

Nearly 100 years of research indicates that alphabet knowledge and phomic awareness are the two best predictors of beginning reading success (Adams, 1990a).

In 1997, the United States Congress asked the director of the National Institute of Child Health and Human Development (NICHD) and the Secretary of Education to convene a national panel to assess the status of research-based knowledge on early reading instruction. The **National Reading Panel,** as it came to be known, issued its report in April 2000 (available free online at www.nationalreadingpanel.org).

Included in this *Report of the National Reading Panel* was a call for improved classroom instruction in several key areas: *alphabetics* (phonemic awareness and phonics instruction), *fluency* (reading rate, accuracy, and intonation), *vocabulary knowledge*, and *text comprehension*. The panel found that effective teachers (a) understand how reading develops in each of these critical areas, (b) have the ability to quickly and efficiently assess each of their students to learn which skills are already known and which are still developing, and (c) use assessment information to plan instruction targeting student needs.

*The **National Reading Panel** assesses the status of research-based knowledge on reading instruction.*

While some have challenged some of the findings of the *Report of the National Reading Panel,* few would question its impact on current policy at the national level and on related federally funded intiatives.

Other Scientific Research on Reading Instruction: Common Findings

In addition to the *Report of the National Reading Panel,* several other important research reports have appeared in recent years describing effective reading instruction. They include the following:

- American Federation of Teachers. (1999). *Teaching reading is rocket science: What expert teachers of reading should know and be able to do.* Washington, DC: Author.
- Armbruster, B. B., Lehr, F., & Osborn, J. (2001). *Put reading first: The research building blocks for teaching children to read.* Washington, DC: The Partnership for Reading—NIL, NICHHD, and U.S. Department of Education.
- Burns, M. S., Griffin, P., & Snow, C. E. (1999). *Starting out right: A guide to promoting children's reading success.* Washington, DC: National Academy Press.

Figure 2.1 Evidenced-based reading skills and practices*

> **"Alphabetics"** (using direct instruction [DI] methods)
>   **-Phonemic awareness**
>   **-Alphabetic principle**
>   **-Phonics**
> **Concepts of print** (Grades EC–1; DI methods)
> **Oral reading fluency** (DI methods)
> **Independent reading practice** (structured "buddy reading")
> **Exposure to a variety of reading materials/genres**
> **Comprehension strategies** (DI methods)
> **Vocabulary** (DI methods)
> **Oral language development** (DI methods)
> **Spelling and word study** (DI methods)
> **Interactive read-aloud** (structured)
> **Technology-assisted reading instruction**
> **Integrated reading, writing, and language instruction**
> **Adequate time for daily reading/writing instruction and practice**

*Note: These recommendations are *minimal* and do not speak to the many other needs of students, such as family involvement or adapting the curriculum to meet the needs of exceptional children.

- Snow, C. E., Burns, M. S., & Griffin, P. (1998). *Preventing reading difficulties in young children.* Washington, DC: National Academy Press.

Reutzel and Cooter (2003) sorted the instructional and programmatic recommendations into categories in order to better understand the elements of a comprehensive reading program. Following is a summary of essential skills and recommended classroom practices (where applicable) drawn from these research reports that directly relate to word identification and supporting (see Figure 2.1).

Teachers Make the Difference

There was one clear finding across all the recent research reports: *In the end, it is teachers, not programs, who make the critical difference whether students achieve and succeed in reading.* Linda Darling-Hammond, executive director of the National Commission on Teaching and America's Future, in a report titled *What Matters Most: Teachers for America's Future* (1996), concluded, "What teachers know and do is the most important influence on what students learn. Competent and caring teaching should be a student right" (p. 6). Likewise, the seminal *Becoming a Nation of Readers Report* nearly two decades ago found that teacher ability was at least five times more important than the adoption of new published reading materials:

> An indisputable conclusion of research is that the quality of teaching makes a considerable difference in children's learning. Studies indicate that about 15 percent of the variation among children in reading achievement at the end of the school year is attributable to factors that relate to the skill and effectiveness of the teacher. In contrast, the largest study ever done comparing approaches to beginning reading found

Optimal word-identification instruction requires a knowledgeable teacher with expertise in assessment to decide which children need which skills, grouping according to student needs, and discernment of best teaching strategies.

Phonemic awareness *is the understanding that spoken words are made up of individual speech sounds.*

Complete the phonemic awareness "anticipation guide" before reading further, then retake the quiz after reading to see if your prereading assumptions were accurate.

Standards Note
Standard 11.5: The reading professional will be able to interpret research findings related to the improvement of instruction and communicate these to colleagues and the wider community. After you read more on evidence-based practices, develop a concise, succinct, jargon-free summary of "best practice" regarding letter-sound instruction for colleagues as well as a wider public audience.

Phonemic awareness refers to the understanding that spoken words are made up of individual sounds, or ***phonemes.***

that about 3 percent of the variation in reading achievement at the end of first grade was attributable to the overall approach of the program. (Anderson, Hiebert, Scott, & Wilkinson, 1985, p. 85)

In other words, the solution for meeting the literacy needs of all children is a knowledgeable and skilled classroom teacher. To that end, we review in this chapter the most potent research currently available for helping students acquire word-identification skills as well as ways of helping children acquire these important skills within a context of rich language and literature.

AN EVIDENCE-BASED SEQUENCE OF INSTRUCTION

One of the continuing challenges for practicing teachers is how to unravel and apply myriad research findings in reading to their classroom teaching. This task has been especially daunting of late in the areas of phonemic awareness, alphabetic principle, and phonics. We are frequently asked to define each of these terms and answer questions like these: Aren't phonics and phonemic awareness basically the same? (Answer: No.) Does it matter when you offer instruction in these three areas? (Answer: Yes!) Is it appropriate to teach all children phonemic awareness and phonics skills every day in grades K–2? (Answer: No, it is *not* appropriate. The *only* thing we recommend for *all* children is good oral hygiene!)

Cooter, Reutzel, and Cooter (1998) developed a simple instructional model to help teachers interpret the research on sequencing phonemic awareness, alphabetic principle, and phonics instruction. Figure 2.2 shows the development of children from the emergent reading stage toward fluent reading, at least in terms of word identification.

Notice the three developmental areas are depicted as a developmental staircase of sorts progressing from (1) the most basic level of **phonemic awareness** (an exclusively oral language activity), to (2) alphabetic principle development (matching elemental sounds and the letters that represent them), and ultimately to (3) phonics (decoding written symbols to speech sounds). This progression from exclusively speech/sound activities to eventually understanding how to decode symbols back to speech sounds is at the heart of recent breakthroughs in reading research.

In the remainder of this chapter, we take a much closer look at phonemic awareness and phonics instruction.

PHONEMIC AWARENESS

An Anticipation Guide on Phonemic Awareness

To begin the study of this topic, please complete the anticipation guide (see Figure 2.3) to discover the extent of your own prior knowledge about phonemic awareness. After reading this section, you should complete the anticipation guide again to see if your opinions and understandings have changed. You may want to use this technique as a tool in future teaching situations as a kind of "action research" experiment.

Research on Phonemic Awareness

Phonemic awareness refers to the understanding that spoken words are made up of individual speech sounds (Pikulski & Templeton, 1997; Burns, Griffin, & Snow,

Figure 2.2   Phonemic awareness, alphabetic principle, and phonics: developmental and instructional progression

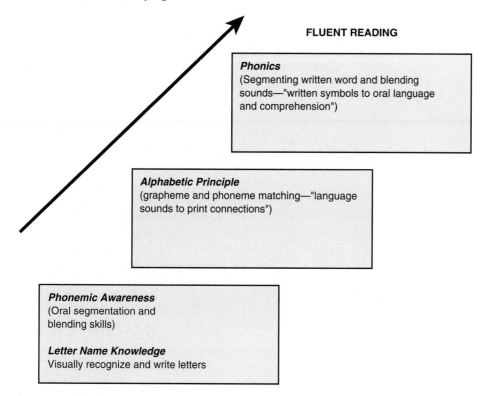

FLUENT READING

> *Phonics*
> (Segmenting written word and blending sounds—"written symbols to oral language and comprehension")

> *Alphabetic Principle*
> (grapheme and phoneme matching—"language sounds to print connections")

> *Phonemic Awareness*
> (Oral segmentation and blending skills)
>
> *Letter Name Knowledge*
> Visually recognize and write letters

EMERGENT READING

From "Sequence of Development and Instruction for Phonemic Awareness" by R. B. Cooter, Jr., D. R. Reutzel, and K. S. Cooter, 1998, unpublished paper.

1999). For example, "no" and "she" each have two speech sounds, or **phonemes.** Phonemes are not the same as letters, by the way; letters *represent* phonemes in the spelling of words. Before children learn to read print, they need to become aware of how the sounds in words work and, as mentioned, that spoken words are made up of phonemes (National Reading Panel, 2000; Armbruster, Lehr, & Osborn, 2001).

When most children begin their schooling, they come equipped with a sizable vocabulary and a fairly well developed knowledge of syntax. However, many lack phonemic awareness. For instance, the word *dog* is known to many 4- and 5-year-olds only as a domestic animal that walks on four legs. They usually lack the awareness that *dog* is composed of three sound units or phonemes, /d/, /o/, and /g/.

Phonemic awareness is an important factor in beginning reading success and in learning to spell (Lyon, 1997; National Reading Panel, 2000; Snow, Burns, & Griffin, 1998). About 20% of students lack phonemic awareness (Adams, 1990), a problem that can be easily resolved through classroom instruction. Numerous studies have shown that while phonemic awareness is an important factor, it is not sufficient alone to ensure reading success (Lyon, 1997). Rather, instruction in phonemic awareness should be viewed as an important element of a comprehensive reading program in the early elementary grades.

Adams (1990a) has identified five essential phonemic awareness tasks for students to acquire. Can you name them?

Figure 2.3 Phonemic awareness

Anticipation Guide

Directions: Read each statement and decide if it is **TRUE** or **FALSE.** Write your response in column A. After reading this part of the chapter on phonemic awareness, reread the statements and respond in column B. Discuss the differences in your responses with a fellow student (or the instructor if you are taking a college course).

A   **B**

_____   1. At least 80% of all children require instruction in   _____
             phonemic awareness in order to be successful in
             learning to read.

_____   2. Phonemic awareness refers to a child's awareness of   _____
             sounds that make up words.

_____   3. Measures of phonemic awareness have been found   _____
             to predict success in early reading as well as measures
             of intelligence, general language development, and
             listening comprehension.

_____   4. Phonemic awareness has nothing to do with writing.   _____

_____   5. Children who are low in reading performance rarely   _____
             score low in phonemic awareness.

_____   6. Instruction in phonemic awareness alone is not enough   _____
             to prevent and correct reading problems.

_____   7. If children have acquired phonemic awareness then   _____
             they also understand the alphabetic principle.

_____   8. Individual sounds are easier to hear than syllables, so   _____
             they should be taught first.

_____   9. Phonemic awareness is the same thing as phonics.   _____

_____   10. Blending sounds to produce words is one of the   _____
             easiest phonemic awareness skills.

_____   11. Research indicates a particular sequence for teaching   _____
             phonemic awareness.

_____   12. Matching letters to the speech sounds they represent is   _____
             an appropriate phonemic awareness activity.

What Scientifically Based Research Tells Us About Phonemic Awareness Instruction

In phonemic awareness instruction, teachers help children develop the ability to notice, think about, and work with the individual sounds in spoken words. Numerous studies have now confirmed the kinds of teaching activities that help children develop phonemic awareness. These types of activities will help those of your students who come to school without phonemic awareness fill in that gap and become better readers (Adams, 1990; Blevins, 1997). Further, these activities will pave the way for all students to become better spellers (National Reading Panel, 2000). Here are the research-based categories for you to use in selecting teaching and learning activities:

- *Phoneme isolation*   Recognizing individual sounds in words.

     Teacher: What is the first sound in *boy?*
     Student: The first sound in *boy* is /b/.

- *Phoneme identity*   Hearing the same sound in different words.

   Teacher: What sound is the same in *boy, bake,* and *butter*?
   Student: The first sound /b/ is the same.

- *Phoneme categorization*   Recognizing a word having a different sound in a group of three or four words.

   Teacher: Which word doesn't belong? *run, rake, toy*
   Student: Toy doesn't belong because it begins with /t/.

- *Phoneme blending*   Children listen to phonemes spoken separately, then blend them together to form a word.

   Teacher: What is this word? /m/ /a/ /k/
   Student: /m/ /a/ /k/ is *make.*

- *Phoneme segmentation*   Breaking a spoken word into its separate phonemes while tapping or counting on their fingers each sound.

   Teacher: Say the sounds you hear in the word *cup* slowly.
   Student: cccccccc uhhhhhhhh pppppppp
   Teacher: How many sounds did you count in *cup*?
   Student: *Cup* has three sounds.

- *Phoneme deletion*   Recognizing that a phoneme can be removed from a spoken word and that part of the word remains.

   Teacher: If I take away the sound /b/ in the word *brook,* what word is left?
   Student: *Brook* without /b/ is *rook.*

- *Phoneme addition*   The ability to create a new word by adding a phoneme.

   Teacher: If I add the sound /s/ to the end of the word *tree,* what new word would I have?
   Student: *Tree* with /s/ added to the end would be *trees.*

- *Phoneme substitution*   Exchanging a phoneme for one in a spoken word to create a new word.

   Teacher: The word is *run.* Change /n/ to /t/. What's the new word?
   Student: The new word is *rut.*

Some Misunderstandings About Phonemic Awareness

One of the most common misunderstandings about phonemic awareness is that it is the same as *phonics.* It's not. As we learned earlier, phonemic awareness is the understanding that *spoken words* are made up of individual speech sounds, or what are called phonemes. Phonics, on the other hand, is the understanding that letters and letter combinations *represent* phonemes that can be blended to create spoken words (of course, words that are "sounded out" using phonics are not actually spoken when we read to ourselves, but you see what we mean).

One thing is certain: having children learn phonemic awareness will help them acquire phonics later on, as you will see later in this chapter. The reason is simple, really. When students are phonemically aware and can hear individual sounds (phonemes) in spoken words, then learning that alphabet letters or letter combinations

Phonics is not the same as phonemic awareness; on the contrary, it is the understanding that letters and letter combinations represent phonemes that can be blended to create spoken words.

represent these same speech sounds makes perfect sense—there is a relationship between sounds and letters. The introduction of phonics becomes the next logical step in learning to read. Phonics knowledge helps children reverse the process and translate written symbols back into phonemes or speech sounds, hence the age-old term "sounding out."

Phonological Awareness

Another misunderstanding is that phonological awareness and phonemic awareness are synonymous terms. Again, this is not so. Phonological awareness is a broader term that goes beyond simple awareness and manipulation of speech sounds; phonemic awareness is only one part of phonological awareness. **Phonological awareness** includes identifying and manipulating larger parts of spoken language, such as words, syllables, onsets and rimes (discussed later in this chapter), rhyming, and alliteration (Armbruster, Lehr, & Osborn, 2001; National Reading Panel, 2000).

As with phonemic awareness, children can demonstrate their phonological awareness in a number of ways (Armbruster et al., 2001), including the following:

- *identifying and making rhymes orally*
  "Hickory, dickory **dock,**
  The mouse ran up the **clock.**"
- *identifying and working with syllables in spoken words*
  "I can tap out the sounds in *kindergarten:* **kin-der-gar-ten!**"
- *identifying and working with onsets and rimes in spoken syllables or one-syllable words* (Note: An *onset* is the part of a syllable that comes before the vowel; the *rime* is the rest (Adams, 1990b, p. 55).
  The first sound in *tall* is **/t/**,
  and the last part is **-all**.
- *identifying and working with individual phonemes in spoken words*
  The first sound in *dog* is **/d/**.

The Instructional Sequence for Phonemic Awareness Instruction

In all instruction, teachers should move from the simplest, most basic concepts toward the more complex. Figure 2.4 shows that the most basic starting point is helping students understand that spoken words are made up of individual speech sounds. Word-stretching activities, such as "word rubber-banding," can help students begin to hear individual speech sounds or phonemes. Once this most basic level of awareness begins to emerge, teachers should help students begin to develop simple segmenting and blending skills using compound words. For example, children are able to catch on quickly that simple compound words like *airport, bloodhound, clothespin,* and *rainbow* are just two smaller words "glued" together. They can hear and segment the two spoken words easily! If the compound words are chosen so that each word part is a one-syllable word that carries a meaning students easily understand, both the sound and meaning connections can be understood at once by most students. Learning simple segmenting and blending with compound words is the first major jump into phonemic awareness.

Phonological awareness includes identifying and manipulating larger parts of spoken language, such as words, syllables, onsets and rimes, rhyming, and alliteration.

Describe how "word rubber-banding" activities can help students learn to hear speech sounds.

Phonemic awareness instruction tackles the segmenting and blending of simple compound words first.

Figure 2.4   Sequence of development and instruction for phonemic awareness

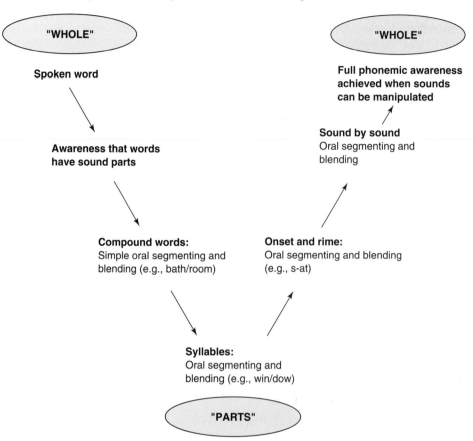

From "Sequence of Development and Instruction for Phonemic Awareness" by R. B. Cooter, Jr., D. R. Reutzel, and K. S. Cooter. 1998, unpublished paper.

Syllables are the next speech sound unit for students to orally segment and blend. This step moves students from simply segmenting smaller words in compound words to dividing words by sound units that seem more abstract. Clapping or counting syllables heard in words like *window* and *kindergarten* helps them segment sound elements (i.e., win-dow, kin-der-gar-ten). Blending activities such as "I will say the first part of a word, then the rest of the word. Say the word as a whole. /sha/ . . . dow. What is the word? (*shadow*)," help students further develop phonemic awareness.

The next phonemic awareness level calls for segmenting and blending *onsets* and *rimes*. As noted earlier, an onset is the part of a syllable that comes before the vowel; the rime is the rest (Adams, 1990b, p. 55). For example, in the word *sat*, "s" is the onset, and "-at" is the rime. Similarly, in the first syllable of the word *turtle*, "t" is the onset and, "-ur" is the rime. This activity is easily done in the context of poetry (teaching rimes with *rhymes*).

Segmenting spoken words sound by sound is the next and most abstract level of phonemic awareness and is a necessary forerunner of letter-by-letter sounding out in phonics. The difference here is that we segment, then blend, individual sounds in spoken words. This final stage of phonemic awareness development helps children use

Segmenting and blending syllables moves students into the realm of dividing words by sound units.

What are some of the more important tips for planning phonemic awareness instruction offered by Blevins (1997)?

phonemic segmentation and blending in more sophisticated and fun ways. Now your students will be ready for such activities as phonemic manipulation: e.g., categorization, deletion, addition, and substitution tasks, described earlier.

Some Tips for Planning Instruction in Phonemic Awareness

Blevins (1997, pp. 7–8) has summarized some useful points on phonemic awareness that are important for teachers in kindergarten through grade 2 to keep in mind as they plan for instruction:

- *Phonemic awareness is not related to print.*   Oral and aural (listening) activities are what phonemic awareness teaching and learning are all about. Once children can name and identify the letters of the alphabet, they are ready to move into learning the *alphabetic principle.*

- *Many, if not most, poor readers in the early grades have weak phonemic awareness skills.*   Thus, phonemic awareness may be an important issue (on a limited basis) for teachers well beyond the K–2 years. Indeed, phonemic awareness training may well be indicated throughout K–12 education for students considered "remedial" readers.

- *Model, model, model!*   Children need to observe their teacher and other students actually doing the phonemic awareness activities.

Several other recommendations have been suggested (National Association for the Education of Young Children, 1986; Yopp, 1992) for the selection of phonemic awareness activities:

- *Learning activities should help foster positive feelings toward learning through an atmosphere of playfulness and fun.*   Drill activities in phonemic awareness should be avoided, as should rote memorization.

- *Interaction among children should be encouraged through group activities.* Language play seems to be most effective in group settings.

- *Curiosity about language and experimentation should be encouraged.* Teachers should react positively when students engage in language manipulation.

- *Teachers should be prepared for wide differences in the acquisition of phonemic awareness.*   Some children will catch on quickly, whereas others will take much longer. Teachers should avoid making quick judgments about children on the basis of how they perform in phonemic awareness activities.

REMINDER: Now that you have finished reading about phonemic awareness, go back and complete the anticipation guide in Figure 2.3.

Strategies for Teaching Phonemic Awareness

Following are selected strategies we recommend from our text *Strategies for Reading Assessment and Instruction* (Reutzel & Cooter, 2003b), which is intended as a companion text to this book.

Playing with Rhymes and Alliteration

As teachers get to know their students' phonemic and alphabet needs, they often search for opportunities to teach these concepts in books, songs, or poems. When the teacher consciously searches for and locates books, songs, poems, or other print opportunities to teach language concepts like rhyming and alliteration, this act is called *language watching* (Reutzel, 1992). Books, songs, and poems typically contain many examples of rhyming and alliterative words that may be used to teach the concepts of rhyming and alliteration.

> *Option 1:* Select a poem, such as "Sister for Sale" (Silverstein, 1976), for a shared reading experience. After reading, analyze the poem. It provides an excellent opportunity to demonstrate the alliterative beginning sound associated with the letter /s/.

> *Option 2:* Select a poem or song such as the song "Do Your Ears Hang Low." After singing, analyze this song for pairs of rhyming words. Then invite the children to think of other words that rhyme with pairs of rhyming words found in the song. Make a "Rhyming Word Wall" from the songs, poems, and stories read in the classroom during shared reading or singing experiences.

Grab the Odd One Out

The purpose of the Grab the Odd One Out game is to help children develop phonemic awareness through a playful "oddity task" activity. The ability to discriminate which spoken word does not fit among three choices relates to the oddity task described in the assessment section of this chapter. This game may focus children's attention on beginning, ending, or middle sounds in words. Once a list of beginning syllable words is created, a list of ending sounds and medial sounds should be created for this game as well.

This game is played by seating a group of children on the floor or table comfortably. Begin by saying that you have a "grab bag" filled with objects while showing children the bag. Next, tell the children that you will be saying three words and that they are to listen carefully for the word that does not fit. If they know the word, they are to raise their hand but not call it out. A child is selected to reach into the grab bag without looking and feel around to find the object. When the object is found, he or she can say the word and show the object to the group. This process continues until all the objects in the grab bag have been used. When an object has been used, it is to be returned to the grab bag for use with the next set of words.

Picture Box Sound Counting

Learning to hear sounds in words requires that students hear syllables and sounds (phonemes). Students need to develop the ability to hear syllables and sounds in words in proper sequence. Counting the number of syllables and sounds in words helps children attend more carefully to the sounds and syllables in words (Yopp and Troyer, 1992). A version of this activity (Elkonin, 1963) has been used successfully for a number of years in successful intervention programs, such as Reading Recovery.

This activity uses a word card with a picture, such as the one shown in Figure 2.5, for the word cat. The teacher begins by pronouncing the word very slowly while placing a chip into a box below for each letter sound heard, progressing sound by sound (ccccc aaaaaaa ttttt). After an initial demonstration, the child is encouraged to join in the activity by saying the next word for the picture on the card while the teacher places a chip into a box below each letter sound.

Figure 2.5   Elkonin Box for Sound Counting

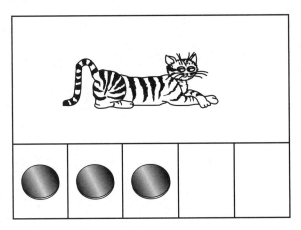

The teacher gradually releases responsibility to the child by exchanging roles. For example, the teacher can pronounce the word, and the child can place chips into the boxes below each letter sound. Finally, the child both says the word and places a chip into a box below each letter sound entirely on his or her own. Eventually, children should be able to count the number of sounds in a word and be able to answer questions about the order of sounds in words (Griffith & Olson, 1992).

Add a Sound/Take a Sound

Adding or substituting sounds in words in familiar songs, stories, or rhymes may help special-needs and younger readers attend to the sounds in their speech. The ability to add or substitute sounds in words in familiar language is easier than segmenting sounds and benefits students in many of the same ways.

Two strategies add enjoyment to developing awareness of phonemes and the alphabetic principle. The first of these is *consonant substitution*. When using this strategy, initial, final, or medial consonants in words found in a phrase or sentence can be exchanged. For example, in the Shel Silverstein poem "Jimmie Jet and His TV Set," change the consonants from /j/ to /n/ or /b/ to produce

Nimmie Net and His TV Set

Bimmie Bet and His TV Set

Another approach is to delete the sound /j/ as follows:

Jimmie Jet and His TV Set

immie et and His TV Set

Young children find the nonsensical result to be both humorous and helpful in understanding how consonants work in connected text. Other consonants may be exchanged in the future to vary the number of consonants exchanged and the position of the consonants in the words.

A second strategy is *vowel substitution*. When using a vowel substitution strategy, a single vowel (and sound) is selected and substituted in key words in the text.

For example, in the poem "Mary Had a Little Lamb," the vowel sounds can be changed to produce a completely nonsensical version with "Miry hid a little limb" by substituting the /i/ short vowel sound in place of the vowels in the original poem.

Children find that adding, changing, or substituting sounds in this way turns learning about letters and sounds into a game. One first-grade Chapter 1 student who had been working with his teacher late one afternoon using these strategies remarked on his way out the door to catch his bus, "Teacher, can we play some more games tomorrow?" This statement sums up the enthusiasm these two strategies generate among young children as they learn to focus their attention on phonemic awareness.

Word Rubber-Banding

Segmenting refers to isolating individual sounds in a spoken word. Segmenting can be one of the more difficult phonemic awareness tasks for students. It is, however, an important skill for children to develop if they are to profit from implicit or indirect instruction related to letter names, sounds, and the connections between the two. Segmenting sounds in words can be done by rubber-banding or stretching a word into its sounds like a rubber band, as described next.

Begin by singing a favorite song, such as "Old MacDonald Had a Farm." Next, ask the children to repeat the first sounds of selected words as follows: "Old m-m-m-MacDonald had a f-f-f-farm, e i e i o, and on this f-f-f-farm he had a c-c-c-cow, e i e i o. With a m-m-m-moo here and a m-m-m-moo there, here a moo there a moo everywhere a moo moo . . . " Children's names can be used in this fashion, such as J-J-J-Jason or K-K-K-Kate. Still another variation involves drawing a sound out or exaggerating the sound, for example, MMMMMaaaaarrrryyyy had a little llllllllaaaaammmmm. Beyond this iterative technique, children can be asked to segment entire words. Yopp (1992) recommends a song set to the tune of "Twinkle, Twinkle Little Star" for this purpose:

> Listen, Listen
> To my word
> Tell me all the sounds you heard: *race* (*pronounce this word slowly*)
> /r/ is one sound
> /a/ is two
> /s/ is last in race
> It's true.

When working with the segmentation of entire words, it is best to use words of no more than three or four sounds because of the difficulty of these tasks for younger or special-needs learners. Children seem to enjoy these tasks and with careful guidance can enjoy high levels of success as they develop phonemic awareness through segmentation tasks.

ALPHABETIC PRINCIPLE

A **grapheme** is the smallest part of *written* language that represents a phoneme in the spelling of a word. A grapheme may be just one letter, such as b, d, f, p, or s, or several letters, such as ch, sh, th, -ck, ea, or -igh (Armbruster et al., 2001, p. 4). When phonemic awareness is combined with letter-sound knowledge, students can attain a new level of understanding called the *alphabetic principle* (Byrne & Fielding-Barnsley, 1989).

*A **grapheme** is the smallest part of written language that represents a phoneme in the spelling of a word.*

Alphabetic princi-
ple is the knowledge
that a letter or letter
combination represents
each of the phonemes,
or speech sounds.

Alphabetic principle is the knowledge that a specific letter or letter combination represent each of the speech sounds (phonemes). Discovery of the alphabetic principle is thought to be necessary for students to progress in their reading development, particularly in learning phonics. Thus, primary-level teachers actively seek out activities that help students learn (1) the alphabet letters and the sounds they represent, (2) that speech is made up of individual sounds that can be represented by specific letters and letter combinations, and (3) that the spellings of words remain generally constant across the various books or texts children encounter (i.e., the word *book* is written using the same letters every time you see it in print).

Using Environmental Print for Learning About Letters

Reutzel and Cooter (2003a) recommend a strategy that uses familiar examples of writing from the students' environment (such as cereal boxes, signs, bumper stickers, and candy wrappers) to help them begin to understand how sounds and letters go together (the alphabetic principle). Hiebert and Ham (1981) have found in their research that children who were taught using environmental print learned significantly more letter names and sounds than did children who learned alphabet letters without using environmental print. Familiar print in the environment can be used in interesting ways to give children confidence in reading and writing and to help them understand how print works.

The only materials needed for this strategy are collectibles from home and school. Can labels, empty cereal boxes, bumper stickers, advertisements from the local papers, and old boxes or containers are usually available in large quantities.

Begin by setting aside a classroom display area, bulletin board, or wall that is designated as an "Environmental Print" wall. Children may be asked to bring environmental print or product logos from home to put on this display wall in random order. Next, environmental print can be taken down and rearranged in an alphabet display with 26 blocks or areas reserved for each alphabet letter as shown in Figure 2.6. For

Figure 2.6 Environmental print chart

Alphabet Wall		Aa	Bb Nestle Butterfinger	Cc Coca-Cola	Dd	Ee
Ff	Gg	Hh	Ii	Jj	Kk	Ll
Mm	Nn	Oo	Pp	Qq	Rr	Ss
Tt	Uu	Vv	Ww	Xx	Yy	Zz

Figure 2.7 Environmental print ring from SRAI

example, specific print items such as Butterfinger, Baby Ruth, and Batman can be placed in a block for the letter "B".

In some cases, children can be asked to bring environmental print to school for a specific letter name or sound. After discussing and displaying letter specific environmental print, teachers and children can cut and paste environmental print items onto 5- by 7-inch plain index cards (see Figure 2.7). These letter environmental print collections are often bound together to be read in small groups or by individuals in an alphabet and letter play center.

Selected letters can be taught from known environmental print items, such as "C" in Figure 2.7. Environmental print logos can be collected and bound together to represent selected letter, such as *S*nicker, *S*prite, and *S*ugar. Other possibilities for using environmental print to produce letter knowledge include cutting up environmental print to compose new words or making letter collages for an art activity.

How might the interaction among children develop their language skills?

Phonics instruction emphasizes how spellings are related to speech sounds in systematic and predictable ways.

PHONICS INSTRUCTION IN COMPREHENSIVE READING CLASSROOMS

A Phonics Prereading Quiz

Surveys conducted by the International Reading Association found that phonics is one of the most talked about subjects in the field of reading education (second only to the topic of comprehensive reading instruction). Reutzel and Cooter (2003a) have developed a kind of phonics "quick test" so that you can see just how much you may already know about the subject (see Figure 2.8). Please complete the exercise in the figure *before* reading further (the results may surprise you). As with the anticipation guide on phonemic awareness, you may benefit from retaking the Phonics Quick Test *after* you have finished reading this section.

Phonics: What We Know from Research and Practice

Phonics instruction emphasizes how spellings are related to speech sounds in systematic and predictable ways (Burns, Griffin, & Snow, 1999; Reutzel & Cooter, 2003a). Research confirms that systematic and explicit phonics instruction is more effective than nonsystematic or programs that ignore phonics (National Reading

Figure 2.8   The Phonics Quick Test*

1. For the word *sparkle,* it is divided between _____ and _____ . The <u>a</u> has an _____ controlled sound, and the <u>e</u> _____ .

2. In the word <u>small,</u> *sm-* is known as the *onset,* and *-all* is known as the _____ .

3. <u>Ch</u> in the word *chair* is known as a _____ .

4. The letter <u>c</u> is the word *city* is a _____ sound, and in the word cow is a _____ sound.

5. The letters <u>bl</u> in the word *blue* are referred to as a consonant _____ .

6. The underlined vowels in the words <u>*au*</u>*thor,* *spr*<u>*ea*</u>*d,* and *bl*<u>*ue*</u> are known as vowel _____ .

7. The words *tag, run, cot,* and *get* have which vowel pattern? _____

8. The words *glide, take,* and *use* have the _____ vowel pattern.

9. The single most powerful phonics skill we can teach to emergent readers for decoding unfamiliar words in print is _____ sounds in words. We introduce this skill using <u>consonant or vowel (?)</u> (choose one) sounds because they are _____ .

10. The word part <u>work</u> in the word *working* Is known as a _____ .

11. The word part <u>-ing</u> in the word *working* is known as a _____ .

12. Cues to the meaning and pronunciation of unfamiliar words in print are often found in the print surrounding the unfamiliar—which is to say, in the _____ .

*Answers to the *Phonics Quick Test* are found in Figure 2.11 later in this chapter.

Panel, 2000). When delivered as part of a comprehensive reading program—one that includes expansive vocabulary instruction, reading practice in great books, and writing development, all delivered by a skillful teacher—phonics instruction can help children become enthusiastic lifelong readers.

Marilyn Jager Adams (1990b), in her exhaustive review of phonics and other factors essential to word identification titled *Beginning to Read: Thinking and Learning About Print,* found that approaches in which systematic code instruction was included with the reading of meaningful connected text resulted in superior reading achievement overall for both low-readiness and better-prepared students. (p. 125) Adams also noted that these conclusions seem to hold true regardless of the instructional approach through which reading is taught. However, it should be noted that very few if any studies have been conducted comparing comprehensive reading strategies with more traditional skills instructional models or with basal readers for that matter. Nevertheless, one cannot deny that there is a compelling need to include systematic phonics as an important part of a comprehensive reading program.

Approaches to Phonics Instruction

Several approaches to phonics instruction have found support in the research (National Reading Panel, 2000). These approaches are sometimes modified or combined in reading programs.

Synthetic Phonics Instruction—Traditional phonics instruction in which students learn how to change letters or letter combinations into speech sounds, then blend them together to form known words (i.e., sounding out).

Embedded Phonics Instruction—Teaching students phonics by embedding phonics instruction in text reading, a more implicit approach that relies to some extent on incidental learning (National Reading Panel, 2000, p. 8).

Analogy-Based Phonics—A variation of onset and rime instruction that has students use their knowledge of word families to identify new words that have that same word part. For example, students learn to pronounce *light* by using their prior knowledge of the *-ight* rime from three words they already new: *right, might,* and *night.*

Analytic Phonics Instruction—A variation of the previous two approaches, students study previously learned whole words to discover letter-sound relationships. For example, *Stan, steam,* and *story* all include the *st* word element (*st* is known as a consonant blend).

Phonics Through Spelling—Students segment spoken words into phonemes and write letters that represent those sounds to create the word in print. For example, *rat* can be sounded out and written phonetically. This approach is often used as part of a *process writing* program.

Arguments *For* and *Against* Intensive Phonics Instruction

Those who support the use of intensive phonics instruction in beginning reading have traditionally cited several benefits of this practice (Adams, 2001; Chall, 1967; Flesch, 1955, 1981). One argument is that English spelling patterns are relatively consistent;

Standards Note
Standard 6.2: The reading professional will be able to use phonics to teach students to use their knowledge of letter-sound correspondence to identify sounds in the construction of meaning. Juel, Blancarosa, Cohen, and Deffes (2003) espouse *anchored word instruction* so that children are taught letter-sound knowledge and vocabulary meaning. They state, however, that current visitations found most teachers focusing on phonological awareness and decoding skills without attention to meaning. Where do you stand? Are you overcorrecting? Can we have it both ways?

List some approaches to phonics instruction.

therefore, phonics rules can aid the reader in approximating the pronunciation of unfamiliar words. As a result, phonics rules can assist the reader in triggering meaning for unfamiliar words if they are in the reader's listening and speaking vocabulary. It is felt that when phonics knowledge is applied first and then makes use of semantic (meaning) and syntactic (grammar) cues in the passage, the reader can positively identify unknown words in most elementary-level reading materials.

Those opposing intensive phonics instruction cite a number of justifications for their position as well. The chief complaint is that the English language is *not* all that regular and that phonics generalizations often have many exceptions (Harris & Sipay, 1990). Focusing on ambiguous details in words to the exclusion of such comprehension-based strategies as using context clues can cause some children to miss appropriate meaning and language order clues.

The question in building a comprehensive reading program is not whether one should teach phonics strategies. Rather, we need to ask *which phonics strategies should be taught* and *how we should teach them.* The next section partially answers the "which phonics skills" question.

List some problems with using phonics instruction.

Some Important Phonics Generalizations to Teach

Scope and sequence guides help coordinate instruction across states, which can be especially helpful in maintaining continuity for highly mobile students.

Most states and local school districts have developed their own "scope and sequence" guides to help teachers know which reading skills should be taught at each grade level. The primary value of these scope and sequence guides is that they help coordinate instruction across the state, which can be especially helpful in maintaining continuity in learning for highly mobile students. Texas, California, Mississippi, Kansas, and Oklahoma are just a few of the states that have developed their own curriculum guides. Eventually, there is likely to be a national curriculum detailing the essential knowledge and skills to be learned by students at each grade level.

Following are a few research-proven phonics skills that seem to be included in virtually all curriculum guides.

Beginning Consonant Sounds in Words

Arguably the single most efficient phonics generalization to teach is *beginning consonant sounds in words.* When used in conjunction with context clues and the reader's background knowledge, beginning consonant sounds can help students identify up to 90% of words typically found in elementary reading materials through about grade 2 or 3. This is because consonant sounds tend to be the most constant or reliable as compared to vowels, which account for much (but not all) of the variance in English.

The C Rule

The letter *c* is an irregular consonant letter that has no phoneme of its own. Instead, it assumes two other phonemes found in different words, *k* and *s*. In general, when the letter *c* is followed by *a, o,* or *u,* it will represent the sound we associate with the letter *k,* also known as the *hard c* sound. Some examples are the words *cake, cosmic,* and *cute.*

On the other hand, the letter *c* can sometimes represent the sound associated with the letter *s.* This is referred to as the *soft c* sound. The *soft c* sound is usually produced when *c* is followed by *e, i,* or *y.* Examples of the *soft c* sound are found in the words *celebrate, circus,* and *cycle.*

The G Rule

G is the key symbol for the phoneme we hear in the word *get* (Hull, 1989, p. 35). It is also irregular, having a *soft* and a *hard g* sound. The rules remain the same as they are for the letter *c*. When *g* is followed by the letters *e, i,* or *y,* it represents a *soft g* or *j* sound, as with the words *gently, giraffe,* and *gym.* If *g* is followed by the letters *a, o,* or *u,* then it usually represents the *hard* or regular sound, as with the words *garden, go,* and *sugar.*

The CVC Generalization

When a vowel comes between two consonants, it usually has the short vowel sound. Examples of words following the CVC pattern include *sat, ran, let, pen, win, fit, hot, mop, sun,* and *cut.*

Vowel Digraphs

When two vowels come together in a word, the first vowel is usually long and the second vowel silent. This occurs especially often with the *oa, ee,* and *ay* combinations. Some examples are *toad, fleet,* and *day.* A common slogan used by teachers that helps children remember this generalization is "when two vowels go walking, the first one does the talking."

The VCE (Final E) Generalization

When two vowels appear in a word and one is an *e* at the end of the word, the first vowel is generally long and the final *e* silent. Examples include *cape, rope,* and *kite.*

The CV Generalization

When a consonant is followed by a vowel, the vowel usually produces a long sound. This is especially easy to see in two-letter words, such as *be, go,* and *so.*

R-Controlled Vowels

Vowels that appear before the letter *r* are usually neither long nor short but tend to be overpowered or "swallowed up" by the sound. Examples include *person, player, neighborhood,* and *herself.*

Other Important Phonics Terms and Skills

Even though the phonics generalizations seem to be the most useful, most basal reading programs focus attention on many others. Following are several more terms, definitions, and examples of other phonics skills related to consonants and vowels not already discussed in this chapter.

- *Consonant digraphs*—Two consonants together in a word that produce only one speech sound (*th, sh, ng*).
- *Consonant blends or clusters*—Two or more consonants coming together in which the speech sounds of all the consonants may be heard (*bl, fr, sk, spl*).

Vowels

- *Vowel digraphs*—Two vowels together in a word that produce only one speech sound (*ou, oo, ie, ai*)
- *Schwa*—Vowel letters that produce the *uh* sound (*a* in *America*). The schwa is represented by the upside-down *e* symbol:
- *Diphthongs*—Two vowels together in a word that produce a single, glided sound (*oi* in *oil, oy* in *boy*).

Favorite Strategies for Teaching Phonics

Following are selected strategies we recommend from our text *Strategies for Reading Assessment and Instruction* (Reutzel & Cooter, 2003b), which is intended as a companion text to this book.

Letter-Sound Cards

Letter-sound cards are intended as prompts to help students remember individual and combination (i.e., digraphs and blends) letter sounds that have been introduced during minilessons or other teachable moments. You will need to have a word bank for each child (children's shoe boxes, recipe boxes, or other small containers in which index cards can be filed), alphabetic divider cards to separate words in the word bank, index cards, and colored markers.

The idea is to provide students with their own word cards on which you (or they) have written a key letter sound or sounds on one side and a word that uses that sound on the other. Whenever possible, it is best to use nouns or other words that can be depicted with a picture, so that, for emergent readers, a drawing can be added to the side having the word (as needed). Two examples are shown in Figure 2.9.

Figure 2.9   Letter-sound card examples

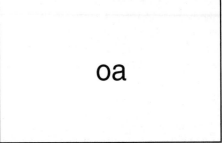

Phonics Fish (or Foniks Phish?) Card Game

Remember the age-old children's card game *Fish* (sometimes called *Go Fish*)? This review activity helps students use their growing visual awareness of phonics sounds and patterns to construct word families (i.e., groups of words having the same phonetic pattern). It can be played in small groups, at a learning center with two to four children, or during reading groups with the teacher.

You will need a deck of word cards. The words can be selected from the students' word banks or chosen by the teacher or parent/teaching assistant from among those familiar to all students. The word cards should contain ample examples of at least three or four phonetic patterns that you wish to review (e.g., beginning consonant sounds, R-controlled vowels, clusters, digraphs, or rime families).

Before beginning the game, explain which word families or sound patterns are to be used in this game of Phonics Fish. Next, explain the rules of the game:

1. Each child will be dealt five cards.
2. The remaining cards (deck of about 50) are placed face down in the middle of the group.
3. Taking turns in a round-robin fashion, each child can ask any other if he or she is holding a word having a particular sound or pattern. For example, if one of the patterns included is the /sh/ sound, then the first student may say something like, "Juanita, do you have any words with the /sh/ sound?" If the student being asked does not have any word cards with that pattern, he or she can say "Go Fish!" The student asking the question then draws a card from the deck.
4. Cards having matching patterns (two or more) are placed face up in front of the student asking the question.
5. The first student to get rid of all his or her cards wins the game.

Stomping, Clapping, Tapping, and Snapping Sound

Helping children hear syllables in words enables them to segment sounds. This knowledge can be used in myriad ways to improve writing and spelling, increase awareness of letter combinations used to produce speech sounds, and apply knowledge of onsets and rimes. All these skills and more enable students to sound out words in print more effectively. For years, teachers have found success in helping children hear syllables by clapping them out when reading nursery rhymes, such as "Mar-y had a lit-tle lamb, lit-tle lamb, lit-tle lamb . . . "

We prefer to use rhyming poetry, songs, chants, or raps for these syllabication activities. Use an enlarged version produced for an overhead projector or a big-book version or simply rewrite the text on large chart paper using a colored ink marker. First, model read the enlarged text aloud in a normal cadence for your students. Reread the selection at a normal cadence, inviting students to join in as they wish. Next, explain that you will reread the selection, but this time you will clap (or snap, or stomp) the syllables in the words. (Note: If you have not already explained the concept of syllables, you will need to do so at this point.) Finally, invite students to clap (or make whatever gesture or sound that you have chosen) as you reread the passage.

Tongue Twisters

Many students enjoy word play. Tongue twisters can be a wonderful way of reviewing consonants (Cunningham, 1995) in a way that is fun for students. We have found that tongue-twister activities can combine reading and creative writing processes to help children deepen their understanding of phonic elements.

There are many traditional tongue twisters in published children's literature that may be used. However, we find that children enjoy creating their own tongue twisters perhaps even more. All you need to do is decide which sounds or letter pattern families are to be used.

Cunningham (1995) suggests that you begin by simply reciting some tongue twisters aloud and inviting students to join in. We recommend that you produce two or three examples on chart paper and post them on the wall as you introduce the concept of tongue twisters. For example, you might use the following:

Silly Sally sat in strawberries.

Peter Piper picked a peck of pickled peppers.
If Peter Piper picked a peck of pickled peppers,
Then how many peppers did Peter Piper pick?
Peter Piper panhandles pepperoni pizza,
With his pint-sized pick-up he packs a peck of pepperoni pizzas,
For Patti his portly patron.

Simple Simon met a pieman going to the fair,
Said Simple Simon to the pieman,
Let me taste your wares!"
Said the pieman to Simple Simon,
Show me first your penny!"
Said Simple Simon to the pieman,
I'm afraid I haven't any."

Children especially love it when teachers create tongue twisters using names of children in the class, such as the following example:

Pretty Pam picked pink peonies for Patty's party.

Finally, challenge students to create their own tongue twisters to "stump the class." It may be fun to award students coupons that can be used to purchase take-home books for coming up with clever tongue twisters.

Creating Nonsense Words

Many of the most popular poets, such as Shel Silverstein and Jack Prelutsky, have tapped into children's fascination with word play in their very creative poetry. For instance, when Silverstein speaks of "gloppy glumps of cold oatmeal," we all understand what he means, even though *gloppy* and *glumps* are really nonsense words. Getting students to create nonsense words and apply them to popular poetry is a motivating way to help students practice phonic patterns.

First decide which phonic letter-sound families you wish to emphasize. For instance, it may be appropriate to review the letter-sound families represented by *-ack, -ide, -ing,* and *-ore.* Also needed are books of poetry or songs with rhyming phrases, chart paper or overhead transparencies, and markers.

As with all activities, begin by modeling what you expect students to do. On a large sheet of chart paper or at the overhead projector, write the word family parts that you wish to emphasize (for this example, we used -ack, -ide, -ing, and -ore). Illustrate how you can convert the word parts into nonsense words by adding a consonant, consonant blend, or consonant digraph before each one, such as shown by the following:

-ack	-ide	-ing	-ore
gack	spide	gacking	zore
clack	mide	zwing	glore
chack	plide	kaching	jore

In the next phase of the demonstration, select a poem or song that rhymes and review it with students first (use enlarged text for all of your modeling). Next, show students a revised copy of the song or poem in which you have substituted nonsense words. Here is one example we have used with the song "I Know an Old Lady Who Swallowed a Fly." We show only the first verse here, but you could use the entire song, substituting a nonsense word in each stanza:

Original version:
I know an old lady who swallowed a fly,
I don't know why,
she swallowed the fly,
I guess she'll die.
Nonsense word version:
I know an old lady who swallowed a **zwing,**
I don't know why,
she swallowed the **zwing,**
I guess she'll die.

The Vowel Song

Coauthor Ray Reutzel discovered while teaching first grade that his students needed a way to remember the fundamental vowel generalizations. He wrote the "Vowel Song," which can be sung to the tune of "Twinkle, Twinkle, Little Star," and it was an instant success. After sharing it with coauthor Robert Cooter, who was also teaching first grade at the time, Cooter decided to introduce the "Vowel Song" as a chant with hand gestures (claiming that his singing voice was not nearly as good as Reutzel's—who had studied music in college!). Cooter reproduced the "Vowel Song" onto chart paper, laminated it, and placed it in a prominent place in his classroom. Once again, the "Vowel Song" was a hit with 6-year-olds, this time on the other side of the United States. Following is Reutzel's "Vowel Song" for your own uses. Enjoy!

The Vowel Song*

The vowels we know
And you will see,
That we can say each perfectly,
ă as in apple
ā as in ate
And don't you think that we are great!
ĕ as in egg
ē as in eat
And don't you think that we are neat!
ĭ as in it

ī as in ice
And don't you think that we are nice!
ŏ as in pot
ō as in no
And don't you think it's time to go!
ŭ as in cut
ū as in cute
Now it's time to light the fuse!
Boom!!!

Onset and Rime

Adams (1990b) states that linguistic researchers have proposed an instructionally useful alternative form of word analysis known as *onsets* and *rimes*. As noted earlier, an **onset** is the part of the syllable that comes before the vowel; the **rime** is the rest (Adams, 1990b, p. 55). Although all syllables must have a rime, not all will have an onset. In the following list are a few examples of onsets and rimes in words:

Word	Onset	Rime
A	—	A
in	—	in
aft	—	aft
sat	s-	-at
trim	tr-	-im
spring	spr-	-ing

One may wonder what the usefulness of onset and rime is in the classroom, at least as far as word identification instruction is concerned. First, some evidence indicates that children are better able to identify the spelling of whole rimes than of individual vowel sounds (Adams, 1990b; Barton, Miller, & Macken, 1980; Blevins, 1997; Moustafa, 1997; Treiman, 1985). Second, children as young as 5 and 6 years of age can transfer what they know about the pronunciation of one word to another that has the same rime, such as *call* and *ball* (Adams, 1990b). Third, although many traditional phonics generalizations with vowels are very unstable, even irregular phonics patterns seem to remain stable within rimes. For example, the *ea* vowel digraph is quite consistent within rimes, with the exceptions of *-ear* in *hear* compared to *bear* and *-ead* in *bead* compared to *head* (Adams, 1990b). Finally, there appears to be some utility in the learning of rimes for children. Nearly 500 primary-level words can be derived through the following set of only 37 rimes (Adams, 1990b; Blachman, 1984):

-ack	-at	-ide	-ock
-ain	-ate	-ight	-oke
-ake	-aw	-ill	-op
-ale	-ay	-in	-or
-all	-eat	-ine	-ore
-ame	-ell	-ing	-uck
-an	-est	-ink	-ug
-ank	-ice	-ip	-ump
-ap	-ick	-ir	-unk
-ash			

The application of onset and rime to reading and word identification seems obvious. Students should find it easier to identify new words in print by locating familiar rimes and using the sound clue along with context to confirm the words' pronunciation. Spelling efficiency may also increase as rimes are matched with onsets to construct "invented" spellings (we prefer to call them "temporary" spellings so that children and parents understand that we intend to develop correct spellings).

One teacher recently remarked that the easiest way to teach rimes is through *rhymes.* She was exactly right. Children learn many otherwise laborious tasks through rhymes, songs, chants, and raps. Any of these that use rhyming words can be very useful to teachers. For example, a teacher may wish to use an excerpt like the one shown next from the book *Taxi Dog* by Debra and Sal Barracca to emphasize the -*ide* and -*ill* rimes. The rimes are noted in bold type for easy identification by the reader.

Rhymes, songs, and raps are fun ways to teach onsets and rimes.

It's just like a dream,
Me and Jim—we're a team!
I'm always there at his s**ide.**
We never stand st**ill,**
Every day's a new thr**ill**—
Come join us next time for a r**ide!** (1990, p. 30)

Structural Analysis of Words: An Important Next Step

Another way readers decode unfamiliar words in print is called *structural analysis.* Rather than attacking words on the letter-phoneme level, this kind of word identification uses a reader's knowledge of meaning "chunks" in words. Here's how it works. A reader encounters a word that is unknown to him in print (i.e., the word is known to him when he hears it, just not familiar in print). Let's say the word is *unbelievable.* Our reader in this example has heard the word part *believe* dozens of times in conversations and seen it in print (e.g., in sentences like "Yes, I believe you" or "I believe that all children should have a nice birthday party.") and immediately recognizes it. The prefix *un-* is likewise very familiar to the reader from other words he has learned, such as *untie, unreal,* and *unhook.* He is able to infer from his prior knowledge of words that *un-* means something like "not" or "to reverse." Finally, the reader's mind focuses briefly on the suffix (and word) -*able* and its obvious meaning also deduced from his prior knowledge of words like *workable.* In our example, then, the reader has found a new way of decoding words at something larger than the sound-symbol level. He progressed from the root word (*believe*), to the prefix (*un-*), to the suffix (-*able*). Furthermore, it was the meaning of these word parts that led to successful decoding. Structural analysis of words takes phonological awareness to a new and higher level.

Structural analysis uses a reader's knowledge of meaning "chunks" in words to identify familiar elements.

Comprehending prefixes, suffixes, and root words is a structural analysis skill.

How Structural Analysis of Words Works

Words are made up of basic meaning units known as **morphemes.** Morphemes may be divided into two classes: *bound* and *free. Bound morphemes* must be attached to a *root word* (sometimes called a *base word*) to have meaning. Prefixes and suffixes are bound morphemes (e.g., *pre-, un-, dis-, en-, inter-, extra-, -ed, -ies, -er, -ing*). *Free morphemes* (*base words or root words*) are meaning units that can stand alone and have meaning. The word *replay* has both a bound and a free morpheme: *re-,* the bound morpheme (prefix) meaning "again," and *play,* the free morpheme that has meaning on its own. Sometimes two free morphemes combine to form a new compound word, such as dog*house,* out*doors,* play*ground,* and to*night.* Studying words to identify familiar word elements is known as **structural analysis.**

***Morphemes** are the basic meaning units of words.*

The two classes of morphemes are bound *and* free.

As children become more proficient using word-identification strategies and context clues, they become more confident in "attacking" unknown words in print.

Teachers can help children begin to practice structural analysis of words in the same ways as for onset and rime. The idea to get across to students is that whenever a good reader comes to a word she cannot identify through phonics alone, she sometimes looks within the word for a recognizable base (root) word and its accompanying prefix, suffix, or endings (Durkin, 1989; Lass & Davis, 1985). In other words, we are telling our students to "look for something you know within the word."

The following selected examples of affixes are adapted from *The Reading Teacher's Book of Lists* (Fry, Polk, & Fountoukidis, 1984).

Prefixes

Prefix	Meaning	Example	Prefix	Meaning	Example
intro-	inside	introduce	ad-	to, toward	adhere
pro-	forward	project	para-	beside, by	paraphrase
post-	after	postdate	pre-	before	predate
sub-	under	submarine	per-	throughout	pervade
ultra-	beyond	ultramodern	ab-	from	abnormal
dis-	opposite	disagree	trans-	across	transatlantic

Suffixes

Suffix	Meaning	Example(s)	Suffix	Meaning	Example(s)
-ant	one who	servant	-ee	object of action	payee
-ist	one who practices	pianist	-ary	place for	library
-ence	state/quality of	violence	-ity	state/quality of	necessity
-ism	state/quality of	baptism	-ette	small	dinette
-s, -es	plural	cars	-ard	one who	coward
-kin	small	napkin	-ing	material	roofing

Putting It All Together: A Sequence of Word Identification Skills

Based on the research summarized thus far in this chapter, it is now possible for us to suggest a general listing of early literacy skills that directly relate to word identification. This sequence of early literacy milestone skills (see Figure 2.10) proceeds from emergent levels of phonemic awareness through phonics and other decoding skills. Children who become proficient in these abilities and practice them regularly in pleasurable reading will attain a high degree of fluency.

Summary

Recent research has confirmed the necessity of teaching children phonemic awareness, alphabetic principle, and phonics skills explicitly. In this chapter, we have described a research-supported sequence for teaching phonemic awareness skills, moving from a simple understanding that spoken words are made up of sound parts

Figure 2.10 Early literacy milestone skills

Stage 1: Phonemic Awareness
Simple awareness that spoken words have individual sound parts
Compound words: simple oral segmenting and blending
Syllables: oral segmenting and blending
Onset and rime: oral segmenting and blending
Individual sound by sound: oral segmenting and blending
Advanced phonemic awareness skills: oddity tasks and sound manipulation

Stage 2: Alphabetic Principle
Alphabet learning
Sound/symbol associations (awareness of phoneme/grapheme relationships)

Stage 3: Reading: Phonics and Decoding Strategies Development
Context clues (as a meaning-based word attack strategy)
Context clues plus the structural analysis skills
• compound words (segmenting and blending)
• syllabication (segmenting and blending)
• onset and rime (segmenting and blending)
Context clues plus letter-by-letter analysis (segmenting and blending)
• beginning sounds in words, plus . . .
• ending sounds in words, plus . . .
• medial sounds in words

Standards Note
Standard 6.1: The reading professional will be able to teach students to monitor their own word identification through the use of syntactic, semantic, and graphophonic relations. This chapter focuses on one of the three major cuing systems. After reading, prepare notes on how you would teach children to best self-monitor word identification. Be specific as to what they'll need to do at the word level when repair strategies are needed.

Check your understanding of chapter concepts by using the self-assessment for Chapter 2 on our Companion Website at www.prenhall.com/reutzel.

to the most abstract level of sound by sound segmentation, blending, and sound manipulation. As competence in phonemic awareness is reached, students are helped to gain an understanding that the sounds in spoken words can be symbolically represented by letters (alphabetic principle). This level of understanding brings students to the point of development where they are ready to acquire basic phonics skills.

After basic phonics skills have been learned, readers are ready to learn an even higher level of word identification called structural analysis. Here the reader uses his or her prior knowledge of word parts and their meaning to both pronounce and understand unfamiliar words in print. Thus, a great deal of this chapter presented a practical sequence of instruction leading to a fluent level word identification. In later chapters, we present research-proven strategies teachers can use to teach each of these important reading skills.

Figure 2.11   The Phonics Quick Test Answer Key

1. The word *sparkle* is divided between <u>r</u> and <u>k</u>. The *a* has an <u>r</u>-controlled sound, and the *e* <u>is silent</u>.

2. In the word *small, sm-* is known as the "onset" and *-all* is known as the <u>rime</u>.

3. *Ch* in the word *chair* is known as a <u>consonant digraph</u>.

4. The letter *c* in the word *city* is a <u>soft</u> sound, and in the word *cow* it is a <u>hard</u> sound.

5. The letters *bl* in the word *blue* are referred to as a consonant <u>blend</u>.

6. The underlined vowels in the words *<u>au</u>thor, spr<u>ea</u>d,* and *bl<u>ue</u>* are known as vowel *digraphs.*

7. The words *tag, run, cot,* and *get* have which vowel pattern? <u>Consonant — vowel — consonant (CVC)</u>

8. The words *glide, take,* and *use* have the <u>vowel — consonant — "e"</u> vowel pattern.

9. The single most powerful phonics skill we can teach to emergent readers for decoding unfamiliar words in print is <u>beginning</u> sounds in words. We introduce this skill using <u>consonant</u> sounds first because they are <u>the most constant (or "dependable" or "reliable')</u>.

10. The word part *work* in the word *working* is known as a <u>root (for " base" or "unbound morpheme") word</u>.

11. The word part *-ing* in the word *working* is known as a <u>suffix (for "bound morpheme")</u>.

12. Cues to the meaning and pronunciation of unfamiliar words in print are often found in the print surrounding the unfamiliar—which is to say, in the <u>context</u>.

Grading Key for Teachers

Number correct	Evaluation
12	Wow, you're good! (You must have had no social life in college.)
10–11	Not too bad, but you may need a brush-up (i.e., read this chapter).
7–9	Emergency! Take a refresher course, quick (i.e., read this chapter)!
0–6	Have you ever considered a career in telemarketing?! (Just kidding, but read this chapter . . . right away!)

Concept Applications

In the Classroom

1. Using the information summarized on the National Reading Panel find-ings, develop an informal test you can use with kindergarteners to as-sess their current phonemeic awareness abilities. It should include activities in each of the following areas:

   - Phoneme isolation
   - Phoneme identity
   - Phoneme categorization
   - Phoneme blending
   - Phoneme segmentation
   - Phoneme deletion
   - Phoneme addition
   - Phoneme substitution

2. Conduct a library and Internet search for books that could be used to help you introduce *alphabetic principle* to emergent readers. After lo-cating and reading each, prepare an annotated bibliography to share with a group of your colleagues in class. If at least five persons share their annotated bibliographies, you will each have a marvelous resource for your future teaching.

3. Go online and find the Web page for your state's education department. Locate and print out the scope and sequence of recommended skills in the areas of phonemic awareness, alphabetic principle, and phonics. Compare this list to the curriculum guide from the school district in which you plan to have your internship (student teaching). Prepare a "Comprehensive Decoding Checklist" for you to use in profiling each child's decoding abilities. This will be useful to you later when we discuss reading assessment in this text. More important, you will have created a valuable tool for informing your teaching.

In the Field

1. Using one of the following recommended resources, develop and teach to a small group of children several lessons for the following phonemic awareness skills:

   - Simple oral segmenting and blending of compound words
   - Oral segmenting and blending of syllables
   - Oral segmenting and blending of onsets and rimes
   - Sound by sound oral segmenting and blending

2. Now take advantage of the work you accomplished in activities 1 and 3 of the "*In the Classroom*" section. Arrange to work one on one with several emergent readers in kindergarten or grade 1. Administer the informal

assessment you created for activity 1 to determine each child's level of phonemic awareness. Then, using the "Comprehensive Decoding Checklist" you created for activity 3, chart each student individually using your findings. Share your results with the cooperating classroom teacher who has these students in her room to see to what extent your findings are in agreement with her perceptions. (Note: Remember that the classroom teacher has spent much more time with these children and may have some different perceptions. Sometimes it's a bit like comparing a snapshot with a color movie: the teacher's is a much more comprehensive viewpoint.)

Classroom Resources for Teachers

Blevins, W. (1997). *Phonemic awareness activities for early reading success.* New York: Scholastic.

Fry, E. B., Polk, J. K., & Fountoukidis, D. (1984). *The reading teacher's book of lists.* Englewood Cliffs, NJ: Prentice Hall.

Reutzel, D. R., & Cooter, R. B. (2003). *Strategies for reading assessment and instruction: Helping every child succeed* (2nd ed.). Upper Saddle River, NJ: Merrill/Prentice Hall.

Recommended Readings

American Federation of Teachers. (1999). *Teaching reading is rocket science: What expert teachers of reading should know and be able to do.* Washington, DC: Author.

Armbruster, B. B., Lehr, F., & Osborn, J. (2001). *Put reading first: The research building blocks of teaching children to read.* Jessup, MD: National Institute for Literacy/ED Pubs.

Burns, M. S., Griffin, P., & Snow, C. E. (1999). *Starting out right: A guide to promoting children's reading success.* Washington, DC: National Academy Press.

Center for the Improvement of Early Reading Achievement. (1998). *Every child a reader.* Ann Arbor, MI: Author.

Flippo, R. F. (2001). *Reading Researchers in Search of Common Ground.* Newark, DE: International Reading Association.

Freeman, D. E., & Freeman, Y. S. (1994). *Between worlds: Access to second language acquisition.* Portsmouth, NH: Heinemann.

National Education Association. (2000). *Report of the National Education Association's Task Force on Reading 2000.* Washington, DC: Author.

National Reading Panel. (2000). *Report of the National Reading Panel: Teaching children to read.* Washington, DC: National Institute of Child Health and Human Development. Available online at **www.nationalreadingpanel.org**.

Snow, C. E., Burns, M. S., and Griffin, P. (1998). *Preventing reading difficulties in young children.* Washington, DC: National Academy Press.

3 Increasing Vocabulary and Word Knowledge

Focus Questions

When you are finished studying this chapter, you should be able to answer these questions:

1. What are the four acquired vocabularies? Give examples of each.

2. Word learning happens by degree. What are the three levels of vocabulary learning?

3. There has been a great deal of scientific research on vocabulary learning in recent years. What are the "evidence-based" principles listed in this chapter?

4. Not all words are created equal. Which words are worth teaching?

5. Why are some words more difficult to learn than others? What strategies can teachers use to help children learn them?

6. How can we help English language learners acquire new vocabularies for reading, writing, and speaking?

7. How does the study of various word functions (e.g., synonyms, euphemisms, and onomatopoeia) enable students to better communicate and understand the messages of others?

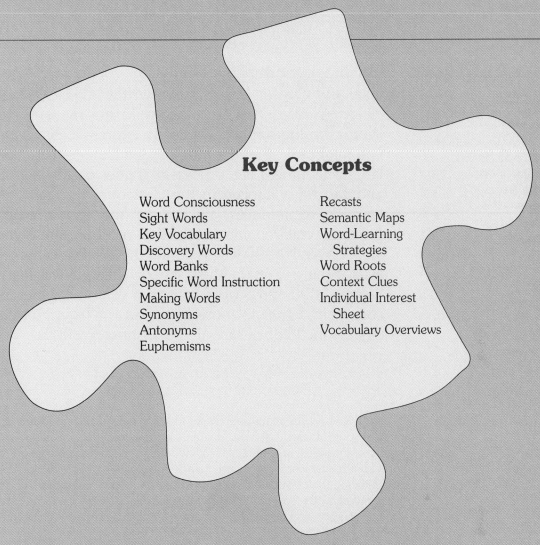

Key Concepts

Word Consciousness
Sight Words
Key Vocabulary
Discovery Words
Word Banks
Specific Word Instruction
Making Words
Synonyms
Antonyms
Euphemisms

Recasts
Semantic Maps
Word-Learning
  Strategies
Word Roots
Context Clues
Individual Interest
  Sheet
Vocabulary Overviews

Recognizing and understanding written vocabulary is essential to reading. Indeed, unless children are able to understand word meanings as they read, the process is reduced to mindless decoding (Fountas & Pinnell, 1996). Children who come to school with thousands of "words in their head"—words they can hear, understand, and use in their daily lives—are already on the path to learning success (Allington & Cunningham, 1996). Similarly, children who have small listening, speaking, and reading vocabularies—from what could be termed "language deprived backgrounds"—must receive immediate attention if they are to have any real chance at reading success (Johnson, 2001; National Research Council, 1998).

Visit Chapter 3 of our Companion Website at www.prenhall.com/reutzel to look into the chapter objectives, standards, and principles, and pertinent Web links associated with increasing vocabulary and word knowledge.

On the importance of building vocabulary knowledge, Reutzel and Cooter (2003) have written the following:

Words are the symbols we use to express ideas; *captions,* you might say, that describe our life experiences. Vocabulary development is a process that goes on throughout life and can be enhanced in the classroom through enticing learning experiences. Except for the economically deprived or children with disabilities, most acquire a vocabulary of over 10,000 words during the first five years of their lives (Smith, 1987). Most school children will learn between 2,000 and 3,600 words per year, though estimates vary from 1,500 to more than 8,000 (Nagy, Herman, & Anderson, 1985; Clark, 1993; Johnson, 2001).

HOW DO STUDENTS ACQUIRE NEW VOCABULARY?

The truth is, there are many sources for learning new words, and some of them may surprise you—at least, just a bit. Students learn a great deal of their new vocabulary from conversations, independent reading, and even from the media. However, they do not learn new words from each source equally, nor is each source of equal value in expanding their vocabularies. To illustrate the point, here are some selected statistics revealing the sources of rare words (i.e., *new* or *unfamiliar* words) found in various language and text forms that are commonly accessed by children and adults (Cunningham & Stanovich, 1998; Rasinski, 1998):

Source	Number of "rare" (uncommon) words per 1,000
Adult speech (expert testimony)	28.4
Adult speech (college graduates to friends)	17.3
Prime time adult television	22.7
Mister Rogers and *Sesame Street*	2.0
Children's books—preschool	16.3
Children's books—elementary	30.9
Comic books	53.5
Popular magazines	65.7
Newspapers	68.3
Adult books	52.7
Scientific article abstracts	128.0

Were you surprised by any of these findings? How about the number of rare words used by college graduates in their conversations with friends compared to the number commonly found in comic books or, for that matter, the number of uncommon words found in comic books compared to elementary children's books? Perhaps there is a case to be made for daily reading for children in self-selected books including comics and popular magazines.

In this chapter, we take a careful look, an *evidence-based* one, at how children learn new words, the kinds of vocabulary they should learn, and ways in which new vocabulary should be taught. As you will see, vocabulary knowledge is an essential building block of reading and writing processes.

RESEARCH ON VOCABULARY LEARNING

In reviewing recent research on vocabulary learning and its role in reading, one conclusion becomes crystal clear: reading and writing activities, obviously, are dependent on words. Indeed, all good readers have a large store of high-frequency words they can read and spell instantly and automatically (Allington & Cunningham, 1996). So what do we know about vocabulary learning? To partially answer this question, we discuss in the following section key findings supported by recent research (Adams, 1990; Allington & Cunningham, 1996; Burns, Griffin, & Snow, 1999; Guthrie, 1982; Johnson, 2001; Krashen, 1993; Beck & McKeown, 1985; Nagy et al., 1985; National Reading Panel, 2000; National Research Council, 1998; Partnership for Reading, 2001; Stahl & Fairbanks, 1986; Stahl, Hare, Sinatra, & Gregory, 1991; Stahl & Jacobson, 1986; Templeton, 1995).

Vocabulary Is Built Through Language Interactions

Children who are exposed to advanced vocabulary through conversations learn words needed later on to help recognize and comprehend while reading. Burns et al. (1999) explain it this way:

> Vocalization in the crib gives way to play with rhyming language and nonsense words. Toddlers find that the words they use in conversation and the objects they represent are depicted in books—that the picture is a symbol for the real object and that the writing represents spoken language. In addition to listening to stories, children label the objects in books, comment on the characters, and request that an adult read to them. In their third and fourth years, children use new vocabulary and grammatical constructions in their own speech. Talking to adults is children's best source to exposure to new vocabulary and ideas. (p. 19)

Reading and being read to also increase vocabulary learning. Books give us challenging ideas, colorful descriptive words and concepts, and new knowledge and information about the world in which we live. Conversely, children who come to school with limited vocabularies, because of either second-language learning or the effects of poverty (Cooter, 2003), struggle to take even their first steps in reading and understanding texts. Burns et al. (1999) ask, "How can they understand a science book about *volcanoes, silkworms,* or *Inuits*? What if they know nothing of *mountains, caterpillars,* or *snow and cold climates*?" (p. 70). As teachers, we must make sure that *no child is left behind* because of weak vocabulary development.

Children from disadvantaged backgrounds, where frequently books and language-oriented games are not part of their daily lives, are at greater risk for reading failure.

Research Findings by the National Reading Panel

To determine how vocabulary can best be taught and related to the reading comprehension process, the National Reading Panel examined more than 20,000 research citations identified through electronic and manual literature searches. From this set, citations were removed if they did not meet predetermined scientific criteria. Fifty studies dating from 1979 to the present were reviewed in detail.

The studies reviewed suggest that vocabulary instruction does not necessarily lead to gains in comprehension unless the methods used are appropriate to the age and ability of the reader. The use of computers in vocabulary instruction was found to be more effective than some traditional methods in a few studies and is clearly emerging as a potentially valuable aid to classroom teachers in the area of vocabulary instruction.

Vocabulary also can be learned incidentally in the context of storybook reading or in listening to others read. Learning words before reading a text is also helpful. Techniques such as task restructuring and repeated exposure (including having the student encounter words in various contexts) appear to enhance vocabulary development. In addition, substituting easy words for more difficult words can assist low-achieving students.

Four Types of Vocabulary

The four types of vocabulary are listening, speaking, reading, and writing.

Though we often speak of vocabulary as if it were a single thing, it is not; human beings acquire four types of vocabulary. They are, in descending order according to size, *listening, speaking, reading*, and *writing. Listening vocabulary,* the largest, is made up of words we can hear and understand. All other vocabularies are subsets of our listening vocabulary. The second-largest vocabulary, *speaking vocabulary,* is comprised of words we can use when we speak. Next is our *reading vocabulary,* or words we can identify and understand when we read. The smallest is our *writing vocabulary,* or words we use in writing. These four vocabularies are continually nurtured in the effective teacher's classroom.

Levels of Vocabulary Learning

Be sure and go to the National Reading Panel Web site on the Internet at www.nationalreadingpanel.org *for a free copy of their conclusions.*

The truth is, words are *not* either "known" or "unknown." As with most new learning, new vocabulary words and concepts are learned by degree. The Partnership for Reading (2001), in summarizing conclusions drawn by the National Reading Panel, described three levels of vocabulary learning: *unknown, acquainted,* and *established.* Definitions for each of these three levels are presented in Figure 3.1. Bear in mind that these levels or "degrees" of learning apply to each of the four vocabulary types—listening, speaking, reading, and writing—so helping children build strong reading and writing vocabularies can sometimes be a formidable task indeed.

If you think about it, sometimes we learn new meanings to words that are already known to us. The word *race,* for example, has many different meanings (to run a race, a group of people, and so on). One of the most challenging tasks for students

Figure 3.1   Levels of vocabulary learning (Partnership for Reading, 2001)

Level of Word Knowledge	Definition
Unknown	The word is completely unfamiliar, and its meaning is unknown.
Acquainted	The word is somewhat familiar; the student has some idea of its basic meaning.
Established	The word is very familiar; the student can immediately recognize its meaning and use the word correctly.

can be learning the meaning of a new word representing an unknown concept. According to the research,

> Much of learning in the content areas involves this type of word learning. As students learn about *deserts, hurricanes,* and *immigrants,* they may be learning both new concepts and new words. Learning words and concepts in science, social studies, and mathematics is even more challenging because each major concept often is associated with many other new concepts. For example, the concept *deserts* is often associated with other concepts that may be unfamiliar, such as cactus, plateau, and mesa. (Partnership for Reading, 2001, p. 43)

WHAT RESEARCH TELLS US ABOUT *TEACHING* VOCABULARY

Most vocabulary is learned indirectly, but some vocabulary *must* be taught directly. The following conclusions about indirect vocabulary learning and direct vocabulary instruction are of particular interest and value to classroom teachers (National Reading Panel, 2000):

Children learn the meanings of most words indirectly through everyday experiences with oral and written language.

There are typically three ways children learn vocabulary indirectly. First, they participate in oral language every day. Children learn word meanings through conversations with other people, and as they participate in conversations, they often hear words repeated several times. The more conversations children have, the more word words they learn.

Another, indirect way children learn words is by being read to. Reading aloud is especially powerful when the reader pauses during reading to define an unfamiliar word and, after reading, engages the child in a conversation about the book. Conversations about books help children learn new words and concepts and relate them to their prior knowledge and experience (Partnership for Reading, 2001).

The third way children learn new words indirectly is through their own reading. This is one of many reasons why many teachers feel that daily independent reading practice sessions of 10 to 20 minutes are so critical (Krashen, 1993). Put simply, the more children read, the more words they'll learn. There is a caveat to mention on this point, however. Struggling readers are often incapable of sitting and reading on their own for extended periods of time. For best results, many readers will get much more from their practice reading when working with a "buddy" who has greater ability. In Chapter 7, we offer specific strategies that can help you implement buddy reading in your classroom.

From the evidenced-based reading research, we can conclude that students learn vocabulary indirectly when they hear and see words used in many different contexts. Conversations, read-aloud experiences, and independent reading are essential.

Students learn vocabulary when they are taught individual words and word-learning strategies directly.

Direct instruction helps students learn difficult words (Johnson, 2001), such as words that represent complex concepts that are not part of the students' everyday experiences (National Reading Panel, 2000). We also know that when a teacher *preteaches* new words that are associated with a text the students are about to read, better reading comprehension results.

As mentioned previously, direct vocabulary instruction should include specific word learning as well as teaching students word-learning strategies they can use on their own.

Children learn most of their vocabulary indirectly by having conversations with others, by being read to, and while doing their own reading.

Repeated readings of familiar books and passages (e.g., songs and poetry) can help students in their vocabulary learning.

Vocabulary instruction results in an increase in word knowledge and reading comprehension.

Developing "word consciousness" can boost vocabulary learning.

Word consciousness learning activities stimulate an awareness and interest in words, their meanings, and their *power*. Word-conscious students enjoy words and are zealous about learning them. In addition, they have been taught how to learn new and interesting words.

The key to capitalizing on word consciousness is through wide reading and use of the writing process. When reading a new book aloud to students, call their attention to the way the author chooses his or her words to convey particular meanings. Imagine the fun you can have discussing some of the intense words used by Gary Paulsen (1987) in his book *Hatchet,* Shel Silverstein's (1974) clever use of rhyming words in his book of poetry *Where the Sidewalk Ends,* or the downright "magical" word selection employed by J. K. Rowling (1998) in *Harry Potter and the Sorcerer's Stone.* Encourage your students to play with words, such as with puns or self-created raps. Help them research a word's history and search for examples of a word's usage in their everyday lives.

PRINCIPLES OF EFFECTIVE VOCABULARY INSTRUCTION

From the research cited previously, as well as that conducted by Stahl (1986) and Rasinski (1998), we have developed a list of principles for effective vocabulary instruction for teachers to consider:

Principle 1:   Vocabulary is learned best through *direct,* hands-on experience.

Context helps readers choose the correct meaning for multiple-meaning words. The old adage that "experience is the best teacher" is certainly true in vocabulary learning. The next-best way to learn new vocabulary is through indirect, vicarious experiences through daily reading in interesting and varied texts (Rasinski, 1998). Marilyn Jager Adams (1990) put it this way:

> The best way to build children's visual vocabulary is to have them read meaningful words in meaningful contexts. The more meaningful reading that children do, the larger will be their repertoires of meanings, the greater their sensitivity to orthographic structure, and the stronger, better refined, and more productive will be their associations between words and meanings. (p. 156)

Principle 2:   Teachers should offer both *definitions* and *context* during vocabulary instruction.

As children learn new words, they do so in two ways. First, students learn basic definitions or information that helps determine the connections of the new word to known words (i.e., elaboration). This step can be accomplished by simply providing the definition, building with students semantic maps linking the known with the new, and through other comparisons, such as synonyms, antonyms, classification schemes, word roots, and affixes.

Second, context information has to do with knowing the basic core definition of a word and how it varies or is changed in different texts. For example, the word *run* is generally thought of as a verb meaning "to move swiftly." When looking for this simple word in the dictionary, one quickly realizes that the word *run* has approximately 50 definitions. There is the word *run,* as in "running a race," "a run of bad luck," or the "run" women sometimes get in their hosiery. Context helps the reader know which definition the author intends. In fact, without context, it is impossible to say with certainty which meaning of the word *run* is intended. Thus, it is important for teachers to help students understand both the *definitional* and the *contextual* relations of words. Vocabulary instruction should include both aspects if reading comprehension is to benefit.

Principle 3: Effective vocabulary instruction must include a depth of learning component as well as a breadth of word knowledge.

Deep processing connects new vocabulary with students' background knowledge. Depth of learning, or "deep processing" of vocabulary, has two potential meanings: relating the word to information the student already knows (elaboration) and spending time on the task of learning new words (expansion). Stahl (1986) defines three levels of processing for vocabulary instruction:

1. *Association processing:* Students learn simple associations through synonyms and word associations.

2. *Comprehension processing:* Students move beyond simple associations by doing something with the association, such as fitting the word into a sentence blank, classifying the word with other words, or finding antonyms.

3. *Generation processing:* Students use the comprehended association to generate a new or novel product (sometimes called *generative comprehension*). This process could involve a restatement of the definition in the student's own words, creating a novel sentence using the word correctly in a clear context, or comparing the definition to the student's personal experiences. One caution relates to the generation of sentences by students: Sometimes students generate sentences without really processing the information deeply, as with students who begin each sentence with "This is a . . . " (Pearson, 1985; Stahl, 1986).

Principle 4: Students need to have *multiple exposures* to new reading vocabulary words.

Notice that multiple exposures to new vocabulary improve comprehension.

Vocabulary learning requires repetition. To learn words thoroughly, students need to see, hear, and use words many times in many contexts (Rasinski, 1998). Providing students with multiple exposures in varied contexts appears to significantly improve reading comprehension. The amount of time spent reading these new words also seems to be a relevant factor for improving comprehension.

WHICH WORDS SHOULD WE TEACH?

McKeown and Beck (1988) have addressed an important issue in their research: *Which vocabulary should be taught in elementary classrooms?* They point out that one problem with traditional vocabulary instruction in basal readers has been the equal treatment of all categories of words. As an example, a mythology selection in a basal reader about *Arachne,* who loved to weave, gives the word *loom* as much attention as the word *agreement.* McKeown and Beck point out that although the word *loom* may be helpful in understanding more about spinning, it is a word of relatively low use compared to the word *agreement,* which is key to understanding the story and of much higher utility as students move into adult life.

Not all words are created equal, especially in terms of difficulty in elementary classrooms. As McKeown and Beck (1988) explained,

Memorizing long lists of isolated words is a relatively ineffective way to teach new vocabulary. In fact, students learn new vocabulary some 10 times faster by reading than through intensive vocabulary instruction with word lists (Krashen, 1993; Nagy et al., 1985).

Standards Note
Standard 2.6: The reading professional will understand that children need opportunities to integrate their use of literacy through reading, writing, listening, speaking, viewing, and visually representing. This chapter is clear about the fact that multiple exposures to new words are necessary. As you read, plan an integrated unit focusing on vocabulary learning, using all six of the language arts.

When selecting new words to teach, consider the importance of the word to understanding the selection.

The choice of which words to teach and what kind of attention to give them depends on a variety of factors, such as importance of the words for understanding the selection, relationship to specific domains of knowledge, general utility, and relationship to other lessons and classroom events. (p. 45)

Why You Shouldn't Try to Teach *All* Unknown Words

There are several good reasons why you should not try to directly teach *all* unknown words. For one thing, the text may have too many words that are unknown to your students, far too many for direct instruction. You'll want to limit your vocabulary teaching time to no more than 5 to 10 minutes so that they can spend the bulk of their time actually reading. Most of your students will be able to handle a fair amount of new words, up to 5%, simply by using context clues in the passage. Also, your students need many opportunities to *practice and use* the word-learning strategies you are teaching them for learning unknown words on their own.

Words You *Should* Teach

Realistically, you will probably be able to teach thoroughly only a few new words (8 to 10) per week, so you need to choose the words you teach carefully. Focus your energies on high-utility words and words that are important to the meaning of the selections you will be reading in class. A logical place to begin vocabulary instruction is the teaching of *sight words*.

Sight Words

Sight words occur frequently in most texts and account for a majority of written words. Understanding text relies in part on the immediate recognition of these "high frequency" words. Studies of print have found that just 109 words account for upward of 50% of all words in student textbooks, and a total of only 5,000 words accounts for about 90% of the words in student texts (Adams 1990b; Carroll, Davies, & Richman, 1971). Knowledge of high-frequency sight words, logically, can help readers manage text in a more fluent way. Many of these words, such as *the, from, but, because, that*, and *this*, sometimes called *structure words*, carry little meaning but do affect the flow and coherence of the text being read. The actual meaning of the text depends on the ready knowledge of less frequent words, or *lexical words*, such as *automobile, aristocrat, pulley, streetcar, Martin Luther King*, and *phantom*. Adams et al. (1991) concluded that

> while the cohesion and connectivity of English text is owed most to its frequent words (e.g., *it, that, this, and, because, when, while*), its meaning depends disproportionately on its less frequent words (e.g., *doctor, fever, infection, medicine, penicillin, Alexander, Fleming, melon, mold, poison, bacteria, antibiotic, protect, germs, disease*). (p. 394)

Sight words are high-frequency words that students recognize immediately by sight.

It is critical that you, the teacher, make sure that all your students learn to instantly recognize sight words, so you should have a reliable list of these words as a resource. Figure 3.2 presents the Fry (1980) word list of the 300 most common words in print. The Fry list is widely regarded as the best-researched list of sight words in the English language.

Figure 3.2 Fry new instant word list

Teach these words any way you can. Teaching suggestions might include: 1. Flashcards for flashing and sorting. 2. Word Walls. 3. Pocket charts for short sentences or stories using Instant Words. 4. Teacher written cooperative stories written on the chalk board. 5. Spelling lessons. 6. Games such as Bingo or board games. 7. Lots of easy reading. 8. Give a copy of this sheet to the student for home study.

Test these words by asking the students to read them instantly. If they can cross out the word. Test each student beginning, mid-year, and end-year.

First Hundred				Second Hundred				Third Hundred			
1–25	26–50	51–75	76–100	101–125	126–150	151–175	176–200	201–225	226–250	251–275	276–300
the	or	will	number	over	say	set	try	high	saw	important	miss
of	one	up	no	new	great	put	kind	every	left	until	idea
and	had	other	way	sound	where	end	hand	near	don't	children	enough
a	by	about	could	take	help	does	picture	add	few	side	eat
to	words	out	people	only	through	another	again	food	while	feet	face
in	but	many	my	little	much	well	change	between	along	car	watch
is	not	then	than	work	before	large	off	own	might	mile	far
you	what	them	first	know	line	must	play	below	close	night	Indian
that	all	these	water	place	right	big	spell	country	something	walk	really
it	were	so	been	year	too	even	air	plant	seem	white	almost
he	we	some	call	live	mean	such	away	last	next	sea	let
was	when	her	who	me	old	because	animal	school	hard	began	above
for	your	would	am	back	any	turn	house	father	open	grow	girl
on	can	make	its	give	same	here	point	keep	example	took	sometimes
are	said	like	now	most	tell	why	page	tree	begin	river	mountain
as	there	him	find	very	boy	ask	letter	never	life	four	cut
with	use	into	long	after	follow	went	mother	start	always	carry	young
his	an	time	down	thing	came	men	answer	city	those	state	talk
they	each	has	day	our	want	read	found	earth	both	once	soon
I	which	look	did	just	show	need	study	eye	paper	book	list
at	she	two	get	name	also	land	still	light	together	hear	song
be	do	more	come	good	around	different	learn	thought	got	stop	being
this	how	write	made	sentence	farm	home	should	head	group	without	leave
have	their	go	may	man	three	us	America	under	often	second	family
from	if	see	part	think	small	move	world	story	run	later	it's

From "The New Instant Word List," by Edward Fry, *The Reading Teacher*, December 1980, pp. 284–289. Reprinted with permission of Edward Fry and the International Reading Association.

Figure 3.3   Cornejo's high-frequency word list for Spanish (graded)

Pre-Primer	Primer	1st	2nd	3rd	4th	5th
a	alto	bonita	ayer	amar	árbol	amistad
azul	flor	arriba	aqui	aquí	bandera	azucar
bajo	blusa	fruta	año	debajo	abeja	contento
mi	ella	globo	cerca	familia	escuela	corazón
mesa	ir	estar	desde	fiesta	fácil	compleaños
pan	leche	café	donde	grande	fuego	edad
mamá	más	letra	hacer	hermana	hacia	escribir
lado	niño	luna	hasta	jueves	idea	felicidad
la	padre	luz	hijo	lápiz	jardín	guitarra
papá	por	muy	hoy	miércoles	llegar	estrella
me	si	noche	leer	once	manzana	igual
no	tan	nombre	libro	quince	muñeca	invierno
esa	sobre	nosotros	martes	sábado	naranja	orquesta
el	sin	nunca	mejor	semana	saludar	primavera
en	tras	ojo	mucho	silla	sueño	recordar
cuna	color	pelota	oir	sobrino	señorita	respeto
dos	al	porque	papel	vivir	tierra	tijeras
mi	día	rojo	paz	zapato	traer	último
de	bien	té	quien	tarde	ventana	querer
los	chico	taza	usted	traje	queso	otoño

From Cornejo, R. (1972). *Spanish High Frequency Word List*. Austin, TX: Southwestern Educational Development Laboratory. Used by permission.

Sight Words for Bilingual Classrooms (Spanish)

Just as the most common sight words have been identified in English, high-frequency words have also been identified for Spanish (Cornejo, 1972). This popular word list is divided by grade and presented in Figure 3.3.

Key Vocabulary

Key vocabulary are organic or lexical words that come from within the child and his or her own experiences.

Silvia Ashton-Warner, in her classic book *Teacher* (1963), described **key vocabulary** words as "organic," or *lexical,* words that come from within the child and his or her own experiences. Ashton-Warner states that key vocabulary words act as "captions" for important events in life that the child has experienced.

Here's how the process works. Children come to the teacher individually at an appointed time or during a group experience and indicate which words he or she would like to learn. For instance, the teacher may ask, "What word would you like to learn today?" The child responds with a lexical word—perhaps a word like *police, ghost,* or *sing.* Once the child has told the teacher a word she would like to learn, the teacher writes the word on an index card or a small piece of tagboard using a dark marker. The student is then instructed to share the word with as many people as possible during the day. After the child has done so, the word is added to her writing folder or "word bank" for future use in writing.

Ashton-Warner found that the most common categories of key vocabulary words children wanted to learn were *fear words* (*dog, bull, kill, police*), sex (as she called them) or *affection words* (*love, kiss, sing, darling*), *locomotion words* (*bus, car, truck, jet*), and a *miscellaneous* category that generally reflects cultural and other considerations (*socks, frog, beer, Disneyland, Dallas Cowboys*).

Ashton-Warner (1963) referred to key vocabulary as "one-look words" because one look is usually all that is required for permanent learning to take place. The reason that these words seem so easy for children to learn is that they usually carry strong emotional significance and, once seen, are almost never forgotten. This process helps children begin to build a significant cadre of "lexical sight words."

Discovery Words

During the course of a typical school day, students are exposed to many new words. These words are often discovered as a result of studies in the content areas. Words such as *experiment, algebra, social, enterprise, conquest, Bengal tiger, spider,* and *cocoon* find their way into students' listening and speaking vocabulary. Every effort should be made to add these **discovery words** to the word bank as they are discussed in their natural context. Such words often appear in new student compositions. Developing vocabulary in content areas can help children discover words in their natural context.

Discovery words are words that students are exposed to throughout a day, often as a result of studies in the content areas.

Which Words Are The Most Difficult to Learn?

Here are some examples of words that can be especially difficult for your students (National Reading Panel, 2000):

• *Words with multiple meanings* are quite challenging for students. They sometimes have trouble understanding that words with the same spelling and/or pronunciation can have different meanings, depending on their context. For example, note the different uses of *run* in the following sentences: "Molly complained when she found a *run* in her hose" versus "Jeff Johnston plans to *run* for Congress." Or, again, note the different uses and pronunciation of the word *read* in the following sentences: "I will *read* the story later today" versus "I *read* the story yesterday." Words with multiple meanings and/or pronunciations can be confusing for students. When they notice in the dictionary that a number of different definitions are possible; choosing the context-specific definition can be confusing.

Some of the most difficult words to learn are words with multiple meanings and idiomatic expressions.

• *Idiomatic expressions* also can be especially difficult for language-deficient students in inner-city settings and for students who are English language learners (Cooter, 2003). Because idiomatic expressions do not match literal meanings of the words used, you may need to explain to students expressions such as "chocolate moose," "gorilla war," "airplane hangers," or "get the picture." A great book to use as a catalyst for discussing idioms is Fred Gwynne's (1970) *A Chocolate Moose for Dinner.*

COMMON STRATEGIES USED IN VOCABULARY INSTRUCTION

An important question for teachers is this: *How can we help students increase their vocabulary knowledge?* In this section, we present a few of the most common and successful methods. In later chapters, we add to this methodological base for each grade-level range. We begin this discussion with *word banks*, a tool with which we have had much success.

Word Banks

Word banks are used to help students collect and review sight words. They can also be used as personal dictionaries. A word bank is simply a student-constructed box, file, or notebook in which newly discovered words are stored, reviewed, and used in their writing. In the early grades, teachers often collect small shoe boxes from local stores for this purpose. Children at the beginning of the year decorate the boxes to make them their own. In the upper grades, more formal-looking word banks are used to give an "adult" appearance; notebooks or recipe boxes are generally selected.

Alphabetic dividers can also be used at all levels to facilitate the quick location of word bank words. Alphabetic dividers in the early grades help students rehearse and reinforce knowledge of alphabetical order. Figure 3.4 shows an example of a word bank.

Specific Word Instruction

Specific word instruction can deepen students' knowledge of word meanings and, in turn, help them understand what they are hearing or reading (Johnson, 2001). It also can help them use words accurately in speaking and writing. Three

Figure 3.4   A word bank

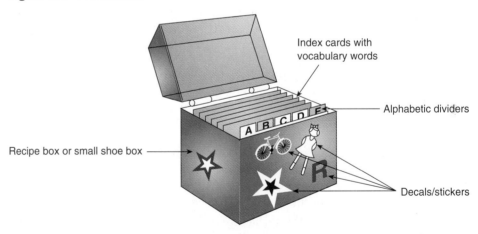

A word bank is a box in which children keep/file new words they are learning. The words are usually written in isolation on one side of the card and in a sentence on the back of the card (usually with a picture clue).

Example:

Front	Back
bicycle	Jason rode his bicycle to school.

ways of providing specific word instruction have been drawn from the research evidence (National Reading Panel, 2000; Partnership for Reading, 2001): *preteaching vocabulary, extended instruction,* and *repeated exposures.*

What Specific Word Instruction Looks Like in the Classroom

The Partnership for Reading, a federally funded collaborative effort of the National Institute for Literacy, the National Institute of Child Health and Human Development, and the U.S. Department of Education, published in 2001 a booklet titled *Put Reading First: The Research Building Blocks for Teaching Children to Read.* This document was constructed to help disseminate data from the 2000 report of the National Reading Panel and covers the topics of phonemic awareness instruction, phonics instruction, fluency instruction, vocabulary instruction, and text comprehension instruction. In order to help you better understand what each of the three specific word instruction components might look like in the classroom, we include examples after each definition borrowed from the *Put Reading First* booklet.

> **Preteaching vocabulary:** *Before students read, it is helpful to teach them specific words they will see in the text for the first time. Teaching vocabulary before reading helps students learn new words and comprehend the text.*

AN EXAMPLE OF CLASSROOM INSTRUCTION:

Preteaching Vocabulary*

A teacher plans to have his third-grade class read the novel *Stone Fox* by John Reynolds Gardiner. In this novel, a young boy enters a dogsled race in hopes of winning prize money to pay the taxes on his grandfather's farm. The teacher knows that understanding the concept of taxes is important to understanding the novel's plot. Therefore, before his students begin reading the novel, the teacher may do several things to make sure that they understand what the concept means and why it is important to the story. For example, the teacher may:

- engage students in a discussion of the concept of taxes; and/or
- read a sentence from the book that contains the word *taxes* and ask students to use context and their prior knowledge to try to figure out what it means.

To solidify their understanding of the word, the teacher might ask students to use *taxes* in their own sentences.

* From *Put Reading First: The Research Building Blocks for Teaching Children to Read* (2001). Noncopyrighted material published by the National Institute for Literacy. Available online at www.nifl.gov.

> **Extended instruction:** *Students should be saturated (marinated!) with word learning activities spread over an extended period of time. These should be activities that actively engage students (as opposed to passive learning tasks).*

AN EXAMPLE OF CLASSROOM INSTRUCTION:

Extended Instruction*

A first-grade teacher wants to help her students understand the concept of *jobs,* which is part of her social studies curriculum. Over a period of time, the teacher engages students in exercises in

Three ways of providing **specific word instruction** *are preteaching vocabulary, extended instruction, and repeated exposures.*

You can obtain Put Reading First: The Research Building Blocks for Teaching Children to Read *(2001) online free at www.nifl.gov. The report of the National Reading Panel,* Teaching Children to Read: An Evidence-Based Assessment of the Scientific Research Literature on Reading and Its Implications for Reading Instruction, *is likewise available online at* www.nationalreadingpanel.org.

which they work repeatedly with the meaning of the concept of jobs. The students have many opportunities to see and actively use the word in various contexts that reinforce its meaning.

The teacher begins by asking the students what they already know about jobs and by having them give examples of jobs their parents have. The class might have a discussion about the jobs of different people who work at the school.

The teacher then reads the class a simple book about jobs. The book introduces the idea that different jobs help people meet their needs and that jobs either provide goods or services. The book does not use the word *goods* and *services*; rather, it uses the verbs *makes* and *helps*.

The teacher then asks the students to make up sentences describing their parents' jobs by using the verbs *makes* and *helps* (e.g., "My mother is a doctor. She helps sick people get well.")

Next, the teacher asks students to brainstorm other jobs. Together, they decide whether the jobs are "making jobs" or "helping jobs." The job names are placed under the appropriate headings on a bulletin board. They might also suggest jobs that do not fit neatly into either category.

The teacher might then ask the students to share whether they think they would like to have a making job or a helping job when they grow up.

The teacher then asks the students to talk with their parents about jobs. She tells them to try to bring to class two new examples of jobs—one making job and one helping job.

As the students come across different jobs throughout the year (e.g., through reading books, on field trips, or through classroom guests), they can add the jobs to the appropriate categories on the bulletin board.

* From *Put Reading First: The Research Building Blocks for Teaching Children to Read* (2001). Noncopyrighted material published by the National Institute for Literacy. Available online at www.nifl.gov.

> ***Repeated exposures to vocabulary:*** *You will find that the more students use new words in different contexts, the more likely they are to learn the words permanently. When children see, hear, and work with specific words, they seem to learn them better.*

AN EXAMPLE OF CLASSROOM INSTRUCTION:

Repeated Exposures to Vocabulary*

A second-grade class is reading a biography of Benjamin Franklin. The biography discusses Franklin's important role as a scientist. The teacher wants to make sure that her students understand the meaning of the words *science* and *scientist*, both because the words are important to understanding the biography and because they are obviously very useful words to know in school and in everyday life.

At every opportunity, therefore, the teacher draws her students' attention to the words. She points out the words *scientist* and *science* in textbooks and reading selections, particularly in her science curriculum. She has students use the words in their own writing, especially during science instruction. She also asks them to listen for and find in print the words as they are used outside the classroom—in newspapers, in magazines, at museums, in television shows or movies, or on the Internet.

Then, as they read the biography, she discusses with students in what ways Benjamin Franklin was a scientist and what science meant in his time.

* From *Put Reading First: The Research Building Blocks for Teaching Children to Read* (2001). Noncopyrighted material published by the National Institute for Literacy. Available online at www.nifl.gov.

Making Words

Making Words (Cunningham & Cunningham, 1992) is an excellent word-learning strategy that helps children improve their phonetic understanding of words through invented or "temporary spellings" while also increasing their repertoire of vocabulary words they can recognize in print (Reutzel & Cooter, 2003a). Making Words will be a familiar strategy for anyone who has ever played the popular crossword board game Scrabble.

Making Words begins when students are given a number of specific letters with which to make words. They begin by making two- or three-letter words using the letters during a set amount of time, then progress to words having more letters until they finally arrive at a specific word that uses all the letters. This final word is usually the main word to be taught for the day, but the other words discovered may be new for some students. By manipulating the letters to make two-, three-, and four-letter words (or longer) using temporary or "transitional" spellings, students have an opportunity to practice their phonemic awareness skills. Making words is recommended as a 15-minute activity when used with first and second graders. Tables 3.1, 3.2, and 3.3 summarize and adapt the steps in planning and teaching a Making Words lesson suggested by Cunningham and Cunningham (1992).

Table 3.1 Planning a making words lesson

1. Choose a word to be the final word to be emphasized in the lesson. It should be a key word that is chosen from a reading selection to be read by the class, fiction or nonfiction, or may be of particular interest to the group. Be sure to select a word that has enough vowels and/or one that fits letter-sound patterns useful for most children at their developmental stage in reading and writing. For illustrative purposes, we will use the word *thunder* in these instructions, as suggested by Cunningham and Cunningham (1992).
2. Make a list of shorter words that can be spelled using the main word to be learned. For the word *thunder,* one could derive the following words: *red, Ted, Ned/den/end* (note: these all use the same letters), *her, hut, herd, turn, hunt, hurt, under, hunted, turned, thunder.*

   From the words you were able to list, select 12 to 15 words that include such aspects of written language as (a) words that can be used to emphasize a certain kind of pattern, (b) big and little words, (c) words that can be made with the same letters in different positions (as with *Ned, end, den*), (d) a proper noun (if possible) to remind them when we use capital letters, and especially (e) words that students already have in their listening vocabularies.
3. Write all these words on large index cards and order them from smallest to largest words. Also, write each of the individual letters found in the key word for the day on large index cards (make two sets of these).
4. Reorder the words one more time to group them according to letter patterns and/or to demonstrate how shifting around letters can form new words. Store the two sets of large single-letter cards in two envelopes—one for the teacher and one for children participating during the modeling activity.
5. Store the word stacks in envelopes and note on the outside the words/patterns to be emphasized during the lesson. Also, note clues that you can use with the children to help them discover the words you desire. For example, "See if you can make a three-letter word that is the name of the room in some people's homes where they like to watch television." (*den*)

Making Words *is a word-learning strategy that helps children improve their phonetic understanding of words through temporary spellings while increasing the amount of vocabulary words they can recognize in print.*

Standards Note
Standard 6.5: The reading professional will be able to teach students to recognize and use various spelling patterns in the English language as an aid to work identification. As you learn about "making words," list on a T chart the advantages and disadvantages of onset and rime teaching as opposed to traditional letter-sound relationships.

Table 3.2   Teaching a making words lesson

1. Place the large single letters from the key word in a the pocket chart or along the chalkboard ledge.
2. For modeling purposes the first time you use Making Words, select one of the students to be the "passer" and ask that child to pass the large single letters to other designated children.
3. Hold up and name each of the letter cards and have students selected to participate in the modeling exercise respond by holding up their matching card.
4. Write the numeral 2 (or 3 if there are no two-letter words in this lesson) on the board. Next, tell the student "volunteers" the clue you developed for the desired word. Then tell the student volunteers to put together two (or three) of their letters to form the desired word.
5. Continue directing the students to make more words using the clues provided and the letter cards until you have helped them discovered all but the final key word (the one that uses all the letters). Ask the student volunteers if they can guess what the key word is. If not, ask the remainder of the class if anyone can guess what it is. If no one is able to do so, offer them a meaning clue (e.g., " I am thinking of a word with letters that means . . . ").
6. Repeat these steps the next day with the whole group as a guided practice activity using a new word.

Table 3.3   Making words: additional examples

Sample Making Words lessons (Cunningham & Cunningham, 1992)

Lesson using one vowel:
Letter cards: uknrst
Words to make: us, nut, rut, sun, sunk, runs, ruts/rust, tusk, stun, stunk, trunk, *trunks* (the key word)
You can sort for: rhymes, "s" pairs (run, runs; rut, ruts; trunk, trunks)

Lesson using big words:
Letter cards: aaaeibchllpt
Words to make: itch, able, cable, table, batch, patch, pitch, petal, label, chapel, capital, capable, alphabet, *alphabetical* (the key word)
You can sort for: el, le, al, -itch, -atch

Table 3.3 provides details necessary for making two more Making Words lessons suggested by Cunningham and Cunningham (1992) that may be useful for helping students learn the procedure.

Function (Four-Letter) Words

Many words are very difficult for students to learn because they carry no definable meaning. Words in this category include *with, were, what,* and *want.* Referred to as *structure words* (also known as *functors, glue words,* and *four-letter words*), these words are perhaps the most difficult to teach because they cannot be explained in a concrete way for children. Imagine trying to define or draw a picture of the word *what.*

Patricia Cunningham (1980) developed the *drastic strategy* to help teachers solve this difficult instructional problem. Here is her six-step process:

Step 1: Select a function word and write it on a vocabulary card for each child. Locate a story for storytelling or spontaneously create a story in which you use the word many times. Before you begin your story, ask the children to hold up their card every time they hear the word printed on their card. As you tell the story, pause briefly each time you come to the word in the text.

Step 2: Ask children to volunteer to make up a story using the word on their card. Listeners should hold up their card each time they hear their classmate use the function word.

Step 3: Ask the children to study the word on their card. Next, go around to each child and cut the word into letters (or have the children do it for themselves). Have the children try to arrange the letters to make the word. Check each child's attempt for accuracy. They should mix up the letters and try to make the word again several times; each child should be able to do this before moving on to the next step. Put the letters into an envelope and write the word on the outside. Children should be encouraged to practice making the word during free times.

Step 4: Write the word on the chalkboard and ask children to pretend their eyes are like a camera and to take a picture of the word and put it in their mind. Have them close their eyes and try to see it in their mind. Next, they should open their eyes and check the board to see if they correctly imagined the word. They should do this three times. The last activity is for them to write the word from memory after the chalkboard has been erased, then check their spelling when it is rewritten on the chalkboard. This should be done three times.

The drastic strategy is useful for teaching "function words," or those that have no meaning; such as what, with, and that.

Developing vocabulary in content areas can help children discover words in their natural context.

Step 5: Write several sentences on the board containing a blank in the place of the word under study. As you come to the missing word in the sentences, invite a child to come to the board and write the word in the blank space provided.

Step 6: Give children real books or text in which the function word appears. Ask them to read through the story, and whenever they find the word being studied, they should lightly underline (in pencil) the new word. When they have done this, read the text to them and pause each time you come to the word so the students can read it chorally.

We recommend one final step to the drastic strategy: Add the word under study to the child's word bank for future use in writing.

There is one drawback to the drastic strategy: *time*. Sometimes it is not necessary to teach every step in the drastic strategy for all words. A careful assessment of your students' vocabulary knowledge and needs, coupled with years of classroom experience, will help you decide when certain steps can be omitted.

Teaching Word Functions and Changes

Synonyms

Synonyms are words that have similar meanings.

Can you find examples of interesting reading materials that might be used to teach synonyms?

Synonyms are words that have similar but not exactly the same meanings (D. D. Johnson & Pearson, 1984). No two words carry exactly the same meaning in all situations. Thus, when teaching children about new words and their synonyms, teachers should provide numerous opportunities for students to see differences as well as similarities. As with all reading strategies, this is best done within the natural context of real books and authentic writing experiences.

One very productive way to get children interested in synonyms in the upper elementary grades is to teach the use of a thesaurus with their writing. Children can begin to see how using a thesaurus can "spice up" their writing projects. This tool is best used during revising and editing stages of the writing process when children sometimes have problems coming up with descriptive language in their writing. For example, let's say a character in their story was tortured by hostile savages (sorry to be so violent in our example!), but the child writes that the victim felt *bad*. If this word is targeted for thesaurus research, then the child may come up with synonyms for *bad* such as *in pain, anguished, in misery, depressed,* or *desperate.*

Following are several common words that children overuse that could be researched using a thesaurus.

good	big	thing
pleasant	vast	object
glorious	grand	item
wonderful	enormous	like
delightful	huge	organism

One way to get children involved with synonyms is to take text from some of their "old favorite" books and revise selected words. Teachers might want to develop a modified cloze passage, deleting only certain kinds of words, and then let the children use synonyms to complete the blanks. Take, for example, the following excerpt from a book well suited for this purpose with early to intermediate grade readers, *The Grouchy Ladybug* (Carle, 1986):

Good morning," said the friendly ladybug.
Go away!" shouted the grouchy ladybug. "I want those aphids."
We can share them," suggested the friendly ladybug.
No. They're mine, all mine," screamed the grouchy ladybug.
Or do you want to fight me for them?"*

*From The Grouchy Ladybug by E. Carle, 1977, 1986. New York: HarperCollins.
Reprinted by permission.

One option is to delete words following a statement (e.g., *said, shouted, suggested, screamed*) and put them in a list on the chalkboard with possible synonyms, such as *hinted, greeted, growled, yelled, reminded, mentioned, pointed out*, and *offered*. The resulting rewrites may look something like the following:

Good morning," *greeted* the friendly ladybug.
Go away!" *growled* the grouchy ladybug. "I want those aphids."
We can share them," *hinted* the friendly ladybug.
No. They're mine, all mine," *yelled* the grouchy ladybug.
Or do you want to fight me for them?"

Class discussions might relate to how the use of different synonyms can alter meaning significantly, thus showing how synonyms have similar meanings but not the exact same meanings. For example, if we took the sentence

Go away!" *shouted* the grouchy ladybug.

and changed it to read

Go away!" *hinted* the grouchy ladybug.

it would be easy for children to understand how the author's message had been softened considerably. This cross training with reading and writing experiences helps synonyms take on new relevance as a literacy tool in the hands of children.

Antonyms

Antonyms are word opposites or near opposites. *Hard–soft, dark–light,* and *big–small* are examples of antonym pairs. Like synonyms, antonyms help students gain insights into word meanings. When searching for ideal antonym examples, teachers should try to identify word sets that are mutually exclusive or that completely contradict each other.

Several classes of antonyms have been identified (Johnson & Pearson, 1984) that may be useful in instruction. One class is called *relative pairs*, or *counterparts*. Examples include *mother–father, sister–brother, uncle–aunt, and writer–reader* because one term implies the other. Other antonyms reflect a complete opposite or reversal of meaning, such as *fast–slow, stop–go,* and *give–take.* Complimentary antonyms tend to lead from one to another, such as *give–take, friend–foe,* and *hot–cold.*

Antonym activities, as with all language-learning activities, should be drawn from the context of familiar books and student writing samples. By using familiar text with clear meanings, it is easy for children to see the full impact and flavor of differing word meanings. Remember, in classroom instruction involving minilessons, teaching

Word opposites, or near opposites, are **antonyms.**

from whole text to parts (antonyms in this case) is the key. Thus, if the teacher decided to develop an antonym worksheet for students, then the worksheet should be drawn from a book that has already been shared (or will be shared) with the whole class or group. One example of a fun book for this exercise is *Weird Parents* by Audrey Wood (1990), which could yield sentences like the following (in the space provided, students write in antonyms for the underlined words):

1. There once was a boy who had <u>weird</u> (   ) parents.
2. In the <u>morning</u> (   ), the weird mother always walked the boy to his bus stop.
3. At 12 o'clock when the boy <u>opened</u> (   ) his lunch box, he'd always have a weird surprise.

Another possibility is to ask children to find words in their writing or reading for which they can think of antonyms. A student in sixth grade reading *A Wrinkle in Time* (L'Engle, 1962) might create the following list of book words and antonyms:

Wrinkle Words/Page No.	Antonyms
punishment/13	reward
hesitant/63	eager
frightening/111	pleasant

If a student in third grade had written a story about his new baby sister, he might select some of the following words and antonyms:

Baby Story Words	Opposites
asleep	awake
cry	laugh
wet	dry

One way to assess students' ability to recognize antonyms is through multiple-choice and cloze exercises. The idea is to choose sentences from familiar text and let students select which word is the correct antonym from among three choices. The choices may include one synonym, the correct antonym, and a third choice that is a different part of speech. Following are two examples taken from the book *The Glorious Flight* (Provensen & Provensen, 1983):

1. Like a great swan, the *beautiful* (attractive, <u>homely</u>, shoots) glider rises into the air . . . .
2. Papa is getting *lots* (<u>limited</u>, from, loads) of practice.

Of many possible classroom activities, the most profitable will probably be those in which students are required to generate their own responses. Simple recognition items, as with multiple-choice measures, do not cause children to go within themselves nearly as deeply to find and apply new knowledge.

Euphemisms

According to Tompkins and Hoskisson (1995, p. 122), **euphemisms** are words or phrases that are used to soften language to avoid harsh or distasteful realities (e.g., *passed away*), usually out of concern for people's feelings. Euphemisms are certainly

---

Learning ***euphemisms*** *(words or phrases used to soften language to avoid harsh or distasteful realities) can improve students' writing versatility and reading comprehension.*

worth some attention because they not only help students improve their writing versatility but also aid in reading comprehension.

Two types of euphemisms include *inflated* and *deceptive* language. Inflated language euphemisms tend to make something sound greater or more sophisticated than it is. For example, *sanitation engineer* might be an inflated euphemism for *garbage collector*. Deceptive language euphemisms are intentional words and phrases meant to intentionally misrepresent. Children should learn that this language often is used in advertisements to persuade an unknowing public. Several examples of euphemisms based on the work of Lutz (cited in Tompkins & Hoskisson, 1995, p. 122) follow:

Euphemism	Real Meaning
dentures	false teeth
expecting	pregnant
funeral director	undertaker
passed away	died
previously owned	used
senior citizen	old person
terminal patient	dying

Onomatopoeia and Creative Words

Onomatopoeia is the creation of words that imitate sounds (*buzz, whir, vrrrrooom*). Some authors, such as Dr. Seuss, Shel Silverstein, and others, have made regular use of onomatopoeia and other creative words in their writing. One instance of onomatopoeia may be found in Dr. Seuss's book *Horton Hears a Who!* (1954) in the sentence "On clarinets, *oom-pahs* and *boom-pahs* and flutes." A wonderful example of creative language is found in Silverstein's (1974, p. 71) poem "Sarah Cynthia Sylvia Stout Would Not Take the Garbage Out" in the phrase "Rubbery *blubbery* macaroni .... "

Children can be shown many interesting examples on onomatopoeia and creative words from the world of great children's literature. The natural extension to their own writing comes swiftly. Children may want to add a special section to their word banks for onomatopoeia and creative words to enhance their own written creations.

Shared Reading Experiences and Vocabulary Learning

Senechal and Cornell (1993) studied ways vocabulary knowledge can be increased through *shared reading experiences* (where adults and children read stories together). The methods investigated included reading the story verbatim (read-alouds), asking questions, repeating sentences containing new vocabulary words, and what has been referred to as *recasting* new vocabulary introduced in the selection.

Recasts build directly on sentences just read that contain a new word the teacher (or parent) may want to teach the child. Verbs, subjects, or objects are often changed to recast the word for further discussion and examination. Thus, if a child says or reads, "Look at the *snake*," the adult may recast the phrase by replying, "It is a large striped *snake*." In this example, the same meaning of the phrase was maintained, but adjectives were added to enhance understanding of the word *snake*.

Interestingly, Senechal and Cornell concluded that teacher questioning and recasts were about as *effective* as reading a book aloud to a child as a word learning tool. Thus, reading passages aloud to students can often be just as potent as direct

Onomatopoeia is the creation of words that imitate sounds, like zzzoooom, buzz, or vrrrroooom.

Teachers use the shared reading experience known as **recasting** to repeat a word just read in a new way for further understanding and examination.

teaching strategies. We need to do both: read aloud regularly *and* discuss passages containing new vocabulary with students in challenging ways.

MEETING THE NEEDS OF ENGLISH LANGUAGE LEARNERS

English language learners often need assistance with unfamiliar vocabulary encountered while reading.

A growing percentage of students in our schools are learning to read in a second language: *English*. According to the National Center for Education Statistics (1999), about 17% of all students are classified as Hispanic (14%) or Asian/Pacific Islander (3%). Many of these students speak a language other than English as their native tongue. As it was in the earliest days of our country for most newcomers, learning to read and write in English can be a formidable challenge but one that must be successfully addressed if all our students are to reach their potential. *Literacy is, in so many ways, the gateway to social equity.*

One of the common needs of English language learners (ELL) is assistance with unfamiliar vocabulary they encounter while reading. Peregoy and Boyle (2001), in their book *Reading, Writing, and Learning in ESL,* recommend some guidelines for vocabulary development:

- First, select words to emphasize that you consider important to comprehending each assigned passage.
- Next, create several sentences loaded with context using these target words. This will give them an opportunity to use context to predict the meaning of the target words.
- Teacher modeling of prediction strategies using context is a must for students to grasp this strategy.
- Follow these modeling and guided practice sessions with discussion using excerpts from the text they will be assigned in which the target words appear.

Two vocabulary development activities are highly recommended for ELL students (May & Rizzardi, 2002; Peregoy & Boyle, 2001; Reutzel & Cooter, 2001b): the *vocabulary cluster strategy* and *semantic maps*.

Using the Vocabulary Cluster Strategy with ELL Students

It is especially important that ELL students who struggle with reading use the context of the passage, their background knowledge, and the vocabulary they know to understand new words in print. This is true whether English is their second language or their first (as is the case with children from language-deprived backgrounds). English language learners and students who have language deficiencies because of poverty are two large groups of students who benefit from direct instruction of this kind (Peregoy & Boyle, 2001). With the vocabulary cluster strategy, students are helped to read a passage, gather context clues, and then predict the meaning of a new word targeted for learning by you, the teacher. Here's how it works.

First, you will need to gather multiple copies of the text students are to read, an overhead transparency and projector, and erasable marking pens for transparencies. Select vocabulary you want to teach from the text you will use; it could be a poem, song, excerpt from a chapter book (novel), or nonfiction textbook. Gather your students around the overhead projector and draw their attention to the transparency

Figure 3.5 Vocabulary cluster* based on *Harry Potter and the Prisoner of Azkaban:* target word *irritable*

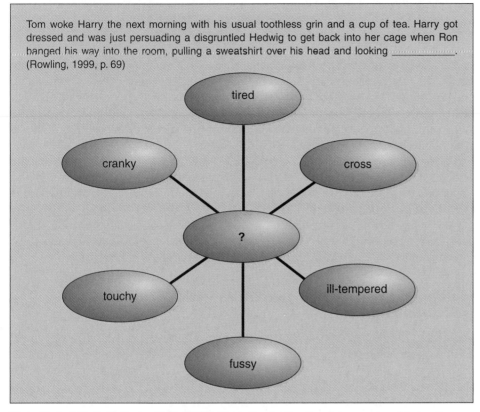

Tom woke Harry the next morning with his usual toothless grin and a cup of tea. Harry got dressed and was just persuading a disgruntled Hedwig to get back into her cage when Ron banged his way into the room, pulling a sweatshirt over his head and looking _____. (Rowling, 1999, p. 69)

tired

cranky

cross

?

touchy

ill-tempered

fussy

*From Reutzel, D. R., & Cooter, R. B. (2003). *Strategies for Reading Assessment and Instruction: Helping Every Child Succeed, 2nd Ed.* Upper Saddle River, NJ: Merrill/Prentice-Hall. ISBN: 0–13–098899–5. Used with permission.

you have prepared. The transparency should contain an excerpt from the text with sufficient context to help students predict what the unknown word might be. The target word(s) should have been deleted and replaced with a blank line, much the same as with a cloze passage. Figure 3.5 shows a passage prepared in this way along with a vocabulary cluster supporting the new word to be learned. This example is based on the book *Harry Potter and the Prisoner of Azkaban* (Rowling, 1999). Through discussion, you will lead students into predicting what the unknown word might be. If the word is not already in the students' listening vocabulary, as with ELL students or those with otherwise limited vocabularies, then you will be able to introduce the new word quite well using the context and synonyms provided in the vocabulary cluster.

Semantic Maps

Semantic maps are essentially a kind of "schema blueprint" in which students sketch out or "map" what is stored in their brain about a topic. Semantic maps help ELL students relate new information to schemata and vocabulary already in the brain, integrate new information, and restructure existing information for greater clarity (Yopp & Yopp,

Semantic maps are useful in tying together new vocabulary with prior knowledge and related terms (Johnson & Pearson, 1984; Monroe, 1998; Reutzel & Cooter, 2003).

1996). For students having learning problems, using semantic maps prior to reading a selection has also proven to promote better story recall than traditional methods (Sinatra, Stahl-Gemake, & Berg, 1984). Writing materials are the only supplies needed.

There are many ways to introduce semantic mapping to students, but the first time around you will want to use a direct instruction approach with a lot of teacher modeling, guided practice, and independent practice.

One way is to introduce semantic maps through something we call "wacky webbing." The idea is to take a topic familiar to all, such as the name of one's home state, and portray it in the center of the web. Major categories related to the theme are connected to the central concept using either bold lines or double lines. Details that relate to the major categories are connected using single lines. Figure 3.6 shows a semantic web for the topic "Tennessee."

Semantic webs can also be constructed that relate to a story or chapter book the students are reading. Figure 3.7 shows an example (Reutzel & Cooter, 2003b) of a semantic web from a story in the book *Golden Tales: Myths, Legends and Folktales from Latin America* (Delacre, 1996).

Certainly, any of the strategies found in this chapter can be adapted for ELL students, as long as you are direct and explicit in your teaching. Direct instruction helps ELL students create mental scaffolding for support of new vocabulary and concepts.

Linking Multicultural Experiences with Vocabulary Development

Vocabulary development in spoken and written English is at the heart of literacy learning (Wheatley, Muller, & Miller, 1993). Because of the rich diversity found in

Figure 3.6　Tennessee semantic web

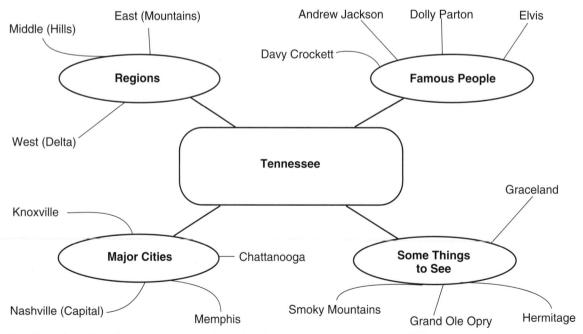

From Reutzel, D. R., & Cooter, R. B. (2003). *Strategies for Reading Assessment and Instruction: Helping Every Child Succeed, 2nd Ed.* Upper Saddle River, NJ: Merrill/Prentice-Hall. ISBN: 0–13–098899–5. Used with permission.

Figure 3.7 Semantic map "Guanina"

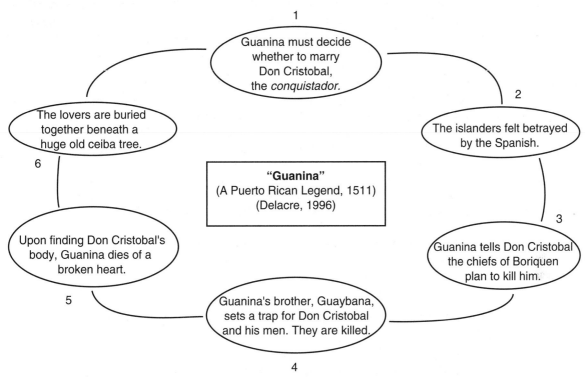

1

Guanina must decide whether to marry Don Cristobal, the *conquistador.*

2

The islanders felt betrayed by the Spanish.

The lovers are buried together beneath a huge old ceiba tree.

6

"Guanina"
(A Puerto Rican Legend, 1511)
(Delacre, 1996)

3

Guanina tells Don Cristobal the chiefs of Boriquen plan to kill him.

Upon finding Don Cristobal's body, Guanina dies of a broken heart.

5

Guanina's brother, Guaybana, sets a trap for Don Cristobal and his men. They are killed.

4

* From Reutzel, D. R., & Cooter, R. B. (2003). *Strategies for Reading Assessment and Instruction: Helping Every Child Succeed, 2nd Ed.* Upper Saddle River, NJ: Merrill/Prentice-Hall. ISBN: 0–13–098899–5. Used with permission.

American classrooms, teachers need to consider ways of adapting the curriculum so that all children can learn to recognize and use appropriate and descriptive vocabulary. In this section, we consider three possible avenues proven to be successful in multicultural settings.

1. *Linking vocabulary studies to a broad topic or novel.* We know that there is a limit to the number of words that can be taught directly and in isolation. K. Au (1993) tells us that students in multicultural settings learn vocabulary best if the new words are related to a broader topic. Working on vocabulary development in connection with students' exploration of content area topics is a natural and connected way to learn new words and explore their various meanings. Later we go into further detail about how vocabulary instruction can be conducted in content units, including the use of special computer-assisted programs.

2. *Wide reading as a vehicle for vocabulary development.* Reading for enjoyment on a daily basis helps students increase their vocabulary knowledge, not to mention myriad other reading abilities. Teachers can help students become regular readers by assessing their reading interests, then locate books that "fit the reader." Matching books and students is a simple way of encouraging the kinds of reading behaviors that pay dividends. Helping students learn how to choose books on their developmental level is an important way students can learn to independently select books.

3. *The Village English activity.* Delpit (1988) writes about a method of teaching Native Alaskan students new vocabulary that works well in many multicultural settings.

This *Village English activity* respects and encourages children's home languages while helping them see relationships between language use and social/professional realities in the United States (Au, 1993).

The Village English activity begins with the teacher writing "Our Language Heritage" at the top of half a piece of poster board and "Standard American English" at the top of the second half. The teacher explains to students that in America people speak in many different ways and that this makes our nation as colorful and interesting as a patchwork quilt. For elementary students, we think this would be a good time to share *Elmer* by David McKee (1990), a book about an elephant of many colors (called a "patchwork elephant") and how he enriched his elephant culture.

The teacher explains that there are many times when adults need to speak in the same way so that they can be understood, usually in formal situations. In formal situations, we speak Standard American English. When at home or with friends in our community, we usually speak the language of our heritage. It is like the difference between a picnic compared to a "dressed up" formal dinner. On the chart, then, phrases used in the native dialect can be written under the heading "Our Language Heritage," and comparative translations are noted and discussed on the side labeled "Standard American English." These comparisons can be noted in an ongoing way throughout the year as part of a special *word wall.* The Village English activity can be an interesting way to increase vocabulary knowledge while also valuing language differences.

HELPING STUDENTS ACQUIRE NEW VOCABULARY INDEPENDENTLY

The ultimate task for teachers is to help students become independent learners. The ongoing learning of new vocabulary throughout life is unquestionably a key to continued self-education. In this section, we feature ways students can become independent learners of new words.

Word-Learning Strategies

Word-learning strategies are skills such as how to use dictionaries and other reference aids, how to use information about word parts to figure out the meanings, and how to use context clues to determine meanings.

Students must determine the meaning of words that are new to them when these words are discovered in their reading. The key is to develop effective **word-learning strategies,** such as how to use *dictionaries and other reference aids,* how to use *information about word parts* to figure out the meanings of words in text; and how to use *context clues* to determine word meanings.

Using Dictionaries and Other Reference Aids

Students must learn how to use dictionaries, glossaries, and thesauruses to help broaden and deepen their knowledge of words. In preparation for using these tools, students must learn such things as alphabetical order, ordinal language (i.e., first, second, third, and so on), and *guide words.* The most helpful dictionaries and reference aids include sentences providing clear examples of word meanings in context.

Using Information About Word Parts

We learned earlier in the book that *structural analysis* involves the use of word parts, such as *affixes* (prefixes and suffixes) and *base words,* to figure out the meaning of new words in print. Students can likewise use structural analysis skills independently as a meaning-based, word-learning tool just as effectively as they would as a decoding strategy. For example, learning the four most common prefixes in English (*un-, re-, in-, dis-*), can provide helpful meaning clues for about two thirds of all English words having prefixes. Prefixes are relatively easy to learn because they have clear meanings (e.g., *un-* means "not" and *re-* means "again"); they are usually spelled the same way from word to word. Suffixes can often be a bit more challenging to learn than prefixes. For one thing, quite a few suffixes have confusing meanings (e.g., the suffix *-ness,* meaning "the state of," is not all that helpful in figuring out the meaning of *tenderness*).

Students should also learn about **word roots,** or words having their origins from other languages. About 60% of all English words have Latin or Greek origins (Partnership for Reading, 2001, p. 39). Latin and Greek word roots are common to the subjects of science and social studies and also form a large share of the new words for students in their content-area textbooks. Teachers should teach the highest-frequency word roots as they occur in the texts students read.

Using Context Clues to Determine Word Meanings

Context clues are meaning cues found in the words, phrases, and sentences that surround an unknown word. It is not an overstatement to say that the ability to use context clues is fundamental to reading success. This is because most word meanings will be learned indirectly from context. Following is another classroom example from the publication, *Put Reading First,* this time demonstrating the use of context clues as a word-learning strategy.

AN EXAMPLE OF CLASSROOM INSTRUCTION:

Using Context Clues*

In a third-grade class, the teacher models how to use context clues to determine word meanings as follows:

Student (*reading the text*): When the cat pounced on the dog, the dog jumped up, yelping, and knocked over a lamp, which crashed to the floor. The animals ran past Tonia, tripping her. She fell to the floor and began sobbing. Tonia's brother Felix yelled at the animals to stop. As the noise and confusion mounted, Mother hollered upstairs, "What's all that **commotion?**"

Teacher: The context of the paragraph helps us determine what **commotion** means. There's yelping and crashing, sobbing, and yelling. And then the last sentence says, "as the **noise** and **confusion** mounted." The author's use of the words noise and confusion gives us a very strong clue as to what **commotion** means. In fact, the author is really giving us a definition there, because **commotion** means something that's noisy and confusing—a disturbance. Mother was right; there was definitely a **commotion!**

*From *Put Reading First: The Research Building Blocks for Teaching Children to Read* (2001). Non-copyrighted material published by the National Institute for Literacy. Available online at www.nifl.gov.

Students can use their knowledge of word parts—affixes (prefixes and suffixes), base words, and root words—to figure out unfamiliar words in print.

Word roots *are words that have their origins from other languages.*

Standards Note
Standard 6.3: The reading professional will be able to teach students to use context to identify and define unfamiliar words. Telling students to use context to figure out new words is not sufficient. Develop five specific examples of context clues, using specific vocabulary to illustrate each.

Context clues *are meaning cues found in the words, phrases and sentences that surround an unknown word.*

Encouraging Wide Reading

Wide reading is a powerful way for students to build vocabulary knowledge independently.

Reading is a cognitive skill that in some ways mirrors physical skill development. As with physical skills, the more one practices reading, the more reading ability increases. Over the years in our work with at-risk students, we have come to realize that if we can simply get children to read every day for at least 15 to 20 minutes, their reading ability will increase quickly and exponentially. In one study, Reutzel and Hollingsworth (1991c) discovered that allowing children to read self-selected books 30 minutes *every day* resulted in significantly improved scores on reading comprehension tests. These children performed as well as students who had received 30 minutes of direct instruction on the tested reading comprehension skills. Their results suggest that regular daily reading is probably at least as effective as formal reading instruction, and the children can do it on their own. Encouraging children to read books that match their interests can motivate them to read independently and grow their vocabulary.

Surveying student interests with an **individual interest sheet** *(IIS) helps teachers select free-reading materials. An ISS lists topics that appear to be of interest to a child and suggests related books that are available in the school library*

What Are Some Ways Teachers Can Encourage Wide Reading?

How can teachers encourage children to read independently on a regular basis? The answer lies in helping children become aware of their own interests and in finding books they can read. The interest issue can be resolved in two steps. First, the teacher should administer an *interest inventory* to the class at the beginning of the year to determine what types of books are indicated for classroom instruction. These results, however, could be taken a little further: As the second step, we suggest that the teacher start an **individual interest sheet** (IIS) for each child based on these results and present them to children during individual reading conferences (discussed more in later chapters). The IIS sheet simply lists topics that appear to be of interest to the child and suggests books available in the school library. Over time, the children can list additional topics they discover to be of interest and can look for books in those areas. The principle is much the same as having children keep a list of topics they would like to write stories about. Figure 3.8 shows a sample IIS, with new interests written in by the student.

A useful reference for teachers attempting to match children's interests with quality literature is Donna Norton's (1998) book *Through the Eyes of a Child: An In-*

Figure 3.8 Sample individual interest sheet (IIS)

> ***Individual Interest Sheet***
>
> **Mrs. Harbor's Sixth Grade**
>
> **Sunnydale School**
>
> Name: Holly Ambrose
>
> Things I am interested in knowing more about, or topics that I like . . .
>
> | **Topics** | **Books to consider from our library** |
> | --- | --- |
> | horses | *The Red Pony* (J. Steinbeck) |
> | getting along with friends | *Afternoon of the Elves* (J. Lisle) |
> | romantic stories | *The Witch of Blackbird Pond* (E. Speare) |
> | one-parent families | *The Moonlight Man* (P. Fox) |

troduction to Children's Literature. Most high-interest topic areas are discussed in this text and are matched to several possible book titles. Book suggestions include brief descriptions of the main story line to help in the decision-making process.

Computer-Assisted Vocabulary Learning

As computers become more accessible to students and teachers, the question arises: Can some of the new computer applications available help students learn new vocabulary? Reinking and Rickman (1990) studied the vocabulary growth of sixth-grade students who had computer-assisted programs available to them. They compared students who read passages on printed pages accompanied by either a standard dictionary or a glossary (the traditional classroom situation) with students who read passages on a computer screen. These computer-assisted programs provided either *optional* assistance (on command) for specific vocabulary words or *mandatory* (automatic) assistance. Two very interesting things were learned from their research. First, students reading passages with computer assistance performed significantly better on vocabulary tests that focused on the words emphasized than did students in traditional reading groups. Second, students receiving automatic computer assistance with the passages also outperformed the more traditional reading group on a passage comprehension test relating to information read in the experiment. These results suggest that computer programs that offer students passages to read with vocabulary assistance can be helpful. Further, they suggest to us another possible advantage of the computer: teaching students to use what might be termed a *vocabulary enhancer,* such as a thesaurus program, with their writing, which could help students discover on their own new synonyms and antonyms for commonly used words. Most word processing programs, such as Microsoft Word, have a thesaurus program already installed for easy use.

Name and describe two ways teachers can enhance vocabulary learning.

Computer-assisted vocabulary instruction can provide motivational word-learning instruction in a classroom learning center.

Encouraging children to read books that match their interests can motivate them to read independently and grow their vocabulary.

Vocabulary Overview

Vocabulary overviews help students decide which words they will learn. In classroom settings, teachers can usually anticipate vocabulary that may be troublesome during reading and teach these words through brief minilessons. But when children read independently, they need to find ways to learn new words on their own. One activity that serves this purpose is the vocabulary overview, which helps students select unfamiliar words in print, then use context clues and their background knowledge to determine word meaning.

One way of helping students develop their own vocabulary overviews is Haggard's (1986) *vocabulary self-selection strategy* (VSS). Our version of the VSS begins with a small-group minilesson to learn the process. Students are asked to find at least one word they feel the class should learn. Next, they define the word to the best of their ability on the basis of context clues and any clues from their own background knowledge. On the day the words are presented, each child takes turns explaining (a) where each word was found, (b) his or her context-determined definition for the word, and (c) reasons why the class should learn the word.

Word Maps

A **word map** (Schwartz & Raphael, 1985) is a graphic rendering of a word's meaning. It answers three important questions about the word: *What is it? What is it like? What are some examples?* Answers to these questions are extremely valuable because they help children link the new word or concept to their prior knowledge and world experiences, a process known to have an effect on reading comprehension (Stahl et al., 1991). An example of a word map is shown in Figure 3.9.

Figure 3.9   Word map

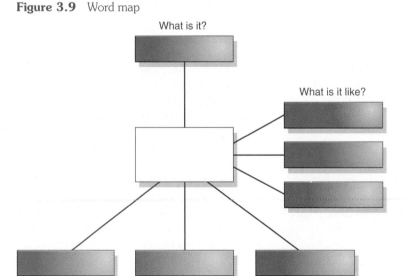

Introducing this vocabulary-acquisition strategy to students is a relatively easy task. First, the teacher presents the idea of using this kind of graphic organizer to understand new word meanings and models the word map as one example. Next, students work with the teacher in a guided practice format to organize familiar information using the three key questions used in the word map.

Simple concepts should be used in initial guided practice exercises to help students learn how to use the map. For example, a practice map might be constructed using the word *car.* Answers for each of the story map questions that might be offered by elementary students follow:

Word: *car*

What is it? (transportation, movement)

What is it like? (four wheels, metal, glass, lights, moves, steering wheel)

What are some examples? (Honda, station wagon, Thunderbird, convertible)

After working through several examples with the whole group or class, teachers should give students opportunities to practice using the word map. In the beginning, whole-class practice works best, followed by independent practice using narrative and expository texts of the students' or teacher's choosing.

Summary

Dale Johnson (2001, pp. 41–48), an eminent researcher in the field of vocabulary development, provided valuable insights in his book titled *Vocabulary in the Elementary and Middle School,* that wonderfully encapsulates information presented in this chapter. First, we know that word knowledge is essential for reading comprehension. Evidenced-based research tells us that vocabulary instruction should utilize activities (like the ones found in this chapter) that link word learning to concept and schema development. We should also teach specific word-learning strategies to our students as well as strategies they can use on their own to understand unfamiliar words in print.

Wide reading should be encouraged and made possible in the classroom. Literally thousands of words are learned through regular and sustained reading. Time should be set aside each day for this crucial learning activity. As an example, Johnson (2001) advocated the use of a program called "Read-a-Million-Minutes," which was designed to foster wide reading throughout Iowa. All students set their own in-school and out-of school reading goal that contributes to the school's goal.

Direct instruction should be used to teach words that are necessary for passage comprehension. Considering how critical some words are for comprehending a new passage, teachers should not leave vocabulary learning to incidental encounters but rather should plan regular direct instruction lessons to make sure that essential words are learned. Active learning activities yield the best results. According to research conducted by Stahl (1986), vocabulary instruction that provided only definitional information (i.e., dictionary activities) failed to significantly improve comprehension. Active learning opportunities; such as creation of word webs, playing word games, and discussing new words in reading groups or literature circles, are far more effective in cementing new knowledge and improving comprehension.

Check your understanding of chapter concepts by using the self-assessment for Chapter 3 of our Companion Website at www.prenhall.com/ reutzel.

We also know that students require a good bit of repetition to learn new words and integrate them into existing knowledge (schemas). In some cases, students may require as many as 40 encounters to fully learn new vocabulary. To know a word well means knowing what it means, how to pronounce it, and how its meaning changes in different contexts. Repeated exposures to the word in different contexts is the key to successful learning.

Students should be helped to develop their own strategies for word learning from written and oral contexts. This includes the use of context clues, structural analysis (word roots, prefixes, and suffixes), and research skills (use of the dictionary, thesaurus, and so on).

Finally, parents can help their children succeed in expanding concept and vocabulary knowledge by exposing them to new experiences and helping them to read about and discuss new ideas in the home.

Concept Applications

In the Classroom

1. Design a lesson plan introducing a chosen word-learning strategy to third-grade students. You should be certain that the lesson includes rich literature examples, teacher modeling, and ample guided practice for students.
2. Create a "Deceptive Language" bulletin board that shows various uses of euphemisms in advertising aimed at children as consumers. Create a second board showing how these same tactics are used on adults through advertising (and perhaps by political leaders).
3. Prepare a lesson plan for second-year (*not* the same as second grade) ELL students introducing one of the vocabulary-learning strategies provided in this chapter. You will need to identify the age of the students and their first language and consider the background knowledge they might have to help them use the new strategy. As always, be certain that the lesson includes rich literature examples, teacher modeling, and ample guided practice for students.

In the Field

1. Do an interest inventory with five students in a local elementary school. Next, prepare an IIS that matches at least four of their interests to popular children's literature. Ideas for the books should be recommended by the school librarian or drawn from D. Norton's (1998) book *Through the Eyes of a Child: An Introduction to Children's Literature*. Finally, present the IIS forms to each child and explain how they are to be used. Copies of both forms should be turned in to your college instructor, along with a journal entry explaining how each child reacted.
2. Prepare and teach a minilesson demonstrating the VSS for multicultural classes. Develop a simple handout for the students with helpful hints about collecting new words for investigation.
3. Locate an elementary classroom in which the writing process is practiced. Working with two child volunteers, prepare a minilesson on synonyms and antonyms using samples they permit you to borrow from their writing folders.

Recommended Readings

Cunningham, P. M., & Cunningham, J. (1992). Making words: Enhancing the invented spelling-decoding connection. *The Reading Teacher, 46*(2), 106–115.

Fry, E. B., Kress, J. E., & Fountoukidis, D. L. (2000). *The reading teacher's book of lists* (3rd ed.). New York: Jossey-Bass.

Johnson, D. D. (2001). *Vocabulary in the elementary and middle school.* Boston: Allyn and Bacon.

Peregoy, S. F., & Boyle, O. F. (2001). *Reading, writing, and learning in ESL.* New York: Longman.

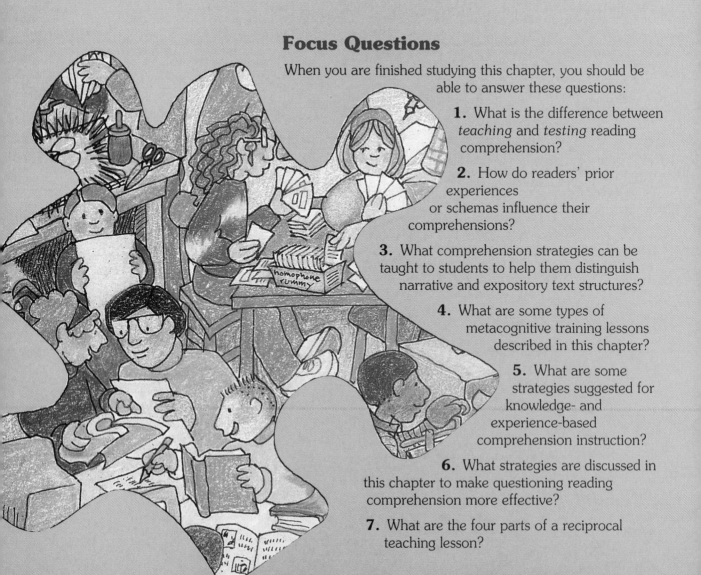

Improving Reading Comprehension

Focus Questions

When you are finished studying this chapter, you should be able to answer these questions:

1. What is the difference between *teaching* and *testing* reading comprehension?

2. How do readers' prior experiences or schemas influence their comprehensions?

3. What comprehension strategies can be taught to students to help them distinguish narrative and expository text structures?

4. What are some types of metacognitive training lessons described in this chapter?

5. What are some strategies suggested for knowledge- and experience-based comprehension instruction?

6. What strategies are discussed in this chapter to make questioning reading comprehension more effective?

7. What are the four parts of a reciprocal teaching lesson?

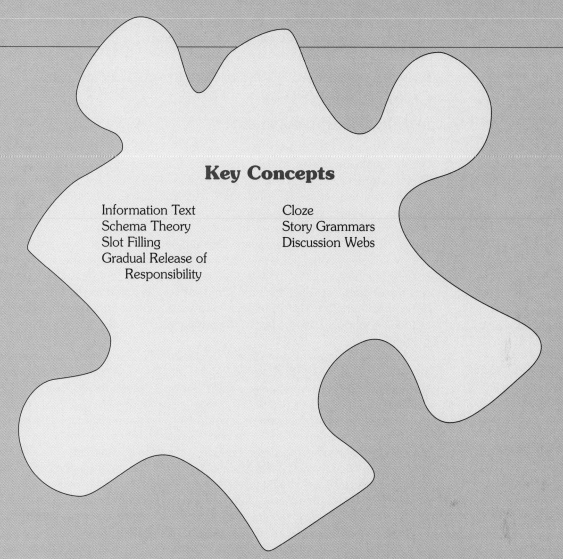

Key Concepts

Information Text
Schema Theory
Slot Filling
Gradual Release of
  Responsibility

Cloze
Story Grammars
Discussion Webs

Reading comprehension is the very heart and soul of reading (Collins-Block, Gambrell, & Pressley, 2003; Collins-Block & Pressley, 2002; Keene & Zimmerman, 1997. Although learning to recognize letters, learning to connect letters with sounds, and then blending these elements into words is extremely important (Johnson, 2001; Pressley, 2000), teachers must never lose sight of the ultimate goal of reading instruction—comprehending the text! From their very first encounters with print, teachers should help children discover meaning from print by providing effective comprehension instruction (Pearson & Duke, 2002).

Visit Chapter 4 of our Companion Website at www.prenhall.com/ reutzel to look into the chapter objectives, standards and principles, and pertinent Web links associated with improving reading comprehension.

RESEARCH ON TEACHING READING COMPREHENSION

Instruction *or* Assessment?

During the late 1960s and throughout the 1970s, reading comprehension was largely taught by asking students questions following reading or by assigning skill sheets as practice for reading comprehension skills such as getting the main idea, determining the sequence, following directions, noting details, and cause and effect relationships. In 1978, Dolores Durkin reported findings from reading comprehension studies conducted in public school classrooms. After observing a variety of "expert" teachers engaged in reading instruction in both reading and social studies classrooms, Durkin concluded that these teachers spent very little time actually teaching children how to understand texts. *In fact, less than 1% of total reading or social studies instructional time was devoted to the teaching of reading comprehension.* Unfortunately, many researchers conclude that the situation in today's schools has not improved appreciably over the last 25 years (Collins-Block et al., 2003).

So, what is happening in America's classrooms with respect to comprehension instruction? Durkin (1978) provided insights into that question as well. Teachers, she said, do not teach comprehension skills, but only "mention" or "question." Durkin defined a *mentioner* as a teacher who says "just enough about a topic [e.g., unstated conclusions] to allow for a written assignment to be given" (Durkin, 1981a, p. 516). Furthermore, attention to new vocabulary words was often brief, even "skimpy" (p. 524). Basal reader teacher's manuals were usually consulted for only two purposes: (a) to study the list of new vocabulary words and (b) to ask the comprehension questions following the reading of a selection. Worksheets, in reality nothing more than informal tests, dominated classroom reading comprehension instruction.

Durkin conducted a second study (1981b) in which she investigated the comprehension instruction found in five nationally published basal reading series. Her conclusions in this study essentially supported her earlier study: Publishers, like teachers, failed to understand the differences between teaching and testing reading comprehension. Basal reader teachers' manuals offered little or no help for teachers about *how to teach* children to comprehend text. Instead, the main resources were reading comprehension worksheets mislabeled as instruction. Durkin concluded that teachers often have difficulty telling the difference between *teaching* and *testing* when it comes to reading comprehension.

If mentioning and questioning are not the qualities of effective comprehension instruction, then what is? Durkin (1978) suggested that effective comprehension instruction includes helping, assisting, defining, demonstrating, modeling, describing, explaining, providing feedback, thinking aloud, and *guiding* students through learning activities. Simply asking students to respond to a worksheet or to answer a list of comprehension questions does nothing to develop new comprehension skills. Research has shown that reading comprehension improves when teachers provide explicit comprehension strategy instruction (Bauman & Bergeron, 1993; Brown, Pressley, Van Meter, & Schuder, 1996; Dole, Brown, & Trathen, 1996; Morrow, 1985) and when they provide instructional activities that support students' understanding of the texts they will read (Dowhower, 1987; Eldredge, Reutzel, & Hollingsworth, 1996; Hansen, 1981; Reutzel, Hollingsworth, & Eldredge, 1994; Tharp, 1982).

Durkin (1978) observed that less than 1% of total reading or social studies instructional time was devoted to the teaching of reading comprehension.

Basal teacher's manuals offered little or no help for teachers about how to teach children to comprehend text.

Teaching Comprehension in the Primary Grades

Recently most early literacy research has been directed toward the issues of word identification, particularly phonemic awareness and phonics instruction (National Reading Panel, 2000; RAND Reading Study Group Report, 2001; Snow, Burns, & Griffin, 1998). This is so much the case that "the terms *comprehension instruction* and *primary grades* do not often appear in the same sentence" (Pearson & Duke, 2002, p. 247). But more recently, leading reading authorities, corporately sponsored study groups such as the RAND Reading Study Group, and federal government agencies concluded that young children can and should be taught reading comprehension strategies from the onset of reading instruction.

Teaching Comprehension in the Information Age

Information text (nonfiction) presents different kinds of comprehension obstacles for younger readers. Unlike stories (fiction), information texts are written to explain new concepts, historical events, and previously unknown vocabulary. Text organizations used by authors (e.g., cause/effect, comparison/contrast, problem/solution, description, listing) help structure their ideas depending on their purpose (Alexander & Jetton, 2000). These structures are used extensively in the areas of mathematics, the sciences, historical texts, and the social sciences. Many young readers have trouble following these organizational structures, which can lead to knowledge deficits in critical areas and a widening achievement gap among young children (Neuman, 2001).

In spite of the growing need for content knowledge in the Information Age, the vast majority of reading materials in grades K–3 are *narrative* or story in form. Duke (2000) took a closer look at the reading instruction of children in 20 first-grade classrooms from very low and very high socioeconomic-status school districts (i.e., school districts having a lot of poor families versus districts with a lot of upper-class families). She found very few informational texts in any of these classrooms, particularly the low socioeconomic-status schools. The most startling finding was children in low socioeconomic classrooms, "poor kids," in other words, were asked to read information books only about 3.6 minutes per day on average. Clearly, teachers must spend much more time helping children read and understand nonfiction informational text if they are to excel. Similarly, reading researchers need to devote more energy to this critical topic (Pearson & Duke, 2002).

Comprehension Strategy Instruction: Single Strategies or Multiple Strategies?

The National Reading Panel (NRP; 2000) examined research evidence supporting the teaching of 16 reading comprehension strategies. From this examination, the NRP identified a set of seven comprehension strategies as having sufficient research evidence to recommend implementation in every classroom: *story and text structure, graphic or semantic organizers, question answering, question generation, comprehension monitoring, cooperative learning,* and *summarization.* This information is intended not to narrow the scope of comprehension strategies taught in classrooms but rather to highlight these seven comprehension strategies as essential based on the existing scientific evidence. Every teacher of comprehension should teach these seven comprehension strategies at a minimum but may also choose from others where appropriate. Each of these comprehension strategies is covered within the pages of this chapter.

In many classrooms the idea that children learn to read before reading to learn is evidenced in a lack of comprehension instruction in the primary grades.

There is little time spent teaching comprehension strategies using information texts in the primary grades.

Research has yet to determine whether teaching comprehension strategies singly or as a set of multiple strategies is most effective for young children.

Pressley (2002a) pointed out another vexing issue concerning comprehension strategy instruction in his *Turn-of-the-Century Status Report*. Teachers are increasingly aware that they need to explicitly teach comprehension strategies to children. But *which strategies*, taught in *what order?* Should they be taught singly or in combination? In one approach to teaching comprehension strategies, Keene and Zimmerman (1997) in their book *Mosaic of Thought* encouraged teachers to teach children single comprehension strategies, one at a time, from a list of seven research validated strategies. These single strategies are to be taught in separate "mini-lessons" in which the teacher demonstrates the use of the strategy and gradually releases the application of the strategy to the students. Later, students are taught ways of applying the strategy in other reading situations.

Another approach for teaching comprehension strategies has been described in Palincsar and Brown (1984) and Pressley (2002). Here children practice using *multiple* comprehension strategies as a set or *package* as they read, then discuss what they've learned in small groups with teacher support. The idea is to teach children a "routine" for working through texts using a specific set of comprehension strategies. Research has yet to determine if explicitly teaching a combination of comprehension strategies as a set is preferable to explicitly teaching a series of single strategies. One thing is certain: children need to be taught comprehension strategies.

COMPREHENDING TEXT: SCHEMA THEORY

Schema theory explains how knowledge is stored in the mind. A *schema* (the plural is *schemata* or *schemas*) can be thought of as a mental file folder of categorical knowledge *(chairs, birds, ships)*, events *(weddings, birthdays, funerals)*, emotions *(anger, frustration, joy, pleasure)*, and roles *(parent, judge, teacher)* drawn from the reader's life experiences (Rumelhart, 1981). Schemas do not exist in the mind in any tangible form. Rather, schemas are abstract representations of how knowledge is structured in the mind.

If schemas are like file folders for different concepts, then each concept "folder" has parts inside; these are called *semantic features*. For example, the semantic features associated with the concept of *bird* may include examples, such as *eagles, robins,* and *blue jays;* attributes of birds, such as wings, feathers, and beaks; and a category in which a particular bird belongs, such as *pets* or *birds of prey.* Hence, schemas are organized in our minds by *associations, categories, examples,* and *meaning,* and each are found in our memory much like looking up a topic in an encyclopedia. For example, when looking up the topic of *birds* in an encyclopedia, one typically encounters information about birds, including attributes, categories, and examples of birds.

Schemas are also linked together when there are related meanings (Anderson & Pearson, 1984; A. M. Collins & Quillian, 1969; Lindsay & Norman, 1977; Reznitskaya & Anderson, 2002). Each schema is connected to another related schema, forming a vast interconnected network of knowledge and experiences within the mind of the individual. The size and content of each schema are influenced by past experiences.

Figure 4.1   First grader's bird schema network

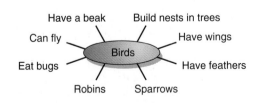

Figure 4.2 High school student's bird schema network

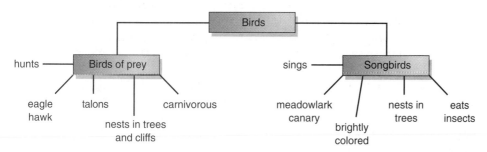

Thus, younger children predictably possess fewer, less well-developed schemas than mature adults. For example, consider Figure 4.1, which represents a first-grader's schema about birds; then in Figure 4.2, compare the first grader's bird schema with that of a freshman high school student just completing a biology class.

Because individuals have their own unique life experiences stored in memory, teachers must not assume that all children in a classroom possess identical knowledge for a given concept, event, or experience. Although readers' schemas often have common features, as shown in Figures 4.1 and 4.2, the first grader's schema, for example, is less developed than the high school student's. Schemas are never complete; they simply provide a flexible place (a mental "file folder") for storing new information. One concept fundamental to schema theory is the idea of adding new information to a schema through a process called **slot filling.** In conclusion, a schema can be thought of as a flexible and growing cognitive framework with slots that can be filled in by the personal and vicarious experiences of a reader.

Pearson, Hansen, and Gordon (1979) found that children who already know a great deal about a given topic before reading about that topic, such as *spiders* prior to reading a text on spiders, remembered more from their reading than did children who knew little or nothing about the topic. This study demonstrates that teachers must be as concerned about building children's knowledge across a wide variety of topics at the same time they are helping students gain control over comprehension strategies. In this way, we can close both the knowledge gap and the reading achievement gap (National Assessment of Educational Progress, 2000; Neuman, 2001).

COMPREHENDING TEXT: A PROCESS OVERVIEW

Comprehending text is a complicated process. Based on schema theory, we see comprehension as a five-stage model that includes *searching, selecting, applying, evaluating,* and *composing.*

1. *Searching* for an appropriate schema, a specific "mental file folder," by paying attention to meaning clues taken from the text (i.e., words, sentences, and paragraphs)
2. *Selecting* an appropriate schema based on the clues found in the text
3. *Applying* the information in that mental file folder (schema) to help the reader figure out the author's message
4. *Evaluating* whether the schema chosen was the correct one or if it should be discarded and replaced with another schema that seems to make more sense
5. *Composing* a new or revised understanding (memory) that is added to the existing schema or used to create a new schema

Younger readers generally possess less well-developed schemata than older readers.

*Adding new information to an incomplete schema is called **slot filling.***

***Comprehending** can be thought of as a five-step process: searching, selecting, applying, evaluating, and composing.*

Figure 4.3   A schema-based explanation of processing text information

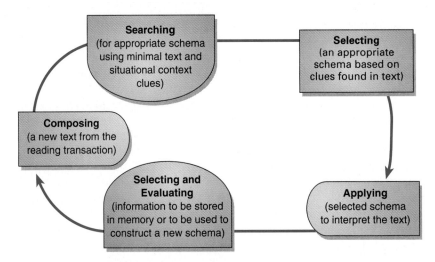

Schemas guide the construction of each word meaning as well as the meaning of the entire text.

This process is illustrated in Figure 4.3.

When readers begin reading a text, they bring along all of their schemas to help them get meaning from the print. What readers expect to find when they begin reading a selection, in terms of content, vocabulary, and format, is influenced by two factors: (a) the *function* of the reading materials, such as labels, road signs, bus schedules, books, or newspapers, and (b) the *situational context* in which the act of reading takes place, such as a supermarket, a car, a bus terminal, a bookstore, or an easy chair at home. In this way, context factors—*function* and *situation*—help readers efficiently select a tentative schema for interpreting the print.

As an example, consider the following. Imagine that you are going to a local laundromat to wash your clothes for the first time. Since you are new at this, you will probably look around the laundromat for information to help you accomplish the task. On a nearby wall, you see a large sign posted above the washing machines. The text reads as follows:

> The procedure is actually quite simple. First you arrange the items into different groups. Of course, one pile may be sufficient, depending on how much there is to do. If you have to go somewhere else due to lack of facilities, that is the next step, otherwise you are pretty well set. It is important not to overdo things. It is better to do too few things at once than too many. In the short run this may not seem important, but complications can easily arise. A mistake can be expensive as well. At first, the whole procedure will seem complicated. Soon, however, it will become just another facet of life. It is difficult to foresee any end to the necessity for this task in the immediate future, but then, one never can tell. After the procedure is complete, one arranges the materials into different groups again. Then they can be put into their appropriate places. Eventually they will be used once more and the whole cycle will then have to be repeated. However, that is part of life. *(Bransford & Franks, 1971, p. 719)*

If you had not read these directions on a sign in a laundromat, you may have had greater difficulty limiting your search for the correct schema to interpret the sign to the act of washing clothes. Thus, the function of a sign and the situational context of reading, in this case the laundromat, helped you limit your search to the most likely schema—washing clothes.

Once the most likely schema is selected for interpreting a text, it is applied. In the laundromat scenario, you would interpret the word *procedure* in the text to mean *the act of,* or *steps involved in,* washing clothes. If you had selected a postmaster schema by mistake, then the word *procedure* may have been interpreted as the act of, or steps in, sorting letters into post office boxes. Thus, the selected schema can be used to guide the interpretation of each word in the text as well as the collective meaning of all the words in the text.

Schemas also provide a framework for absorbing new information found in the text. Empty slots in a novice's laundry schema are filled in using information found in the sign. Connections are also made between existing knowledge about doing laundry and the new information learned in the sign. By contrasting new information to already known schemas, readers automatically decide which information is important to remember for future use.

During this ongoing process, readers create a newly revised schema that includes new information learned in this case, new knowledge gained from reading the laundry sign. In a way, comprehending text is a bit like creating a *new* text (Tierney & Pearson, 1983). In other words, one change resulting from the reading "transaction" above is that the reader is changed—he now possess greater knowledge about doing the laundry than he did before reading the sign on the wall. The sign on the wall has changed, in a sense, because it has been transformed in the mind of the reader. Hence, the act of comprehending a text can be thought of in terms of a dialogue between reader and author that takes place in a specific situational context.

COMPREHENSION DIFFICULTIES

Comprehension difficulties can be traced to four schema-related problems (Rumelhart, 1984). Each of these problems is discussed with examples to help you gain an understanding by experiencing firsthand the difficulties students may encounter in comprehending.

• *Difficulty 1: Students may not have the necessary schema to understand a specific topic. Without a schema for a particular concept, they simply cannot understand the text.*

In the passage below, for example, readers not having the needed schema cannot understand individual word meanings and have trouble comprehending the overall text.

A—Machine-baste interfacing to WRONG side of one collar section 1/2 inch from raw edges. Trim interfacing close to stitching. B—Clip dress neck edge to stay stitching. With RIGHT sides together, pin collar to dress, matching centers back and small dots. Baste. Stitch. Trim seam; clip curve. Press seam open. *(Gibson & Levin, 1975, p. 7)*

Although individuals with a sewing schema readily interpret this passage, those who don't possess a sewing schema experience greater difficulty making sense of certain specialized words *(baste, interfacing)* in the text and the text as a whole.

• *Difficulty 2: Readers may have well-developed schemas for a topic, but authors may fail to provide enough information or clues for readers to locate or select a given schema.*

In some cases a reader may already know a great deal about the topic to be read. However, the author may fail to provide enough information in the text that connects with the reader's schema. For example, read the following text to see if you can locate your schema on this well-known topic.

> Our hero bravely defied all scornful laughter that tried to prevent his scheme. "Your eyes deceive," he had said, "An egg not a table correctly typifies this planet." Now three sturdy sisters sought proof, forging along sometimes through calm vastness. *(Bransford & Johnson, 1972)*

The authors failed to include explicit clues in the text, such as *explorer, ships,* and *America,* making the selection of a *Christopher Columbus* schema much more difficult. Without these important clues being placed in the text, it will be hard for readers to call up specific "slots" (associations) found in the Columbus schema.

   • *Difficulty 3: Readers may hastily select a schema for interpreting a text, only to discover later that the text information does not match the known information for that schema.*

When this comprehension difficulty occurs, readers usually shift from using the first schema to the appropriate one to correctly comprehend the text. You may recall the following example from Chapter 2. Read this scenario again and think how your schema changes with new information.

> John was on his way to school.
>
> He was terribly worried about the math lesson.
>
> He thought he might not be able to control the class again today.
>
> It was not a normal part of a janitor's duties.
>
> *(Sanford & Garrod, 1981, p. 114)*

Did you experience several shifts to select the appropriate schema to interpret the text? Not only do schemas help readers interpret what they read, but also the information found in the text helps readers decide which schemas are selected.

   • *Difficulty 4: The cultural and experiential background of readers may affect their perspective when selecting a schema to interpret a text. This sometimes leads to an "understanding" of the text but a misunderstanding of the author.*

To illustrate this comprehension difficulty, Lipson (1983) conducted a study showing that Catholic and Jewish children comprehended texts better when they were compatible with their own religious beliefs than when the texts went against their religious schemas. Other studies (Alvermann, Smith, & Readence, 1985; Reutzel & Hollingsworth, 1991a; Read & Rosson, 1982) have also shown that students' schemas that are based on their prior knowledge, attitudes, and experiences have a strong influence on how well students comprehend and *remember* information from their readings.

To illustrate this difficulty further, Anderson, Reynolds, Schallert, and Goetz (1977) asked people in a study to read the following paragraph:

> Tony slowly got up from the mat, planning his escape. He hesitated a moment and thought. Things were not going well. What bothered him most was being held, especially since the charge against him had been weak. He considered his present sit-

uation. The lock that held him was strong but he thought he could break it. He knew, however, that his timing would have to be perfect. Tony was aware that it was because of his early roughness that he had been penalized so severely—much too severely from his point of view. The situation was becoming frustrating; the pressure had been grinding on him for too long. He was being ridden unmercifully. Tony was getting angry now. He felt he was ready to make his move. He knew that his success or failure would depend on what he did in the next few seconds. (p. 372)

Most people in the study thought the passage described a convict planning his escape. There *is*, however, another possible interpretation. When physical education majors in this study read the passage above, they thought it was about wrestling. Thus, the experiential background of the readers influenced their understanding of what they read.

A MODEL FOR EFFECTIVE COMPREHENSION INSTRUCTION

Gradual Release of Responsibility Instruction Model

Pearson and Gallagher (1983) designed a model for effective comprehension instruction called the **gradual release of responsibility.** In Figure 4.4, the diagonal line from the upper-left-hand corner extending downward toward the lower-right-hand corner represents varying degrees of responsibility teachers and children *share* in learning and using comprehension strategies or completing comprehension tasks. The upper-left-hand corner in Figure 4.4 shows teachers carrying the major share of the responsibility for comprehension task completion, and the lower-right-hand corner shows students carrying the major share of the responsibility.

The concept of *gradual release* shown in this instructional model can be used as a planning guide for any of the comprehension strategy lessons presented in the remainder of this chapter.

Students may need assistance to help them locate and use their schemata to comprehend text. For example, sometimes a picture can be very helpful.

*The **gradual release of responsibility model** depicts the idea that responsibility for comprehension tasks should be shifted gradually over time from the teacher to the student.*

Figure 4.4 The gradual release of responsibility model of instruction

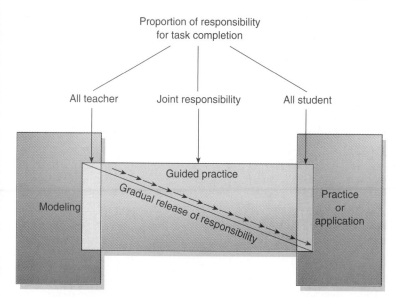

Proportion of responsibility for task completion

All teacher　　Joint responsibility　　All student

Modeling　　Guided practice　　Gradual release of responsibility　　Practice or application

Source: From "The Instruction of Reading Comprehension" by P. D. Pearson and M. C. Gallagher, 1983, *Contemporary Educational Psychology, 8*(3), pp. 317–344. Copyright 1983 by Academic Press. Reprinted by permission.

It is important at this point to recall again Vygotsky's (1962) *zone of proximal development,* which reminds us that children need to be helped to do those things they cannot yet do independently.

How Gradual Release of Responsibility Works in the Classroom: The Teacher's Job

It is assumed that, before any kind of comprehension skill lesson is planned, the teacher has assessed her students to find out which strategies are needed. This is what we refer to as *class profiling,* and is discussed in-depth later in Chapter 7. The teacher then sets about planning learning activities for each strategy.

The first step, as indicated in Figure 4.4, is for the teacher to *model* how the skill is used in a reading situation. Modeling involves repeated examples where the teacher, as a master user of the new strategy to be learned, demonstrates how the strategy "looks" when she uses it. Modeling should be done until the teacher is reasonably sure that the student(s) have an understanding of what is expected of them.

Teachers need to model the use of comprehension strategies using think-alouds.

In the early stages of the next phase, *guided practice,* the teacher continues to model how the strategy is used in reading situations, but she now invites students to try it themselves. Thus, in the early stages of guided practice, as the model in Figure 4.4 indicates, most of the responsibility for using the strategy still rests with the teacher, but it is becoming a "joint responsibility." Students are starting to "get their hands dirty" as they try out the strategy with the help of the teacher. You might say that the teacher is shifting from serving as a *model* to being a supportive *coach.* You will need to plan for numerous practice activities during the guided practice stage; one or two lessons will not be enough.

As guided practice continues and the students gain confidence in using the new strategy, teachers begin to slowly phase out their direct support. Practice sessions can be planned in which students, working in pairs, practice using the strategy. Students only call on the teacher now when they have a problem they cannot solve for themselves. This allows you to move about the classroom making "house calls" as needed and to conduct informal assessments of their learning.

One caution for new teachers: be sure and have students *overlearn* the new strategy. One of our teacher friends calls this "marinating" students in the new knowledge (i.e., have them overlearn until the new knowledge is "soaked to the bone"). Teachers tend not to provide enough guided practice on new skills, which can result in only temporary or short-term learning. "Marinating" takes care of this problem.

In the final stage of the gradual release of responsibility model, students use the strategy independently—with little or no support. Activities planned now are essentially "all student" in nature. Again, much practice is needed to make sure the new skill has *crystallized* in students' minds. Before moving on and starting instruction on a new comprehension skill, the teacher ends the way she began—by assessing whether students are now proficient in using the skill.

How Gradual Release of Responsibility Works in the Classroom: The Student's Job

Much of what is expected of students can be inferred from the description above, but let's take a few moments to clarify their role. It may be helpful if you think of students in learning situations as *apprentices* and you yourself as a skilled craftsman.

At the beginning of a comprehension strategy lesson, when the teacher is busy modeling (demonstrating) the new strategy to be learned, the student's job is to *observe*. Learners should attend to the teacher demonstration and ask questions to clarify as necessary. During the guided practice phase, the student's job is to *experiment* with the new strategy.

In the final stages of learning, independent practice, students *demonstrate* for teachers how they can now use the newly acquired strategy on their own. New comprehension abilities are best demonstrated by students using language (Benson & Cummins, 2000): postreading discussion, written summaries (e.g., reading response journals), oral retellings, and construction of graphic organizers that show key concepts and vocabulary, just to name a few possibilities. Student-generated language responses help teachers get a closer look at thinking processes that have been developed as a result of the learning activities.

COMPREHENSION INSTRUCTION: PHRASES AND SENTENCES

Comprehension instruction proceeds from an understanding of individual words in context to comprehending phrases and sentences. In this section of the chapter, we discuss how teachers can help children derive the meaning of individual words in text and "chunk" into meaningful phrases and sentences.

"Clozing" in on Comprehension: Deriving the Meaning of Words in Text

One of the more potent ways of teaching children how to use the context of a sentence to guess the identity of an unknown word is a teaching method known as *cloze*. The **cloze** procedure is "the use of a piece of writing in which certain words have been deleted and the pupil has to make maximum possible use of context clues available in predicting the missing words" (D.E.S., 1975, p. 93). According to Rye (1982), the cloze procedure is a useful instructional strategy because "the human mind has a tendency to complete incomplete patterns or sequences." (p. 2) When cloze was first introduced by W. L. Taylor in 1953, it was proposed as a means of measuring reading ability. Since that time, a variety of instructional uses have been developed using cloze to improve children's ability to comprehend word meanings in text. Here are several instructional uses of cloze.

The most familiar version of cloze involves an *every-nth-word* deletion pattern. Typically, every 5th or 10th word in a passage of 250 words is deleted and left for students to complete using the context or surrounding familiar words in the sentence. Look at the following example, which uses an *every-5th-word* deletion pattern.

Students need to assume responsibility for using comprehension strategies with teacher guidance and support.

Standards Note
Standard 7.1: The reading professional will provide direct instruction and model when and how to use multiple comprehension strategies, including retelling. After reading each of the comprehension strategies presented, plan a direct instruction lesson for one comprehension strategy that includes gradually releasing responsibility for using the strategy to a group of children.

*The **cloze** is a teaching method in which students identify missing words in a piece of writing by using context clues.*

The most familiar version of cloze involves an every-nth-word deletion pattern.

Many scientists believe that there are other forms of intelligent life somewhere in space. These forms may not _____ the way we do. _____ often show life forms _____ space with silly-looking _____ . Movies often show them _____ frightening monsters. But have _____ ever wondered what those _____ life forms might think _____ us?

Primary-aged children experience greater success with an every-10th-word deletion pattern because children are given more context clues to use before encountering the next deletion.

Watson and Crowley (1988) describe another approach using the cloze procedure called *selected deletions*. The advantage to this approach is that teachers can delete selected words depending on their instructional goals and the needs of their students. For example, different categories of words may be selected for deletion: words signaling the sequence of text *(first, second, next, before, after)*, words referring back to or ahead to other words in the text *(he, she, this, those, which)*, words showing location *(behind, on, under, next to)*, words signaling an explanation *(thus, because, so, therefore, as a result)*, words signaling comparisons *(but, yet, although, similarly)*, and words signaling an example *(such as, for example, that is, namely)*. Here is one example of selected deletions:

> Many scientists believe that there are other forms of intelligent _____ somewhere in space. These _____ may not look the way we do. Movies often show life _____ from space with silly-looking _____ . _____ often show them as frightening monsters. But have you ever wondered what those other _____ forms might think of us?

Phrasing for Comprehension: "Chunking" and "Readers' Theater"

To comprehend well, students must be able to mentally *chunk* words into meaningful phrases. Chunking develops best when children are given multiple opportunities to practice reading a text several times with increasing fluency (Irwin, 1996). We have also found that wide reading of easy materials across a variety of genre (e.g., mysteries, information texts, biography, poetry, short stories) is very useful—particularly information texts.

Students can practice *chunking* in a number of ways. One method is to rewrite a passage into chunks. An example taken from the book *The World of Matter* by Ron Cole (1997) is found in Figure 4.5.

Readers' theater is another great task for practicing phrasing and fluency. In reader's theater, children practice reading from a script in preparation for sharing an oral performance with classmates and selected audiences (Hill, 1990b); Sloyer, 1982. Unlike a play where students memorize lines, practice actions, and use elaborate stage sets to make their presentation, emphasis is placed on presenting a dramatic oral reading of a text for an audience who imagines setting and actions.

Typically, readers' theater works best when easy texts are selected for practice. Information texts such as *The Popcorn Book* (dePaola, 1978) and *The Magic School Bus Lost in the Solar System* (Cole, 1990) may be used effectively as readers' theater practice scripts (Young & Vardell, 1993). Also, scripts based on quality narratives,

*With **selected deletions,** teachers delete selected words, depending on their instructional goals and the observed needs of their students.*

One way to practice "chunking" is to rewrite a passage into visual chunks for fluency practice.

Readers' theater is a very useful task for practicing phrasing and fluency.

Figure 4.5   Chunking an information text

> Big or small/ hot or cold/ shiny or dull/ visible or invisible/ every living thing/
> And nonliving thing/ in our universe/ is made up of the stuff/ we call **matter.**/
> Matter can be defined/ as anything that takes up space. (p. 1)

stories, and poems are good choices. Readers' theater selections should be packed with action, contain an element of suspense, and include an entire meaningful story or episode. A few examples of such texts are Martin and Archambault's (1987) *Knots on a Counting Rope,* Viorst's (1972) *Alexander and the Terrible, Horrible, No Good, Very Bad Day,* and Barbara Robinson's (1972) *The Best Christmas Pageant Ever.*

Hennings (1974) describes a simple procedure for preparing readers' theater scripts for classroom performance. First, the text to be performed is read silently by the individual students. Second, the text is read again orally, sometimes using choral reading in a group. After the second reading, either children choose their parts, or the teacher assigns parts to the children. (We suggest that students be allowed to select their three most desired parts, write these choices on a slip of paper, and submit them to the teacher and that teachers do everything possible to assign one of these three choices.) The third reading is also an oral reading with students reading their parts with scripts in hand. Students may have several rehearsal readings as they prepare for the final reading or performance in front of the class or a special audience.

COMPREHENSION INSTRUCTION: CONNECTING INFORMATION AND MAKING INFERENCES

An important part of reading comprehension involves the ability to make connections between words and ideas in text. This leads to the ability of making inferences or "reading between the lines" (Hollingsworth & Reutzel, 1988; Keene & Zimmerman, 1997; Pearson & Duke, 2002). Drawing inferences requires readers to link words and ideas between sentences and then connect key ideas found in several sentences. Therefore, let's first take a look at the *connectives* that link ideas between sentences. Next, we will discuss what are called *slot-filling* inferences—those that connect ideas across several sentences.

*Words that link sentences together are called **cohesive ties.***

Connecting Ideas Among Sentences

Important ideas between sentences are "glued" together by words known as *cohesive ties* (Moe & Irwin, 1986). Some examples of these "glue words" or cohesive ties follow:

Cohesive Ties (categories)	Example
Reference	
Includes many pronoun types, location words, and time words	Austin went to the park. He climbed the slide. "Mom, look at that car! Can we go over there?"
Substitution	
Replacing a word or phrase with another	"My dress is old. I need a new one." "Tom already knows." "Everyone does."
Ellipsis	
Omitting a word or phrase resulting in an implied repetition	"Were laughing?" "No, I wasn't." "Dylan wears expensive sneakers. His look nicer."

Conjunction

Connects phrases and sentences using additive, adversative, causal, and temporal ties	"Denver ate ice cream after dinner. He didn't eat fish *because* he dislikes them."

Lexical

Using synonymous or category terms to establish ties in text	The bear went fishing. This large mammal likes to eat fish.

Some students struggle with comprehension because they do not understand cohesive ties. As always, you should assess your students to see who may be having trouble understanding cohesive ties. We suggest beginning your assessment with referential ties (see previous text—especially common pronouns.)

Teaching Cohesive Ties

Here are some tips for effective cohesive ties lessons (an example lesson is shown in Figure 4.6 inspired by Pulver [1986] and Baumann and Stevenson [1986]).

- Directly explain each cohesive tie and give examples of how it works in text (Reutzel & Morgan, 1990).
- Think aloud by describing your own thought processes as a reader on how a cohesive tie works in text.
- Ask questions to encourage discussion and description of students' thoughts about each cohesive tie.
- Practice each cohesive tie during group activities.
- Practice each cohesive tie during independent activities.

Drawing Inferences: Making Connections Across Sentences in Text

As children read a text, they must often fill in information that the author did not include; this is called *drawing inferences* or *making an inference*. Missing information in texts are like empty slots left by the author to be filled in by the reader (Fillmore, 1968; Kintsch, 1974; Trabasso, 1980). These slots can be filled in by identifying relevant clues from the sentence context and answering questions like the following:

Instigator	=	Who did it?
Action	=	What was done?
Object	=	To whom or what was it done?
Location	=	Where was it done?
Instrument	=	What was used to do it?
Result	=	What was the result or goal?

The ***Generating Reciprocal Inferences Procedure (GRIP)*** *is an approach aimed at helping students learn to make a variety of slot-filling inferences.*

Other slot-filling inferences are shaped by the situation including the character's motivation, cause and effect factors, and time/space relationships.

Hollingsworth and Reutzel (1988) developed an approach for helping students learn to make a variety of *slot-filling inferences* called GRIP (Generating Reciprocal Inferences Procedure). To begin a GRIP lesson, the teacher models how a particular

Figure 4.6 Example cohesive ties lesson—Reference ties

Purpose for Learning the Strategy: This strategy will help you make connections between words and ideas in sentences. By using this strategy, you will improve your understanding of text information.

Objective: Learn to identify pronouns that refer back to another person, place, thing, or idea.

Teacher Explanation & Modeling: This strategy begins preparing several pairs of sentences that show a pronoun replacing a noun in another sentence. For example:

Carter jumped on the bunk bed.
He was playing like Spiderman.

Place these sentences and others you have prepared on an overhead transparency.

Read the first pair of sentences aloud. Underline the word 'he' and ask aloud, "I wonder what the word 'he' refers to in this other sentence? Does 'he' refer to the bunk bed? No, that doesn't make sense. Maybe 'he' refers to Carter. That makes sense. I guess the "he" refers to another person, place, thing, or idea in a neighboring sentence."

Draw an arrow showing the backward reference of "he" to Carter

Carter jumped on the bunk bed. He was playing like Spiderman.

Guided Application: Now let's try these next sentences together. Underline the word "she" in the second sentence. Ask, "I wonder what word in the other sentence the word 'she' is telling us about? Can anyone help me?" (Allow the children to pick out the referenced term, Candice.)

Invite a student to come forward and draw an arrow between the words "she" and "Candice."

Candice liked to ride horses. She dreamed one day of riding in a parade.

Continue with another example set of sentences. This time invite students to find the word to underline, "They." Next ask them to find the referenced term. Then invite a student to come and draw the arrows between the referenced ties.

Individual Application: "Now I want you to finish this handout in pairs. Begin by underlining the words that are referencing each other and then draw an arrow between the words. When you are finished, I want you to come up here record and your work on the overhead transparency. I will number you off into pairs. Remember your number because that is the number of the sentence pair you will record on the overhead transparency up here. So, if your pair number is '6,' you and your partner will come up and complete sentence pair number 6. Do you all understand?"

Assessment: After the children complete their handouts and the numbered item on the overhead, bring the group together. Project the overhead transparency, and invite pairs to come forward and explain how they identified the reference terms.

type (Instigator, Action, Object, etc.) of *slot-filling inference* is made. She starts by reading aloud and highlighting key words in the text, as highlighted in this example:

The *elevator ride* was great fun. Now Kathy and Becky *looked down* through the wire fence as the wind whistled in their ears. The *people* and the *cars on the street looked* just like *tiny* toys. Although they were *very high up,* the girls were not frightened. It was exciting to *see the whole city* spread out before them.

This passage helps readers understand "location" inferences. Where were Kathy and Becky? The teacher, in her modeling, makes the inference that Kathy and Becky were on a high building, perhaps a skyscraper, overlooking a city—the location. Next, the teacher thinks aloud and explains how she used the underlined clue words in the passage to justify the inference she made.

Notice how teachers model the process of making an inference in the first stage of the GRIP strategy.

To gradually release the responsibility for making an inference from the teacher to the students, the GRIP lesson continues using at least four more paragraphs. In the second paragraph, the teacher highlights the words, the children make the inference, and the teacher justifies the inference the students made. In the third paragraph, the children highlight the key words, the teacher makes the inference, and the students justify the inference—the roles have now reversed. In the fourth and final passage, students highlight the key words, make the inference, and justify the inference; the teacher assesses whether they are now proficient in the skill.

To *crystallize* this new knowledge children have gained from the GRIP method, a final step could be to have them *generate* their own reciprocal inferences. This is done by having students, working in pairs, create a list of five or more key words and write their own text. You will need to model how a writer can insert the clues into a text without giving away the inference to be made. After writing their texts, students exchange texts, mark key words, make an inference, and justify their inferences to the peer authors. Another variation to this approach involves a game board activity (Figure 4.7) with directions for playing the game (Figure 4.8).

In the second stage of the GRIP strategy, students compose inferential text for peers to make inferences.

Figure 4.7   Generating Reciprocal Inferences Procedure (GRIP) game board

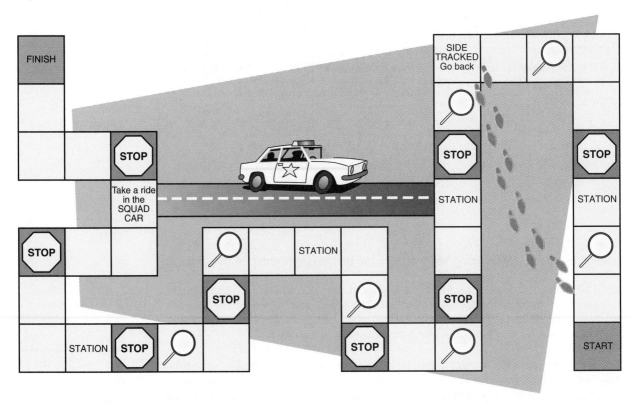

Source: From "Get a GRIP on Comprehension" by P. M. Hollingsworth and D. R. Reutzel, 1988, *Reading Horizons, 29*(1), p. 78. Copyright 1988 by Reading Horizons. Reprinted by permission.

Figure 4.8   Directions for Generating Reciprocal Inferences Procedure (GRIP) game board

---

Children play the GRIP board game in pairs. Before the game begins, each child needs to understand the rules for playing the game and follow them carefully. We begin by discussing the game rules with the children:

1. Requires two players to play the game.
2. Write four sentences that go together to make a story. Underline the clue words in each sentence.
3. Select a marker.
4. Place marker on START.
5. Throw the die, letting the highest start the game.
6. Each player moves his/her marker the number of spaces shown on the die.
7. If you land on STATION, have the other player read a sentence.
8. If you land on MAGNIFYING GLASS, move to the nearest STATION, have the other player read a sentence.
9. A different sentence is read at each STATION.
10. You must be on STATION to guess, and you get only one guess.
11. If you land on STOP SIGN, go back to the space from which you started your turn.
12. You can be on the same space as the other player.
13. If you land on SIDETRACKED, follow the feet.
14. If you land on SQUAD CAR, follow the road.
15. Whoever guesses what the story is about is the winner, and the game is over.

When the GRIP board game is introduced, play the game with one child while the other children in the classroom watch. This makes the transition from discussing the rules to playing the game easier.

Source: From "Get a GRIP on Comprehension" by P. M. Hollingsworth and D. R. Reutzel, 1988. *Reading Horizons, 29*(1), pp. 76–77. Copyright 1988 by Reading Horizons. Reprinted by permission.

COMPREHENSION INSTRUCTION: TEACHING STUDENTS ABOUT TEXT STRUCTURES

Understanding Stories: Narrative Text Structure

Understanding the way in which authors organize and structure their ideas in texts is key to good reading comprehension (Simmons & Kameenui, 1998; Pressley, 2000; Pearson & Duke, 2002). One of the most important aspects of teaching young children to comprehend narrative texts is to teach them story structure (Vallecorsa & de-Bettencourt, 1997). The elements of story structure have been captured in a system of rules called **story grammars** (Mandler & Johnson, 1977; Stein & Glenn, 1979; Thorndyke, 1977). Story grammars are the rules, necessary elements to make a story, and the expected sequence for these elements. Researchers generally agree on the following elements and sequence of elements in a story grammar: *setting, problem, goal, events,* and *resolution.*

Developing a sense of how stories are written and organized helps readers predict what is coming next with greater skill, store information in schemas more efficiently, and recall story elements with increased accuracy and completeness. Several

Story grammars *is a system of rules necessary for making a story.*

Figure 4.9   Story grammar map

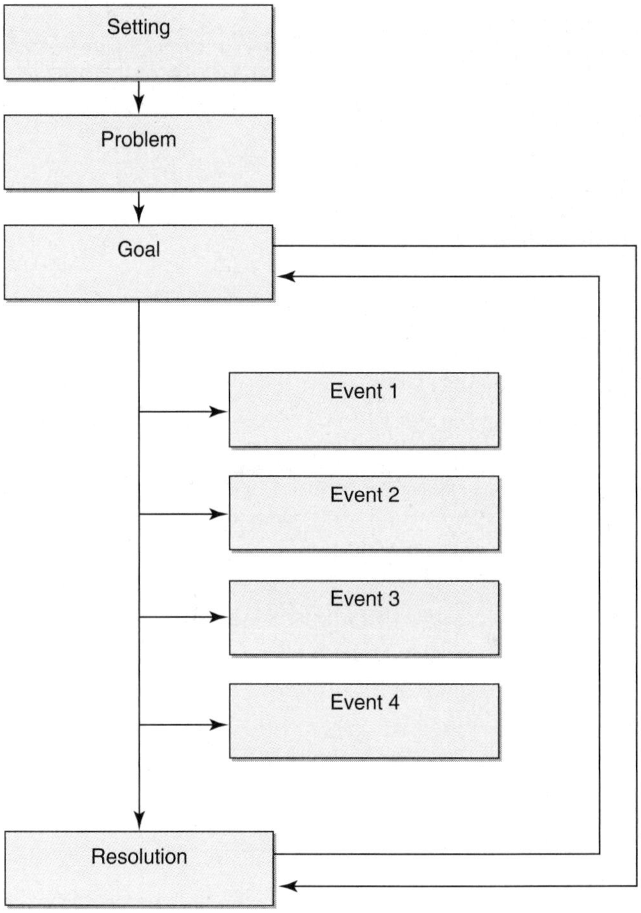

researchers have described effective teaching procedures for developing readers' story grammar knowledge (Gordon & Braun, 1983; Hagood, 1997).

Story grammars can be enhanced by teaching students the major structural elements of stories.

1. Instruction in story structure is most effective when it makes use of well-formed stories such as *Jack and the Beanstalk, Cinderella, The Three Billy Goats Gruff,* and *The Little Red Hen.* Visual organizers can be used to guide the introduction of the concept of story structure (see Figures 4.9 and 4.10). For the first story used in story structure instruction, read the story aloud, stop at key points in the story, and discuss the missing information needed to fill in the empty parts of the story grammar map or story structure clothesline. For stories read after introducing the concept of story schema, use visual organizers to introduce and elicit predictions about the story before reading. During and after reading, the visual organizer such as a story map (shown later in this chapter) can be used to guide a discussion.
2. Set the purposes for reading by asking questions related to the structure of the story. Questioning designed to follow the story's structure will focus students' attention on major story elements.
3. After questioning and discussing story structure, specific questions about the story content can be asked.

Figure 4.10 Clothesline

4. For continued instruction, gradually introduce less well-formed stories so that students will learn that not all stories are "ideal" in organization.
5. Extend this instruction by encouraging children to ask their own questions using story structure and to apply this understanding in writing their own stories.

Another effective method for developing story structure awareness is asking children to read stories and talk about the story structure in small discussion and cooperative learning groups (Gersten, Fuchs, Williams, 2001; Mathes, 1997; Simmons & Kameenui, 1998). In the following sections, we describe several instructional strategies shown to improve comprehension of narrative text.

Narrative Graphic Organizers: Story Maps and Discussion Webs, and Schema Stories

Story Maps. Story maps are diagrams that show the elements (title, setting, problem, events, resolution) and sequence of story events. According to Reutzel (1985b, 1986c), story maps help teachers accomplish two major comprehension goals. First, by creating story maps, teachers become involved in thinking about the structure of stories and how story elements are related to one another. Such involvement in making story maps leads to increased planning and better organization of comprehension instruction. Second, when story mapping is used, students are helped to understand the important parts of stories as well as how these parts relate to one another.

To design a story map, Reutzel (1985b) lists the following steps:

1. Preread the story. Construct in sequence a listing of the major elements that make up the plot of the story.
2. Place the title of the story in the center of the story map.

Story maps help teachers and students think about the important elements of stories and visualize the story structure.

Story maps can be used before, during, and after reading to improve comprehension by helping children visualize the organization of a story.

Figure 4.11   Story Map of *The Paper Bag Princess* (Munsch, 1980).

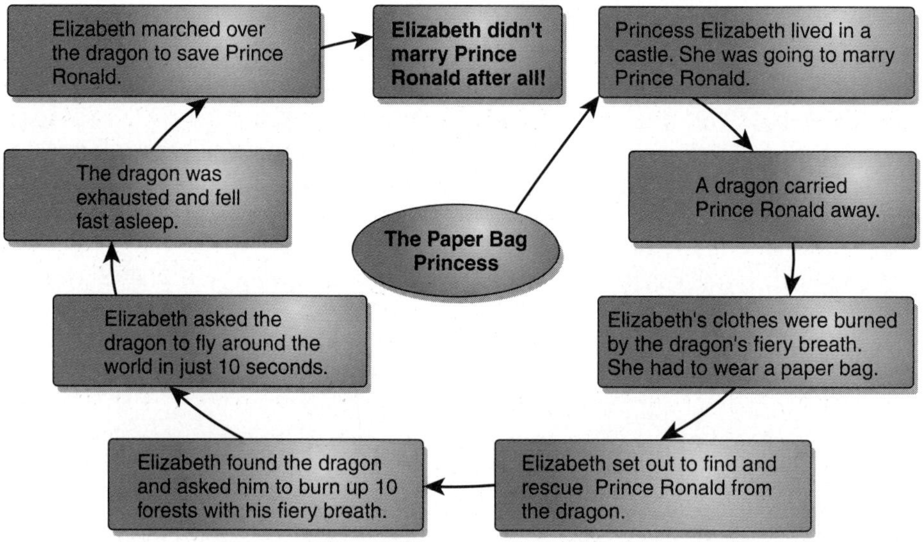

3. Draw enough ties projecting out symmetrically from the center of the map to accommodate the major elements of the story's plot (setting, problem, goal, events, and resolution).
4. Attach information from the summary listing to each of the ties in clockwise rotation around the story map.

After creating a story map as shown in Figure 4.11 for the *Paper Bag Princess* (Munsch, 1980), introduce children to the story by viewing a copy of the story map on an overhead projector, large chart paper, or at the board. While pointing to the center of the story map, ask children, "What do you think the story will be about today?" Children focus their attention on the title of the story at the center of the story map to guide their predictions and discussion. Next, move the pointer to the setting circle and ask students to predict details in the story map such as "Who do you think the characters are in the story, or what can we tell about the characters in the story?" After discussing the setting, move the pointer to the circle where the story problem is shown. Ask students to read the information in the story map and ask them why they think this may be a problem for the characters in the story. Move the pointer around the story map discussing the information found in each story element tie. Children read the story after the discussion of the story map to see if their predictions were accurate.

Story maps can be used with a variety of ages, text structures, and reading strategies to improve reading comprehension.

During reading, children will often reference the unfolding story against the information contained in the story map (Reutzel, 1985b). In this way, the story map acts as a metacognitive aid to help students determine whether they comprehend the elements and sequence of the story events as well as the relationship among these events. After reading, students are asked to write (for older students) or dictate (for younger students) a summary of the story without the story map. They can also be asked to fill in the details in an incomplete story map handout.

Story maps may be used before, during, and after reading a text to make predictions, discuss story elements, or review the sequence of events in a story. By visually representing the major elements of the story plot and the relationships among those elements, teachers plan and implement more purposeful, focused reading lessons, which lead to increased student memory for and comprehension of text.

Discussion Webs. Discussion plays an important part in guiding students' comprehension and interpretation of reading selections (Alvermann, Dillon, & O'Brien, 1987; Gambrell & Almasi, 1996). Children are encouraged during discussions to examine more than one point of view as well as to refine their own comprehension of a text. **Discussion webs** are an adaptation of the cooperative teaming approach by McTighe and Lyman (1988) known as *Think–Pair–Share.* The aim of using discussion webs is to encourage children to adopt a listening attitude, to think individually and critically about ideas, and to involve typically less verbal children in the ongoing discussion of a reading selection.

*The purpose of using **discussion webs** is to encourage children to discuss issues from more than a single point of view.*

Alvermann (1991) describes a five-step process for using discussion webs:

1. Begin by preparing students to read a selection by activating their background for the selection, introducing unfamiliar vocabulary terms and concepts, and setting a purpose for reading. An example may be based on the story *Tales of a Fourth Grade Nothing* (Blume, 1972), as shown in Figure 4.12.

Notice five steps for using discussion webs.

2. After reading the selection, students are introduced to the discussion web. Students are placed in pairs and asked to discuss the pros and cons of the question in the center of the web, "Was Fudge really a bad kid?" Children take turns jotting down reasons for the yes and no continuum of the web.

3. Once children have had sufficient time to discuss the question in pairs and jot their ideas down on the web, one pair of students is placed with another pair of students. This group of four students discusses and shares its thinking around the central question in the discussion web. Children are told to keep an open mind and to listen carefully during this part of the sharing. They are also reminded that it is appropriate to disagree with others in appropriate ways. The children work as a group toward a concluding statement that can be placed in the web.

4. When each group of four has reached a conclusion, a spokesperson is selected to represent the conclusion during the general group discussion. Spokespeople are encouraged to represent dissenting points of view as well as the group's majority conclusion.

Figure 4.12 Discussion web based on *Tales of a Fourth Grade Nothing* (Blume, 1972)

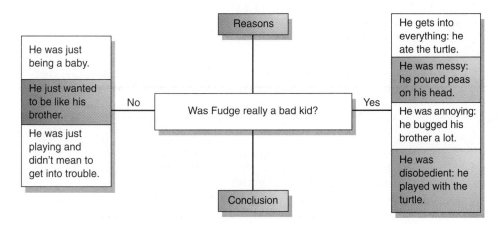

5. As a follow-up, children are asked to complete their own discussion webs by filling in their own ideas as well as those of the groups with whom they participated. These individual responses in the discussion webs should be prominently displayed in the classroom when completed.

Discussion webs help teachers lead students to deeper understandings of characters, story outcomes, how two sides of an issue may be considered, and using critical thinking strategies to make reasoned judgments.

Schema Stories. Watson and Crowley (1988) describe a strategy lesson called schema stories where children use what they know about story structure to reconstruct cut-apart elements of a story. The key to this lesson is to select text that contains highly predictable structures such as "once upon a time" and "they lived happily ever after." After selecting a well-formed story, such as *Elbert's Bad Word* (Wood & Wood, 1988), prepare the lesson by photocopying the text, then physically cutting the story into sections (each of which is long enough to contain at least one main idea). One or two paragraphs will usually be sufficient in length to accomplish this purpose. To begin the lesson, each section of text is distributed to a small group of students (five to eight students).

A student is selected in each group to read the text aloud. The teacher asks for the group that thinks it has the beginning of the story to raise their hands. Members of the group must explain why they believe they have the requested part of the story. A consensus must be reached by the class before proceeding to a discussion of the next text segment. This procedure continues as described until all of the segments of the text have been put in order. An example of a schema story lesson is found in Figure 4.13.

Schema story lessons make excellent small-group or individual comprehension lessons that can be placed into a center or station devoted to comprehension strategies. All the segments of a text can be placed into an envelope and filed in the center. Two children, or individuals, can come to the center and select an envelope and

Schema stories are used to teach children to predict and confirm story predictions.

Figure 4.13 Schema story using text from *Elbert's Bad Word*

- "Come with me young man!" Elbert's mother said with a frown. In the lavatory Elbert's mother handed him a bar of soap.
- One afternoon at an elegant garden party, young Elbert heard a word he had never heard before.
- Elbert knew something had to be done.
- He ran down a cobbled path and knocked at the gardener's cottage. The gardener, who was a practicing wizard, opened the door.
- He baked the words into a little cake. Elbert ate every last crumb.
- Soon the trouble began anew.
- Then with a terrible thud, the mallet landed on Elbert's great toe.
- "My stars! Thunder and lightning! Rats and blue blazes! Suffering cats! Blistering hop toads! Zounds and gadzooks!" he shouted.
- Everyone breathed a sigh of relief and gave Elbert three rousing cheers.
- He saw something that looked like a little spider scurry down a dark hole, and disappear.
- Forgetting about it, the boy went on his way. But the word waited patiently.
- Then with a terrible thud, the mallet landed on Elbert's great toe. Elbert opened his mouth to scream, but the bad word sprang out, bigger and uglier than before.
- Opening his desk, the gardener pulled out a drawer filled with words that crackled and sparkled. Use these words, and perhaps you won't get into trouble.

Source: Wood, A., & Wood, D. (1988). *Elbert's bad word*. New York: Harcourt Brace.

work on reconstructing the story. A key for self-checking can be included to reduce the amount of teacher supervision.

Accessing Information: Information Text Structure

Nearly 85% of all adult reading is with information texts (i.e., nonfiction). Information texts contain facts, details, descriptions, and procedures that are necessary to understand concepts and events in the world around us. Authors structure information texts using several well-known text patterns or structures. Armbruster and Anderson (1981) and Meyer (1979) researched text patterns most used by authors of information texts. These include time order (putting information into a chronological sequence), cause and effect (showing how something occurs because of another event), problem and solution (presenting a problem along with a solution to the problem), comparison (examining similarities and differences among concepts and events), simple listing (registering in list form a group of facts, concepts, or events); and descriptions.

Simply put, readers who understand an author's organizational pattern recall more from reading information texts than readers who do not (Bartlett, 1978; Meyer, Brandt, & Bluth, 1980). Research has also shown that poor or struggling readers are less likely to be able to identify and use an author's organization of text to recall information. Thus, teachers need to teach children how to identify the author's organizational pattern or text structure and use this knowledge.

Information text structures include time order, cause and effect, problem and solution, comparison, simple listing, and descriptions.

Using Background Knowledge to Comprehend Information Texts

Elaborative interrogation is an intervention especially well suited to information text comprehension. By using "why" questions to promote active processing of factual reading materials (Wood, Pressley, & Winne, 1990), students are encouraged to activate their prior knowledge and experiences and use these to create relationships linking facts together from text. Facts linked together into a network of relationships improve students' understanding and memory for text information.

Asking "why" questions helps students process information text more effectively, resulting in better understanding and memory.

It is important that "why" questions be asked in such as way as to orient students to activate prior knowledge supporting the facts they need to learn—otherwise, such questions will not enhance comprehension and memory for text. We describe the elaborative interrogation strategy using the trade book *My Picture Book of the Planets* (Krulik, 1991) in a model lesson shown in Figure 4.14.

Menke and Pressley (1994) state that, "*Answering why questions is as good as constructing images to boost memory for facts, providing the questions are well focused*" (p. 644). The elaborative interrogation strategy has been validated to improve readers' comprehension of factual material ranging from elementary school ages to adult. It is recommended that teachers use elaborative interrogation when they train struggling students to access relevant prior knowledge in situations where they typically do not do so spontaneously to improve information text comprehension.

Information Text Graphic Organizers: Highlighting Text Structure

Instruction in higher-level text organization not only enhances students' retention of major ideas in text but also improves their retention of lower-level text details in information texts (Williams, Brown, Silverstein, & deCari, 1994). Dickson, Simmons, & Kameenui (1998) describe a six-principle instructional framework for providing effective text structure strategy instruction: (a) introduce the big ideas, (b) explicit instruction

Figure 4.14   Example lesson on elaborative interrogation

Purpose for Learning the Strategy: This strategy will help you relate your own experiences and knowledge to the facts you read in books and other information texts. By using this strategy, you will improve your understanding of and memory for text information.

Objective: Learn to respond to statements in text as if they were stated as "why" questions.

Teacher Explanation & Modeling: This strategy begins by reading a section of text. For example, *My Picture Book of the Planets,* I would begin by reading the title. Then, I might ask myself, "Why would someone write a book about the planets?" My answer might include such ideas as the author wanted to teach others and me about planets as compared with stars, or I might wonder if other planets can support life like on Earth, etc. Next, I read about the first planet, Mercury, in the book. "Mercury is the planet closest to the sun. It is very hot and dry" (Krulik, 1991). I might ask myself the why question, "Why is Mercury so hot?" I read on, "Because it is so close to the sun, Mercury takes the shortest amount of time of any of the planets to circle the sun." I ask myself, "Why is closeness to the sun related to a shorter time needed to circle the sun?"

Guided Application: Now let's try this strategy together. Mariann, come read this statement aloud for the class. After she has read this statement, I will make a "why" question from the statement. O.K. read this statement. Mariann reads, "Mercury is gray and covered with craters." My question is, "Why would Mercury be gray and covered with craters?" Students are invited to use their knowledge and background to answer this "why" question.

Now let's reverse the roles. I will read aloud the next statement and you make this statement into a "why" question. Teacher reads aloud, "Some of Mercury's craters are bigger than the whole state of Texas!" Children raise their hands. Benji is called upon. He asks, "Why are the craters on Mercury so big?" A discussion ensues to potentially answer these "why" questions.

Individual Application: Now I want you to read the rest of this book. When you get to the end of each page, pick one statement to write a "why" question in your notebooks. Next, see if you can answer the question from your own knowledge or experiences. If not, try using the book to answer your question. If neither source can answer your question, save it for our discussion of the book when we are all finished reading. Now, go ahead and read. If you forget what I want you to do, look at this poster for step-by-step directions. The teacher displays the following poster at the front of the room on the board.

> **Using the Elaborative Interrogation Strategy**
> - Read each page carefully.
> - Stop at the end of each page and pick a statement.
> - Write a "why" question for the statement you pick in your reading notebooks.
> - Think about an answer to the "why" question using your own knowledge and experiences.
> - If you can, write an answer to your "why" question.
> - Read the pages again looking for an answer. Read on to another page to look for the answer.
> - If you can, write an answer to your "why" question.
> - If you can't write an answer to your "why" question, save it for our group discussion after reading.

(continued)

Source: From "Hitting the Wall: Helping Struggling Readers Comprehend;" by D. R. Reutzel, K. Camperell, and J. A. Smith, 2002, in L. B. Gambrell, and M. Pressley (eds.), *Improving Comprehension Instruction: Advances in Research, Theory, and Classroom Practice,* pp. 340–341, Hoboken, NJ: John Wiley & Sons.

Notice the six instructional principles for providing highly effective text structure instruction with information texts.

of strategies, (c) mediated scaffolding, (d) strategic integration, (e) primed background knowledge, and (f) judicious review cycles.

The first principle for helping students identify and use text structure is understanding the "big ideas." Two "big ideas" associated with teaching text structure are

Figure 4.14   *continued*

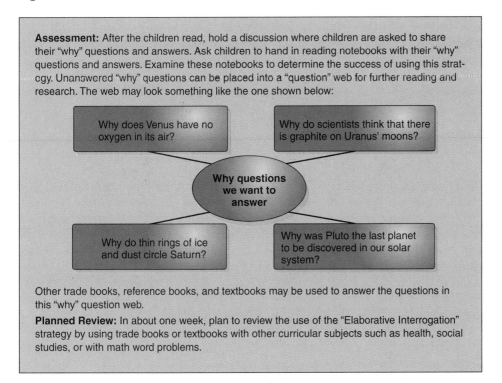

Assessment: After the children read, hold a discussion where children are asked to share their "why" questions and answers. Ask children to hand in reading notebooks with their "why" questions and answers. Examine these notebooks to determine the success of using this strategy. Unanswered "why" questions can be placed into a "question" web for further reading and research. The web may look something like the one shown below:

> Why does Venus have no oxygen in its air?
>
> Why do scientists think that there is graphite on Uranus' moons?
>
> **Why questions we want to answer**
>
> Why do thin rings of ice and dust circle Saturn?
>
> Why was Pluto the last planet to be discovered in our solar system?

Other trade books, reference books, and textbooks may be used to answer the questions in this "why" question web.

Planned Review: In about one week, plan to review the use of the "Elaborative Interrogation" strategy by using trade books or textbooks with other curricular subjects such as health, social studies, or with math word problems.

(a) the physical presentation of text and (b) text structures. The physical presentation of text deals with how well the physical presentation of text highlights importance of information and the relationship among various levels of information within the text. Physical text features affect the comprehensibility of text. When authors write, they use a variety of typographic features. Comprehension instruction about the physical presentation of text should include attention to headings, subheadings, signal words, topic sentences, and paragraph organization. Aside from these text features, authors will sometimes use italics, bolded text, bullets, or boxes to highlight text features and make text more reader friendly. We suggest that teachers draw attention to these features during group readings to heighten students' awareness of their presence and functions in text.

The higher-level structure of text deals with well-organized patterns that establish the flow, organization, and relationship of information within an entire text, that is, descriptive structure, listing structure, sequential structure, compare/contrast structure, problem/solution structure, or a collection of explanations structure. Identifying and using higher-level text structure helps all readers, good and poor, more effectively organize their recall of important ideas and details in text.

To make comprehension strategies explicit as described in the second principle, teachers need to define and explain the strategy components, inform students about when and why the strategies are helpful as well as the expected benefits of using the strategies, model the strategy use, ask students to verbalize the strategy, and provide feedback, coaching, and guidance during the learning process. Teachers will explicitly teach students various patterns of text organization, tell students how learning these patterns will help them understand and remember text, model how to identify text patterns, and provide them written prompts or lists to help them identify text patterns in their reading materials.

The third principle, mediated scaffolding for teaching information text structure, is focused on two types or targets of scaffolding: (a) controlling the difficulty of the content and task and (b) controlling the difficulty of the reading materials. Mediated content and task scaffolding occurs when teachers structure the learning to proceed from easy to more difficult content or tasks. Mediated material scaffolding guides students' thinking as they work through a task or new content base within a leveled text. Using guidance and leveled texts is best exemplified in practices associated with guided reading (Fountas & Pinnell, 1996, 2001). When providing mediated scaffolding of text structures, teachers use "think-alouds," lists of procedures, graphic organizers, and structured questions to elicit and focus attention on the text's top-level structure.

Strategic integration of comprehension strategies, the fourth principle, means pulling together a collection or set of related strategies and applying these in natural and novel settings. For example, instruction on information text structure is applied in actual texts to be read by students under the guidance of the teacher rather than using these strategies only in adapted texts or text "snippets" during whole class strategy lessons. Maximum transfer for automatic, student-initiated strategy use has been demonstrated to occur when natural, novel settings are (a) scheduled in different subject areas and (b) at different periods in the school day outside the traditional literacy instructional block (Block, 1993; Block & Mangieri, 1995, 1996).

The fifth principle, priming background knowledge, refers to activating students' prior knowledge about the content and the structure of a text to be read in order to facilitate comprehension of text. Teachers may use graphic organizers to show the relationship between main ideas and the parts of a story. We remind you that using the elaborative interrogation strategy is an effective strategy to prime background knowledge and experience as well.

Judicious review, the sixth and final principle for providing effective comprehension text structure strategy instruction, refers to closely spaced and shorter reviews where students apply strategy instruction to a variety of text structures and organization. We provide a model lesson on teaching text structure in Figure 4.15. We continue using the information picture book *My Picture Book of the Planets* in order to demonstrate how teachers can not only increase students' factual recall of the text but also increase their awareness of the text structure used by the author to organize the text.

Experience-Text-Relationships (E-T-R): Discussing Information Texts

Tharp (1982) developed Experience-Text-Relationships (E-T-R) as a structure for lessons to improve comprehension of information text. An E-T-R lesson is organized around three steps. First, student experiences related to the text to be read are discussed. *How are caterpillars and butterflies related? Which comes first, the caterpillar or the butterfly?* Second, information text requires special instructional attention because it contains heavy concept and vocabulary loads, placing unusual demands on the reader. To help with this task, an E-T-R lesson uses reading and questioning. Students read to assigned points in the text and stop to discuss questions posed by the teacher and/or the students. *What is the difference between a cocoon and a chrysalis?* Third, information text structure is less familiar for young readers than narrative text, prompting comprehension difficulties (Pearson & Duke, 2002). To help younger readers to make connections between their own experience and the text, a discussion following the reading of the text focuses on making the connections

Figure 4.15 Using graphic organizers to teach information book text structure

Purpose for Learning the Strategy: This strategy will help you recognize the pattern(s) authors use to organize their ideas when they write stories, books, or other printed materials.

Objective: To learn to use the knowledge of text structures to organize study, note taking, and memory for reading a variety of texts.

Teacher Explanation & Modeling: When I read, I try to think about how the author has organized the information so that I can remember it better. In *My Picture Book of the Planets* (Krulik, 1991), the author presents a list of planets in the solar system from the planet nearest the sun to the planet farthest from the sun. I also notice that with each planet the author writes a description of the planet with several interesting facts. So, I have drawn a graphic organizer to show how this author has written the book. Look at what I have drawn up here on the board.

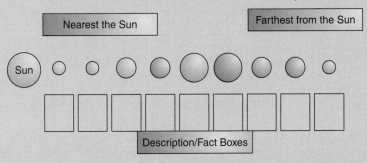

By using this text structure/ graphic organizer strategy, I can read, take notes, and remember how this book works much better.

Guided Application: Let's look through our copies of the book to see if the graphic organizer on the board properly shows the order of the book's organization. What is the first planet that is closest to the sun? Mercury. Is that the planet shown first in the graphic organizer? Yes. Good. What is the second planet in the graphic organizer at the board? Venus. Is that the second planet in the book? Yes. Good. Now look through the rest of the book and check to see if the graphic organizer properly shows the author's organization.

Individual Application: I am giving each of you a copy of the graphic organizer for *My Picture Book of the Planets* (Krulik, 1991). As you read about each planet, write down two to three facts about each planet in the descriptive box underneath each planet in the graphic organizer to help you remember what you have read. Please notice that the author has organized the book to be a "collection or list" of descriptions about each planet.

Assessment: Ask students to turn in their completed graphic organizers. Check to see what they have done and how they have used the graphic organizer. Also, you may want to give them a blank organizer to fill in after the discussion of the book. This will help them and you to see how this strategy creates a mental organizer for the book's structure and the facts about each planet.

Planned Review: In about one week, plan to review the use of the "Text Structure-Graphic Organizer" strategy by using trade books or textbooks with other curricular subjects, such as health, social studies, or with math word problems.

Source: From "Hitting the Wall: Helping Struggling Readers Comprehend," by D. R. Reutzel, K. Camperell, and J. A. Smith, 2002, in L. B. Gambrell, & M. Pressley (eds.), *Improving Comprehension Instruction: Advances in Research, Theory, and Classroom Practice,* pp. 342–343. Hoboken, NJ: John Wiley & Sons.

explicit. *So what did you learn from reading this text about butterflies that you will think about the next time you see a butterfly or a caterpillar?*

An E-T-R lesson is composed of four stages: (a) planning, (b) concept assessment and development, (c) guided reading of the text, and (d) application, during which the teacher helps students draw relationships between the text information and their own

There are four stages of an E-T-R lesson: planning, concept assessment and development, guided reading of the text, and application.

Figure 4.16   To structure a lesson based on the E-T-R strategy, a teacher might create a visual organizer such as this one for *The Life of the Butterfly* (Drew, 1989)

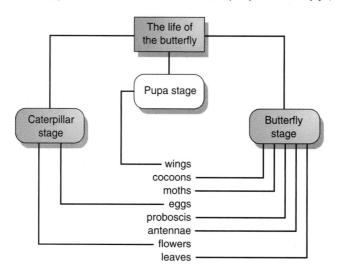

background experiences. To clarify the E-T-R lesson structure, a lesson as well as a graphic organizer based on the book *The Life of the Butterfly* (Drew, 1989) is presented in Figure 4.16.

Planning an E-T-R Lesson

To plan an E-T-R lesson, the teacher follows three steps. First, preread the information book to determine the major concepts and main ideas in the text. Second, look for major points to bring up during the discussion, formulate attention-focusing questions, and note important vocabulary concepts that may need to be pretaught. When planning an E-T-R lesson, we have found it useful to plan the lesson around a graphic organizer like the one found in Figure 4.16. The final step in planning involves thinking about ways information in the text about the life of a butterfly can be shared, used, and extended into other related curriculum areas.

Eliciting Student Knowledge and Experience

Tharp (1982) explains that capturing children's interest and activating their prior knowledge and experience at the outset of the lesson are critical to success. This can be accomplished by asking questions that invite students to engage in dialogue about their own background experiences in interesting and imaginative ways. For example, while teaching an E-T-R lesson using *The Life of the Butterfly* (Drew, 1989), you might begin the lesson with the following introduction and questions:

> **Teacher:** (while holding the book up for the children to see) In this book, we will learn about how a caterpillar becomes a butterfly. Can you tell me what you know about caterpillars and butterflies?

After this initial discussion, subsequent questions could focus attention on critical or potentially unfamiliar concepts and vocabulary related to butterflies and caterpillars. For example, children may need to learn the vocabulary terms *spiracles, pupa, antennae,* and *proboscis.*

Text Reading and Study

At this point in the lesson, the teacher moves into guided reading of predetermined parts of the text. Through questioning and discussion, teacher and children negotiate a purpose for reading each segment of the book. The lesson proceeds by alternating purpose setting, silent reading, and discussion for each segment of the text. A visual organizer plays a central role in the alternating activities of purpose setting, reading, and discussion. By displaying an organizer, the teacher directs reading and discussion toward filling in the organizer. So, for each cycle of the lesson, the teacher fills in the organizer with additional information until it is complete. The lines are drawn in after the discussion to show which of the items previously discussed belonged with the phases of the life of a butterfly. In this way, the teacher represents the author's structure for conveying the information in the text. Thus, the text information is mapped onto the organizer, which visually depicts the organization and content of the information the author presented in the text.

Again, we encourage you to look for opportunities to teach other useful concepts and vocabulary not presented in the text. Teachers should remain alert to opportunities to build or elaborate on children's existing butterfly schemas; for example, explaining that moths build cocoons and butterflies develop in a chrysalis is a topic with which the text deals only briefly.

Application

After the entire text has been read, help students draw relationships between the text and their own background knowledge. By using the graphic organizer, students may be encouraged to synthesize and summarize the information discussed throughout the lesson. On another occasion, students may become involved in other research and extension activities. These may range from something as simple as illustrating their favorite butterfly to something as complex as building a three-dimensional diorama of collected and labeled butterflies. By following the steps in elaborative interrogation and E-T-R lessons, coupled with text structure lessons using graphic organizers, students will experience quality comprehension instruction for processing information texts on a variety of topics and levels of reading challenge.

COMPREHENSION INSTRUCTION: INTERPRETATION AND ELABORATION

Activating students' background knowledge in preparation for reading is critical for promoting reading comprehension. In fact, many teacher's guides and editions contain a section titled "Building Background for the Story" or "Building Background Knowledge." One well-known and highly useful strategy is called K-W-L. Ogle (1986), the originator of K-W-L, asserts that this strategy is best suited for use with information texts.

K-W-L

Step K: What I Know

K-W-L strategy lessons begin with step K, *what I know*. This step is composed of two levels of accessing prior knowledge: (a) brainstorming and (b) categorizing information. Ask children to brainstorm about a particular topic (in the case of a narrative, brainstorm a particular theme or message). For instance, you might ask children what they know about bats. A list of associations is formed through brainstorming. When students make a contribution, Ogle (1986) suggests asking them where or how they got their information to challenge them to use higher levels of thinking.

Notice three steps for using K-W-L.

Next, ask students to look for ways in which the brainstorming list can be reorganized into categories of information. For example, you may notice that the brainstorming list shows three related pieces of information about how bats navigate. These can be reorganized into a "navigation" category. Encourage children to look at the list and think about other categories represented in the brainstorming list.

Step W: What Do I Want to Learn?

During step W, students recognize gaps, inaccuracies, and disagreements in their prior knowledge to decide what they want to learn. You, the teacher, can play a central role in pointing out these problems and helping students frame questions for which they would like to have answers. Questions can be framed by using the stem "I wonder." After children generate a series of questions to be answered from the reading, they are to write down personal questions for which they would like answers. These are often selected from those questions generated by the group.

Step L: What I Learned

After reading, ask students to write down what they learned. This can take the form of answers to specific questions they asked or a concise written summary of their learning. These questions and answers may be discussed as a group or shared between pairs of students. In this way, other children benefit from the learning of their peers as well as from their own learning. In summary, K-W-L has been shown to be effective in improving reading comprehension by causing students to activate, think about, and organize their prior knowledge as an aid to reading comprehension (Dewitz & Carr, 1987).

Imagery: Elaborating the Meaning of Text

When students make visual images about what they read, they make mental "movies." Making visual images within the mind as one reads provides an effective framework for organizing, remembering, and constructing meaning from text (Sadoski & Quast, 1990; Wilson & Gambrell, 1988). Struggling readers do not spontaneously create mental images as they read. As a consequence, struggling readers often miss out on the comprehension-monitoring boost that mental imagery can give them (Gambrell & Bales, 1986). Wilson and Gambrell (1988) indicate specific ways to instruct children in how and when to apply *imagery* as a comprehension tool in Figure 4.17.

Since research on visual imagery indicates that some students do not spontaneously use visual imagery, but can when directed to do so, teachers need to provide guidance and practice in the use of imagery during reading. Wilson and Gambrell (1988) recommend the following considerations when selecting materials to be used to encourage visual imagery:

1. For modeling and teacher-guided practice activities, select brief passages of about paragraph length.
2. Choose passages that have strong potential for creating "mental movies" (i.e., those that typically contain rich descriptions of events and objects).

Figure 4.17   Hints for making visual images during reading

1. Inform students that making pictures in their minds can help them understand what a passage is about. Specific directions, depending on whether the text is narrative or information text, may be helpful. For example, "Make a picture in your mind of the interesting characters in this story." "Make pictures in your mind about the things that happened in this story." "Make a picture in your mind of the human skeleton with each of the bones labeled." Using visual imagery in this manner encourages students to integrate information across the text as they engage in constructing the meaning.
2. Inform students that, when something is difficult to understand, it sometimes helps to try to make a picture in their minds. Using visual imagery can help students clarify meaning, and it encourages them to think about whether they comprehend or not.
3. Encourage students to make visual images about texts they want to remember. Tell them that making pictures in their minds can help them remember. As a follow-up to story time or silent reading, invite students to think about the visual images they made and encourage them to use their images to help them retell the story to a partner. This activity will help students realize the value of using visual imagery to enhance memory.

Point out that not all text material is easy to visualize—especially when the material is about unfamiliar and abstract concepts. Tell students that in those instances they should select another strategy that would be easier to use and more helpful (be prepared with suggestions that better fit some of the text types they are likely to encounter). With minimal guidance and practice, students can learn and enjoy using visual imagery to enhance their reading experiences.

Affective Responses: Interpreting and Elaborating Meaning

Discussion and dialogue are critical aspects of effective comprehension instruction (Gambrell & Almasi, 1996). One widely recognized and recommended approach to discussion and dialog about text is called *reader response*, which invites students to take a much more active role (Bleich, 1978; Rosenblatt, 1978, 1989). Reader response theories suggest there are many possible meanings in a text, depending on the reader's background and reaction to the text. Rosenblatt's (1978) *transactional theory* described reading and literature study as a carefully orchestrated relationship between reader and text (Clifford, 1991).

Rosenblatt (1978) describes two stances—efferent and aesthetic—in discussing how readers may choose to focus their attention during reading. When readers focus their attention on information to be remembered from reading a text, they are taking an *efferent stance*. When readers adopt an aesthetic stance, they draw on past experiences, connect these experiences to the text, often savor the beauty of the literary art form, and become an integral participant in the unfolding events of the text.

Discussion of or dialogue about texts in small groups is often called *literature circles* or *book clubs* that lead students into *grand conversations* about books (Daniels, 1994; Peterson & Eeds, 1990; McMahon & Raphael, 1997; Raphael, Pardo, Highfield, & McMahon, 1997; Tompkins, 2003). Grand conversations about books motivate students to extend, clarify, and elaborate their own interpretations of the text as well as learn to consider alternative interpretations offered by peers.

Figure 4.18 Alternative affective responses to books

1. Prepare a condensed or simplified version of the text to read aloud to younger readers.
2. Draw a map of the journey of characters in a story.
3. Talk to your teacher or a peer about the book.
4. Make a wanted poster for a character in the text.
5. Make an information poster for an information book.
6. Select a part of the book to read aloud to others.
7. Send a letter to your parents, a friend, or your teacher telling about a book and why they should read it.
8. Write a classified newspaper ad for a book.
9. Rewrite a story or part of a story as a reader's theater.
10. Make transparencies about the story to use on the overhead projector.
11. Make a power point slide computer presentation about an information book.
12. Make a character report card on your favorite character.
13. Make a passport application as your favorite character.
14. Write a "Dear Abby" column as your favorite character.
15. Write a missing persons report about a story character.
16. Draw a part of the book and ask others to tell about what part of the story is illustrated.
17. Write a newspaper headline for a book or story.
18. Write a newspaper report for a story character or about information you have learned in an information book.
19. Write to the author to describe your responses to a book.
20. Illustrate a book using a variety of art mediums or techniques.
21. Write a letter to the librarian suggesting why he or she should or should not recommend a book to someone.
22. Study about the author and write a brief biography.
23. Compose a telegram about the book to tell someone why he or she must read this book.
24. Make a TV commercial and videotape it.
25. Plan a storytelling session for kindergarten children.
26. Interview a story character and write the interview.
27. Compare and contrast characters settings, or facts in a book using a Venn diagram.
28. Construct a game of Trivial Pursuit using facts in an information book.
29. Construct a game of Password using clues about characters or events in a story.
30. Compose an imaginary diary that may be kept by a book character.

There are many ways to invite students to respond to text to increase comprehension.

There are many ways to invite students to respond to texts they read. One of the most common is to ask children to write in a response journal (Parsons, 1990). We have developed a listing of affective responses to text that represent both aesthetic and efferent stances as described by Rosenblatt (1978) in Figure 4.18.

COMPREHENSION INSTRUCTION: STRATEGIES FOR EFFECTIVE QUESTIONING

Asking questions is not enough; teachers must help students learn how to answer questions.

Questions are an integral part of life both in and out of school. From birth, we learn about our world by asking questions and then by testing our answers against the realities in our environment. In school, teachers ask questions to motivate children to become involved in learning and to assess the quality of their learning. Because questions are so much a part of the schooling process and can affect the quality of children's comprehension, teachers must know how to effectively use questioning to deliver quality reading comprehension instruction.

Figure 4.19   Illustrations to explain question–answer relationships (QARs) to students

In the Book QARs

Right There

The answer is in the text, usually easy to find. The words used to make up the question and words used to answer the question are **Right There** in the same sentence.

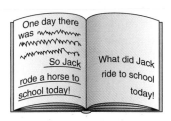

Think and Search (Putting It Together)

The answer is in the story, but you need to put together different story parts to find it. Words for the question and words for the answer are not found in the same sentence. They come from different parts of the text.

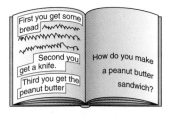

In My Head QARs

Author and You

The answer is *not* in the story. You need to think about what you already know, what the author tells you in the text, and how it fits together.

On My Own

The answer is *not* in the story. You can even answer the question without reading the story. You need to use your own experience.

Source: Figure from "Teaching Question Answer Relationships, Revisited" by Taffy E. Raphael. *The Reading Teacher,* February 1986. Reprinted with permission of Taffy E. Raphael and the International Reading Association.

Question–Answer Relationship

Raphael (1982, 1986) describes four question–answer relationships (QARs) to help children identify the connection between the type of question asked and the information sources necessary and available for answering questions: (a) right there, (b) think and search, (c) author and you, and (d) on my own. Figure 4.19 shows examples of each of these four types of QARs.

Instruction using QARs begins by explaining to students that when they answer questions about reading there are basically two places they can look to get information: *in the book* and *in my head.* This concept should be practiced with the students by reading aloud a text, asking questions, and having the students explain or show where they found their answers. Once students understand the two-category approach,

QARs help students learn to identify types of questions asked and where to get information necessary to answer questions.

expand the *in the book* category to include *right there* and *putting it together.* The distinction between these two categories should be practiced under the guidance of the teacher with several texts, gradually releasing responsibility to the students. For older students, Raphael (1986) suggests that students be shown specific strategies for locating the answers to *right there* questions. These include looking in a single sentence or looking in two sentences connected by a pronoun. For *putting it together* questions, students can be asked to focus their attention on the structure of the text, such as cause–effect, problem–solution, listing–example, compare–contrast, and explanation.

Next, instruction should be directed toward two subcategories within the *in my head* category: (a) *author and me* and (b) *on my own.* Here again, these categories can be practiced as a group by reading a text aloud, answering the questions, and discussing the sources of information. To expand this training, students can be asked to identify the types of questions asked in their basal readers, workbooks, content area texts, and tests as well as to determine the sources of information needed to answer these questions. Students may be informed that certain types of questions are asked before and after reading a text. For example, questions asked before reading typically require that students activate their own knowledge. Therefore, questions asked before reading will usually be *on my own* questions. However, questions asked after reading will make use of information found in the text. Therefore, questions asked after reading will typically focus on the *right there, putting it together,* and *author and me* types of questions.

Using the QARs question–answering training strategy is useful for at least two other purposes. First, it can help teachers examine their own questioning with respect to the types of questions and the information sources students need to use to answer their questions. Second, some teachers may find that by using QARs to monitor their own questioning behaviors they are asking only *right there* types of questions. This discovery should lead teachers to ask questions that require the use of other information sources. Students can use QARs to initiate self-questioning before and after reading. Children may be asked to write questions for each of the QARs categories and answer these questions. Finally, a poster displaying the information in Figure 4.19 can heighten children's and teachers' awareness to the types of questions asked and the information sources available for answering those questions.

Raphael and Pearson (1982) provided evidence that training students to recognize these question–answer relationships resulted in improved comprehension and question-answering behavior. In addition, evidence also shows that teachers find the QARs strategies productive for improving their own questioning behaviors.

Questioning the Author

Research has shown that many young readers construct very little meaning from the information they read in textbooks. Several features in the text combine to create a number of obstacles for young children's comprehension of information text. These include (a) incoherence, (b) lack of clear descriptions and explanations, (c) unrealistic assumptions on the level of background knowledge, (d) the objective nature of the language used, and (e) the "authority" that places it above criticism (McKeown, Beck, & Worthy, 1993). These "inconsiderate" features of a textbook's organization and content inhibit comprehension, and the textbook's authority causes students to attribute these difficulties to their own inadequacies. As a result, younger readers feel reluctant to persist in using their natural "problem-solving" abilities in the face of these perceptions (Anderson, 1991; Schunk & Zimmerman, 1997).

A *questioning the author* lesson attempts, "in a sense to 'depose' the authority of the textbook through actualizing the presence of an author." (McKeown, et al., 1993, p. 561). Children are taught that the information in textbooks is just someone's thoughts written down and that sometimes these ideas are not written as well or as clearly as they might be. Next, the teacher prompts the children as they read a text using a series of questions such as the following:

- What is the author trying to tell you?
- Why is the author telling you that?
- Is that said clearly?

Asking children to search out answers to these questions encourages them to actively engage the ideas in the text. As children encounter difficulties in understanding the text, they are encouraged, again through teacher questioning, to recast the author's ideas in clearer language. Questions used for this purpose include the following:

- How could the author have said the ideas in a clearer way?
- What would you want to say instead?

Asking children to "revise" the author's ideas and writing causes them to "grapple" with the ideas and problems in a text. In this way, children engage texts in ways that successful readers use to make sense of complex ideas and texts.

Recent research has shown that *questioning the author* results in increased length and complexity of recalled ideas from text and answers to comprehension questions as compared with other forms of book discussions (Sandora, Beck, & McKeown, 1999).

> **Questioning the author** *prompts students to "depose" the authority of text by asking the author questions as if the author were present.*

COMPREHENSION INSTRUCTION: MONITORING AND SELF-REGULATION

Metacognition and Fix-Up Strategies

In addition to activating, elaborating, or modifying prior knowledge to improve comprehension, readers must learn to monitor and self-regulate the status of their own ongoing comprehension and know when comprehension breaks down. The act of monitoring one's unfolding comprehension of text is called metacognition, or sometimes *metacomprehension*. The ability to plan, check, monitor, revise, regulate, and evaluate one's unfolding comprehension is of particular importance in reading. If a child fails to detect a comprehension breakdown, then she will take no action to correct misinterpretations of the text. However, if a child expects the text to make sense and has the ability to strategically self-correct comprehension problems, then reading can progress as it should.

To help students develop the ability to monitor their own comprehension processes, Carr (1986) suggested a strategy called "click or clunk." This strategy urges readers to reflect at the end of each paragraph or section of reading by stopping and asking themselves if the meaning or message "clicks" for them or goes "clunk." If it clunks, what is wrong? What can be done to make sense of it?

Although the ability to detect when comprehension breaks down is important, it is equally important to know which *fix-up* strategies to select in repairing broken comprehension and when to use these strategies. Consequently, students may know

> **Metacognition** *involves readers in checking the status of their own understanding and taking steps to repair failing comprehension when necessary.*

that they need to take steps to repair comprehension but may not know which steps to take or when to take them. As a consequence, children should be introduced to the options available to them for repairing broken comprehension. Collins and Smith (1980) suggest the following fix-up or repair strategies for use by readers who experience comprehension failure:

An online Reading Instructional Handbook has wonderful material on monitoring comprehension. Readers can link to this site from Chapter 4 on our Companion Website at www.prenhall.com/ reutzel.

- Ignore the problem and continue reading.
- Suspend judgment for now and continue reading.
- Form a tentative hypothesis using text information and continue reading.
- Look back or reread the previous sentence.
- Stop and think about the previously read context; reread if necessary.
- Seek help from the environment, reference materials, or other knowledgeable individuals.

To help students develop a sense for when to select these strategies for repairing failing comprehension, teachers may consider using a think-aloud modeling procedure. Begin a think-aloud by reading part of a text aloud. Comment on your own thinking as the teacher. By revealing to students your thinking, the hypotheses you form for the text, and anything that strikes you as difficult or unclear, you demonstrate for the students the processes successful readers use to comprehend a text. Next, remind students of the click or clunk strategy. Gradually release the responsibility for modeling metacognitive strategies to the children during follow-up lessons. It also helps if you display the fix-up repair strategies on a poster prominently placed in the classroom to draw students' attention to these strategies throughout the year.

For students needing additional help with metacognitive strategy development, we recommend Baumann, Jones, and Seifert-Kessell's (1993) think-aloud lessons. In think-aloud lessons, students are explicitly taught what the strategies of metacognition are through definition, description, and examples. Next, children are told why learning these strategies is important for helping them become better readers. Finally, students are taught how to use these strategies through a sequence of instruction using (a) verbal explanation, (b) teacher modeling, (c) guided practice, and (d) independent practice. The think-aloud lesson centered on the following topics:

- Self-questioning
- Sources of information (see question–answer relationships and QARs previously in this chapter)
- Think-aloud modeling introduction (see GRIP, previously in this chapter)
- Think-aloud review and extension (see GRIP)
- Predicting, reading, and verifying
- Understanding unstated information
- Retelling a story
- Rereading and reading on (see fix-up strategies)
- Think-aloud/comprehension-monitoring application

We recommend this procedure because it brings together in an integrated fashion all the elements of excellent, research-based metacognitive reading instruction, which has been shown to be very effective in helping students acquire a broad range of metacognitive strategies.

Figure 4.20 Situational context diagram

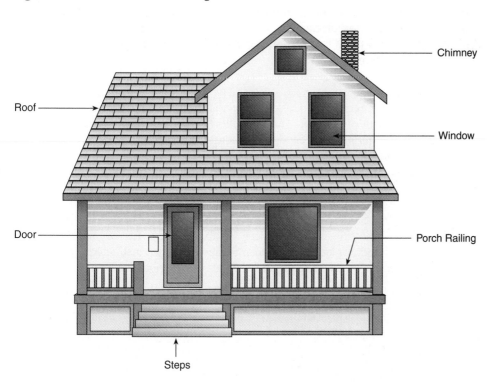

COMPREHENSION INSTRUCTION: MEETING THE
NEEDS OF SECOND-LANGUAGE LEARNERS
===

Contextual Diagrams: Labeling the Situational Context

For many second-language learners, pictures or diagrams of social or situational settings wherein objects and actions are labeled are of significant help for acquiring ability to speak, listen, read, and write in a largely unfamiliar language (Freeman &
Freeman, 2000). The purpose of contextual diagrams, such as the one shown in
Figure 4.20, is to allow students to learn language for settings outside the school classroom. Diagrams of the kitchen, bedroom, or bathroom at home can help students begin to learn and associate second-language terms with familiar or even somewhat
unfamiliar objects in another setting. Diagrams of stores, libraries, mechanic shops, or
hospitals wherein objects and actions are labeled can move students' potential for language comprehension well beyond the physical and social confines of the school classroom. Hence, diagrams of whole, meaningful, and naturally occurring situations serve
a purpose of expanding the language learning contexts of English-as-second-language
(ESL) and limited-English-proficiency (LEP) students in schools.

*Contextual diagrams al-
low LEP students to
learn needed vocabulary
before entering an unfa-
miliar societal setting.*

COMPREHENSION INSTRUCTION: MEETING THE
NEEDS OF STRUGGLING READERS
===

Palincsar and Brown (1985) designed and evaluated an approach to improve the reading comprehension and comprehension monitoring of students who scored 2 years
below grade level on standardized tests of reading ability and reading comprehension.

Reciprocal teaching is a useful strategy for helping students who have difficulties with comprehension and monitoring.

Their results, along with many others (Rosenshine & Meister, 1994; Loranger, 1997), suggest a teaching strategy that is useful for helping students who have difficulties with comprehension and comprehension monitoring called *reciprocal teaching*. Essentially, this strategy involves teachers and students in exchanging roles, which increases student involvement in the lesson.

The reciprocal teaching lesson is composed of the following four phases or steps:

1. *Prediction:* Students are asked to predict from the title and pictures the possible content of the text. The predictions are recorded by the teacher.
2. *Question generation:* Students generate purpose questions after reading a predetermined segment of the text, such as a paragraph or page.
3. *Summarizing:* Students write a brief summary for the text by starting with "This paragraph was about . . ." (p. 299). Summarizing helps students capture the gist of the text.
4. *Clarifying:* Students and teacher discuss a variety of reasons a text may be difficult or confusing, such as difficult vocabulary, poor text organization, unfamiliar content, or lack of cohesion. Students are then instructed in a variety of comprehension fix-up or repair strategies (as described earlier in this chapter).

Once teachers have modeled this process with several segments of text, the teacher assigns one of the students (preferably a good student) to assume the role of teacher for the next segment of text. The teacher may also, while acting in the student role, provide appropriate prompts and feedback when necessary. When the next segment of text is completed, the student assigned as teacher asks another student to assume that role.

Teachers who use reciprocal teaching to help students with comprehension difficulties should follow four simple guidelines suggested by Palincsar and Brown (1985). First, assess student difficulties and provide reading materials appropriate to students' decoding abilities. Second, use reciprocal teaching for at least 30 minutes per day for 15 to 20 consecutive days. Third, teachers should model frequently and provide corrective feedback. Finally, student progress should be monitored regularly and individually to determine whether the instruction is having the intended effect.

Hoyt (1999) describes a process using cards for teaching children the four interrelated processes of *reciprocal teaching*. Prepare children to use *reciprocal teaching cards* by modeling the process with several segments of text. Next, have students use the cards shown below in small groups. The group leader shows the cards.

Card #1: Please get ready to read to _____ .

Card #2: I predict this part will be about _____ . (Leader speaks.)

Card #3: Does anyone else have a prediction? (Group members speak.)

Card #4: Please read silently to the point we selected.

Card #5: Are there any words you thought were interesting? (Group.)

Card #6: Are there any ideas you found interesting or puzzling? (Group.)

Card #7: Do you have comments about the reading? (Group.)

Card #8: Summarize (in 2 or 3 sentences): This was about _____ . (Discussion Leader.)

Palincsar and Brown (1985) and many others (Loranger, 1997; Rosenshine & Meister, 1994) have reported positive results for this intervention procedure by demonstrating dramatic changes in students' ineffective reading behaviors. While reciprocal teaching was originally intended for use with information text, this intervention strategy may be used with narrative texts by focusing discussion and reading on the major elements of stories.

With minor changes, reciprocal teaching can be used with narrative as well as expository texts.

Summary

Teaching comprehension, unlike assessing comprehension, involves teaching behaviors such as modeling, explaining, thinking aloud, demonstrating, and defining. Teachers must not assume they are teaching children to comprehend text when they mention or assign comprehension skill practice sheets. Comprehension instruction in the early grades is both inconsistent and infrequent (Taylor, Pearson, Clark, & Walpole, 2000). In fact, comprehension instruction in the early grades is often neglected in favor of developing automatic decoding abilities in young children. Also, there is considerable concern that children are learning *about* comprehension rather than acquiring knowledge *through* comprehension (Neuman, 2001). Access in the early years to information texts is also an issue of current concern among researchers (Duke, 2000a, 2000b). And finally, there is considerable debate around whether comprehension strategy instruction is best taught as single or multiple strategies.

Schema theory, a theory about one's storehouse of prior knowledge and experience and how these influence the ability to comprehend text, was depicted in the context of a simplified model of text comprehension involving searching, applying, selecting and evaluating, and composing.

The gradual release of responsibility model of instruction was discussed to provide a comprehensive framework for effective comprehension instruction. Other effective instructional strategies for improving comprehension of narrative text and information text as well as focusing on comprehending text parts such as sentences, words, and typographic features were highlighted throughout the chapter.

Finally, readers were shown effective strategies for teaching comprehension at the phrase and sentence levels, making inferences, using text structure to improve comprehension, activating prior knowledge, elaborating and responding to texts, effective questioning practices, self-monitoring and fix-up strategies, helping LEP/ESL students, and assisting readers with comprehension difficulties.

Check your understanding of chapter concepts by using the self-assessment for Chapter 4 on our Companion Website at www.prenhall.com/ reutzel.

Concept Applications

In the Classroom

1. Pick a favorite story. Describe the story grammar parts of your selection. Make a story map, a schema story lesson, or design a story grammar questioning map.
2. Select a chapter from an elementary science, health, math, or social studies text. Identify the organizational pattern used by the authors. Make a graphic organizer.
3. Choose a literature or basal textbook selection. Design two metacognitive monitoring lessons of the 10 possible lessons described by Baumann et al. (1993) in this chapter. Be sure to include each of the lesson parts, that is, (a) verbal explanation, (b) teacher modeling, (c) guided practice, and (d) independent practice.

4. Take a 250-word passage from a story or an information text. Show how you could use two cloze techniques on this passage by preparing two cloze lessons.
5. Make some group response cards or boards for use in your classroom to respond to questions.
6. Evaluate the recommendations for background building in a basal reader. If necessary, describe how you would alter the recommendations.

In the Field

1. Make arrangements to visit a public school classroom. Carefully observe and record the time devoted to teaching versus testing reading comprehension.
2. Visit with a classroom teacher about the skills she thinks are important for helping students become skilled readers. Summarize these views in a brief essay.
3. Devise a lesson to train children to use *questioning the author* with an information book or content textbook. Try it out in an elementary school classroom. Reflect on this experience by making an entry in your professional journal.
4. Prepare a reciprocal teaching lesson using the reciprocal lesson cards. Make arrangements to visit a local resource or Title I classroom to teach your lesson.
5. Prepare a situational context diagram. Make arrangements to work with LEP or ESL students in an elementary school classroom. Use your diagram to teach a language lesson and report on your findings.

Recommended Readings

Alexander, P. A., & Jetton, T. L. (2000). Learning from text: A multidimensional perspective. In M. L. Kamil, P. B. Mosenthal, P. D. Pearson, and R. Barr (Eds.), *Handbook of reading research* (Vol. 3, pp. 285–310). Mahwah, NJ: Erlbaum.

Anderson, R. C., & Pearson, P. D. (1984). A schema-theoretic view of basic processes in reading. In P. D. Pearson (Ed.), *Handbook of reading research* (pp. 255–292). New York: Longman.

Collins-Block, C., Gambrell, L. B., & Pressley, M. (2003). *Improving comprehension instruction: Advances in research, theory, and classroom practice.* San Francisco: Jossey-Bass.

Collins-Block, C., & Pressley, M. (2002). *Comprehension instruction: Research-based best practice.* New York: Guilford Press.

Keene, E. O., & Zimmermann, S. (1997). *Mosaic of thought: Teaching comprehension in a reader's workshop.* Portsmouth, NH: Heinemann.

Pearson, P. D., & Duke, N. (2002). Comprehension instruction in the primary grades. In C. Collins-Block & M. Pressley (Eds.), *Comprehension instruction: Research-based best practices* (pp. 247–258). New York: Guilford Press.

Pressley, M. (2000). What should comprehension instruction be the instruction of? In M. L. Kamil, P. B. Mosenthal, P. D. Pearson, & R. Barr (Eds.), *Handbook of reading research* (Vol. 3). Mahwah, NJ: Erlbaum.

Simmons, D. C., & Kameenui, E. J. (1998). *What reading research tells us about children with diverse learning needs: Bases and basics.* Mahwah, NJ: Erlbaum.

Taylor, B. M, Graves, M. F., & Van den Broek, P. (2000). *Reading for meaning: Fostering comprehension in the middle grades.* New York: Teachers College Press.

5 Developing Reading Fluency

Focus Questions

When you are finished studying this chapter, you should be able to answer these questions:

1. What are the characteristics of fluent reading according to evidence-based research?

2. Is there a relationship between fluency and reading comprehension? Explain.

3. Describe the grade level expectations for reading fluency.

4. How is reading fluency developed?

5. What is the Fluency Formula for organizing classroom instruction? How are repeated readings and guided oral reading incorporated in this plan?

6. What is *guided reading* instruction (Fountas & Pinnell, 1996), and how is it organized?

Key Concepts

Reading Fluency
Automaticity
Quality
Rate
Fluency Formula
Fluency Pyramid
Decodable Text
Orthography
Guided Oral Reading
Guided Reading
Leveled Books
Choral Readings

Partner Reading
Neurological Impress
   Method
Book Buddies
Repeated Readings
Sustained Silent
   Reading
Performance
   Reading
Reader's theater

Storytelling was the life's blood of communications in the early history of our country, a time when many could neither read nor write. Then, as literacy trickled down the socioeconomic pyramid, stories kept alive for generations were written down. Some 20 years ago we discovered Donald D. Davis, an enthralling storyteller from North Carolina. Davis had recorded a splendid video in which he told a story, the *Crack of Dawn,* about wonderful life lessons learned from his Aunt Laura Henry, "the oldest living thing I'd ever seen." Later, his book *Listening for the Crack of Dawn* was released. Amazingly, the story he had told on the video and the written version were virtually identical! We then realized that our favorite storyteller was not only a great teller of tales verbally but also a fluent *reader.* He had READ the tale on the video so fluently we thought it must be extemporaneous! No . . . Donald Davis is a fluent reader. He knows when to slow down or add voice intonations and reads with such automaticity it seems like natural speech.

Figure 5.1 A model of fluent reading
Adapted from Chall (1967)

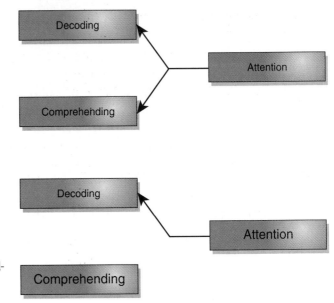

Figure 5.2 Less fluent readers focus mostly on decoding
Adapted from Chall (1967).

Visit Chapter 5 of our Companion Website at www.prenhall.com/reutzel to look into the chapter objectives, standards and principles, and pertinent Web links associated with developing reading fluency.

Fluent readers are better able to comprehend the author's message.

WHAT IS READING FLUENCY?

Reading fluency involves the ability to read text smoothly and at a reasonable rate. When fluent readers read aloud, they do so effortlessly with speed, accuracy, and proper expression as though they are speaking. Because of the "automatic" nature of their reading, fluent readers are able to focus their attention on the ideas in the text and comprehend the author's message. In Figure 5.1 we present a model reflecting the *automaticity* of fluent readers.

On the other hand, less fluent readers struggle along through text in a very labored, word-by-word way. They must focus most of their attention on decoding the words, so comprehension suffers. Figure 5.2 shows how comprehension can be virtually ignored when readers must devote most of their mental energies on decoding. Thus, fluency is important because it provides a kind of bridge between word recognition and reading comprehension (National Reading Panel, 2000; Rasinski, 1985; Reutzel & Hollingsworth, 1993).

What Skills Do Fluent Readers Possess?

There seems to be agreement among researchers as to the skills one must develop to become a fluent reader (Allington, 2001; Juel, 1991; National Reading Panel, 2000; Richards, 2000). They include the following:

- **Automaticity** involves translating letters to sounds to words effortlessly and accurately.
- **Quality** refers to the reader's ability to use proper intonation or expression (i.e., "prosodic features"—pitch, juncture, and stress) in one's voice.
- **Rate** involves attaining appropriate reading speed according to the reader's purpose or the type of passage. What is an appropriate rate? Figure 5.3 presents some suggested guidelines.

Figure 5.3 Oral reading fluency end-of-year goals for grade levels 1–5: Words per minute (wpm)—Instructional level (adequate) text

Grade Level	*Minimum* Words per Minute* (wpm)	Fluent Oral Reading (wpm)
Grade 1	60 wpm	80 wpm
Grade 2	70 wpm	100 wpm
Grade 3	80 wpm	126 wpm**
Grade 4	90 wpm	162 wpm**
Grade 5	100 wpm	180 wpm

*Adapted from *Texas Essential Knowledge and Skills,* 2002, at the Texas Education Agency Web site www.tea.state.tx.us.
**Source: *Listening to Children Read Aloud.* Washington, D.C., U.S. Department of Education, National Center for Education Statistics. 1995, 1/p. 44.

Figure 5.4 Fluency benchmark standards*

Kindergarten:
"Reads" familiar texts emergently, i.e., not necessarily verbatim from the print alone.

Grade 1:
Reads aloud with accuracy any text that is appropriately designed for the first half of grade 1.

Grade 2:
Accurately decodes orthographically regular multisyllable words and nonsense words.

Accurately reads many irregularly spelled words and such spelling patterns as diphthongs, special vowel spellings, and common word endings.

Grade 3:
Reads aloud with fluency any text that is appropriately designed for grade level.

*Criteria derived for the research by the Committee on the Prevention of Reading Difficulties in Young Children. Snow, C. E., Burns, M. S., & Griffin, P. (Eds.). (1998). *Preventing reading difficulties in young children.* Washington, DC: National Academy Press.

Armed with these three abilities, a fluent reader can decode words in a text accurately, with correct phrasing and intonation, and at a rate that facilitates text comprehension.

Reading Fluency "Standards"

In 1998, the federally sponsored Committee on the Prevention of Reading Difficulties in Young Children conducted an exhaustive study of evidence-based reading research. Included in its report *Preventing Reading Difficulties in Young Children* (Snow, Burns, & Griffin, 1998) were desired "benchmarks accomplishments" for kindergarten through third grade in reading and writing. Figure 5.4 presents excerpts that pertain to reading fluency from the report. They help us to better understand what we hope to achieve in our teaching of normally developing children at each of these grade levels.

Fluent readers have learned the following skills: automaticity, quality, and rate.

Fluency Is Sometimes Ignored in Basal Reading Programs

Basal reading programs often ignore the need to develop reading fluency.

Standards Note
Standard 4.3: The reading professional will be well versed in individual and group instruction and interventions targeted toward those students in greatest need or at low proficiency levels. Basal programs rarely address fluency, and fluency is a major problem for struggling readers. Pick one good fluency builder (e.g., readers' theatre) and develop specific plans for your present or future class, meeting the range but targeting your struggling readers.

For many years reading fluency has been acknowledged as an important goal in becoming a proficient and strategic reader (Allington, 1983, 1984, 2001; Klenk & Kibby, 2000; National Reading Panel, 2000; Opitz & Rasinski, 1998; Rasinski, 2000; Rasinkski & Padak, 1996). But as important as fluency is to reading success, it is often neglected in basal reading programs (i.e., published series adopted by each state—more on basal readers is found in Chapter 6). In fact, an analysis of basal programs during the 1990s (Stein et al., 1993) concluded that very few programs emphasized the development of reading fluency (Snow, et al., 1998). Since many teachers rely heavily on basal readers as the foundation for their instructional program, particularly in the first 5 years of their career, fluency instruction can be virtually overlooked. This is unfortunate, concluded the National Reading Panel (2000), because

> if text is read in a laborious and inefficient manner, it will be difficult for the child to remember what has been read and to relate the ideas expressed in the text to his or her background knowledge. Recent research on the efficacy of certain approaches to teaching fluency has led to increased recognition of its importance in the classroom and to changes in instructional practices. (p. 11)

Our recent visits to many elementary school classrooms likewise reveal little attention to reading fluency in daily instruction. As we continue in this chapter, we offer some important insights from the very best research as to how you can help all students become more fluent readers and, in turn, better *comprehenders*.

DEVELOPING READING FLUENCY

How Readers Develop Fluency

Fluency instruction must be well organized and consistently delivered. Several researchers (Allington, 1983, 2001; Rasinski, 1989; Rasinski & Padak, 1996; Richards, 2000) have identified classroom practices that help most students develop the ability to read fluently. Here are the practices they identified.

Provide Direct Instruction Using Guided Oral Reading

Students need structure and support in new learning. When the National Reading Panel (2000) conducted its review of research in the area of fluency, it concluded that guided oral repeated reading procedures

> that included guidance from teachers, peers, or parents had significant and positive impact on word recognition, fluency, and comprehension across a range of grade levels. These studies were conducted in a variety of classrooms in both regular and special education settings with teachers using widely available instructional materials. (p. 12)

When students practice a single text repeatedly, their oral reading becomes fluent. Supporting students using such strategies as choral reading, buddy or dyad reading, and computer-assisted reading can be most effective in a well-conceived reading fluency program. We will take a closer look at these and other strategies later in the chapter and throughout the remainder of the book.

Use a Good Deal of Modeling

Being exposed to rich and varied models of fluent reading helps many children. In this case, parents or siblings spend significant amounts of time reading aloud to these children. Through this process of modeling fluent reading, children learn the behaviors of fluent readers. Other researchers have documented the significant impact of modeling on the acquisition of fluent reading (Amarel, Bussis, & Chittenden, 1977; Durkin, 1966, 1974). Observing, listening to, and imitating fluent reading models help students learn how to become fluent readers themselves. Modeling fluent reading for students and pointing out specific behaviors as texts are read aloud, as well as providing constructive feedback, can also help students become fluent.

Students Need Massive Amounts of Practice

The more we can help students spend significant time reading—on their own with books of high interest, "buddy reading" with a classmate, and in guided oral reading— the greater their fluency will become. The research on this point is clear: Proficient readers spend more time reading silently than do students having reading problems (Allington, 1980; National Assessment of Educational Progress, 2000).

Good readers are given more opportunities to read connected text and for longer periods of time than are students having reading problems. This dilemma leads Allington (1977) to muse, "If they don't read much, how they ever gonna get good?"

Struggling readers usually benefit more from paired or "buddy reading" than reading on their own.

Provide Students with Access to Easy Reading Materials

Proficient readers spend more time reading easier texts than students having reading problems (Gambrell, Wilson, & Gnatt, 1981). Reading easy books may help proficient readers make the transition from word by word reading to fluent reading, while poorer readers spend more time reading materials that are relatively difficult. This practice denies students with reading problems access to reading materials that could help them develop fluent reading abilities.

ORGANIZING FOR INSTRUCTION: THE FLUENCY FORMULA

Careful planning is always crucial for successful teaching. In fluency instruction, as with most reading skill areas, the teacher must choose a "balanced diet" of reading materials for practice exercises (i.e., stories, nonfiction materials, poetry) and provide adequate teacher modeling, student practice with peers, and independent practice.

The **Fluency Formula** (summarized in Figure 5.5), developed for Title I reading teachers in Kansas, is an effective model for organizing fluency instruction that includes these elements (Cooter & Cooter, 2002). Sample lesson plan forms are shown in Figure 5.6 for your own uses. In the description that follows, you will see how important research-based elements have been included. While you may not wish to use the Fluency Formula in its entirety, its components should be strongly considered as you make transitions toward comprehensive reading instruction.

*The **Fluency Formula** (Cooter & Cooter, 2002) contains all the essential ingredients of research-based fluency instruction. Try incorporating its components as you are making transitions toward comprehensive reading instruction.*

Planning for Instruction

An effective teacher always maps out her teaching plan well before reaching the schoolhouse; none of this *shooting from the hip* or *random acts of teaching* for us! Lesson planning always begins with the decision about an appropriate objective. Objectives for

Figure 5.5   The Fluency Formula

Planning for Instruction
A. Identify Instructional Standards (Objectives)
B. Selection of Passages for Modeling and for Guided Oral Reading (Fluency Pyramid)
C. Develop Lesson Plans

Step I: Passage Introduction & Modeling
A. Introducing the Passage & Concepts
  • Introduce Vocabulary
  • Introduce New Concepts
  • Introduce the Fluency Skill to Be Learned
B. Teacher Modeling of the Targeted Fluency Skill

Step II: Guided Oral Reading Practice
A. Guided Oral Reading Strategies: *Teacher with Kids*
  • Guided Reading Strategy (Fountas & Pinnell, 1996)
  • Choral Reading
B. Peer Supported Practice: *Kids Helping Kids*
  • Partner or "Buddy" Reading
  • Neurological Impress Method (NIM)
  • Book Buddies

Step III: Independent Practice Reading
  • Repeated Readings
  • Sustained Silent Reading or DEAR Time

Step IV: Performance Reading for Fluency Assessment
  • Readers' Theatre
  • Evening Newscast
  • Radio Reading
  • Dialog Retellings

fluency instruction, as with anything else in the curriculum, should be drawn from three sources:

1. A careful review of grade levels expectations and state *standards*
2. An assessment of each child's abilities and *individual needs* relative to the standards
3. A collation of all students' needs into a classroom profile to better understand more universal group needs

Identifying Standards for Fluency Instruction

Standards for fluency have been developed by most states for each grade level and by the U.S. Department of Education. Figures 5.3 and 5.4 are examples of these kinds of standards. Standards almost invariably pertain to one of three principle areas: automaticity, quality, and reading rate. These three areas are described later in the description of step 1 of the Fluency Formula.

Selecting Reading Materials: Varying Literary Genre

Once you have selected a fluency objective, reading materials should be selected for (a) reading aloud (modeling) and (b) instruction (guided oral reading). Your primary goal in the first part of fluency instruction should be to *model* fluent reading behav-

The primary goal in the first part of fluency instruction is to model fluent reading behavior for students.

Figure 5.6 Lesson planning form: The Fluency Formula

Fluency Standard or Objective to be taught (i.e., state standard; Automaticity, Quality, or Rate):
_____

Passage(s) to be used: _____
_____

Step I: Passage Introduction & Modeling
Goal: Share a new passage modeling fluent reading behavior.
A. **Vocabulary and Concepts to be introduced:**

   Method of Instruction (for A)

B. **Methods for Introducing and Modeling the New Fluency Skill:**
   1. **Teacher Input:** (Preteaching—State in your own words the skill/task you expect students to perform.)
   2. **Modeling:** (Specify which part of the reading selection you will use to model this aspect of fluency, and how you will model it.)

Step II: Guided Oral Reading Practice
A. **Guided Oral Reading Strategies:** *Teacher Helping Kids*
   1. **Strategy to be used:**
   2. **Procedures for teaching** (step-by-step):
   3. **Materials Needed:**
   4. **Assessment Strategies** (Specific standards-based criteria for how you will know when learning occurs):
B. **Peer-Supported Practice:** *Kids Helping Kids*
   1. **Strategy to be used** (e.g., buddy reading, NIM, etc.):
   2. **Student assignments/pairings** (Attach assignment sheet):
   3. **Procedures for teaching** (step-by-step):
   4. **Materials Needed:**
   5. **Assessment Strategies** (Specific standards-based criteria for how you will know when learning occurs):

Step III: Independent Practice Reading
Specify the strategy and texts to be used for each Fluency Group:
Group: _____
Strategy (Repeated readings, SSR, Assisted-SSR, etc.): _____
_____
Text: _____
Group: _____
Strategy (Repeated readings, SSR, Assisted-SSR, etc.): _____
_____
Text: _____
Group: _____
Strategy (Repeated readings, SSR, Assisted-SSR, etc.): _____
_____
Text: _____

Step IV: Performance Reading for Fluency Assessment
Specify the fluency performance task the students will use, when ready: _____
_____
_____
_____

ior. As the teacher, you are theoretically the *best* reader in the room, and your young charges want to see and hear what fluent reading behavior is like. Because you will have a wide range of reading ability represented in your class, you will want to think about modeling for students in two venues—whole class and small groups based on reading level (i.e., guided reading groups).

Figure 5.7 Fluency pyramid for passage selection and modeling: Grades K–2

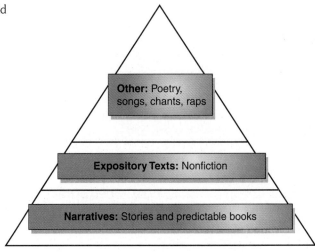

For whole-group modeling, remember the "balanced diet" idea mentioned above: *model reading from a variety of genre in children's literature.* In reality, the selection of reading passages may not be all that balanced (sorry to throw you a curve ball). Here's what we mean. Think of the balanced diet at each grade level as more like the famous food pyramid.

In grades K–2, the bottom of the **fluency pyramid** (i.e., where most of the emphasis is placed) has narrative selections or stories. Thus, much of your oral reading to the class for modeling should come from high-quality books like *The Polar Express* (Van Allsburg, 1985); *Alexander and the Terrible, Horrible, No Good, Very Bad Day* (Viorst, 1987); and *When Lightening Comes in a Jar* (Polacco, 2002). At the center of the pyramid for grades K–2 should be interesting nonfiction books that not only provide a medium for modeling fluency but also help children develop an understanding of new concepts and vocabulary. Notice that expository text examples are almost equal in proportion to narrative texts. At the top of the pyramid, less frequent in comparison to the first two types, is some extra spice for their fluency diet: songs, poetry, chants, and raps. Figure 5.7 shows a fluency pyramid scheme for passage selection in the early grades.

In grades 3–6, the pyramid changes significantly. Nonfiction or *expository text* becomes the staple for modeling and practice. This should not be a return to the narrative forms of the early grades but selections that bridge between nonfiction information and the creative images of novelists. Historical fiction is perhaps the clearest example of these kinds of narratives for modeling and practice. For example, Linda Sue Park (2001) won the 2002 Newbery Medal for her book *A Single Shard.* It is a book set in 12th-century Korea and talks about how the central character, Tree-ear, an orphan who lives under a bridge, becomes involved with a community of pottery makers. This book makes for fine modeling and will have your students crying out for you to continue when your time for modeling each day has expired. Along the way they will also learn more about another culture, art, and enjoy a good bit of drama. Figure 5.8 shows our conception of a fluency pyramid for grades 3–6.

Selecting Reading Materials: Readability and Target Word Frequency

Passages *only* read aloud by the teacher during modeling can be at reading levels well above the abilities of the listeners. In these cases, the teacher is simply demonstrating how a passage can be read with proper intonation and rate. But when passages

---

*The **fluency pyramid** shows the appropriate balance of a variety of genre needed by grade level.*

Just as children get a balanced diet from the offerings on the food pyramid, the fluency pyramid offers a balanced selection of narratives, expository texts, and miscellany such as poetry, songs, chants, and raps.

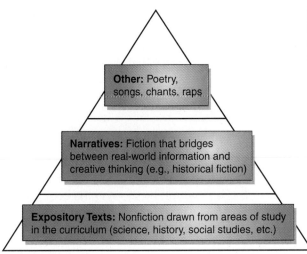

Figure 5.8—Fluency pyramid for passage selection and modeling: Grades 3–6

are selected for children to read themselves, whether with the teacher or with another student, then the passages should conform to certain guidelines.

- *Use selections within the decoding range of the learner*—ninety-five percent or better accuracy in decoding. A good rule of thumb is that the range of readers in a classroom is usually equal to plus or minus the grade-level designation. For example, in second-grade classrooms there can be a range of readers from a preprimer level to fourth grade. In a fourth-grade classroom there can be struggling readers at emergent or first-grade levels and some students reading at an eighth-grade level.

- *Text type and your objective should be a good match*—The objective of your lesson, depending on the needs of your student, will fall within the domain of either automaticity, quality, or reading rate. If your purpose is to practice automaticity, then you may want to choose what is called **decodable text.** Decodable texts are usually short books that use common spelling patterns, or **orthography.** If, on the other hand, your objective is to help readers adjust their reading speeds according to their purpose or type of text, then you may want to choose a variety of text samples, such as stories, mathematics word problems, history readings, and poetry, for demonstration and practice sessions.

- *Word overlap*—New vocabulary to be emphasized should appear multiple times.

- *Target rates*—Have been identified using benchmarks for the grade level as minimums.

- *A variety of literary genres*—Should be used and in appropriate proportions for the grade level (see the fluency pyramid in Figures 5.7 and 5.8).

Develop Your Lesson Plan

Once you have completed the above tasks, lesson planning begins. Using the template for planning provided in Figure 5.6, you will be able to map out in some detail the flow of fluency instruction to be offered. It is important that new teachers work through this process so that instruction is presented in a seamless way. *Scaffolding*

A good rule of thumb for anticipating the range of reading ability in a classroom is that the range is usually equal to plus or minus the grade-level designation. Thus, a fifth-grade classroom can have struggling readers at emergent or first-grade levels as well as fluent readers at the 10th-grade level.

*Decodable texts are written using common spelling patterns, or **orthography** (such as are found in words like call, ball, tall, and wall). Words containing the pattern(s) being emphasized appear throughout decodable text to help readers develop automatic and rapid decoding.*

of instruction is used to help students work through their individual zones of proximal development. Verbal instructions and explanations to students make sense, and nothing important is omitted. Even long-time veteran teachers who are new to fluency instruction should fully complete the template since they are first-time teachers in this area. Once you get your sea legs with this model, lesson planning can become less detailed in terms of language, but the steps should always be followed to insure comprehensive instruction.

Step I: Passage Introduction and Modeling

The Fluency Formula (Cooter & Cooter, 2002) begins in earnest with the teacher introducing the selection much like a *book talk*. Start off by showing the book jacket, telling a little about the author, and explaining why you chose this selection. Children should feel enticed and even excited about hearing the selection.

Introduce Important Vocabulary

Standards Note
Standard 5.1: The reading professional will be able to create a literacy environment that fosters interest and growth in all aspects of literacy. List four activities for your present or future classroom that promote fluency—be general, but cite titles that you'll use.

Next, introduce any new vocabulary that may not be familiar to the students. There are actually three levels of vocabulary knowledge (National Reading Panel, 2000): unknown words, acquainted, and established. *Unknown* words are completely unfamiliar to students whether they hear or attempt to read the word. *Acquainted* words are those students have some familiarity with but need some kind of review. *Established* words are known to students when they hear them spoken or see them in print. Unknown and acquainted words that are important in the selection you plan to model are the ones you will need to introduce before reading aloud. In Chapter 3, which deals with vocabulary instruction, there is much more detail on this point.

Introduce the Targeted Fluency Skill

Scooping is a strategy for helping students to learn to "chunk," or read in meaningful phrases, as a means for attaining good fluency in reading.

Finally, before reading the text, draw students' attention to the fluency skill you plan to emphasize—whether they are seeing it for the first time or as a review. As noted earlier, the three main areas of fluency delineated in scientifically based reading research are automaticity, quality, and reading rate. Name and describe the fluency skill you will be modeling before reading, then return to the skill after reading. Reread short portions of the selection "thinking out loud" how you are using the fluency strategy. Thinking out loud for students is the essence of modeling. You should use many examples, *saturating* students, if you will, with examples drawn from your reading.

For instance, one of the fluency skills you will want to develop is the ability to "chunk text"—read in meaningful phrases. *Scooping* (Hook & Jones, 2002) is a strategy for helping students learn to chunk phrases as a means of attaining good fluency in reading. The "Scooping" box gives a description of moving the activity from teacher modeling to independent reading.

Step II: Guided Oral Reading Practice

This phase of the Fluency Formula (Cooter & Cooter, 2002) provides students with repeated and monitored oral reading experiences. These **guided oral reading** sessions are at the heart of the Fluency Formula and are based on the very best reading research. In the summary of the *Report of the National Reading Panel* (2000), the authors noted;

SCOOPING*

1. The teacher orally introduces the text after first having a discussion about the content and important vocabulary. She also sets up a listening center with a tape-recording of the modeled passage for students' use for comparisons.

2. Students then read selected phrases from the paragraph while scooping under them with a finger or a pencil.

In the tree   on the lawn

3. Next, students read selected sentences from the paragraph individually while scooping phrases (with spaces between phrases).

Meg told Jim   her kite was stuck   in a tree

4. Students then read the paragraph while scooping phrases within the passage (with spaces between the phrases.)

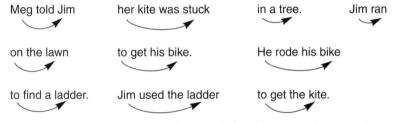

Meg told Jim   her kite was stuck   in a tree.   Jim ran

on the lawn   to get his bike.   He rode his bike

to find a ladder.   Jim used the ladder   to get the kite.

5. Students then read the paragraph as a whole *without* scooping and without spaces.

6. This reading is compared to the first reading in terms of fluency (accuracy, speed, and rhythm). In the beginning, timing a student as she reads connected text may not be as important as monitoring that she is applying prosodic features and chunking the text into syntactic units. Timing may be incorporated once rhythm has been clearly established.

Adapted from Hook and Jones, The Importance of Automaticity and Fluency for Efficient Reading Comprehension in *Perspectives*, 28(1), 9–14, 2002. The International Dyslexia Association.

[Guided oral reading] encourages students to read passages orally with systematic and explicit guidance and feedback from the teacher. . . . On the basis of a detailed analysis of the available research that met NRP methodological criteria, the Panel concluded that guided repeated oral reading procedures that included guidance from teachers, peers, or parents had a significant and positive impact on word recognition, fluency, and comprehension across a range of grade levels. These studies were conducted in a variety of classrooms in both regular and special education settings with teachers using widely available instructional materials. . . . These results also apply to all students—good readers as well as those experiencing reading difficulties. (p. 12)

Two kinds of guided oral reading are provided in Step II of the Fluency Formula. The first is done with the aid and guidance of the teacher. The second involves repeated readings with a peer. In each case, the student has ample practice rereading texts for fluency and for getting feedback from a more fluent reader.

In the following sections, we highlight some of the most successful strategies used for guided oral reading practice. In the realm of teacher-assisted instruction, we will

Two kinds of effective **guided oral reading** *are repeated readings with a peer and reading with the aid of a teacher.*

examine a procedure known as *guided reading* (Fountas & Pinnell, 1996) and *choral reading*. The student-assisted strategies we describe include *partner* or buddy reading (Eldredge & Quinn, 1988; Greene, 1970) and the *Neurological Impress Method* (Heckleman, 1966, 1969).

Guided Reading

The major purposes of **guided reading** *are to develop reading fluency strategies and to move children toward independent reading.*

Guided reading is an essential part of a comprehensive reading program (Fountas & Pinnell, 1996; Mooney, 1990). The major purposes of guided reading are (a) to develop reading fluency strategies and (b) to move children toward independent reading. Children are grouped by developmental levels that reflect a range of competencies, experiences, and interests. The strategy centers on developing the child's ability to successfully process text with limited teacher guidance and interaction.

Guided reading groups typically include four levels of children's reading development: (a) early emergent, (b) emergent, (c) early fluency, and (d) fluency. Guided reading groups are composed of six to eight children who work together for a period of time under the direct guidance of the teacher.

It is important to note that the membership of guided reading groups changes as children progress during the year. This is a crucial point because failure to modify groups as students progress can result in static ability groups much like the "Eagles, Bluebirds, and Buzzards" as practiced in earlier days. The static nature of these ability groups caused children to suffer self-esteem damage and have lowered academic expectations, particularly struggling readers left in the "lower" developmental groups.

Leveled Books

Leveled books *are books categorized by their difficulty so as to be matched up to a student's appropriate reading level.*

Offering fluency instruction for students hinges on their being correctly placed in books on their reading level. Thus, the notion of **leveled books,** books categorized according to their difficulty so that they can be matched to students at that level, is an important one for fluency instruction. Before a guided reading group is begun, the teacher must take great care to match the levels of text with the identified needs of a group of children to ensure that the group can enjoy and control the story throughout the first reading. Texts chosen for each leveled group should present children with a reasonable challenge but also with a high degree of potential success.

See the listing of criteria typically used for leveling books for guided reading instruction in the accompanying box on page 149. In Table 5.1 we include a useful reading level cross-referencing guide comparing grade levels to guided reading levels, to Reading Recovery levels (a popular remedial reading program for first-grade students), and to the stages of reading.

Lesson Planning for Guided Reading

The basic lesson pattern employed in guided reading lessons consists of seven phases that are listed and explained in Figure 5.9.

Teacher Feedback During Instruction

Understanding the nature, quantity, and quality of teacher feedback during guided oral reading, as well as in other "coaching" situations, is a crucial part of helping students become fluent readers. The self-assessment questions on the bottom of Figure 5.9 for teachers are provided to assist in this process.

LEVELS 1–4 (A–D)
- Repeating language patterns.
- Illustrations that match and explain most of the text. Actions are clearly presented without much in the way of extraneous detail that might confuse the reader.
- Whole meaning or story that is likely to match the experiences and conceptual knowledge common to most beginning readers.
- The language of the text developmentally matches syntax and organization of most young children's speech for whom the text is intended.
- Sentences and books themselves are comparatively short (e.g., 10–60 words).
- Print is carefully laid out so that it consistently appears on the same place on the page throughout each book.

Assumption at this level:

That when students encounter an unknown word in print they can easily use context from known words and illustrations along with language pattern cues and early word analysis skills for successful decoding.

LEVELS 5–8 (D–E)
- One often sees predictable, repetitive language patterns, but without allowing the same pattern to dominate the entire text.
- There is now more variation of language patterns, as opposed to one or two word changes, for example.
- Words and phrases may appear to express different meanings through varying sentence structures.
- By the end of these stages, the syntax is more typical of written or "book" language. Illustrations provide minimal support for readers determining exact language.

LEVELS 9–12 (E–G)
- Variation in sentence patterns is now the norm.
- Longer sentences with less predictable text.
- Written language styles and genre become more prominent, including the use of some verb forms not often used by young children in oral settings.
- The average sentence length in texts increases (double that found in levels 5–8).
- Events in a story may continue over several pages.
- Illustrations provide only moderate support to the meaning of the stories.

LEVELS 13–15* (G–H)
(*Consider these characteristics as enhancements to the description for levels 9–12.)
- There is a greater variety of words and the inclusion of more specialized vocabulary.
- Pictures provide some support for the overall meaning of the story, but cannot be used by the reader to interpret the precise message.

LEVELS 16–20 (I–K)
- Now there are longer stories or sequences of events.
- Story events are developed more fully than texts at lower levels.
- Vocabulary is progressively more rich and varied.
- Illustrations are used to help to create the atmosphere and setting, rather than to specifically depict the content of the text.
- It is now common to have full pages of print.

General Explanation of Criteria for Determining the Reading Levels of Texts: Levels 1–20 (A–K) The language of the text developmentally matches syntax and organization of most young children's speech for whom the text is intended.

Table 5.1 Guided reading leveling comparisons

Here is a handy guide to help you translate books from publishers using Guided Reading ratings to leveling systems common in one-to-one tutorial programs (i.e., Reading Recovery, Cooter and Cooter's *BLAST* program, etc.).

Grade Level (Basal)	Guided Reading Level (Fountas-Pinnell)	One-to-One Tutoring Level	Stages of Reading
Kindergarten	A B	A 1 2	Emergent
Pre-Primer	C D E	3 4 6–8	Emergent / Early
Primer	F G	10 12	Early
1st Grade	H I	14 16	Early / Transitional
2nd Grade	J–K L–M	18–20 24–28	Transitional
3rd Grade	N O–P	30 34–38	Transitional / Fluent/Extending
4th Grade	Q–R	40	Fluent/Extending
5th Grade	—	44	Fluent/Extending
6th Grade	—	—	Fluent/Extending

Figure 5.9 Guided reading lesson overview

Picture Talk • Walk through a new book by looking at the pictures. Ask children, "What do you see?"

First Reading • Depending on the students' developmental levels, the first reading is initially done by the teacher with children following the lead. Later, the teacher gradually releases responsibility for the first reading to the children by sharing the reading role and then fading into one who encourages children to try it on their own.

Language Play • In this phase of the guided reading lesson, the teacher carefully analyzes the text to find specific elements associated with written language to teach children how language works. For early emergent readers, this may mean letter identification, punctuation, or directionality. In the fluency stage, children might identify text genre or compound words.

Rereading • Children read the text again with the assistance of the teacher, a peer, or a mechanical device such as a computer or tape. Novice readers are encouraged to point to the text as they read, whereas fluent readers are encouraged to "read the text with your eyes" or silently.

Retelling • Children retell what they have read to their teacher or to their peers. Typically we say, "Can you tell me what you've read?" Sometimes we probe children's retellings with other questions to prompt recall.

Follow-up • The most effective follow-up activity to a guided reading lesson is to invite children to take guided reading books home for demonstrating their ability to parents and siblings. This provides needed practice time and promotes increased confidence and self-esteem among young readers.

Extensions • Extending books through performances, murals, artwork, and even music helps children deepen their understandings and increase their interpretations of text.

1. Am I more often telling the word than providing a clue?
2. What is the average self-correction rate of my students?
3. Do I assist poor readers with unknown words more often than good readers? If so, why?
4. Am I correcting miscues even when they do not alter the meaning of the text? If so, why?
5. Does one reader group tend to engage in more self-correction than other groups? If so, why?
6. Does one reading group have more miscues that go unaddressed than other groups?
7. What types of cues for oral reading errors do I provide, and why?
8. What is *my* ultimate goal in reading instruction?
9. How do I handle interruptions from other students during oral reading? Do I practice what I preach?
10. How does my feedback influence the self-correction behavior of students?
11. Does my feedback differ across reader groups? If so, *how* and *why?*
12. Would students benefit more from a form of feedback different from that which I normally offer?
13. Am I allowing students time to self-correct (3–5 seconds)?
14. Am I further confusing students with my feedback?
15. Do I digress into "mini-lessons" mid-sentence when students make a mistake? If so, why?
16. Do I analyze miscues to gain information about the reading strategies students employ?
17. Does the feedback I offer aid students in becoming independent, self-monitoring readers? If so, how?
18. Do I encourage students to ask themselves, "Did that make sense?" when they are reading both orally and silently? If not, why not?
19. Do students need the kind of feedback I am offering them?

Source: Adapted from "Teacher Interruptions During Oral Reading Instruction: Self-Monitoring as an Impetus for Change in Corrective Feedback," by M. Shake, *Remedial and Special Education, 7*(5), 1986, pp. 18–24.

Choral Reading

Choral readings of text can be done in three ways. Wood (1983) recommends *unison reading* and *echo reading*. Unison reading is where everyone reads together. Echo (sometimes called *echoic*) reading has the teacher or a student read a passage aloud, then everyone else "echoes" by repeating it. A third method we have found useful is *antiphonal* reading. Derived from ancient monastic traditions, antiphonal reading has two groups. The first reading group reads a passage aloud (usually a sentence or two), and the second group echoes the reading.

Student-Assisted Strategies: Partner or Buddy Reading

Partner reading or buddy reading has a student reading aloud with a more fluent partner or, sometimes, a reader of equal fluency. The partner provides the model of fluent reading in place of the teacher, provides useful feedback, and helps, when needed, with word recognition.

Usually the partners take turns reading an assigned passage aloud to one another, with the more developed reader reading first, thus providing the model for fluent reading. Then, the second reader rereads the passage in the same way as the first. The more fluent reader offers feedback on how his partner can read the passage more fluently, and the less fluent reader rereads the passage until he can do so independently.

Readers of about the same ability are sometimes paired for this exercise. The difference is that both readers first hear the teacher reading the passage as the model, then the two buddies take turns reading to each other and offering feedback until they can each read the passage fluently.

Student-Assisted Strategies: Neurological Impress Method

The **neurological impress method** (NIM) involves the student and a more fluent reader in reading the same text aloud simultaneously (Heckleman, 1966, 1969). Unlike other partner reading examples described before, NIM has the student and more fluent model reading in unison at the same volume at first, and then the model's voice gradually fades as the student becomes more confident.

The use of multiple sensory systems associated with using NIM is thought to "impress" the fluent reading patterns of the teacher onto the student through direct modeling. It is assumed that exposing students to numerous examples of texts (read in a more sophisticated way than struggling readers could achieve on their own) will enable them to achieve automaticity in word recognition more naturally. This assumption stands to reason when viewed in light of more recent advances in learning theory, especially those espoused by Vygotsky (1978).

Each NIM session is aimed at reading as much material as is possible in 10 minutes. Reading material selected for the first few sessions should be easy and predictable and make sense for the reader. However, other more challenging materials that are on the student's normal guided reading level can be used rather quickly.

To use the NIM, the student sits slightly in front and to one side of the teacher as they hold the text. The more fluent reader moves her finger beneath the words as they are spoken in near-unison fashion. Both try to maintain a comfortably brisk and continuous rate of oral reading. The more fluent reader's role is to keep the pace when the student starts to slow down. Pausing for analyzing unknown words is not permitted. The more fluent reader's voice is directed at the student's ear so that the words are seen, heard, and said simultaneously.

Since many struggling readers have not read at an accelerated pace before, their first efforts often have a mumble-like quality. Most struggling readers typically take time to adjust to the NIM; however, within a few sessions they start to feel more at ease. Many struggling readers say they enjoy the NIM because it allows them to read more challenging and interesting material like "good readers."

At first, the more fluent reader's voice will dominate the oral reading, but in later sessions it should be reduced gradually. This will eventually allow the student to assume the vocal lead naturally. Usually 3 sessions per week are sufficient to obtain noticeable results. This routine should be followed for a minimum of 10 consecutive weeks (Henk, 1983).

The NIM can also be adapted for group use (Hollingsworth, 1978). Here the teacher tape-records 10 minutes of his or her own oral reading in advance. Individual students can read along with the tape while following the text independently, or the tape can be used in a listening center to permit the teacher to spend individual time with each student as others participate in reading with the tape. Despite the advantages of the prerecorded tape format, teachers' or more fluent peer's one-to-one interactions with individual students result in a better instructional experience.

Book Buddies

In the **book buddies** strategy, students improve reading fluency with the help of a classroom volunteer tutoring in a one-to-one setting (Invernizzi, Juel, & Rosemary 1997). The four-part lesson uses *repeated readings* of a familiar text, *word study* (phonics and structural analysis), *writing for sounds,* and reading a new book.

Book buddies enlists the aid of a volunteer classroom tutor in a one-on-one setting with a student.

In the word study portion of the lesson, students principally focus on beginning consonants, middle and ending consonant sounds, and finally vowel sounds. This program leads students to a better understanding of "speech to print" concepts for improved automaticity and the beginning of a sight vocabulary (Snow et al., 1998).

Research on book buddies has been very positive indeed. In one study (Invernizzi et al., 1997), three groups of 358 first- and second-grade students participated. First graders who scored in the bottom quartile of the Title I referral list were assigned tutors using this method. University faculty members provided the assessments and lesson plans for the tutors. Results were very positive for developing automaticity, in fact, on a par with coaching by professionally trained teachers.

Step III: Independent Practice

Developing students as readers is in some ways like a coach developing an Olympic swimmer. There are numerous skills to be developed and learned to the point of automaticity. If the student, or swimmer, is to become proficient, then there must be many hours of practice. You might say, then, that independent practice is intended to provide students with ample opportunities to become *Olympic readers*—strong, capable, and fluent. Two of the more productive strategies for independent practice are repeated readings (Dowhower, 1991; Samuels, 1979) and sustained silent reading.

Repeated Readings

Repeated readings engage students in reading interesting passages orally over and over again to enhance students' reading fluency (Dowhower, 1987; Samuels, 1979). Although it might seem that reading a text again and again could lead to boredom, it can actually have just the opposite effect.

Repeated readings help improve students' comprehension, vocabulary recognition, and oral reading performance.

In the beginning, texts selected for repeated readings should be short, predictable, and easy. When students attain adequate speed and accuracy with easy texts, the length and difficulty of the stories and poems can gradually be increased.

Repeated readings help students by expanding the total number of words they can recognize instantaneously and help improve students' comprehension and oral elocution (performance) with each succeeding attempt. Improved performance quickly leads students to improved confidence regarding reading aloud and positive attitudes toward the act of reading. Additionally, because high-frequency words (e.g., *the, and, but, was,* etc.) occur in literally all reading situations, the increase in automatic sight word knowledge developed through repeated readings transfers far beyond the practiced texts.

Research indicates that repeated readings are most effective when students are supported during independent reading. Audiotapes, tutors, or peer feedback are supports shown to be most effective during repeated reading practice sessions (National Reading Panel, 2000). For example, try providing a tape-recorded version of the story or poem to be practiced. Students can read along with an audiocassette tape to develop fluency similar to the model on the tape (probably your voice). Also, students can tape-record their oral reading performance as a source of immediate feedback. If two audiocassette tape players are available, ask students to listen and read along with the taped version of the text using headphones. At the same time, use the second recorder for recording the student's oral reading. The child can then replay his version simultaneously with the teacher-recorded version to compare or simply listen to his own rendition alone. Either way, the feedback can be both instant and effective.

You may use taped recordings of repeated readings for further analysis of each reader's improvement in fluency and comprehension. Also, using a tape recorder frees the teacher to work with other students, thereby conserving precious instructional time and leaving behind an audit trail of student readings for later assessment and documentation. On occasion, teachers should listen to the tape with the reader present. During this time the teacher and student can discuss effective ways of reducing word recognition errors and increasing reading rate.

Sustained Silent Reading

Sustained Silent Reading (SSR), or Drop Everything and Read Time (DEAR Time), works by allowing students to choose a book that interests them and orchestrating timed periods each day for them to read said book.

Sustained Silent Reading (SSR), also known as *DEAR Time* (Drop Everything And Read) is a very popular method of independent reading practice in our schools. The way it works is simple. Students first self-select a book of interest to them from the library, then check to make sure it won't be too hard for them using a strategy known as *rule of thumb* (ROT). Here are the steps in ROT:

ROT Strategy for Choosing "Just Right" Books

1. Choose a book that looks interesting.
2. Open the book to any page that has lots of words on it.
3. Begin reading aloud or silently. When you come to a word you don't know, hold up your small finger.
4. If you come to another word you don't know, hold up your next finger. If you use up all of your fingers on one hand (and come to your thumb) on one page, then the book is *too hard,* and you should put it back. Just find another book you like just as well and repeat the ROT exercise to make sure it's just right for you.

Once students have chosen their books, they are ready for DEAR Time. The goal is for students to read a total of 20 minutes per day in a self-selected book. For younger students you may need to have several 5-minute periods for DEAR Time. Teachers will usually set an egg timer for the amount of time they wish, then *everyone* reads (including the teacher). Some principals even have daily schoolwide DEAR Time.

The research on SSR or DEAR time has been somewhat inconclusive. There is no real question that students must have a good deal of practice if they are to become fluent readers. The question really is, What kind of practice? For struggling readers in particular, SSR may not be very effective. If a struggling reader is truly *struggling* with basic word recognition skills, for instance, sitting alone and staring at a book he is unable to decode will do little to develop his fluency.

In many cases, SSR will be far more effective if a form of buddy reading is used rather than having students reading in isolation. This is especially so with emergent readers in the early grades who have not yet mastered the alphabetic principle and/or basic decoding skills and with struggling readers (National Reading Panel, 2000).

A teacher in Kansas once remarked, "I've been an ice skater all my life. I recently had a chance to go see Dorothy Hamill in the *Ice Capades.* You know, just being around Dorothy Hamill won't make me as good an ice skater as Dorothy Hamill. Its like struggling readers during SSR if they don't have any support; just being around great readers won't make them great readers . . . it takes much more."

Another exception has to do with the teacher's role during SSR. While it is certainly a desirable goal for teachers to participate in SSR themselves by reading and modeling their enjoyment of reading, it may not always be in some students' best interest. For example, some struggling readers lack initiative or a desire to read. In these cases, a teacher may need to intervene during SSR and give the student a motivating purpose to read or a task to fulfill. Some examples might include the following:

"I'd like you to draw me a picture of your favorite character when you finish reading this story."

"Find five _____ (e.g., color, describing, number, etc.) words for me as you read."

"I will want you to act out one of the characters when you finish, and I'll see if I can guess which one it is!"

Sustained silent reading is most effective with readers who have mastered basic word-recognition skills. Emergent and struggling readers will benefit most from SSR when they can participate in a paired reading format.

Step IV: Performance Reading for Fluency Assessment

Performance reading has students reading aloud for the teacher and/or an audience so that the teacher can monitor each student's fluency growth. Students prepare for the exercise, regardless of format, by orally rereading the text to be performed until they can read it with maximum fluency. There are several ways this can be done that have found support in evidence-based research. Before we get to those, we should first examine a very well-known approach that you should *not* use—"round-robin reading."

Long ago, teachers commonly relied on an activity commonly known as *round-robin reading* as a means of listening to students read aloud. Students would sit in a circle. The teacher would call on a child to begin reading from a story in the basal reader, and the other children would follow along. After the first student read a paragraph or two, the teacher would stop her, call on the next student to the first one's right, and ask her to continue reading. This process was repeated until every child in the circle had a chance to read.

*In **performance reading,** students read aloud for the teacher or an audience so that the teacher can assess each student's fluency levels.*

Round-robin reading is not an effective method to use in your classroom for fluency development.

Though the simplicity of round-robin is very appealing, research has revealed it to be far less effective than other available strategies for monitoring fluency development, and it can even have a negative impact on some children (Eldredge, Reutzel, & Hollingsworth, 1996). Round-robin fails to give children adequate opportunities for repeated readings before performing, defeats comprehension (i.e., when a student realizes the paragraph he'll be asked to read is three ahead of the current student in the "hot seat," he'll tend to look ahead and start silently reading his passage feverishly hoping that he won't "mess up" when it's his turn), and causes some students embarrassment when they are unable to read their paragraph fluently. Our advice? Please don't use round-robin in your classroom; there are better alternatives that will help you monitor fluency development, improve student development, and protect fragile egos in the process. There are effective alternatives that can be used for performance reading.

Reader's Theater

Reader's Theater involves students in rehearsing and performing a script before an audience.

Perhaps the most successful performance reading strategy, in terms of the research (National Reading Panel, 2000; Partnership for Reading, 2001; Sloyer, 1982) is reader's theater. **Reader's theater** involves rehearsing and performing a script that is rich with dialogue before an audience. The script itself may be one from a book or, in the upper elementary or middle school grades, could be developed by a group of students working in collaboration as part of a literature response activity (Cooter & Griffith, 1989).

Stayter and Allington (1991) tell about a reader's theater activity for which a group of heterogeneously grouped seventh graders spent 5 days reading, rehearsing, and performing short dramas. After a first reading, students began to negotiate about which role they would read. More hesitant students were permitted to opt for smaller parts, but everyone was required to participate. As time passed, the students critiqued each others' readings and made suggestions as to how they should sound (e.g., "You should sound like a snob"). The most common response in this experience was how repeated readings through drama helped them better understand the text. One student said,

> The first time I read to know what the words are. Then I read to know what the words *say* and later as I read I thought about how to say the words. . . . As I got to know the character better, I put more feeling in my voice. (Stayter & Allington, 1991, p. 145)

Literature selected for reader's theater is often drawn from tales from the oral tradition, poetry, or quality picture books designed to be read aloud by children. However, nonfiction passages can also be adapted and written to be more like a documentary. Selections should, whenever possible, be packed with action, have an element of suspense, and comprise an entire, meaningful story or nonfiction text. Also, texts selected for use in reader's theater should contain sufficient dialogue to make reading and preparing the text a challenge and involve several children as characters. A few examples of narrative texts we have seen used include Martin and Archambault's *Knots on a Counting Rope* (1987), Viorst's *Alexander and the Terrible, Horrible, No Good, Very Bad Day* (1972), and Barbara Robinson's *The Best Christmas Pageant Ever* (1972).

Here is an easy procedure to follow. If a story is selected for reading, students should be assigned to read characters' parts. If poems are selected for a reader's theater, students may read alternating lines or groups of lines. Reader's theater in-the-round, where readers stand around the perimeter of the room and the audience is in the center surrounded by the readers, is a fun and interesting variation for both performers and audience.

Students will often benefit from a discussion prior to reading a reader's theater script for the first time. This discussion helps students make connections between their own background experiences and the text to be read. Also, struggling readers usually benefit from listening to a previously recorded performance of the text as a model prior to their initial attempts at reading the script.

Hennings (1974) described a simplified procedure for preparing reader's theater scripts for classroom performance. First, the text to be performed is read silently by the individual students. Second, the text is read again orally, sometimes using choral reading in a group. After the second reading, either children choose their parts or the teacher assigns parts to the children. We suggest that students be allowed to select their three most desired parts, write these choices on a slip of paper, and submit them to the teacher and that teachers do everything possible to assign them one of these three choices. The third reading is also an oral reading with students reading their parts with scripts in hand. There may be several rehearsal readings as students prepare for the final reading or performance in front of the class or a selected audience.

Reader's theater offers students a unique opportunity to participate in reading along with other, perhaps more skilled readers. Participating in the mainstream classroom with better readers helps students with reading problems feel a part of their peer group, provides them with ready models of good reading, and demonstrates how good readers, through practice, become even better readers. Working together with other readers fosters a sense of teamwork, support, and pride in personal and group accomplishment.

There are numerous variations on reader's theater that possess all the effective elements. Here are three that you may want to try.

- *Evening Newscast* The evening newscast activity offers maximum opportunity for students to practice their roles using the kind of intonation characteristics used by newscasters. Teachers may want to encourage students to adopt and adapt the particular style of a famous personality, such as "Katie Curtsy" or "Bryant Gum-ball."

- *Radio Plays* *Radio plays* is an adaptation of something called "radio reading" (Searfoss, 1975), a procedure for developing oral reading fluency in a group setting, a process that shields students having reading problems from the sometimes harsh emotional consequences from peers due to their limited reading abilities.

Developing a radio play involves virtually the same process as any other student drama and uses a purely oral–aural (i.e., speaking–listening) delivery. Students first write a one-act play based on their book as described in the preceding section. Next, materials are gathered for the purpose of creating needed sound effects (police whistles, recorded train sound effects, door opening/closing, etc.), and different human sounds are practiced (such as a girl's or boy's scream, tongue clicking noise, and throat-clearing). After thorough rehearsal of the script with sound effects, the radio play is taped on a cassette recorder and played over the school's public address system into the classroom.

Teachers may want to obtain recordings of old radio shows, such as *The Shadow,* to help students better understand the concept. A more current source is Garrison Keillor's radio program *A Prairie Home Companion,* which airs every Saturday night on National Public Radio stations and usually has several radio dramas each week.

- *Dialogue Retellings* We recommend that students create *dialogue retellings* by first writing a script retelling the key information and/or dialogue from their

Research shows that reader's theater is one of the most successful performance reading strategies.

selection and then preparing a puppet show for younger students. Participants should rehearse their parts until they are perfectly fluent and should solicit suggestions from other peers before the day of performance. A book like *The Lion, the Witch, and the Wardrobe* by C. S. Lewis (1961) makes a great example for teachers to use in explaining this option. Walley (1993) recommends the use of cumulative stories, those having a minimum of plot and a maximum of rhythm and rhyme, in early elementary grades. Jane Yolen's (1976) *An Invitation to a Butterfly Ball* is one such example.

Summary

Fluency is the ability to read a text accurately with appropriate intonation and phrasing and at a good speed according to the text's purpose. Fluency instruction, since it helps readers achieve automatic decoding, is critical for comprehending the author's message.

Reading fluency can be developed by teacher modeling of fluent behaviors and by having students participate in guided oral repeated reading sessions. It can be further strengthened by massive amounts of practice (i.e., practice reading). Struggling readers and, in fact, all others benefit most from practice reading that provides feedback and direction.

Monitoring and evaluating the development of reading fluency is an important teacher activity. Various forms of the reader's theater were discussed that can be both motivational and informative for teachers and students alike. Careful analysis of students' oral reading in these sessions can help teachers in setting instructional goals.

Concept Applications

In the Classroom

1. In groups of four in your college class or in a small group of teachers from your school, perform the following tasks for a selected grade level:
    a. Identify your state's standards for fluency instruction for the selected grade. These can usually be located on the state's department of education Web site on the Internet.
    b. For each form of reading fluency (automaticity, quality, rate), determine which of these areas are addressed in the state standards and which are not.
    c. Outline the strategies named in this chapter that would be appropriate for improving reading fluency at this level and match each to one of the state standards.
    d. If you are using this book as part of a college class, present your findings for the above to the group. Be sure to provide your classmates with a copy of your findings for future reference in the field.
    e. If you are a small group of teachers from a school working through this exercise, share your findings with another grade-level team and your principal. Determine together whether a renewed emphasis on reading fluency is warranted based on current classroom practices.

In the Field

1. Develop a unit of study using the Fluency Formula presented in this chapter, then teach it to a small group of students (or the class if you al-

Standards Note
Standard 5.4: The reading professional will be able to provide opportunities for learners to select from among a variety of written materials, to read extended texts, and to read for authentic purposes. Create several text sets for your present grade level, leveled appropriately for the readability range.

Check your understanding of chapter concepts by using the self-assessment for Chapter 5 on our Companion Website at www.prenhall.com/ reutzel.

ready have your own classroom). Be sure to pretest students before planning your unit so that you will know which fluency area to emphasize. Also, compare your students' needs to the state's standards for reading fluency and clearly identify in your lesson plan which skill is being addressed.

2. Identify a struggling reader who needs help developing greater fluency. The classroom teacher in charge should easily be able to help you find a good candidate. After determining through assessment or from class records the reading level of the student, select appropriately leveled texts that you can use to plan a neurological impress method (NIM) lesson. Work with this student on a selected passage for a minimum of three sessions per week (about 10–15 minutes each time) until he or she can read at least two passages fluently. Keep a log of your daily lesson plans and results. It is a good idea to tape-record these sessions so that you can replay them later to help add detail to your journal reflections.

Recommended Readings

Fountas, I., & Pinnell, G. S. (1996). *Guided reading.* Portsmouth, NH: Heinemann.

Mooney, M. E. (1990). *Reading to, with, and by children.* Katonah, NY: Richard Owen.

Opitz, M. F., & Rasinski, T. V. (1998). *Good-bye round robin: 25 effective oral reading strategies.* Portsmouth, NH: Heinemann.

Park, L. S. (2001). *A single shard.* New York: Clarion.

Sloyer, S. (1982). *Reader's theatre: Story dramatization in the classroom.* Urbana, IL: National Council of Teachers of English.

chapter 6

Materials and Programs for Literacy Instruction: Basals and Beyond

Focus Questions

When you are finished studying this chapter, you should be able to answer these questions:

1. How have basal readers changed over the years?

2. What are the major components associated with basal readers?

3. What are five strengths and five weaknesses of basal readers?

4. How are basal readers produced and organized?

5. What are at least two ways in which teachers can maximize their use of basal teacher's editions?

6. What are three nationally recognized reading programs for teaching children to read?

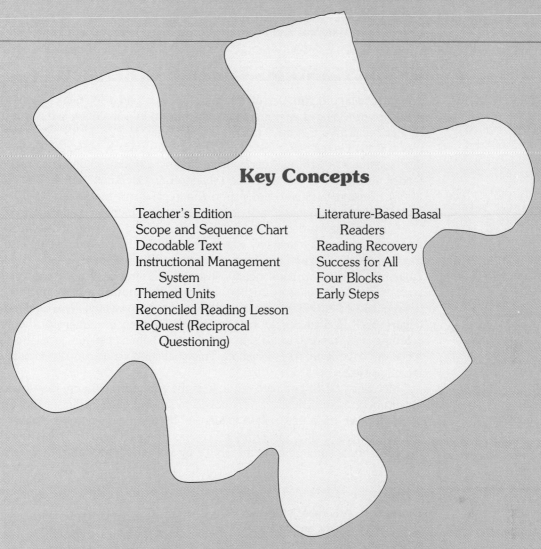

Key Concepts

Teacher's Edition
Scope and Sequence Chart
Decodable Text
Instructional Management
   System
Themed Units
Reconciled Reading Lesson
ReQuest (Reciprocal
   Questioning)

Literature-Based Basal
   Readers
Reading Recovery
Success for All
Four Blocks
Early Steps

Basal readers in one form or another have played an integral role in American reading instruction for centuries and are likely to continue to do so well into the future (Giordano, 2001; Hoffman, 2001; McCallum, 1988; Reutzel, 1991; Robinson, in press). According to *The Literacy Dictionary,* a basal reading program is "a collection of student texts and workbooks, teacher's manuals, and supplemental materials for developmental reading and sometimes writing instruction, used chiefly in the elementary and middle school grades" (Harris & Hodges, 1995, p. 18).

UNDERSTANDING THE BASAL READER

A basal reading program is a set of commercially prepared and marketed resource materials for providing classroom reading instruction in elementary and middle schools. Research indicates that basal readers are used daily in 92% to 98% of primary classrooms in the United States (Flood & Lapp, 1986; Wade & Moje, 2000). More recent data suggest that 85% of intermediate grade classrooms continue to rely on basal reader instruction to some degree (Shannon & Goodman, 1994; Wade & Moje, 2000). These data clearly demonstrate the integral role that basal reader instruction has played and continues to play in contemporary American reading instruction.

Current basal readers have descended from a long ancestry of basal readers. The first in this line of predecessors was the hornbook, the earliest reading instructional material widely used and recorded in American history (Smith, 1986). A cursory examination of the hornbook clearly illustrates the strong religious underpinnings of early American reading instruction (Figure 6.1). Another ancestor of the modern basal published during this era of reading instruction was the *New England Primer* (Figure 6.2). Rooted deeply in the religious freedom movement of the American colonists, early reading instruction was aimed at helping children learn the necessary theology to work out their salvation. This goal could be accomplished only by reading the Bible.

McCallum (1988) pointed out that as the American citizenry moved away from government by the church to civil government, moral character, national interests, and patriotism for a new nation influenced both the aims and the content of basal readers. Consequently, *McGuffey's Eclectic Primer* (Figure 6.3) was introduced to the educational community in the 1830s by William H. McGuffey (Bohning, 1986).

Visit Chapter 6 of our Companion Website at www.prenhall.com/reutzel to look into the chapter objectives, standards and principles, and pertinent Web links associated with materials and programs for literacy instruction: basals and beyond.

Basal readers are used daily in 9 of 10 primary classrooms in the United States.

The hornbook clearly illustrated the strong religious underpinnings of early American reading instruction.

The New England Primer was aimed not only at teaching children to read but also at helping them work out their salvation.

Figure 6.1   A hornbook with the alphabet, a syllabary, and the Lord's Prayer

Photo courtesy of The Horn Book, Inc., www.hbook.com.

Figure 6.2 A page from *The New England Primer*

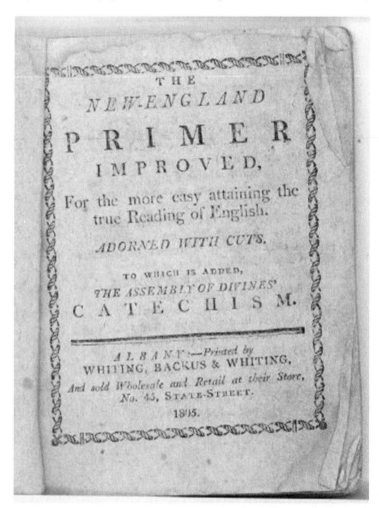

In 1912, the Beacon Street Readers were published by Ginn & Co., located on Beacon Street in Boston. These readers reflected a strong emphasis on phonics, complete with elaborate articulation drills and diacritical markings (Aukerman, 1981; Smith, 1986; Robinson, in press).

The New Basic Readers (Figure 6.4), affectionately known as the "Dick and Jane" readers, principally authored by William S. Gray and Marion Monroe, were originally published by Scott, Foresman and Company in 1941. The Dick and Jane readers conveyed the stereotypic American dream pervasive in the United States during and following World War II and the Korean conflict. The family depicted in the Dick and Jane basals owned a spacious, white, two-story home in a well-cared-for suburban neighborhood. Mother stayed home while Father worked at a successful career, providing for the family's needs. A car and a pet dog and cat also adorned the dream of the American family portrayed in this series. For those who remember the Dick and Jane readers fondly and wish to update their acquaintance, we suggest a modern humorous satire written by Marc Gallant (1986) titled *More Fun with Dick and Jane.*

McGuffey's Eclectic Primer *was intended to inculcate young children with moral character.*

Observe the language in Figure 6.4.

Figure 6.3 Sample pages from *McGuffey's Eclectic Primer,* Revised Edition New York: Henry H. Vail, 1909.

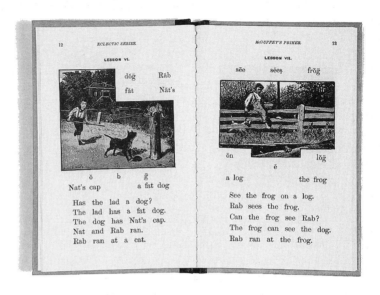

Figure 6.4 Sample pages from the Dick and Jane readers

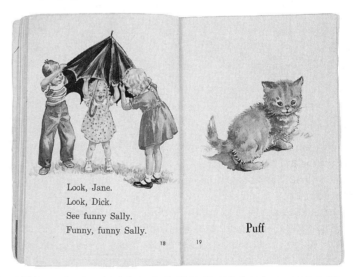

From *The New We Look and See* by W. S. Gray, M. Monroe, A. S. Artley, and M. H. Arbuthnot, Chicago: ScottForesman. Copyright 1956 by ScottForesman.

The basal readers produced during the mid-1960s and through the early 1970s reflected a serious-minded response to a perceived threat to national security by the successful launching of Russia's *Sputnik* into space. This perception prompted a quick return to basic and rigorous academics in American schooling. The publication of Flesch's 1955 book *Why Johnny Can't Read* added fuel to the fire for the hasty return to phonics and basic skill instruction in reading. One well-known basal reading program originally published during this era evidencing the return to basic skills and phonics in reading instruction was *Reading Mastery: DISTAR.*

The basals of the late 1970s into the mid-1980s reflected a continued emphasis on a basic skills approach to reading instruction but was accompanied by a major shift in the composition and content of basal readers. The stereotypic portrayal of men and women in basals was attacked and, as a consequence, revised. The failure of basal readers to represent ethnic minorities fairly was assailed by basal critics. Thus, compilers of the basals of this era reacted by attempting to represent the increasing complexity of modern American society while maintaining a continuing emphasis on back to basics and accountability (Aukerman, 1981).

The basals of the late 1970s and early 1980s reflected an emphasis on back to basics and accountability.

Reading selections found in basal readers of the 1990s and early twenty-first century reflected the influence of the literature-based reading instruction movement of the late 1980s. These basal readers include a substantial number of selections from classical and contemporary children's literature (Reutzel & Larsen, 1995).

The value and the role of the basal reader continue to be the focus of debates (Wade & Moje, 2000). Shannon (1989b, 1992, 1993) asserts that basal readers have contributed to a deskilling of teachers' expertise and decision making related to reflective and thoughtful reading instruction. Baumann (1992, 1993, 1996) asserts on the other hand, that teachers who are otherwise capable and intelligent decision makers are not falling prey to a mindless adherence to basal teacher's editions as Shannon indicates. He says that teachers who otherwise think and make decisions do not stop making decisions when they approach basal reading instruction (Durkin, 1984).

The value and role of the basal reader continue to be debated among reading professionals.

In 1992, the National Assessment of Education Progress (NAEP) surveyed U.S. fourth-grade classroom teachers about their primary resource for providing reading instruction. This survey found that 36% of fourth-grade teachers relied solely on basal readers, 49% relied on a combination of basal readers and trade books, and 15% relied on materials other than basal readers. Researchers have determined that the use of trade books to teach reading steadily decreased with each grade level from 75% in kindergarten to 25% in grade 5 (Fractor, Woodruff, Martinez, & Teale, 1993).

Because of the continued widespread and pervasive use of basal readers in American schools as the core for providing basic reading instruction (Flood & Lapp, 1986; Shannon, 1983; Shannon & Goodman, 1994; Wade & Moje, 2000), it is imperative that preservice and in-service teachers learn to use the basal reader with judgment and skill. The purpose of this chapter is to provide teachers with the information necessary for taking control of their basal reader teacher's editions. Teachers who are in control of reading instruction are empowered to make informed instructional decisions about how, when, and why to use basal readers for providing reading instruction.

Teachers and administrators need to understand the basal reader's purpose to make informed instructional decisions.

ANATOMY OF THE BASAL READING APPROACH

Basal readers are typically composed of a set of core materials. These include (a) a student's text, (b) a teacher's edition, (c) a student's workbook, (d) a teacher's edition workbook, (e) supplemental practice exercises, (f) enrichment activities (usually both of these are in the form of masters that can be duplicated), (g) big books, (h) leveled readers, (i) phonic or decodable readers, and (j) end-of-unit or end-of-book tests. Other supplemental materials can be acquired at additional cost—picture cards, picture with letter cards, letter cards, word cards for display on word walls, pocket charts,

Focus on the core materials that compose basal readers.

Figure 6.5   A basal reading program usually includes a teacher's edition, a student edition, workbooks, and an array of supplemental materials

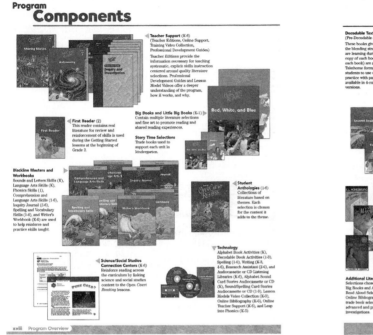

Source: *Open Court Reading: Heritage* (pp. xviii–xix), Level 5, Unit 3, Teacher's Edition, Copyright 2002 by SRA/McGraw-Hill.

*A **scope and sequence chart** describes in detail the range of concepts and skills to be taught in the basal program as well as the order in which these concepts and skills are to be presented.*

classroom trade-book libraries, big books, and technology, including videotapes, CD-ROMs, DVDs, and publisher World Wide Web sites on the Internet. In addition, many basal reading series provide a system for record keeping, management of the reading skills taught and mastered, and assessment. Figure 6.5 shows core components available for Scholastic's *Literacy Place* basal program for grades 3 to 6. Because many teachers will employ a basal series in a school reading program, we will describe each of the most basic basal components along with examples.

The Basal Teacher's Edition

For teachers, perhaps the most important part of the basal reading program is the **teacher's edition** because it contains instructional guidance and support (see Figure 6.6). For many new teachers, the basal teacher's edition is the most important source of initial professional development.

Within the pages of the teacher's edition, one usually finds three important features: (a) the scope and sequence chart of the particular basal reading program, (b) a

Figure 6.6 Example of a 2002 teacher's edition for *SRA Open Court Reading* basal series

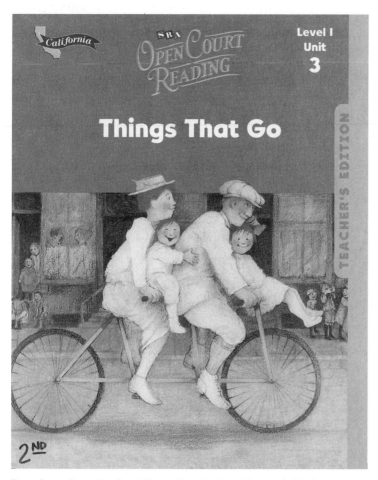

From *Open Court Reading: Things That Go,* Level 1, Unit 3, Teacher's Edition, Copyright 2002 by SRA/McGraw-Hill.

reduced version of the student's text, and (c) lesson plans (see Figures 6.7 and 6.8). A **scope and sequence chart** describes in great detail the range of skills and/or concepts to be taught in a basal program as well as the sequence in which these are to be presented during the school year. The entire student's text, shown as a reduced facsimile, is included for convenience in the teacher's edition. To save the teacher preparation time, lesson plans are included. Current basal readers typically design reading lessons around a modified sequence of the Directed Reading Thinking Activity (Stauffer, 1969).

It is important that teachers and administrators understand that the teacher's edition is a resource to be used with discrimination, not a script to be followed rigidly. Teachers and administrators should not allow the basal teacher's edition to dictate the reading program. Rather, teachers should be encouraged to decide what is and what is not appropriate in the teacher's edition for use with a particular group of children.

Most basal reader programs design reading lessons using a modified lesson framework known as the Directed Reading Thinking Activity.

Figure 6.7 A scope and sequence chart showing the range of skills to be taught in a basal program

Scope and Sequence

Reading

Level: K 1 2 3 4 5 6

Print/Book Awareness (Recognize and understand the conventions of print and books)
- Capitalization
- Constancy of Words
- End Punctuation
- Follow Left-to-right, Top-to-bottom
- Letter Recognition and Formation
- Page Numbering
- Picture/Text Relationship
- Quotation Marks
- Relationship Between Spoken and Printed Language
- Sentence Recognition
- Table of Contents
- Word Length
- Word Boundaries

Phonemic Awareness (Recognize discrete sounds in words)
- Oral Blending: Words/Word Parts
- Oral Blending: Initial Consonants/Blends
- Oral Blending: Final Consonants
- Oral Blending: Initial Vowels
- Oral Blending: Syllables
- Oral Blending: Vowel Replacement
- Segmentation: Initial Consonants/Blends
- Segmentation: Final Consonants
- Segmentation: Words/Word Parts
- Rhyming

How the Alphabet Works
- Letter Knowledge
- Letter Order (Alphabetic Order)
- Letter Sounds
- Sounds in Words

Phonics (Associate sounds and spellings to read words)
- Blending Sounds into Words
- Consonant Clusters
- Consonant Digraphs
- Consonant Sounds and Spellings
- Phonograms
- Syllables
- Vowel Diphthongs
- Vowels: Long Sounds and Spellings
- Vowels: r-controlled
- Vowels: Short Sounds and Spellings

Reading (continued)

Level: K 1 2 3 4 5 6

Comprehension Strategies
- Asking Questions/Answering Questions
- Making Connections
- Monitoring and Clarifying
- Monitoring and Adjusting Reading Speed
- Predicting/Confirming Predictions
- Summarizing
- Visualizing

Comprehension Skills
- Author's Point of View
- Author's Purpose
- Cause and Effect
- Classify and Categorize
- Compare and Contrast
- Drawing Conclusions
- Fact and Opinion
- Main Idea and Details
- Making Inferences
- Reality/Fantasy
- Sequence

Vocabulary
- Antonyms
- Comparatives/Superlatives
- Compound Words
- Connecting Words (Transition Words)
- Context Clues
- Contractions
- Figurative Language
- Greek and Latin Roots
- High-Frequency Words
- Homographs
- Homophones/Homonyms
- Idioms
- Inflectional Endings
- Irregular Plurals
- Multiple Meaning Words
- Multisyllabic Words
- Position Words
- Prefixes
- Question Words
- Base or Root Words
- Selection Vocabulary
- Suffixes
- Synonyms
- Time and Order Words (Creating Sequence)
- Utility Words (Colors, Classroom Objects, etc.)
- Word Families

Legend: ▒ Skills, strategies, and other teaching opportunities ☑ Formal, progress, or informal testing opportunities

48 Appendix   Appendix 49

From *Open Court Reading: Things That Go* (pp. 48–49), Level 1, Unit 3, Teacher's Edition, Copyright 2002 by SRA/McGraw-Hill.

Figure 6.8 Example of the internal pages from a 2002 teacher's edition for *SRA Open Court Reading* basal series

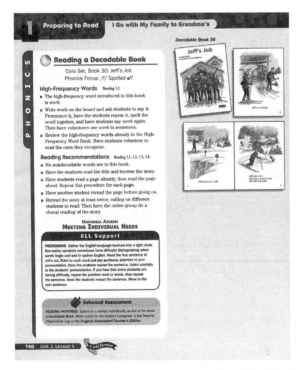

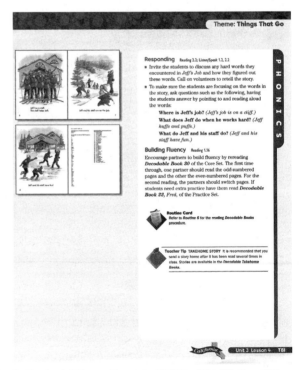

From *Open Court Reading: Things That Go* (pp. T80–T81), Level 1, Unit 3, Teacher's Edition, Copyright 2002 by SRA/McGraw-Hill.

The Student's Basal Text

The student's basal text is an anthology of original contemporary and classic stories, poems, news clips, and expository text selections. Some basal student selections have been created expressly for inclusion in the student's basal reader. Other selections have been adapted from contemporary and classic children's literature or trade books. High-quality artwork generally accompanies the selections. Interspersed throughout the student's text, one may also find poetry selections, jokes, riddles, puzzles, informational essays, and special skill and/or concept lessons. Some basal student texts contain questions children should be able to answer after reading the stories. Upper-level basal readers often contain a glossary of words that students can refer to when decoding new words or so that students can look up the meaning of new words found in the text.

Changes in basal student texts have resulted in a "more engaging basal" than those of two decades ago as judged by students, teachers, and reading experts (Hoffman et al., 1994; McCarthey et al., 1994).

Authentic Trade Literature

A close examination of quality children's literature included in the more recent basal reader revisions reveals few, if any, alterations of the authors' language or word choice. However, one disturbing publishing practice relates to cropping or cutting original artwork in children's picture book stories. Because of costs involved in the reproduction and permission for use of original artwork, basal publishers have engaged in cutting or moving the beautiful artwork that supports and sustains the text in many children's books (Reutzel & Larsen, 1995). The practice of cropping or cutting support artwork may be even more damaging than altering the text for young, emergent readers who may rely more heavily on the pictures for support throughout their initial readings of a new or unfamiliar text at early stages of reading development.

Information Texts

Duke (2000b, pp. 205) defined *information texts* as evidencing several features, including (a) a function to communicate information about the social or natural world; (b) factual content; (c) technical vocabulary; (d) classificatory or definitional material; (e) graphical elements like maps, graphs, and diagrams; (f) varying text structures, for example, cause and effect, problem and solution, compare and contrast, and so on; and (g) repetition of topical themes. Duke (2000) went on to investigate the experiences offered to children in 20 first-grade classrooms selected from very low and very high socioeconomic-status school districts with reading information texts. She found a scarcity of informational texts available in these classrooms—particularly in low socioeconomic-status schools. To compound the scarcity of information texts found in the classrooms, there were relatively few informational texts available in school libraries and on classroom walls and other display surfaces in the schools. As a result, young children in low socioeconomic classrooms read information texts 3.6 minutes per day on average.

In a more recent study, Moss and Newton (2001) investigated the amount of information text available in current second-, fourth-, and sixth-grade basal reading series. These researchers found that 16% to 20% of all selections in current basal readers could be classified as information texts. The preponderance of selections found in current basal readers continue to contain narrative or fiction (66%).

Notice what is included in the student's basal text.

Standards Note
Standard 5.2: The reading professional will use texts and trade books to stimulate interest, promote reading growth, foster appreciation for the written word, and increase the motivation of learners to read widely and independently for information, pleasure, and personal growth. As you read about the different types of reading materials in school reading programs, make a list of five things you can do with such a rich variety of resources to stimulate and motivate children and adolescents to read.

Although many basal readers include well-regarded children's literature, publishers continue to modify or adapt children's books in various ways for inclusion in basal readers.

Information texts need to play a larger role in beginning reading instruction.

Beginning Reading Texts

Controlling Word Difficulty and Frequency

Control over word difficulty in beginning reading texts presumably allows for the systematic introduction of a predetermined number of unfamiliar words in each new story (Hiebert, 1999; Hoffman, 2001). Control of word difficulty is usually achieved by using simpler words or words with fewer syllables in place of longer words and by shortening sentences. Basal publishers have for many years controlled the language of beginning reading texts by using simple, one-syllable words. Town and Holbrook (1857), in the *Progressive Reading* basal reading series, are among the earliest educators to explain the use of controlled texts in beginning reading texts:

Many beginning reading texts are designed to control for word difficulty and frequency.

> The authors, satisfied that the most simple language is best adapted to the class of pupils for whom this Reader is designed, have adhered, as strictly as possible, to the one-syllable system. They have departed from it only when necessary to avoid any stiffness of style, or weakness of expression, which might arise from too closely following it in every instance. (p. 3)

Compare the text from the following 1865 and 2000 basal reader beginning text as shown below:

1865
John stands by his father.
"I will be a good boy, father . . ."

2000
Bob went to the barn for Dad
Dad asked Bob to feed the pigs

Controlling the difficulty of words encountered in basal reader stories supposedly renders text less difficult to read. However, research by Pearson (1974) challenged the idea that shorter sentences are easier to read. Pearson found that short, choppy sentences are actually more difficult to read because explicit connecting or sequencing words such as *because, and, so, then, before,* and *after* are deleted from the text and consequently need to be inferred by the reader to comprehend the text.

Controlling Decoding Difficulty

In some basal reader programs, the earliest books, or *primers,* often contain reading selections known as **decodable text** (Adams, 1990a, 1990b; Beck, 1997; Foorman, Francis, Fletcher, Schatschneider, & Mehta, 1998; Grossen, 1997; Hiebert, 1999). Decodable texts are designed to reinforce the teaching of particular phonic elements such as short *a* by using highly controlled vocabulary in their stories (*Nan* and *Dan*). Decodable texts are frequently sold as supplemental books to school districts to augment basal reader instruction. A decodable text example is shown in the following excerpt (*Scholastic,* Book 14, Phonics Readers, pp. 2–7; Schreiber & Tuchman, 1997):

Decodable beginning reading texts are designed to provide texts for practicing previously taught phonics lessons.

The Big Hit

Who hid? Pig.
Who had a mitt? Pig.

Who did not sit?
Who did hit?
Up. Up. Up.
Who had a big hit? Pig.
Who slid? Pig did!

Although decodable texts can be useful for teaching phonics, children seldom encounter such contrived texts outside of school. As a consequence, the practice of controlling vocabulary to this extent continues to be questioned on the grounds that it tends to result in senseless or inconsiderate texts and tends to cause children to think that reading is primarily a decoding task rather than a search for meaning (Allington, 1997; Armbruster, 1984; Hiebert & Martin, 2001). The lack of real content or presence of a discernable story line in these decodable texts is suspected of causing children to quickly lose interest in reading if overused.

Controlling Language Patterns in Texts

Predictable texts are characterized by the repetition of a syntactic unit that can range from a phrase to a group of sentences, such as "run, run, as fast as you can, you can't catch me, I'm the Gingerbread man." Perhaps the best-known examples of patterned trade books are those authored and advocated by Bill Martin (1967), who wrote books such as *Brown Bear, Brown Bear, What Do You See?* These books have been found to decrease the control over new or unique words as well as adding the presence of engaging illustrations.

Other patterned books are published as part of a total reading program. For example, those published by the Wright Group, but originally from New Zealand, have been well accepted in the United States (Literacy 2000). Books in the *Sunshine Series* begin with simple repetitious phrases accompanied by strong picture or illustration supports, as in the story *"Look"*:

Predictable texts control for language patterns at the phrase and sentence levels.

Look said the birds, cats.
Look said the birds, dogs.
Look said the birds, bread.
Look said the birds, children.

You can clearly see that the difficulty of the language found in patterned beginning readers is still controlled, as in the past. The major difference is that the control is exerted at larger levels of text—phrases and sentences. This approach to beginning reading has produced some interesting research findings. Children who read patterned texts learned a group of sight words as quickly as children who read controlled word difficulty and frequency texts (Bridge, Winograd, & Haley, 1983). However, more recently, Johnston (1998) found that learning new words in first grade was improved when words were learned separate from the text rather than in the context of predictable texts. It seems that controlling text patterns also presents some limitations in providing the texts needed for effective beginning reading instruction.

Leveling Texts

With the availability of enormous varieties of beginning reading texts today (high-frequency words, decodable texts, children's authentic literature, and patterned texts), many teachers are in search of a way to provide a systematic and gradual introduction to beginning reading. Fountas and Pinnell (1999), in their book *Matching*

*Many classroom teach-
ers now use books lev-
eled from A to Z to
provide beginning read-
ing instruction.*

Books to Readers: Using Leveled Books in Guided Reading, K–3 describe the need for a way to level the collection of beginning reading materials in the classroom. Based on their work and that of others (e.g., Flynt & Cooter, 2004; Reutzel & Cooter, 2003), we present a guide titled Selecting Books for Reading Instruction: Reading Level Translations (see Table 6.1).

Many teachers in the primary grades rely heavily on a system for leveling books such as the one shown above to match students with texts that meet their instructional needs. Although leveled books can be an enormously helpful tool in beginning reading instruction, Szymusiak and Sibberson (2001), in *Beyond Leveled Books: Supporting Transitional Readers in Grades 2–5,* warn against the dangers of a "steady diet" of reading in leveled books. They say "When student's reading diet is exclusively a leveled one, their purpose for reading disappears. They read for us. They become eager to reach the next level, instead of being eager to learn more from what they are reading" (pp. 15–16). We know the leveling mania has gone too far when children must read from only leveled materials, when teachers will purchase materials for reading only based on levels, and when children and teachers no longer seek the goal of independence in reading through instruction in self-selection of appropriately challenging and interesting reading materials!

On the other hand, to abandon some controls on text difficulty seems to be, as Holdaway (1979) puts it, "sheer madness." Holdaway reminds us that many children continue to struggle to read authentic texts that are far too difficult for them to handle independently. It is clear that basal readers need to provide a balance of text types, including decodable, leveled, patterned, informational, and authentic story texts, in quantities that allow teachers to choose what works best with each child at various levels of reading development. And finally, Hiebert (1999) makes an impassioned call for authors to produce a new kind of beginning reading text modeled after the creations of Dr. Seuss in books such as *Green Eggs and Ham.* She states,

*Dr. Suess's books are
still viewed by many as
the best model texts for
engaging beginning
readers.*

> Over a decade ago, Anderson and others (1985) called for inventive writers to use Dr. Seuss as a model for creating engaging texts for beginning readers. This call needs to be extended again but, this time, with a clearer mandate—one that derives from a strong vision of what beginning readers need to learn. Such texts require thought to word density ratios and to the repetitions across as well as within texts of words that share phonetic elements. (p. 565)

The Workbook

In years past, the most used part of any basal reading series was the workbook (Osborn, 1985). In fact, if any part of the basal reading lesson was neglected, it was seldom the workbook pages (Durkin, 1984; Mason, 1983). Although clearly less the case today, workbook exercises remain firmly entrenched in many classrooms. It appears that some teachers, administrators, and publishers, as evidenced by the continued inclusion of workbook pages or worksheets as part and parcel of basal reading series, still see seat work as the real "work" of the school literacy program (Allington & Cunningham, 1996) (see Figure 6.9).

*Workbooks are one in-
structional tool that
can assist or inhibit
children's reading
progress.*

Workbook exercises aren't intended to supplant time for structured, well-planned reading instruction or independent reading. Rather, workbook exercises were intended for use by teachers and students to independently practice skills, strategies, and literary understandings previously instructed by the teacher. Also, workbook exercises are often used as a type of formative or ongoing "paper and pencil" assess-

Table 6.1 Selecting books for reading instruction: reading level translations*

Reading Levels (Traditional Designations)	Guided Reading (GR) Levels (extrapolated from Fountas & Pinnell, 1996, 2001)	Common Text Attributes	Exemplar Books & Publishers (Using GR levels)	Approximate Level of Reading Development
Preschool–Kindergarten (Readiness)	A	Wordless picture books	**A**= *Dog Day!* (Rigby)	**Emergent**
	B	Repeated phrases, text-picture matching, experiences common to readers, short (10–60 words)	**B**= *Fun with Hats* (Mondo)	
PP (Preprimer)	C D E	Same as above for B, but repeating phrases don't dominate the book, more language variation, by level E syntax becomes more like regular "book language"	**C**= *Brown Bear, Brown Bear* (Holt) **D**= *The Storm* (Wright Group) **E**= *The Big Toe* (Wright Group)	**Emergent → Early**
P (Primer)	F G	Longer sentences/less predictable text, new verb forms appear, story grammar elements continue over multiple pages, pictures provide only a little support	**F**= *A Moose Is Loose* (Houghton Mifflin) **G**= *More Spaghetti I Say* (Scholastic)	**Early**
Grade 1 **Grade 1 (late in the year)**	H I	As with F and G but there is a greater variety of words and content vocabulary, pictures provide very little to gaining meaning	**H**= *A Zoo Party* (Wright Group) **I**= *There's a Nightmare in My Closet* (Penguin)	**Early → Transitional**
Grade 2 (early) **Grade 2** **Grade 2 (late)**	J K L M	Longer stories with more complicated story grammar elements, varied vocabulary with rich meanings, common to have whole pages of text, more content (nonfiction) selections are in evidence	**J**= *The Boy Who Cried Wolf* (Scholastic) **K**= *Amelia Bedelia* (Harper & Row) **L**= *Cam Jansen and the Mystery of the Monster Movie* (Puffin) **M**= *How to Eat Fried Worms* (Dell)	**Transitional → Fluent**
Grade 3	N–P	Fewer illustrations, more complex nonfiction, complex sentences and challenging vocabulary, higher order thinking begins here	**N**= *Pioneer Cat* (Random House) **O**= *Whipping Boy* (Troll) **P**= *Amelia Earhart* (Dell)	**Fluent (Basic)** *(continued)*

Table 6.1 Selecting books for reading instruction: reading level translations—*continued*

Reading Levels (Traditional Designations)	Guided Reading (GR) Levels (extrapolated from Fountas & Pinnell, 1996, 2001)	Common Text Attributes	Exemplar Books & Publishers (Using GR levels)	Approximate Level of Reading Development
Grade 4	Q–S	Few illustrations, more complex language and concept load, higher order thinking is deepened, appearance of metaphor, topics are farther from student experiences, historical fiction is common, complex ideas are presented	**Q**= *Pony Pals: A Pony for Keeps* (Scholastic) **R**= *Hatchet* (Simon & Schuster) **S**= *Story of Harriet Tubman, Conductor of the Underground Railroad* (Scholastic)	Fluent → Extending to Content Texts
Grade 5	T–V	Fantasy, biographies, historical fiction, and realistic fiction are common; technical figures are used; plots and subplots in fiction, print is smaller (200–300 words per page)	**T**= *Harry Potter and the Sorcerer's Stone* (Scholastic) **U**= *Crocodilians* (Mondo) **V**= *The Riddle of the Rosetta Stone* (Harper)	Fluent → Extending to Content Texts
Grade 6	W–Z	Increasing book length and complexity; science fiction requires more technical knowledge; satire, irony, and higher-order thinking texts sometimes deal with required regularly, content controversial subjects	**W**= *Maya Angelou: Greeting the Morning* (Millbrook) **X**= *Where the Red Fern Grows* (Bantam/Doubleday) **Y**= *The Giver* (Bantam/Doubleday) **Z**= *The Watcher* (Simon & Schuster)	Fluent → Extending to Content Texts
Grade 7	—	Progressively increasing concept load, complexity, and sentence length	*Holes* (Farrar Straus & Giroux)	Fluent → Extending to Content Texts
Grade 8	—	Progressively increasing concept load, complexity, and sentence length	*The House of the Scorpion* (Atheneum)	Fluent → Extending to Content Texts

*Adapted from *The Flynt/Cooter Reading Inventory for the Classroom, 5th Edition*, by E.S. Flynt and R.B. Cooter (2004). Upper Saddle River, NJ: Merrill/Prentice Hall, and *Strategies for Reading Assessment and Instruction: Helping Every Child Succeed*, 2nd Ed., by Reutzel, D.R., & Cooter, R.B. (2003). Upper Saddle River, NJ: Merrill/Prentice-Hall. [E TB.08.001]

Figure 6.9 Many basal reading programs still integrate workbook, seat work, and practice sheets devoted to skill practice into the basal reading program

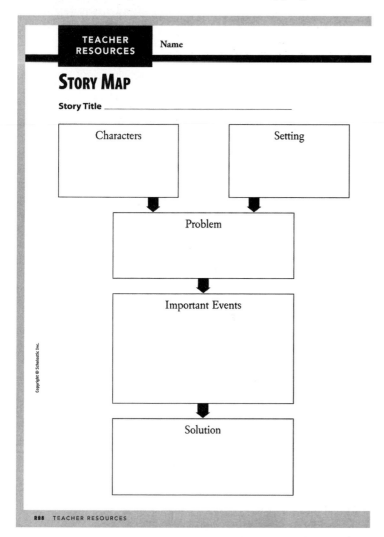

From *Scholastic Literacy Place: Problem Patrol* (p. R88), 2000, New York: Scholastic. Copyright 2000 by Scholastic, Inc. Reprinted by permission.

ment. In addition to these twin purposes, many teachers also use workbook exercises to manage, direct, or focus student activity in independent learning centers when the teacher is actively working with small groups of children in teacher-guided reading groups. Thus, used in these ways, workbook exercises play at least three distinct roles in classrooms—practice, assessment, and management.

Past research revealed that students spend up to 70% of the time allocated for reading instruction, or 49 minutes per day, in independent practice or completing worksheets, like those found in workbooks, whereas less than 10% of the total reading instructional time, or about 7 to 8 minutes per day, is devoted to silent reading in the primary grades. In fact, publishers indicate that there is an insatiable demand for worksheets (Anderson, Hiebert, Scott, & Wilkinson, 1985). More recent studies

The subject of testing and evaluation will be discussed in depth in Chapter 7.

indicate that many teachers assign or provide time for only small amounts of real reading and writing, in some cases less than 5 minutes per day (Knapp, 1991)! Jachym, Allington, and Broikou (1989) and Allington and Cunningham (1996) reported that seat work, that is, using worksheets, is displacing many of the more important aspects of reading instruction, such as the acquisition of good books and time spent reading. Based on these findings, it seems obvious that workbooks have been misused and overused. However, when teachers judiciously select workbook exercises to support and reinforce concepts and skills provided during teacher-guided instruction, students benefit from valuable practice and feedback on their progress in relation to specific reading skills, strategies, and literary understandings. Dole, Osborn, and Lehr (1990, pp. 8–15) provided six guidelines for assessing the worth of workbook and worksheet-type reading tasks in the *Workbooks* subtext for the *Basal Reading Programs: Adoption Guidelines Project.*

To determine the value of workbook tasks, notice the six principles for evaluating workbook tasks.

Some Guidelines for Workbook Tasks:

1. When analyzing the *content of workbook tasks,* look for tasks that:
   - Are integrated with the lessons in the teacher's manual and with the student textbook
   - Relate to the most important (and workbook-appropriate) instruction in the lessons
   - Are based on the reading selections
   - Use vocabulary that is from current or previous lessons
   - Increase in difficulty as grade level increases
2. When analyzing the *content of workbook task design,* look for tasks that require:
   - Students to read all possible choices before selecting an answer
   - Student responses that can be judged correct or incorrect
   - Student responses that indicate to the teacher what the student knows
   - Students be able to successfully complete part two of the task without successfully completing part one
3. When analyzing the *practice and review* tasks, look for tasks that provide:
   - Sufficient practice
   - Independent practice
   - Extra practice
   - Systematic review
4. When analyzing *instructional language,* look for tasks that:
   - Use language consistent with the rest of the program
   - Are accompanied by brief explanations of purpose or explanatory titles that students understand
   - Have clear and easy-to-follow instruction, with attention to consistency, sentence length, and directional steps
5. When evaluating *reading and writing responses,* look for tasks that:
   - Provide opportunities for students to respond in their own words
   - Provide opportunities for students to apply several comprehension strategies or decoding skills in one task
6. When evaluating the *considerateness to students,* look for:
   - Repeated use of task formats
   - Consistent responses
   - Occasional tasks that are fun
   - Few or no nonfunctional tasks

Workbooks can be a valuable resource for teachers and students when used correctly. On the other hand, when they are overrelied on or misused, workbook exercises can be a debilitating deterrent to students' reading progress.

Assessment

Although workbook exercises can be used for formative assessment of reading skill, strategy, and literary understandings development, most basal reading series provide end-of-unit or end-of-book tests for summative evaluation of student learning. These tests are generally criterion-referenced tests, which means that the items measured on these tests are directly related to the specific skills, strategies, or literary concepts taught in that unit, level, or book. Most basal readers now provide suggestions for designing individual assessment portfolios for each student, including the use of running records. Teachers who want to present students' reading demonstrations to parents as evidence for a reading portfolio will need to obtain audiotapes of students' reading and analyze them using something like "running records" analysis for the foreseeable future. As the stakes are raised higher and higher for performance of standardized assessment measures, many current basal readers are correlating skills, strategies, and literary understanding taught with nationally published standardized tests (see Figure 6.10).

Figure 6.10 Many basal teacher's editions show how program elements correspond with nationally published standardized tests

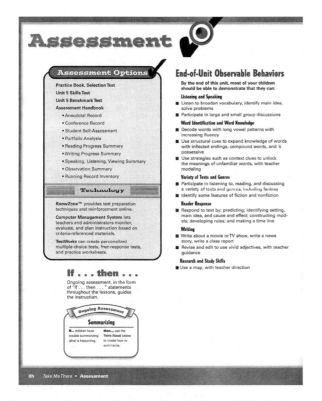

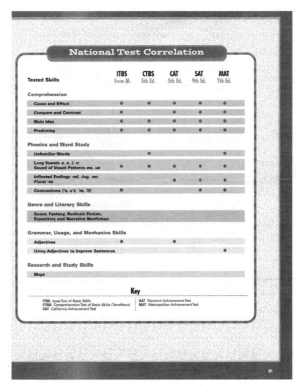

From *Scott Foresman Reading: Take Me There,* 2000 (Teacher's ed., Grade 1, Volume 5, pp. 8h–8i). Copyright © 2000 by Addison-Wesley Educational Publishers, Inc. Reprinted by permission of Pearson Education, Inc.

Just as workbook exercises can be abused, so it is with tests. Tests should provide teachers information about the quantity and quality of children's literacy learning to inform, shape, and direct future instructional choices and selection of interventions. Test results should not be used to label children or embarrass teachers. Two poignant examples of the misuse of test data are found in the books *First Grade Takes a Test* (Cohen, 1980) and *Testing Miss Malarkey* (Finchler, 2001). No single test score should ever form the basis for making important decisions about children's learning or their teachers' competence. Administrators and teachers must be extremely cautious in the use and interpretation of single literacy (reading and writing) test scores.

Record Keeping

An **instructional management system** allows teachers to keep accurate records from year to year regarding each child's progress through the adopted basal reading program's scope and sequence of skills. Maintaining records to document teaching and learning is an important part of accountability. Most basal reading series provide a means for keeping records on children's progress through the skills outlined in the scope and sequence chart of the basal. Most often, the methods of assessment specified are paper-and-pencil testing or worksheet administration. The scores obtained on these exercises are entered into a master list or record available today in CD-ROM form, which follows the children throughout their elementary years. Such a skills management system allows teachers to keep accurate records from year to year regarding each child's progress. Unfortunately, some teachers spend inordinate amounts of time keeping records of this kind, which leads to a most undesirable condition, captured by Pearson (1985):

> The model implicit in the practices of [this teacher] was that of a manager—[a] person who arranged materials, texts, and the classroom environment so learning could occur. But the critical test of whether learning did occur was left up to the child as s/he interacted with the materials.
>
> Children practiced applying skills; if they learned them, fine; we always had more skills for them to practice; if they did not, fine; we always had more worksheets and duplicating sheets for the same skill. And the most important rule in such a mastery role was that practice makes perfect, leading to the ironic condition that children spent most of their time on precisely that subset of skills they performed least well. (p. 736)

To this we would like to add the comment that, disturbingly, teachers under this model spent the bulk of their time running off worksheets, assigning, correcting, and recording rather than guiding, demonstrating, or interacting with children or books. Although increasingly elegant with the addition of CD-ROM technology, record keeping should go well beyond keeping track of worksheet evaluation. Fortunately, many basal readers now recognize this fact and include process and product measures of children's reading and reading habits.

In summary, basal reading series are typically composed of a core of three elements—teacher's edition, student text, and workbooks—as well as a host of available kits, charts, cards, tests, technology, additional practice exercises, and assessment/record-keeping systems to supplement the core elements of the basal series. In an effort to compete with trade-book publishers, basal publishers are also producing big books to complement the already expansive list of purchasable options listed previously. Teachers should be careful not to accept these new "basal" big books without careful examination. In some cases, big books published by basal companies are not big books at all—they are big basals!

Although the basal reader approach offers a resource for helping teachers provide systematic and sequenced reading instruction throughout the elementary and middle grades, teachers must nonetheless be careful to supplement this core program with trade books, silent reading time, group sharing, extensions of reading into writing, speaking, drama, music, and so on and to provide individual assessment of children's reading progress, behaviors, and attitudes. When this goal is understood and achieved, basal readers can provide valuable literacy tools and resources to schools, administrators, teachers, and children. In addition, basals provide a safety net for many teachers, novice and experienced, because they help teachers make personal and professional growth toward implementing balanced, comprehensive reading instruction.

Notice how teachers can supplement the basal reader core program.

PRODUCTION AND ORGANIZATION OF BASAL READERS

Basal reading series are owned by large, diversified business corporations and are produced by a variety of publishing houses from coast to coast. A chief editor oversees the production of a basal reader with the assistance of a senior author team, a group of individuals in the field of reading who are known and respected as experts (see Figure 6.11).

Basal reading programs are often recognized and known by the name of the publishing house that produces the basal. Over the past 20 years, the number of basal publishing companies that have survived the intense business competition, demanding and sometimes invasive state standards, and the vicissitudes of change have dwindled from over 20 companies to half a dozen or less by the time this book was published:

Basal reading programs are typically known by the name of the publishing house that produces the basal.

Harcourt Brace

SRA McGraw-Hill

Houghton Mifflin

Scholastic

Scott Foresman

Minor revisions of basal readers occur every few years; major revision cycles occur every 5 or 6 years. Major revisions are usually slated for completion during the same year Texas and California consider basal readers for statewide adoption. Consequently, the "Texas and California" effect is known to exert considerable influence on the content and quality of new basal readers (Farr, Tulley, & Powell, 1987; 6th, 1981). In reading circles, one often hears the axiom, "as Texas and California go, so goes the nation."

Strengths and Weaknesses of Basal Readers

Although basal readers continue to be the mainstay of reading instruction in American schools, the basal reader approach to reading instruction has not gone unscrutinized. Criticisms of basal readers have ranged from the cultural to the literary, from

Figure 6.11 Title page showing basal authoring team names

TEACHER'S EDITION

SCHOLASTIC

LITERACY PLACE®

UNIT 2

Problem Patrol

LITERACY PLACE AUTHORS

CATHY COLLINS BLOCK
Professor, Curriculum and Instruction, Texas Christian University

LINDA B. GAMBRELL
Professor, Education, University of Maryland at College Park

VIRGINIA HAMILTON
Children's Author; Winner of the Newbery Medal, the Coretta Scott King Award and the Laura Ingalls Wilder Lifetime Achievement Award

DOUGLAS K. HARTMAN
Associate Professor of Language and Literacy, University of Pittsburgh

TED S. HASSELBRING
Co-Director of the Learning Technology Center and Professor in the Department of Special Education at Peabody College, Vanderbilt University

ADRIA KLEIN
Professor, Reading and Teacher Education, California State University at San Bernardino

HILDA MEDRANO
Dean, College of Education, University of Texas-Pan American

GAY SU PINNELL
Professor, School of Teaching and Learning, College of Education, Ohio State University

D. RAY REUTZEL
Provost/Academic Vice President, Southern Utah University

DAVID ROSE
Founder and Executive Director of the Center for Applied Special Technology (CAST); Lecturer, Harvard University Graduate School of Education

ALFREDO SCHIFINI
Professor, School of Education, Division of Curriculum Instruction, California State University, Los Angeles

DELORES STUBBLEFIELD SEAMSTER
Principal, N.W. Harllee Elementary, Dallas, Texas; Consultant on Effective Programs for Urban Inner City Schools

QUALITY QUINN SHARP
Author and Teacher-Educator, Austin, Texas

JOHN SHEFELBINE
Professor, Language and Literacy Education, California State University at Sacramento

GWENDOLYN Y. TURNER
Associate Professor of Literacy Education, University of Missouri at St. Louis

From *Scholastic Literacy Place: Problem Patrol,* 2000, New York: Scholastic. Copyright 2000 by Scholastic, Inc. Reprinted by permission.

the linguistic to the instructional. Because basal readers are used in over 90% of American classrooms, most teachers will inevitably have occasion to make use of the basal reader approach to reading instruction (Baumann, 1993; Flood & Lapp, 1986; Hoffman et al., 1994; McCarthy et al., 1994; Wade & Moje, 2000; Zintz & Maggart, 1989). To make instructional decisions about how, when, and why to use the basal, teachers and administrators must know the strengths and weaknesses of the basal reader approach to reading.

Basal readers contain an organized and systematic plan for teachers to consult in planning reading instruction.

In defense of basal reading series, it must be said that basals possess certain positive qualities that contribute to their enduring popularity in American classrooms. For example, basal readers contain an organized and systematic plan for teachers to consult. Basal readers published more recently often provide teaching suggestions from which comprehensive literacy teachers make decisions about when and how to teach skills that are important to authentic reading-related behaviors. In addition, basal readers are sequenced from grade to grade, thus providing for continuous reading instruction throughout the elementary school years and for continuity both within grades and across grade levels.

The readily available tests and practice exercises found in the workbooks save teachers enormous amounts of time in materials preparation. Reading skills are gradually introduced, practiced, and reviewed through the plan provided in the scope and sequence of the basal. The lesson plans found ready-made in the teacher's editions also save teachers much preparation time. A variety of literary genres is available to teachers and students in current basal readers. The structure provided in basal readers is often very reassuring for novice or beginning teachers. Administrators can manage and provide accountability evidence more easily by adopting and using basal reading series. In short, basal readers possess several characteristics that teachers and administrators find helpful and worthwhile.

Readily available tests and practice exercises found in the basal workbooks save teachers enormous amounts of time in materials preparation.

Advantages of the Basal Reader Approach*

- A sequenced curriculum of instruction is provided by grade level and across grade levels. Instruction is arranged to provide for both initial instruction and a systematic review of skills taught.
- A continuous arrangement of instructional skills and concepts from grade to grade is supplied.
- To save teachers time, a completely prepared set of stories, instructional directions and activities, instructional practice materials, and assessment and management devices is available.
- Student texts are arranged in ascending difficulty.
- Reading skills are gradually introduced and systematically reviewed.
- Teachers are provided lesson plans.
- Students are exposed to a variety of literary genres.
- Organization and structure of basal readers are helpful to beginning teachers just learning about the reading curriculum.
- A variety of beginning reading texts and books are typically available, including trade book libraries, big books, leveled books, and decodable books.
- Organization and structure of basal reading programs are reassuring to administrators and school patrons that important reading skills are being taught.

Limitations of the Basal Reader Approach

- Some new decodable and leveled selections are dull and repetitious.
- Cropping illustrations from original children's trade books renders selections less engaging for readers of all ages.
- Skill instruction is rarely applied in or related to decoding the text or comprehending the selection's content.
- The basal lesson design in teacher's editions very often fails to relate one part of the lesson, such as vocabulary introduction, to subsequent parts of the reading lesson, such as story comprehension discussion.
- Stories often do not relate to students' interests.
- The format of basal readers (hard bound and thick book) is often less appealing than the format of trade books (soft bound and thin book).
- Censorship by special interest groups leads to the selection of content that contain little real subject matter content, that deals with few real-life applications, or that presents little content that advocates ethical living in society.
- Teacher's editions seldom contain useful directions on how to teach/model reading comprehension strategies.

Although popular, basal readers are not without significant deficiencies.

*Based on "Understanding and Using Basal Readers Effectively" by D. R. Reutzel in *Effective Strategies for Teaching Reading* (p. 259), edited by B. Hayes, 1991, Needham Heights, MA: Allyn and Bacon. Copyright 1991 by D. R. Reutzel. Reprinted by permission.

- A rigid adherence to the basal reader leaves little room for teacher creativity and decision making.
- The grading or leveling of basal readers promotes the use of static homogeneous grouping strategies.
- Management demands of the basal program can become so time consuming that little time remains for teachers to reflect on the quality of reading instruction and for students to self-select reading materials.
- Use of the basal reader approach has traditionally been associated with the use of "round robin" reading and ability grouping. Insisting that all children simultaneously attend to the same selection while another child reads orally encourages such practices.

Although popular, basal readers are not without significant deficiencies. Many of the objections voiced about the stories found in the basal readers can be traced to publishers' efforts to produce decodable texts or leveled books.

Basal readers have improved significantly in recent years.

Basal readers have improved significantly in recent years. Although in the past narrative selections in students' basal readers tended in the early grades to be repetitive and boring, recent basal readers have included more high-quality children's literature. However, some are concerned that high-quality literature is beyond the ability of many students to handle independently (Holdaway, 1979). Thus, recent trends have included demands for decodable and leveled texts (Allington, 1997). Although the variety of selections found in basal readers may be considerable, some educators are concerned with what appears to be genre and topic flitting in basal readers. Because of this criticism, most recently published basal readers now organize their selections into similar genres, topic/text pairs (fiction and information), or themed units. Recent basal readers have included more generous exposure to information, nonfiction, or expository selections in comparison to those of generations past.

Basal readers have also been criticized for poorly representing societal groups and concerns. This problem is often attributable to the censorship of various special interest groups that enter into the **basal reader adoption** process, particularly in states that adopt statewide (Marzano, 1993, 1994). Basal teacher's editions continue to be assailed for poor instructional design and content (Ryder & Graves, 1994; Wade & Moje, 2000). Durkin (1981a) found that many teacher's editions contained an abundance of questions and evaluative activities mislabeled as instructional activities. What was labeled as instruction was often found to be nothing more than an assessment exercise. Reutzel and Daines (1987a) found that basal reading skills lessons seldom supported or even related to the selections to be read in the basals. These conclusions supported Mason's (1983) findings that teacher's reading instruction was, more often than not, unrelated to the text that children would be asked to read. In another study the same year, Reutzel and Daines (1987b) reported that even the parts of the reading units had little relation to one another. Although these conditions have improved somewhat in the newer generations of basal readers, with stories that are generally more engaging (Hoffman et al., 1994), problems persist.

Despite limitations, basal reader programs can provide a foundation for classroom reading instruction.

Despite these limitations, the basal "baby" simply cannot be thrown out with the bath water (Baumann, 1993; McCallum, 1988; Winograd, 1989). Basal readers have filled an important niche for many teachers and will likely continue to do so well into the future. As they await continued improvements in the basal, teachers armed with an understanding of their strengths and weaknesses, as described here, can enjoy their benefits while overcoming or avoiding their weaknesses.

Organization of the Basal Reader

Basal readers are designed to take children through a series of books, experiences, and activities toward increasingly sophisticated reading behaviors. Each basal series typically provides several readers or books of reading selections at each level. For example, the *Scott Foresman: Reading* (2000) basal provides the following books organized by theme for each grade level:

Grade 1:	*Good Times We Share*
	Take a Closer Look
	Let's Learn Together
	Favorite Things Old and New
	Take Me There
	Surprise Me!
Grade 2:	*You + Me = Special*
	Zoom In!
	Side by Side
	Ties Through Time
	All Aboard!
	Just Imagine
Grade 3:	*Finding My Place*
	The Whole Wide World
	Getting the Job Done
	From Past to Present
	Are We There Yet?
	Imagination.kids
Grade 4:	*Focus on Family*
	A Wider View
	Keys to Success
	Timeless Stories
	Other Times, Other Places
	Express Yourself!
Grade 5:	*Relating to Others*
	My World and Yours
	A Job Well Done
	Time and Time Again
	Traveling On
	Think of It!
Grade 6:	*Discovering Ourselves*
	The Living Earth
	Goals Great and Small
	The Way We Were—The Way We Are
	Into the Unknown
	I've Got It!

Important features to be found in current teacher's editions are (a) philosophical statements, (b) skills overview for the unit, (c) classroom routines, (d) accommodating special needs, (e) assessment ties to national standards and tests, (f) technology information, (g) themes, (h) projects, (i) assessment benchmarks, (j) glossary,

(k) bibliography, and (l) a scope and sequence chart. The scope and sequence chart is a year-by-year curricular plan, usually in chart form, that includes the instructional objectives and skills associated with a specific basal reading program. Objectives and skills are arranged in the scope and sequence chart by categories and grade levels. It is in the scope and sequence chart that teachers learn about the objectives of the basal program and the sequence of lessons designed to accomplish the objectives.

Most contemporary basal readers are organized into **themed units,** with several selections organized around a selected theme or topic; still others are organized into arbitrarily divided units of instruction. Most basal readers follow a somewhat *modified* version of the Directed Reading Thinking Activity (DRTA) format developed by Stauffer in 1969. This format can be represented in eight discrete parts or steps in the lesson:

*Some contemporary basal readers are organized into **themed units.***

1. Activate prior knowledge and building background
2. Skill lessons on phonics, spelling, vocabulary, and comprehension
3. Previewing and predicting
4. Setting the purpose
5. Guiding the reading
6. Confirm predictions
7. Comprehension discussion questions
8. Skill instruction and practice in oral language, writing, grammar, phonics, handwriting, comprehension, and fluency
9. Enrichment ideas and projects

Lessons are arranged for teachers into a daily planner. It is not intended that teachers will use all of the resources of the basal reader teacher's edition but that they will select those resources on a daily basis that best suit the needs of the children in the classroom. We remind our readers emphatically that basal teacher's editions are *resources* to augment the teacher's knowledge of the reading process and the needs of his or her students, *not* a script to be followed without judgment, skill, and decision making.

A Closer Look at the Anatomy of a Basal Reading Lesson

Activating Prior Experience and Building Background

Activities intended to activate prior experiences and build background involve the teacher and students in a discussion of the topic and unfamiliar concepts to be encountered in the story. Beck (1986, 1995, 1996) directs teachers to focus discussion on the central problem, a critical concept, or an interview with or questioning of the author (see Chapter 4) or to give voice to the story characters. This segment of the basal lesson plan provides students with the necessary lead-in experiences, discussion, and knowledge to facilitate comprehension of the story content. Because comprehension of a story is at least partially dependent on owning the meaning of specific unfamiliar words, teachers are often encouraged in basal reading lessons to focus on activities designed to help students understand how new vocabulary words will be used in the context of the story.

Notice what teachers should focus on when building story background.

Skill Lessons

This part of the basal reading lesson is designed for teaching selected lessons on phonics, vocabulary, or comprehension skills to prepare students to read the theme selection successfully. If a phonics lesson is provided, it will focus on a new phonics element that is necessary to strengthen students' understanding of sound–symbol relationships to facilitate the development of automaticity in decoding. Likewise, if a vocabulary lesson is provided, the teacher will help children anticipate unfamiliar vocabulary terms to be encountered in the upcoming text. And if a comprehension lesson is provided, it will help children anticipate the structure of the upcoming text and any potential challenges or obstacles that may interfere with understanding the selection.

Skill lessons are provided in most contemporary basal readings for each of the essential elements of reading instruction.

Previewing and Predicting

This segment of the basal lesson focuses on helping children develop the ability to survey a text before reading it to determine how the author has arranged and presented the information or story. Typically, the teacher will guide children through the text by reading the story title, heading, subheadings, and looking at the pictures. Students are often encouraged to make predictions from the title, the subheads, and the pictures.

Basal reader lessons also provide teachers guidance for previewing, predicting, setting purposes for reading, guiding reading for selections, and integrating the basal reader with other themes, topics, or content areas.

Setting the Purpose for Reading

This part of the basal reading lesson is devoted to developing a goal or objective for reading and is intended to provide motivation and purpose for reading the story. Teachers are directed to help students read to find the answer to a specific question. Such questions can emanate from (a) the teacher, (b) the student, or (c) both. Many current basal teacher's manuals provide teachers hints on how to help children develop their own, self-questioning competencies. Some basal teacher's editions also provide information to teachers about how to develop students' abilities to "talk back to the text" or "question the author," as described more fully in Chapter 5.

Guiding the Reading of the Selection

During this phase of the basal reading lesson, students read to a predetermined point in the selection. The students are to answer questions or to confirm their predictions. Many teacher's editions suggest that the reading be silent reading. Some teachers, however, especially primary grade teachers, ask that children read stories orally to assess word-decoding abilities and use of decoding and comprehension strategies.

Confirm Predictions

Students review personal or class predictions with the teacher. During this part of the basal lesson, students may be asked to reread portions of the text to justify their predictions. Once the entire selection has been read, a comprehension discussion ensues.

Comprehension Discussion Questions

After reading, students discuss the basal selection by answering questions posed by the teacher. Questions for conducting comprehension discussions are found interspersed throughout and following the story in most teacher's editions.

Skill Instruction and Practice

Skill instruction, application, and practice focus on developing readers' skills in several areas of the reading curriculum: (a) decoding, (b) vocabulary, (c) grammar, (d) writing, (e) handwriting, (f) spelling, (g) fluency, (h) oral language, and (i) comprehension. Individual skill lessons from each of these areas are usually found following the story in the teacher's edition. After instruction and practice, students practice the skills on black line masters or workbook sheets.

Theme Projects

Theme projects bring closure to the topic of study and focus students' efforts on research or creative projects that help them synthesize the information they have gleaned from reading into a personally meaningful product. For example, if children are studying about families, they may be guided into taking an oral history of their grandparents or other senior citizens. They would tape record, transcribe, revise, edit, illustrate, and share the stories of these elderly significant others in their lives and communities.

INSTRUCTIONAL PLANS FOR MORE EFFECTIVELY USING THE BASAL TEACHER'S EDITION

As stated previously, basal readers were never intended to displace the teacher's instructional decision making in the classroom or to supplant opportunities for students to read a wide range of literary genres (Winograd, 1989). Rather, basal readers were intended as an instructional resource to help teachers provide basic, sequenced reading instruction for a wide range of student abilities (Squire, 1989). Although some teachers are content to sample or follow the teacher's edition, effective reading teachers are aware of alternative and research-based reading lesson frameworks for modifying the basal teacher's edition. Because this is often difficult for novice and some experienced teachers, we offer detailed examples of how you can plan reading lessons using a variety of reading lesson frameworks within the familiar confines of the basal reader teacher's edition.

Reconciled Reading Lesson

*The **reconciled reading lesson** (RRL) reverses the traditional basal lesson instructional sequence.*

Most teachers recognize the importance of activating personal experiences and building adequate and accurate background knowledge to prepare readers to successfully process text. The **reconciled reading lesson** (RRL) (Reutzel, 1985a, 1991) is useful for this purpose. (However, with texts for which students already possess adequate background knowledge, RRL may unnecessarily postpone reading the selection. In this case, we recommend using the DRTA.) The RRL recommends that teachers begin the basal lesson with the information at the end of most lessons—the language enrichment and curriculum extenders—and then work backward to vocabulary assessment as the last element in the lesson (Reutzel, 1985a). To begin an RRL, turn to the language enrichment and extension section of the reading lesson in the basal teacher's edition. The activities suggested in this part of the lesson are often excellent for building background knowledge and discussing unfamiliar concepts. In one major basal reader, for example, a lesson on the story "Stone Soup" (Brown, 1947) suggested that teachers make stone soup and have children write a recipe from their experience. Although these ideas could be used as excellent extensions of the story, the activities may be just as appropriate for background building before reading rather than for enrichment after reading.

The second modification that the RRL proposes for the basal lesson sequence centers on the place of reading skill instruction. The RRL recommends teaching reading skills before reading and then relating reading skill instruction to the selection to be read. If this is not possible, teachers should select an appropriate reading skill that relates to the selection. By relating skills to the stories, teachers help children understand that reading skills are to be applied during reading. For example, the vocabulary skill of categorizing words was to be taught with the story in one reading lesson in a major basal reader; however, the words selected for the vocabulary-categorizing activity were unrelated to the words in the story. One must ask the question, Why teach this vocabulary skill in relation to a contrived list of words or using an instructional text snippet (Pearson, 1989a) when the skill could more aptly be applied to words taken from the story itself?

The RRL recommends teaching reading skills before reading and relating them to the selection to be read.

The decoding skill lesson associated with another basal story dealt with teaching children the vowel digraph /oa/. A quick glance over the text revealed that only one word in the entire text contained that vowel digraph. Even worse, the stories preceding and following the story in the lesson contained no words with the /oa/ vowel digraph. This is just one demonstration of the findings that basal lessons seldom relate skill instruction to the selections children are expected to read (Reutzel & Daines, 1987b). Because of this failure on the part of some publishers, the teacher may often need to make explicit the relation between the skills taught and how (or if) these skills can be applied during the reading.

If the story does not lend itself to the reading skills to be taught, then adapt skill instruction to the story. For example, for the story *Good Work, Amelia Bedelia* by Peggy Parish (1963), an appropriate comprehension skill to select for instruction would be understanding figurative or idiomatic expressions. If the teacher's edition did not direct teachers to focus on this skill, the professional decision could be made to teach the prescribed skill lesson—such as getting the main idea—later in the year and to teach figurative or idiomatic expressions with this story. Instructional decisions such as these are characteristic of transitional teachers' taking control of their teacher's editions. In summary, the RRL recommends that skill instruction be taught before reading and be explicitly related to and applied in reading.

If the story does not lend itself to the reading skills to be taught, then adapt skill instruction to the story.

The third step in the RRL involves a discussion of the story intended to foster comprehension. The typical organization of the basal reader teacher's edition provides for comprehension discussion through a list of comprehension questions following the selection in the teacher's edition. The RRL recommends that guided questioning, discussion, and prediction be included as an integral part of the prereading phase of the reading lesson. Questions usually discussed after reading may be discussed before reading. Children are encouraged to predict answers to the questions before reading and then to read to confirm their predictions. Such a practice can help students selectively focus their attention during reading.

Research has shown that the RRL significantly increases students' comprehension and recall of text over the traditional DRA as well as other alternative lesson frameworks.

The remainder of the RRL should be very brief. Students read the selection in the basal. Postreading activities focus primarily on assessment of comprehension and skill application. Questions can be asked, such as, Did the students comprehend? How well did students predict answers to the prequestions? Did students revise their predictions as a result of the reading? Do the students understand the meanings of the new vocabulary words as they were used in the context of the story? In short, assessment is the primary purpose for postreading activities in the RRL. Prince and Mancus (1987) and Thomas and Readence (1988) reported that using the RRL significantly increased students' comprehension and recall of text over the traditional DRA and other alternative lesson frameworks.

Reciprocal Questioning

ReQuest, or **reciprocal questioning,** developed by Anthony Manzo (1969), is a structure for presenting reading lessons in which teachers and children silently read parts of a text and exchange the role of asking and answering questions about that text. The ReQuest procedure can be used with individuals or with groups. The process begins with the teacher and students reading a preassigned portion of a text silently. Both the teacher and the students close the book after reading. Next, the students ask the teacher questions about the text, and the teacher answers these questions clearly and accurately. By answering the students' questions first, the teacher can demonstrate for students effective question-answering behaviors. Next, the teacher and students reverse roles. The teacher and students begin by reading the next part of the text and then close their books. At this point, students try to answer the questions the teacher asks. At some point in the lesson, usually predetermined by the teacher, students are asked to predict the potential events and outcome of the remainder of the text to be read. A list of predictions is constructed through discussion and shown at the board. Students read the remaining text to confirm or correct their predictions. After reading, the teacher leads a discussion to reconsider the original predictions (see Figure 6.12).

Because children are encouraged to construct their own questions for reading, they become active readers to the extent that they (a) select their own purposes for reading and (b) engage in a proven reading strategy involving sampling, prediction, and reading to confirm or correct predictions. ReQuest involves teachers and students equally in the roles of participant and observer in the lesson rather than allowing children spend their time looking on as passive observers. As a result, ReQuest helps children to learn how to compose and answer questions about text through active observation and participation in the reading lesson.

*ReQuest, or **reciprocal questioning,** is a structure for presenting reading lessons in which teachers and children silently read parts of a text and exchange the role of asking and answering questions about that text.*

CONTRASTING DIFFERING PHILOSOPHICAL EMPHASES IN PUBLISHED BASAL READING SERIES

Although current basal readers are alike in many surface respects, they often differ with respect to authoring teams' and publishing/corporate beliefs about how children should be taught to read. Some basal readers, for example, emphasize the acquisition and development of early, automatic decoding skills. Basal reading series created from a decoding emphasis focus first on helping children acquire and apply word-identification skills in decodable texts and then later apply these skills in more authentic texts.

Figure 6.12   Example ReQuest Lesson

Book title: *Franklin in the Dark* (Bourgeois & Clark, 1986).

Read Text: "Franklin could slide down a riverbank all by himself. He could count forwards and backwards. He could even zip zippers and button buttons. But Franklin was afraid of small, dark places and that was a problem because. . . ." (p. 1)
Student 1 question: What's the turtle's name?
Teacher answer: His name is Franklin.
Student 2 question: What are things that Franklin can do?
Teacher answer: Franklin can slide down a riverbank, and button buttons, and zip zippers. Oh, he can also count forward and backward.
Student 3 question: What was Franklin afraid of?
Teacher answer: Franklin was afraid of small dark places.
Teacher question: What kind of animal was Franklin?
Student answer: A turtle.
Teacher question: Why do you think that being afraid of small, dark places can be a problem for a turtle?
Student 1 answer: Because then he wouldn't want to go deep under the water.
Student 2 answer: Because turtles hide in their shells, and if he was afraid of the dark, maybe he wouldn't want to hide in his shell.
Teacher comment: Those are both good answers. Let's read the next page and see why his being afraid is a problem.
Text: "Franklin was a turtle. He was afraid of crawling into his small, dark shell. And so, Franklin the turtle dragged his shell behind him." (p. 2)

After reading the second page of text:

Teacher 1 question: What was Franklin afraid of?
Student answer: He was afraid of getting into his shell because it was dark and small.
Teacher 2 question: What did Franklin do instead of getting into his shell?
Student answer: He had to drag it behind him.
Teacher question: What do you think Franklin could do so that he wouldn't be afraid of hiding in his shell?
Student 1 answer: He could take some medicine that wouldn't make him afraid anymore.
Student 2 answer: He could get a bigger shell so that it wouldn't be so small.
Student 3 answer: He could use a flashlight to light up his shell.
Student 4 answer: He could make a window in his shell so that it wouldn't be so dark.
Teacher comment: You're all really thinking hard about Franklin and his problem. Now let's read on to find out what Franklin does about his fear and see if what we thought was right.

In contrast to a decoding emphasis in basal reading series, other basal reading series emphasize exposure to worthwhile literature and the construction of meaning from text from the very onset of reading instruction. These basal reading series are often referred to as literature-based readers. In literature-based basal readers, children are simultaneously taught sight words, decoding skills, vocabulary skills, and comprehension skills to be applied in the reading of worthwhile children's stories and information selections. Thus, differences in philosophies among basal publishers are typically reflected in both the structure and the content of their published basal reading series.

Although basal readers may be alike in many surface aspects, they often differ with respect to authors' beliefs about how children learn to read and, consequently, how children should be taught to read.

Decoding Emphasis Basal Reading Series

Basal readers founded on a strong decoding belief place an early and strong emphasis on the development and acquisition of decoding, phonics, or "sounding out" skills. In fact, decoding emphasis basal readers are often classified as "phonics first," explicit, or synthetic phonics basal readers (Anderson et al., 1985; Flesch, 1955,

1981). Learning the letter sounds and names until a child has mastered the 26 letter names and the 40-plus sounds those letters represent is considered to be a prerequisite to reading words and connected text from this philosophical point of view.

Once children have learned these letter names and sounds, this knowledge will allow them to crack the written code. Next, they are shown how to blend these sounds together to "sound out" words. For example, a child learns the letters *a, t,* and *c.* Blending sounds from left to right produces *c - a - t, cat.* Although all basal readers provide some type of decoding instruction, decoding emphasis basal readers are distinguished by the following features: (a) teaching grapho-phonic relationships as a prerequisite to reading words and text, (b) teaching the blending of letter-sound elements to make words, and (c) initially reading phonically controlled or decodable texts written to conform to specific phonics generalizations.

Decoding basal readers begins with the smallest units of language first and progresses toward larger, more meaningful units of language (Weaver, 1994). Science Research Associates' (SRA) *Reading Mastery Plus* (Engelmann & Bruner, 2002) pictured in Figure 6.13 is considered by many to represent the epitome of a decoding emphasis basal reading series.

Literature-Based Basal Reading Series

Literature-based basal readers, although committed to decoding skill development, go well beyond the preoccupation with pronouncing words and the construction of meaning from print emphasized in decoding emphasis basal readers. Literature-based basal readers attend to issues of vocabulary development and comprehension, the requisite skills for decoding (Weaver, 1994), and exposure to child classics and contemporary children's literature from the very start of instruction. For example, discussions build experiential background, and demonstrations help children draw on prior knowledge rather than simply teaching a list of new vocabulary words to enhance reading preparation. The Scholastic *Literacy Place* program (Block et al., 2000) shown in Figure 6.14 is one such example. Literature-based basal readers present comprehension, vocabulary, and phonics skill lessons simultaneously from the very start of reading instruction, whereas decoding basal readers will delay emphasis on these components until word-identification and decoding skills have been mastered. Literature-based basal reading series are predicated on the belief that children must be motivated and engaged by the content of the reading to persist in acquiring and applying reading skills of any kind, decoding or comprehension.

ADOPTING AND EVALUATING BASAL READERS

Few professional decisions deserve more careful attention than that of evaluating and adopting a basal reading series. Because you as a teacher will evaluate one or more basal reading series during your professional career, you need to understand how to evaluate and select basal reading programs effectively. Learning about this process will also enable you to help reform, restructure, and strengthen future revisions, editions, and basal reading adoption processes.

Adopting a Basal Reader Program

Twenty-two states have adopted some form of highly centralized, state-level control over the evaluation and selection of basal reading programs. The remaining 28 states

Figure 6.13   Sample page from the SRA *Reading Mastery Plus* program

and the District of Columbia allow individual districts and schools to select basal reading series at the local level (Table 6.2).

Regardless of whether evaluations and selections occur at the state or local level, the task of decision making is most often placed in the hands of a textbook adoption committee. Farr et al. (1987) indicate that these committees often use a locally produced checklist to evaluate basal readers. Unfortunately, most adoption checklists require the evaluators to determine only the presence, rather than the quality, of certain features in basal reading programs. Follett (1985) estimated that the average amount of time textbook adoption committee members spend evaluating basal reading programs is approximately 1 second per page, resulting in what Powell (1986) calls a "Flip Test" approach to evaluation and selection. Farr et al. (1987) proposed several guidelines for improving the basal reader adoption process (see Figure 6.15). Although many of these recommendations will require major changes, improving the basal reader adoption process can itself contribute much to teachers' understanding of the reading curriculum and, as a result, can enhance the overall quality of reading instruction. Dole et al. (1990) at the Center for the Study of Reading developed a comprehensive set of materials for evaluating and adopting basal reader programs titled *A Guide to Selecting Basal Reading Programs*. From our evaluation of checklist,

Because many teachers will evaluate one or more basal reading series during their professional careers, they need to understand how to evaluate and select basal readers effectively.

Figure 6.14   The *Scholastic Literacy Place 2000* basal series draws on contemporary children's literature to build background, preview, and predict

From *Scholastic Literacy Place: Problem Patrol* (pp. 186–187), 2000. New York: Scholastic. Copyright 2000 by Scholastic, Inc. Reprinted by permission.

guidelines, and processes for adopting basal reader programs, the Dole et al. (1990) materials are the most comprehensive, thorough, research-based available today.

Evaluating Basal Readers

According to Simmons and Kameenui (2003), the selection and adoption of an effective, research-based core reading program is a critical step in the development of an effective schoolwide reading initiative. A critical review of core reading programs requires an in-depth and objective analysis of programmatic elements compared against the extant scientific base of reading research, including the reports of the National Reading Panel and the National Academy of Sciences: *Preventing Reading Difficulties in Young Children* (Snow, Burns, & Griffin, 1998). Only after teachers are sufficiently well informed about the characteristics of effective basal reader programs can they act to correct or adjust the use of the basal to benefit their students. Dole, Rogers, and Osborn (1987) recommended that the evaluation of basal readers can be improved by focusing on the following:

Table 6.2   Textbook adoption policies by state

State Adoption	Local Adoption
Alabama	Alaska
Arkansas	Arizona
California	Colorado
Florida	Connecticut
Georgia	Delaware
Hawaii	District of Columbia
Idaho	Illinois
Indiana	Iowa
Kentucky	Kansas
Louisiana	Maine
Mississippi	Maryland
Nevada	Massachusetts
New Mexico	Michigan
North Carolina	Minnesota
Oklahoma	Missouri
Oregon	Montana
South Carolina	Nebraska
Tennessee	New Hampshire
Texas	New Jersey
Utah	New York
Virginia	North Dakota
West Virginia	Ohio
	Pennsylvania
	Rhode Island
	South Dakota
	Vermont
	Washington
	Wisconsin
	Wyoming

1. Identify the facets of effective reading instruction.
2. Delineate criteria related to effective reading instruction to be analyzed in the basal readers.
3. Provide a means for carefully recording how well basal readers measure up to the established criteria.

Notice who is often charged with the responsibility for adopting a new basal reader.

Because many reading teachers are concerned with curriculum changes that reflect a decided move toward more evidence-based or scientifically based comprehensive reading instructional practices in basal readers, we strongly recommend that classroom professionals use *A Consumer's Guide to Evaluating a Core Reading Program Grades K–3: A Critical Elements Analysis,* published at the University of Oregon by Simmons and Kameenui (2003). Developed with federal funds for use in public schools, this public domain document is available for free by going to the Web site http://reading.uoregon.edu/appendices/con_guide_3.1.03.pdf and downloading it in a portable document format (PDF) for use in basal adoption processes. This document describes a core reading program, provides a rationale for why schools

Figure 6.15 Guidelines for basal reader adoption process

Basic Assumptions

1. The selection of a reading textbook series should not be considered the same as the adoption of the total reading curriculum.

2. Basal reading adoptions should be conducted by school districts rather than by states.

3. The final decision regarding textbook selection should reside with the committee that spends the time and energy reviewing the books.

Selection of Reviewers

1. Reviewers should have the respect of other teachers in the school system.

2. We do not recommend in-service training in the teaching of reading, but we do strongly recommend training for reviewers in the review and evaluation of reading textbooks.

Establishing Criteria

1. The adoption committee's most important task is the determination of the basal reading series factors to be used in evaluating the programs.

2. As the selection criteria are established, the committee must agree on the meaning of each factor.

Procedures in Reviewing and Evaluating Basal Readers

1. Committees must be provided an adequate amount of time to conduct thorough evaluations of reading textbooks.

2. Committees should be organized in ways other than by grade level.

3. Procedures used to evaluate basal programs should be tested before the actual evaluation takes place.

4. Whatever evaluation procedures are used, committee members must do more than make a check mark.

5. Any person who wishes to address the entire adoption committee or any individual committee members should be allowed to do so.

6. Reading adoption committees need to consider carefully how much and what contact to have with publishers' representatives.

7. Pilot studies are useful if they are carefully controlled.

8. When the committee has completed its work, a report of the committee's evaluation procedures and findings should be made public.

From "The Evaluation and Selection of Basal Readers" by R. Farr, M. A. Tulley, & D. Powell, 1987, *The Elementary School Journal, 87*(3), pp. 267–281. Published by The University of Chicago Press. Copyright 1987 by The University of Chicago. Reprinted by permission.

Standards Note
Standard 12.2: The reading professional will adapt instruction to meet the needs of different learners to accomplish different purposes. Make a T chart with *same* and *different* as the column heads. Compare selected effective reading programs of national significance.

should adopt a core reading program, and explains the processes and criteria for adopting a core reading program.

Selected Effective Reading Programs of National Significance

In 1998, Pikulski reviewed the effectiveness of several national reading programs designed to prevent reading failure. Although basal readers remain the predominant form of reading instruction in most classrooms, several of these national programs are worth noting here, especially (1) Reading Recovery, (2) Success for All, (3) Four Blocks, and (4) Early Steps.

Reading Recovery

Reading Recovery, developed by clinical child psychologist Marie Clay, is an early intervention program design to reduce reading failure in the first grade for the lowest performing 20% of students. The aim of the program is to help low-achieving children catch up to the level of their age-related peers. Reading Recovery was imported from New Zealand to the United States by faculty at Ohio State University (Allington, 1992). Reading Recovery (RR)-trained teachers enroll in a year-long course of graduate studies with regular follow-up professional development seminars to keep training current and approved (Lyons & Beaver, 1995). Teachers trained in RR must receive training from an approved RR teacher trainer and at one of several approved sites throughout the nation.

The average RR student is recovered from below grade level performance in an average of 12 to 14 weeks. Discontinued children show normal development after release from the program. Students in New Zealand and in the United States demonstrate the substantial positive effects this invention has on young children's reading and writing development (Clay, 1990a; DeFord, Lyons, & Pinnell, 1991; Pinnell, DeFord, & Lyons, 1994).

Children selected for the RR program receive one-on-one, intensive daily reading instruction for 30 minutes. During this 30-minute daily instructional period, teachers and children engage in five major activities in a sequenced and structured format. First is the rereading of at least two familiar books or "familiar rereads" of books they have read previously with the assistance and guidance of the RR teacher. Second, the RR teacher takes a daily "running record" of the student's oral reading of the new book introduced the previous day. During the running record the teacher notes which words are read accurately or inaccurately and analyzes the inaccuracies for the cue system the student used or didn't use to inform upcoming instructional emphasis and planning.

Third, the teacher and students work with letters and words. A typical experience is "making words" using plastic magnetic letters on a cookie sheet. The teacher may show a child the word *ran* and ask the child to blend the sounds to pronounce the word. Then the teacher may remove the *r* and substitute *f* and ask the child to blend the new sound to get the word *fan*.

Fourth, the child dictates a sentence or two called a "story" in RR terminology. Then the teacher helps the child write the "story" by stretching words with the child, encouraging him or her to write the letter for each sound to get each word. After each word is written, the teacher asks the student to reread the previous word(s) until the entire sentence is written. After reading the entire sentence, the teacher will cut the sentence into word strips and ask the student to reorder the word strips into the sentence.

The fifth and final activity in an RR lesson is the introduction of a new story. The teacher has preread the story and noted challenges and obstacles the child might face in reading this book. The teacher will walk the student through the "pictures," introducing new vocabulary, sounding out tricky words with the student (often using a small whiteboard and marker), and discussing any unfamiliar concepts or language prior to the children reading the book with the careful guidance, support, and feedback of the teacher.

Reading Recovery is an effective program for training teachers to help struggling readers succeed.

Some critics of Reading Recovery regard this program as too expensive for widespread adoption and use.

Some educators have suggested that RR may be too expensive to implement on a wide scale in the United States where the reading failure rate exceeds 20%. However, over 80% of children in RR move to discontinuance and grade-level performance in less than a semester of intensive instruction, with continuing acceptable progress. Reductions in referrals to special education services and lowered retention rates indicate that RR is substantially more cost effective than are many of the commonly tried options, including special education, for addressing the needs of low-performing children (Dyer, 1992).

Success for All

Success for All *focuses on providing high-quality literacy instruction and supplementary tutoring in grades K–3.*

Success for All (SFA) is a total school reform program for grades K–3. The goal of the SFA program is to have all children reading on grade level by third grade, with no retentions and referrals to special education for reading problems. Dr. Robert Slavin, director of the Center for Research and Effective Schooling for Disadvantaged Students at Johns Hopkins University, and his colleagues developed the SFA program. The SFA program is grounded in three premises. First, the primary grade classroom is the best place to work on ensuring children's school success. Second, provide needed additional instruction to students as soon as they are identified as needing it. And third, think creatively about the use of school resources, personnel, and instructional time.

SFA focuses on providing quality reading instruction in grades K–3 as well as providing supplementary support in the form of individual tutoring sessions. Children are placed into heterogeneous classroom groupings for most of the day, but when the 90-minute reading instructional block begins, children are regrouped into "ability" groups of 15 to 20 students across the three grade levels 1–3. Regrouping according to reading levels allows whole-group, direct instruction of children and is intended to eliminate the overreliance on seat work and worksheets found in many classrooms.

For students who are not responsive to whole-class instruction in their reading groups, supplementary individual tutoring for 20 minutes per day is provided in the SFA program. Tutoring sessions focus on the same strategies and skills taught in the whole-class sessions, and where possible, the classroom teacher is freed up by the use of classroom aides to provide the tutoring sessions. SFA also recommends that children attend a half-day preschool and a full-day kindergarten to accelerate progress in learning to read successfully. Multiple program evaluations have shown that SFA is an effective program for reducing referrals to special education and grade-level retentions. However, in most of the studies, SFA has not achieved the goal of helping *every* child read on grade level by the end of third grade (Slavin, Madden, Karweit, Livemon, & Dolan, 1990; Slavin, Madden, Dolan, & Wasik, 1996; Slavin, Madder, Karweit, Dolan, & Wasik, 1992).

Four Blocks

*The **Four Blocks** program integrates basal reading programs with time spent writing, working with words, and independent reading.*

The **Four Blocks** (FB) program implemented in Winston-Salem, North Carolina, by P. Cunningham is a program of first-grade reading instruction. The FB program organizes daily reading instruction around four 30-minute blocks of instruction: (a) Basal Block, (b) Writing Block, (c) Working with Words Block, and (d) Self-Selected Reading Block. During the Basal Block, the teacher and children selectively use materials and suggestions provided in the school or district's adopted basal reading program. This means that children read stories, essays, articles, and so on found in the anthology (student's text) of the basal reader program and that the instructional activities found in the basal reader are used during this instructional time.

During the Writing Block, the teacher typically begins with a 5- to 10-minute minilesson on a writing convention, style, or genre. Following the minilesson, children engage in individually selected writing projects, taking these projects through the typical stages and activities of a writer's workshop—drafting, revising, editing, and publishing. The Working with Words Block consists of reading words from the *word wall* and *making words.* Word wall words are high-frequency, phonically irregular words posted on a wall for children to learn to read and spell by sight rather than through pattern analysis or decoding. The making words activities consist of using groups of letters to make as many words as possible. The teacher will usually give children a clue on words that can be made by using two or more of the letters in various combinations. This activity concludes with using all the letters in the group to make a single word known as the *secret word.* The final 30-minute time block, Self-Selected Reading, has students read books of their own choosing, including information books, and complete projects and responses to the books they read to share their experiences and knowledge with other children. Results reported by Cunningham, Hall, and Defee (1998) indicate that the program has been successful with children having a wide range of literacy levels without using ability grouping or leveled grouping.

Early Steps

Early Steps, developed by Darrell Morris (Morris, Shaw, & Perney, 1990), is an early intervention program designed to reduce reading failure in the early years. Children selected for the Early Steps (ES) program receive one-on-one, intensive daily reading instruction for 30 minutes. During this 30-minute daily instructional period, teachers and children engage in four major activities in a sequenced and structured format. To begin a lesson, the children reread familiar leveled books read during a previous day's lesson for 8 to 10 minutes.

Second, for 5 to 6 minutes the tutor takes the student through a series of word sort activities. This is done by the teacher placing three words, such as *hat, man, cap,* horizontally across the table or desktop. After demonstrating the task of sorting several of the words in the pile of words for the student, the student completes the task. Sorting tasks focus initially on sorting words according to "phonograms, word families, or rimes."

For the next 5 to 8 minutes of the lesson, the child writes a sentence from his or her own experience. After a short dialog with the tutor, the child writes by saying aloud each word, stretching the word, and recoding the letter for each sound segmented from the stretched word. After the child is finished writing, the tutor writes the sentence on a sentence strip and cuts it apart for the child to put together and reread.

The fourth and final step in the lesson is the introduction of a new book the child is expected to read the next day without much help. The books are selected in ascending levels of difficulty, thus pushing the child's reading progress forward. Before reading, the tutor helps the child look at the pictures, talk about the unfamiliar vocabulary words, and situate the book in a meaningful frame of reference. During the reading, the tutor coaches the child to use strategies and self-correct. Once this book is completed, it is used the next day for the familiar rereading.

In many ways, ES is very much like RR, only with a more systematic approach to the teaching of phonic decoding strategies. Research by Santa and Heien (1998) showed that ES intervention in grades 1 and 2 helped the most at-risk students

Early Steps is an effective "tutoring" program for struggling readers.

approach the average performance level of their peers within one academic year of instruction. Early Steps boosted scores not only on decoding but also on measures of spelling, word recognition, and comprehension.

HELPING STUDENTS WITH SPECIAL NEEDS SUCCEED WITH BASAL READER INSTRUCTION

Notice three ways to support students with special needs by using the basal reader.

Historically, the basal reader has not been very successful as a tool for reading remediation—for several reasons. First, some teachers find the stories in basal readers to be bland and uninviting, especially for problem readers. What is needed most is literature that turns on the turned-off learner—an order too tall for many basals to fill. Second, if a child is failing to achieve success using one approach to reading instruction, in this case the basal reader, then common sense tells us that what is needed is an alternative strategy—not just more of the same. Finally, basal reader systems frequently do not allow students enough time for real reading. The multifarious collection of skill sheets and workbook pages tends to be so time consuming that little time is left for reading.

Reading the Basal Straight Through

Teachers working with special needs students recognize that what these children need most is regular and sustained reading. We suggest that skill sheets and workbook pages be used judiciously or even avoided to allow for more time spent reading. Children should be allowed to read basals straight through as an anthology of children's stories. The teacher may wish to skip stories that offer little for the reader in this setting.

Repeated Readings

In repeated readings, the teacher typically introduces the story as a shared book or story experience, then students attempt to read the book alone or with a friend (Routman, 1988). If the story has rhyme or a regular pattern, it may be sung or chanted. Repeated readings of stories help children achieve a sense of accomplishment, improve comprehension, and build fluency.

Supported, or Buddy, Reading

The Internet School Library Media Center (ISLMC) Multicultural Page is a metasite that brings together resources for teachers, librarians, parents, and students. You can link to this resource from our Companion Website at www.prenhall.com/ reutzel.

Many times, at-risk readers are very reluctant to become risk takers. Teachers simply must find ways of breaking the ice for them and create classroom safety nets. Supported, or buddy, reading allows students to read basal stories aloud together, either taking turns or in unison. By rereading these supported selections, students' fluency and comprehension improve. Another variation is for teacher–student combinations to read together. Similar to the procedure known as neurological impress (Hollingsworth, 1978), the student and teacher read aloud in unison at a comfortable rate. For first readings, the teacher usually assumes the lead in terms of volume and pace. In subsequent repeated readings, the student is encouraged to assume the lead.

HELPING STUDENTS WITH DIVERSE CULTURAL OR LANGUAGE NEEDS SUCCEED WITH BASAL READERS

Students who do not possess reading and writing ability in a first language should be taught to read and write in their native or first language to support and validate them as worthwhile individuals. In addition, reading instruction in the first language helps students capitalize on what they already know about their primary languages and cultures to build concepts that can facilitate the acquisition of English (Freeman & Freeman, 1992; Krashen & Biber, 1988). In any case, teachers must be sensitive to these students' special needs, which include (a) a need for safety and security, (b) a need to belong and be accepted, and (c) a need to feel self-esteem (Peregoy & Boyle, 1993).

Describe three things that can be done to support second-language learners when using a basal reader.

Teachers should help English-as-a-second-language (ESL) or limited-English-proficiency (LEP) students feel at ease when they arrive in the classroom by assigning them a personal buddy who, if possible, speaks the language of the newcomer. This buddy is assigned to help the new student through the school day, routines, and so on. Another approach is to avoid changes in the classroom schedule by following a regular and predictable routine each day, which creates a sense of security. To create a sense of belonging, assign the student to a home group for an extended period of time. A home group provides a small social unit of concern focused on helping the newcomer adapt to everyday life as well as provides a concerned and caring peer group. Finally, self-esteem is enhanced when an individual's worth is affirmed. Opportunities for the newcomer to share their language and culture during daily events in the classroom provide a useful way to integrate them into the ongoing classroom culture.

To help ESL or LEP students succeed in classrooms where basal readers are the core of instruction, Law and Eckes (1990, p. 92) recommend the following:

- Supplement the basal as much as possible with language experience stories (as discussed previously in this chapter).
- Encourage extensive reading: Gather basal textbooks from as many different levels as possible. Also acquire easier textbooks in content areas as well as trade books to encourage a wide range of reading topics.
- Expose children to the many different types of reading available in the "real" world, such as magazines, *TV Guide,* newspapers, product labels, signs.

Summary

Basal readers over the past two centuries have become a veritable institution in American reading instruction. As social and political aims have changed over the years, basal reader content and structure have been altered to reflect these changing conditions. Modern basal readers are typically composed of several major components, including a teacher's edition, a student's reader, workbooks, assessment, supplementary literature, and technology. For teachers, basal readers represent a structured approach to teaching reading, which can save enormous amounts of preparation time. On the other hand, basal readers can in some instances displace teacher judgment to the degree that the basal becomes the reading program rather than a tool to be used to support the reading program. Large, national commercial publishers produce basal readers. Senior authors on basal series are usually individuals known and respected nationally or internationally in the field of reading.

Check your understanding of chapter concepts by using the self-assessment for Chapter 6 on our Companion Website at www.prenhall.com/reutzel.

Adopting a basal reader for use in schools is a task most teachers will probably face in the course of their professional careers. Hence, it is important for teachers to understand how basal readers have been adopted in the past and know how the adoption process may be improved.

Although basal readers can be useful tools for providing reading instruction, some teachers need to make conscious efforts to take control of their basal teacher's editions by changing the way in which they provide instruction. Suggestions in this chapter included using the balanced reading program, RRL and ReQuest. Other selected, nationally known reading programs that are not considered basal reading programs were also discussed—Success for All, Reading Recovery, Four Blocks, and Early Steps.

Finally, readers with special needs who may be struggling can be helped by reading the basal straight through, allowing repeated readings of self-selected basal stories, and providing buddy or other forms of supported reading. ESL and LEP students can be helped to feel at home as newcomers in a school environment. The teacher can also take steps to supplement and extend basic basal reader text for these students.

Concept Applications

In the Classroom

1. Go to your local school district or university curriculum materials library. Locate two basal readers. Locate the following items in the teacher's edition: (a) the scope and sequence chart, (b) the parts of a directed reading lesson, (c) the skill lessons, (d) the workbooks, and (e) the book tests or assessment materials. Compare the instructional approaches and contents of each using a compare/contrast T chart.

2. Compare the contents of a current basal reader to the contents of the Dick and Jane or McGuffey basal readers. Write a brief essay on the differences you note.

3. Select a basal reader lesson and story. Redesign this lesson on your own by changing it to make use of (a) the RRL, (b) the LEA, (c) ReQuest, or (d) DRTA.

4. Plan Block 1 using the basal reader in the Four Block reading program. Design how you would use the basal for a week for 30 minutes per day.

5. Select a leveled book. Go through the parts of a Reading Recovery lesson and write a plan about how you would introduce this as a new book to a struggling reader.

In the Field

1. Interview a teacher in the field about the strengths and weaknesses of the basal. Find out why this teacher uses or does not use the basal.

2. Visit a classroom in a local elementary school where Success for All is used. Observe a teacher teaching reading. Which parts of the SFA program did the teacher use? Which parts did the teacher omit? Write an essay about your observations.

3. Prepare a basal reading lesson to be taught in the schools. Secure permission to teach this lesson in a local grade-level appropriate classroom. Write a reflective essay on the experience, detailing successes, failures, and necessary changes.

4. Select a basal reading lesson in a teacher's edition. Adapt the lesson in the teacher's edition by rewriting it using a balanced reading program, RRL, ReQuest, or Four Blocks. Secure permission to teach this lesson in a local grade-level appropriate classroom. Write a reflective essay on the experience detailing successes, failures, and necessary changes.

Recommended Readings

Baumann, J. F. (1992). Basal reading programs and the deskilling of teachers: A critical examination of the argument. *Reading Research Quarterly, 27*(4), 390–398.

Cheney, L. V. (1990). *Tyrannical machines.* Washington, DC: National Endowment for the Humanities.

Dole, J. A., Osborn, J., & Lehr, F. (1990). *A guide to selecting basal reading programs.* Urbana, IL: Center for the Study of Reading.

Duke, N. K. (2000). 3.6 minutes per day: The scarcity of informational texts in first grade. *Reading Research Quarterly, 35*(2), 202–224.

Fountas, I. C., & Pinnell, G. S. (1999). *Matching books to readers: Using leveled books in guided reading, K–3.* Portsmouth, NH: Heinemann.

Hiebert, E. H. (1999). Text matters in learning to read. *The Reading Teacher, 52*(6), 552–566.

Hoffman, J. V., McCarthey, S. J., Abbott, J., Christian, C., Corman, L., Curry, C., Dressman, M., Elliott, B., Matherne, D., & Stahle, D. (1994). So what's new in the new basals? A focus on first grade. *Journal of Reading Behavior, 26*(1), 47–73.

McCarthey, S. J., Hoffman, J. V., Christian, C., Corman, L., Elliott, B., Matherne, D., & Stahle, D. (1994). Engaging the new basal readers. *Reading Research and Instruction, 33*(3), 233–256.

Moss, B., & Newton, E. (2001). An examination of the information text genre in basal readers. *Reading Psychology, 23*(1), 1–13.

Perspectives on basal readers. [Special issue]. *Theory Into Practice, 28*(4), 1989.

Reutzel, D. R., & Larsen, N. S. (1995). Look what they've done to real children's books in the new basal readers. *Language Arts, 72*(7), 495–507.

Robinson, A. (2002). *American reading instruction* (Rev. ed.). Newark, DE: International Reading Association.

Shannon, P. (1992). *Becoming political: Readings and writings in the politics of literacy education.* Portsmouth, NH: Heinemann.

Smith, N. B. (1986). *American reading instruction.* Newark, DE: International Reading Association.

Winograd, N., Wixson, K. K., & Lipson, M. Y. (Eds.). (1989). *Improving basal reader instruction.* New York: Columbia Teachers College Press.

7 Assessing Literacy Learning

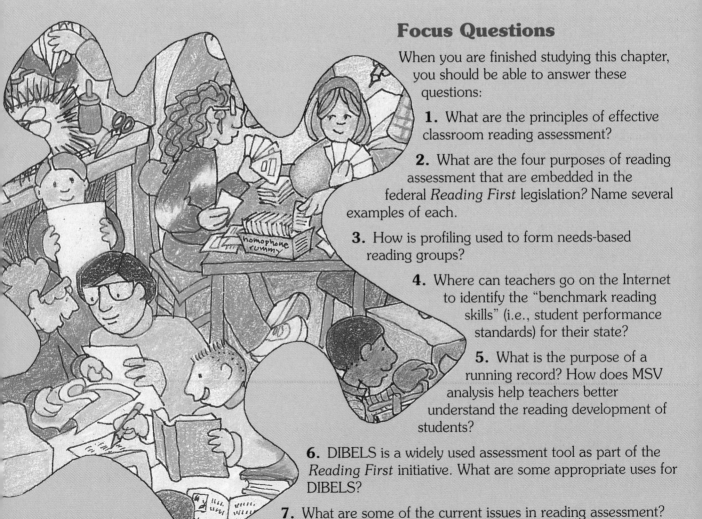

Focus Questions

When you are finished studying this chapter, you should be able to answer these questions:

1. What are the principles of effective classroom reading assessment?

2. What are the four purposes of reading assessment that are embedded in the federal *Reading First* legislation? Name several examples of each.

3. How is profiling used to form needs-based reading groups?

4. Where can teachers go on the Internet to identify the "benchmark reading skills" (i.e., student performance standards) for their state?

5. What is the purpose of a running record? How does MSV analysis help teachers better understand the reading development of students?

6. DIBELS is a widely used assessment tool as part of the *Reading First* initiative. What are some appropriate uses for DIBELS?

7. What are some of the current issues in reading assessment?

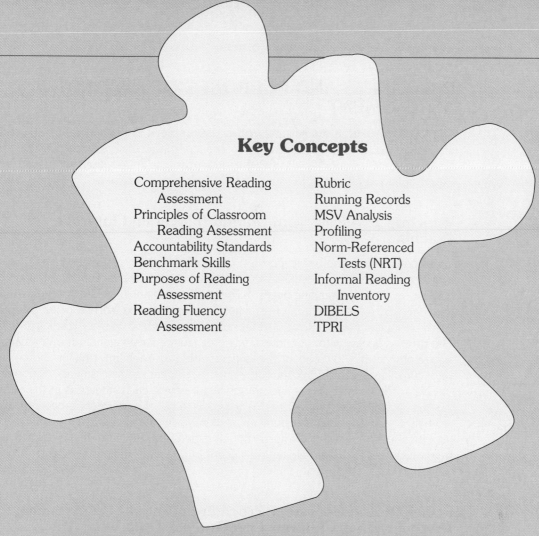

Key Concepts

Comprehensive Reading
    Assessment
Principles of Classroom
    Reading Assessment
Accountability Standards
Benchmark Skills
Purposes of Reading
    Assessment
Reading Fluency
    Assessment

Rubric
Running Records
MSV Analysis
Profiling
Norm-Referenced
    Tests (NRT)
Informal Reading
    Inventory
DIBELS
TPRI

Reading assessment is intended to inform teaching. **Comprehensive reading assessment** strategies satisfy this purpose. The essential assessment tools in your reading teacher's toolbox help you to survey student reading development, make strategic observations of students as they are engaged in reading activities, and gather additional data using informal and commercial assessment tests and procedures. With the array of data you are able to assemble through comprehensive assessment, you will be able to analyze what you see and plan "just-in-time" instruction that meets the need of every student. No child is left behind when the teacher uses comprehensive assessment strategies.

In this chapter, we offer you a kind of primer on the essentials of reading assessment. Let's begin at the beginning, with a brief summary of the governing principles and fundamental purposes of reading assessment.

PRINCIPLES AND PURPOSES OF READING ASSESSMENT

The following **principles of classroom assessment** are intended to help teachers decide which strategies should be adopted to improve their classroom instruction. They are based on our own classroom experiences, current research in the field, and expert opinions expressed to us by successful classroom teachers.

Principle 1: Assessment Should Inform and Improve Teaching

When considering whether to perform any sort of reading assessment, the teacher should ask, "Will this procedure help me make important educational decisions regarding my students' reading needs?" The procedure should yield rich insights as to materials and ways of offering instruction (e.g., skills to be learned next, grouping based on student needs, and so on) that can positively affect students' reading growth. The process begins with an understanding of required state standards and a careful survey of what is known about the students using available information (home surveys, cumulative records, informal assessments, student self-assessments, and so on).

Next, the teacher forms hypotheses about where each student is in his or her reading development (Bintz, 1991). The task is to select assessment procedures that will help the teacher better understand student abilities and confirm or reject earlier hypotheses. Armed with the information obtained from these processes, the teacher teaches lessons aimed at helping the student improve in reading proficiency. Figure 7.1 depicts this assessment-teaching process.

Principle 2: Assessment Procedures Should Help Teachers Discover What Children *Can* Do, Not Only What They Cannot Do

Rather than spending precious classroom time trying to identify all the myriad skills students *cannot* do, many teachers are finding that their time is much better spent finding out what students *can* do, then building on their strengths to add new abili-

Visit Chapter 7 of our Companion Website at www.prenhall.com/ reutzel to look into the chapter objectives, standards and principles, and pertinent Web links associated with assessing literacy learning.

Assessment begins with an understanding of grade-level expectations described in the state's standards.

Figure 7.1   Assessment-teaching process

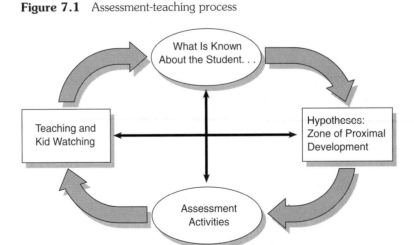

ties. Once teachers understand student strengths in reading, it becomes much easier to decide which new learning experiences should be offered to help them develop further.

Principle 3: Every Assessment Procedure Should Have a Specific Purpose

Sometimes we can fall into the habit of giving reading tests just because they are our "standard operating procedure" rather than selecting assessment activities as an integral part of providing high-quality instruction. For instance, it is common practice in many schools for students identified as having reading problems to be given a "battery" of tests (i.e., a preselected set of tests) to discover what the problem seems to be. This one-size-fits-all approach fails to take into account what is already known about the student's reading ability and the specific purpose of the assessment experience (e.g., diagnostic, providing data for progress reports, or gathering information for parents). Thus, we need to enter into student assessment with a clear purpose.

There Are Four Purposes of Reading Assessment

Because reading assessment removes children from precious instructional time in the classroom, we should be mindful of the **four purposes of reading assessment.** These purposes, by the way, are embedded in the federal *Reading First* legislation and are built on solid scientific research. These purposes are depicted metaphorically in Figure 7.2 as a chalice.

At the open end, or broadest part, of the chalice (since it involves the whole class) is **outcome assessment.** Outcomes are the *results* of our reading program in terms of student test scores and other hard data. The main purpose of outcome assessment is to survey the reading abilities of the class as a whole and provide a snapshot of the reading program's effectiveness when compared to established end-of-year reading benchmarks (standards) for each grade level.

In order to begin planning more specific instruction, your focus will shift to individual students. **Screening assessments** provide initial information about students' reading development. They should be quick and efficient and help teachers place students into preliminary instructional groups based on their general reading abilities and needs. This is an especially critical "first look" for students who may be at risk and in need of special instructional services. Invariably, you will notice that some students are having unusual difficulty with tasks during small-group instruction, or perhaps a parent brings a reading problem to your attention. **Diagnostic assessments** provide in-depth information about each student's particular strengths and needs. These assessments are a bit more involved and take extra time to conduct. Sometimes an educational psychologist, certified diagnostician, or bilingual specialist may be needed to administer some diagnostic tests because administering them requires a hefty investment of time and/or special training. Students requiring special education or Title I programs for reading often undergo diagnostic testing for initial placement or for retention in the program.

Encircling the chalice in Figure 7.2 are **progress-monitoring assessments.** They are an essential part of every reading teacher's daily plan, which is why they surround all other assessments (and students) represented in the figure of the chalice. Progress-monitoring assessments provide ongoing and timely feedback as to how well individual students are responding to your teaching. This allows you to continually reevaluate your instruction and make adjustments as needed.

"Shotgun" approaches to assessment waste valuable time and resources and are stressful to students.

Figure 7.2 Purposes of reading assessment

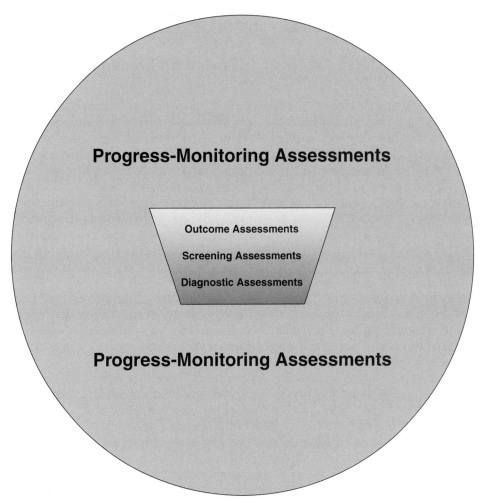

Principle 4: Classroom Assessment Should Be Linked to *Accountability Standards* and Provide Insights into the *Process* of Reading

The passage of the No Child Left Behind Act and other state and federal legislation in reading education has placed even greater emphasis on classroom assessment. **Accountability standards** established by the individual states and professional organizations, such as the International Reading Association (IRA) and the National Council of Teachers of English (NCTE), describe evidence-based reading skills that are typically mastered by the end of each school year. These *benchmark skills* (as they are often referred to) should be monitored on a regular basis.

Principle 5: Assessment Procedures Should Help Identify *Zones of Proximal Development*

Earlier in this book, we discussed Vygotsky's (1962, 1978) notion of a *zone of proximal development,* or the area of potential growth in reading that can occur with ap-

*Accountability stan-dards describe evidence-based reading skills, or **benchmark skills,** that are typi-cally mastered by the end of each school year.*

propriate instruction. To identify students' zones of proximal development, teachers need to determine accurately what children can already do and thus which new skills they may be ready to learn next. For example, in a kindergarten or first-grade classroom, children who can create story lines for wordless picture books and who have been doing so for some time should be ready for books containing simple and predictable text.

Principle 6: Assessment Strategies Should Not Supplant Instruction

State- and locally mandated testing sometimes seems to overwhelm the teacher and take over the classroom. In Texas, for example, a state that has had high-stakes testing since the early 1980s, many principals complain that some teachers virtually stop teaching from January until April in order to drill students on practice tests. If a teacher loses sight of the purpose of classroom assessment, namely, to inform and influence instruction, then he or she may well move into the role of *teacher as manager* rather than *teacher as teacher* (Pearson, 1985). The assessment program should complement the instructional program and grow naturally from it.

Principle 7: Effective Classroom Assessment Makes Use of Both *Valid* and *Reliable* Instruments

Although master teachers are comfortable using many informal assessment processes to gather information about students' reading progress, instruments that possess validity and reliability evidence are necessary. These assessment tools give teachers consistent and trustworthy feedback for adapting or modifying their teaching to meet individual needs.

Reliability evidence demonstrates whether student performance will be measured in a stable and consistent manner. In other words, a reliable test is one that provides the same results with the same children no matter which teacher is giving the test.

Measures of **validity** indicate the degree to which tests measure what the test makers claim they measure. If a test measures reading, then it should measure the complete reading act or at least the specified area of reading (e.g., phonics or reading comprehension), not some other skill, ability, or construct (see the feature "The Reliability-Validity Caveat").

WHERE DO WE BEGIN? A CLASSROOM TEACHER'S PERSPECTIVE

In the remainder of this chapter, we take a closer look at reading assessment from the classroom teacher's point of view. We begin with those assessment tools and strategies that can be administered by busy classroom teachers with a minimum of practice.

It seems logical to us, then, that we should start with the kinds of assessments you might use *every day*. *Screening assessments* useful for the first days and weeks of school and *progress-monitoring assessments* used daily to check the effectiveness of your teaching are the daily bread-and-butter assessment tasks you want to use to validate teaching and learning. Since both assessments may be used more or less

Comprehensive literacy assessment helps teachers understand which reading skills should be introduced next.

Standards Note
Standard 10.1: The reading professional will be able to develop and conduct assessments that involve multiple indicators of early literacy learner progress. Having read the seven principles of reading assessment, list and consider the multiple indicators of early literacy progress that you currently use or would like to use so that you have a truly informative "color movie."

THE RELIABILITY-VALIDITY CAVEAT

Though the selection of reading tests that are *both* reliable and valid is our goal, finding one that meets our highest standards in each category is problematic. There is an important caveat commonly understood in assessment circles (Cooter, 1990): *As test reliability increases, validity usually decreases and vice versa.* For example, informal reading inventories (IRI) are widely used and respected as a *valid* measure of reading ability, but they are also notorious for being rather unreliable (i.e., two teachers giving an IRI to the same child can come to substantially different conclusions about the student's reading needs). Similarly, the Stanford Diagnostic Reading Test (SDRT) is considered to be a very reliable test but not very valid (i.e., the multiple choice format for measuring reading comprehension is very *unlike* normal reading behavior). There are now a number of tests available that report both validity and reliability estimates, but you will discover that the validity-reliability caveat is evident—if the test is high in reliability, it is probably weak in the validity department and vice versa.

How does a teacher overcome the validity-reliability caveat? Simple (well, not really). You will need to develop a *comprehensive* approach to reading assessment, one that includes some tests and procedures that are extremely valid and are counterbalanced with others that are highly reliable.

---

interchangeably, we group them together in the upcoming sections. How will you know which assessment tool is best for screening or progress monitoring? Not to worry. Early in the next section, we provide you with a handy chart that helps you decide.

Screening Students

The first day of school is always magical. It is a day filled with hope, expectation, and, for some, even fear. Your young charges walk slowly into your classroom—some tall and gangly, some short, some smiling, some very cautiously. It is the day when you begin to establish classroom management routines and procedures and get to know each student a little, and they all begin to form opinions about you.

The first week of school should include a basket weave of assessment activities that are quick and efficient and that yield a lot of important information about reading. They should also be pleasant and nonthreatening since some of your students will have had deep experience with failure, and you don't want to lose them.

Screening assessments are essential to use during the first days of school or for students who come to you after the school year has begun. They are easy to administer yet yield a lot of great information. You may actually decide to use many of these same strategies for progress monitoring.

Progress Monitoring in the Reading Classroom

Progress monitoring is an essential part of teaching. As you learn more about your students, you plan instruction that you feel will best meet their needs. In essence, you try to find the zone of proximal development for each reading skill area for each student—not a simple task. Thus, as you offer targeted instruction in small groups, you constantly reassess each student's growth to see if the instruction is working. That is what we mean by progress monitoring. So how do you decide which of the strategies that follow should be used for either screening or progress monitoring? In Figure 7.3, we offer a kind of "if-then" chart to help you choose. *If* you have a particular need that is represented by one of the assessments listed along the left-hand column, *then* you

Figure 7.3 Choosing screening and progress-monitoring assessment strategies

	Appropriate for Screening? (first days/weeks)	Appropriate for Progress Monitoring? (These must be quick and part of daily work!)
Category: Interests and Self-Perception		
Flynt-Cooter Reading Inventory	Yes	No
Burke Interview	Yes	No
Self-Rating Scale—Subject Areas	Yes	No
Background Knowledge	Yes	No
Family Survey	Yes	No
Kid Watching	No	Yes
Screening Checklists	Yes	Yes
Concepts About Print	Yes	No (for emergent readers only)
Category: Phonemic Awareness (PA) and Alphabet Knowledge (AK)		
PA—Recognizing Rhyming Words	Yes (in small groups)	Yes
PA—Oddity Task	Yes (in small groups)	Yes
PA—Same-Different Word Pairs	Yes (in small groups)	Yes
PA—Syllables and Counting Syllables	Yes (in small groups)	Yes
PA—Auditory Sound Blending	Yes (in small groups)	Yes
PA—Segmenting Sounds	Yes (in small groups)	Yes
AK—Alphabet Identification	Yes (in small groups)	Yes
AK—Letter Production	Yes (in small groups)	Yes
Category: Decoding and Word Attack		
Running Records	Yes (first three weeks)	Yes
Category: Vocabulary		
Oral Reading Assessment	No	Yes
Vocabulary Flash Cards	Yes	Yes
Category: Comprehension		
Questioning (Bloom)	Yes	Yes (use mainly higher levels)
Retelling—Story Grammars (Oral)	Yes (in small groups)	Yes
Retelling—Using Graphic Organizers	Yes (in small groups)	Yes
Retelling—Written Summaries	No	Yes
Expository Text Frames	Yes (in small groups)	Yes
Cloze	Yes	Yes
Maze	Yes	Yes
Content Area Reading Inventory (CARI)	Yes (in small groups)	Yes
Category: Fluency		
Multidimensional Fluency Scale (MFS)	Yes (in small groups)	Yes
Rubric for Evaluation	No	Yes
Category: Commercial Tools		
Informal Reading Inventories	Yes (in first three weeks)	Yes (quarterly)
Curriculum-Based Measurements (CBM)	Yes (in first month)	Yes (quarterly)

determine if the particular strategy is appropriate for screening or progress monitoring by checking the appropriate row to the right. Following Figure 7.3 is a detailed description for each strategy. Let's get started!

ASSESSING READING INTERESTS AND SELF-PERCEPTION

On the most basic level, we need to know what kinds of books and materials will be of interest to our students. This helps us choose (or avoid) certain topics for small-group instruction. We also want to be sure and ask the obvious question: Are you a good reader? Why?

Next we share some essential tools for screening students in the areas of interest and self-perception.

Attitude/Interest Inventories

Getting to know students is critical if the teacher is to have insights into background knowledge and oral language abilities and for the selection of reading materials that will be of interest. An interest inventory that is administered either one to one or in small groups is a great tool for getting to know students. However, there are many to choose from, and all interest inventories are not created equally. Further, not all questions on the inventory can tell you what is helpful in choosing appropriate reading materials for instruction.

The Flynt/Cooter Interest Inventory

In Figures 7.4 and 7.5 are two interest inventories developed by Flynt and Cooter (2004) that we find to be helpful. The *Primary Form* is appropriate for students in kindergarten through grade 2, and the *Upper-Level Form* is to be used with students from grade 3 and up.

The Burke Reading Interview

The Burke Reading Interview (Burke, 1987) provides some initial insights into how students see themselves as readers and the reading process in general. The following questions have been adapted from the Burke procedure.

1. When you are reading and come to a word you don't know, what do you do? What else can you do?
2. Which of your friends is a good reader? What makes him/her a good reader?
3. Do you think your teacher ever comes to a word she doesn't know when reading? What do you think she does when that happens?
4. If you knew that one of your friends was having problems with his or her reading, what could you tell your friend that would help?
5. How would a teacher help your friend with reading problems?
6. How do you think you learned to read?
7. Are you a good reader?
8. What would you like to be able to do better as a reader?

Figure 7.4 The Flynt/Cooter Interest Inventory: Primary Form*

PRIMARY FORM

Student's Name: _____ Age: _____

Date: _____ Examiner: _____

Introductory Statement: *[Student's name], before you read some stories for me I would like to ask you some questions.*

Home Life

1. Where do you live? Do you know your address? What is it?

2. Who lives in your house with you?

3. What kinds of jobs do you have at home?

4. What is one thing that you really like to do at home?

5. Do you ever read at home? [*If yes, ask:*] When do you read and what was the last thing you read? [*If no, ask:*] Does anyone ever read to you? [*If so, ask:*] Who, and how often?

6. Do you have a bedtime on school nights? [*If no, ask:*] When do you go to bed?

7. Do you have a TV in your room? How much TV do you watch every day? What are your favorite shows?

8. What do you like to do with your friends?

9. Do you have any pets? Do you collect things? Do you take any kinds of lessons?

10. When you make a new friend, what is something that your friend ought to know about you?

School Life

1. Besides recess and lunch, what do you like about school?

2. Do you get to read much in school?

3. Are you a good reader or a not-so-good reader?
   [*If a good reader, ask:*] What makes a person a good reader?
   [*If a not-so-good reader, ask:*] What causes a person to not be a good reader?

4. If you can pick any book to read, what would the book be about?

5. Do you like to write? What kind of writing do you do in school? What is the favorite thing you have written about?

6. Who has helped you the most in school? How did that person help you?

7. Do you have a place at home to study?

8. Do you get help with your homework? Who helps you?

9. What was the last book you read for school?

10. If you were helping someone learn to read, what could you do to help that person?

*From Flynt, E. S., & Cooter, R. B. The Flynt/Cooter *Reading Inventory for the Classroom,* 5th edition, © 2004. Adapted by permission of Pearson Education, Inc. Upper Saddle River, NJ.

Figure 7.5 The Flynt/Cooter Interest Inventory: Upper-Level Form*

UPPER-LEVEL FORM

Student's Name: _____ Age: _____

Date: _____ Examiner: _____

Introductory Statement: [*Student's name*], *before you read some stories for me I would like to ask you some questions.*

Home Life

1. How many people are there in your family?

2. Do you have your own room or do you share a room? [*Ask this only if it is apparent that the student has siblings.*]

3. Do your parent(s) work? What kinds of jobs do they have?

4. Do you have jobs around the house? What are they?

5. What do you usually do after school?

6. Do you have a TV in your room? How much time do you spend watching TV each day? What are your favorite shows?

7. Do you have a bedtime during the week? What time do you usually go to bed on a school night?

8. Do you get an allowance? How much?

9. Do you belong to any clubs at school or outside school? What are they?

10. What are some things that you really like to do? Do you collect things, have any hobbies, or take lessons outside school?

School Environment

1. Do you like school? What is your favorite class? Your least favorite class?

2. Do you have a special place to study at home?

3. How much homework do you have on a typical school night? Does anyone help you with your homework? Who?

4. Do you consider yourself a good reader or a not-so-good reader?
   [*If a good reader, ask:*] What has helped you most to become a good reader?
   [*If a not-so-good reader, ask:*] What causes someone to be a not-so-good reader?

5. If I gave you the choice of selecting a book about any topic, what would you choose to read about?

6. What is one thing you can think of that would help you become a better reader? Is there anything else?

7. Do you like to write? What kind of writing assignments do you like best?

8. If you went to a new school, what is one thing that you would want the teachers to know about you as a student?

9. If you were helping someone learn to read, what would be the most important thing you could do to help that person?

10. How will knowing how to read help you in the future?

---

*From Flynt, E. S., & Cooter, R. B. The Flynt/Cooter *Reading Inventory for the Classroom,* 5th edition, © 2004. Adapted by permission of Pearson Education, Inc. Upper Saddle River, NJ.

Figure 7.6 Class interests profile sorting table

Student Names	Q1	Q2						

Sorting Out Student Interests

After you have collected student responses to the Flynt/Cooter Interest inventory, create a grid for your class like the one shown in Figure 7.6. List student names along the left-hand column and question numbers along the top row (e.g., "Q1" for question number 1, "Q2" for question number 2, and so on). You may decide that some questions provide more information than others; if so, list only the numbers you plan to survey.

After the entire class has been surveyed, compile the individual responses into a class profile. Record abbreviated answers to each question for each student in the class interests profile. Look over the responses to each question by all the children for categories of interests to be observed in your teaching and for choosing reading materials. Make any changes on the class profile sheet you discover throughout the year. This updated information about your students' reading interests will help you adjust your selection of topics and reading materials as the year progresses.

Don't forget to do the obvious: Ask students what they feel are their reading strengths and needs.

Self-Rating Scales for Subject Area Reading

No one knows better than the reader how he or she is doing in reading. A teacher carrying out an assessment agenda should never overlook the obvious: Ask kids how they're doing! Although this is best achieved in a one-on-one discussion setting, large class sizes frequently make it a prohibitive practice. A good alternative to one-to-one interviews for older elementary children is a student self-rating scale in which students complete a questionnaire tailored to obtain specific information about the reader from the reader's point of view. One example is illustrated in Figure 7.7 for a teacher interested in reading and study strategies used with social studies readings. Whichever reading skills are to be surveyed, remember to keep self-rating scales focused and brief.

Assessing Background Knowledge

Children's background knowledge and experiences are among the most important contributors (or inhibitors) of comprehension. Researchers have determined that students who possess a great deal of background information about a subject tend

Figure 7.7   Self-rating scale: Reading social studies

Reading Social Studies

Name _____ Date _____

1. The first three things I usually do when I begin reading a chapter in social studies are (number 1, 2, 3):

_____ Look at the pictures.

_____ Read the chapter through one time silently.

_____ Look at the new terms and definitions.

_____ Read the questions at the end of the chapter.

_____ Read the first paragraph or introduction.

_____ Skip around and read the most interesting parts.

_____ Skim the chapter.

_____ Preview the chapter.

2. What is hardest for me about social studies is . . .

3. The easiest thing about social studies is . . .

4. The thing(s) I like best about reading social studies is (are) . . .

to recall greater amounts of information more accurately from reading than do students with little or no background knowledge (Carr & Thompson, 1996; Pressley, 2000; Pearson, Hansen, & Gordon, 1979). It is also a well-known fact that well-developed background information can inhibit the comprehension of new information that conflicts with or refutes prior knowledge and assumptions about a specific topic. Thus, knowing how much knowledge a reader has about a concept or topic can help teachers better prepare students to read and comprehend successfully. One way that teachers can assess background knowledge and experience is to use a procedure developed by Langer (1982) for assessing the amount and content of students' background knowledge about selected topics, themes, concepts, and events.

Here's the procedure you will follow. Select a story for students to read. Construct a list of specific vocabulary terms or story concepts related to the topic, message, theme, or events to be experienced in reading the story. For example, students may read the story *Stone Fox* by John R. Gardiner (1980) about a boy named Willy who saves his grandfather's farm from the tax collector. Construct a list of 5 to 10 specific vocabulary terms or concepts related to the story. Use this list to probe

Figure 7.8   Checklist of levels of prior knowledge

Phrase 1	What comes to mind when . . .?
Phrase 2	What made you think of . . .?
Phrase 3	Have you any new ideas about . . .?

Stimulus used to elicit student background knowledge _____

(Picture, word, or phrase, etc.)

	Much - (3)	Some - (2)	Little - (1)
	category labels	examples	personal associations
	definitions	attributes	morphemes
	analogies	defining characteristics	sound alikes
	relationships		personal experiences

Student name			
Maria _____	_____	__X__	_____
Jawan _____	__X__	_____	_____
_____	_____	_____	_____
_____	_____	_____	_____
_____	_____	_____	_____

through discussion background knowledge and experiences of the students about the story's message and plot. Such a list for this story might include the following:

Broke

Taxes

Tax Collector

Dogsled Race

Samoyeds

Students are asked to respond to each of these terms in writing or through discussion. This is accomplished by using one of several stem statements (shown in the previous list), such as, "What comes to mind when you think of paying bills and you hear the term *broke?*" Students then respond. After students have responded to each of the specific terms, the teacher can score the responses to survey the class's knowledge. Awarding the number of points that most closely represents the level of prior knowledge in the response is used to score each item. Divide the total score by the number of terms or concepts in the list (five in our example) to determine the average knowledge level of individual students. These average scores are compared against the Checklist of Levels of Prior Knowledge in Figure 7.8 for each student. By scanning the Xs in the checklist, a teacher can get a sense of the entire class's overall level of prior knowledge. Information thus gathered can be used to inform both the content and the nature of whole-group comprehension instruction.

Family Surveys of Reading Habits

Family surveys are brief questionnaires sent to adult family members to provide teachers insights into reading behaviors at home.

We recently observed a friend of ours who has a heart condition going through his normal daily activities with a small radiolike device attached to his belt. When asked what this gadget was, he indicated that it was a heart monitor. He went on to say that the device constantly measured his heart rate for an entire day to provide the doctor with a reliable account of his normal heart rhythms in the real world of daily activity. Traditional reading assessment has often failed to give teachers such a real-world look at students' reading ability by restricting the assessment to school settings. So the question posed here is, How do we acquire information about a student's reading habits and abilities away from the somewhat artificial environment of the school? One way is to assess what is happening in the home using family surveys.

Standard 5.8: The reading professional will be able to implement effective strategies to include parents as partners in the literacy development of their children. Family surveys are a preliminary step in involving parents, who are their children's "first and best" teachers.

Family surveys are *brief* questionnaires (too long, and they'll never be answered!) sent to adult family members periodically to maintain communications between the home and school. They also remind parents of the importance of reading in the home to support and encourage reading growth. When taken into consideration with other assessment evidence from the classroom, family surveys enable teachers to develop a more accurate profile of the child's reading ability. An example of a family survey is provided in Figure 7.9.

Kid Watching

In **kid watching**, we are looking for positive "movement" in literacy learning (Clay, 1985).

For many teachers, the most basic assessment strategy is systematic observations of children engaged in the reading act, or **kid watching.** Clay, in her classic book *The Early Detection of Reading Difficulties* (1985), explains her philosophy concerning observations:

> I am looking for movement in appropriate directions. . . . For if I do not watch what [the student] is doing, and if I do not capture what is happening in records of some kind, Johnny, who never gets under my feet and who never comes really into a situation where I can truly see what he is doing, may, in fact, for six months or even a year, practice behaviours that will handicap him in reading. (p. 49)

Teachers must have a thorough understanding of how reading develops for kid watching to be instructive.

Thus, observation is a critical tool at the teacher's disposal for the early assessment of students and their abilities.

But Do You Know *What* to Look For?

Think of ways that you could make kid watching a regular part of your teaching schedule.

One semester, a young student teacher was busily making anecdotal notes on a clipboard as she watched second graders working away. The students were engaged in activities such as reading, planning writing projects, working at a computer station, listening to books on tape while following along in small books, and several other reading/learning tasks. When the student teacher was asked by the visiting college supervisor what she was working on, she said, "I'm trying to figure out where the children are in their reading development." The supervisor responded, "That's great! How do you know what to watch for?" The student teacher appeared bewildered, so the supervisor said, "If you have time later, I'd like to share with you information about reading milestones. They are observable learning stages that can be noted as part of your assessment profiling system." The student teacher quickly accepted the offer and welcomed the information enthusiastically.

Figure 7.9 Family survey

September 6, 200___

Dear Adult Family Member:

As we begin the new school year, I would like to know a little more about your child's reading habits at home. This information will help me provide the best possible learning plan for your child this year. Please take a few minutes to answer the questions below and return in the self-addressed stamped envelope provided. Should you have any questions, feel free to phone me at XXX–XXXX.

Cordially,

Mrs. Shelley

---

1. My child likes to read the following at least once a week (check all that apply):

Comic books _____   Sports page _____

Magazines (example: *Highlights*) _____   Library books _____

Cereal boxes _____   Cooking recipes _____

TV Guide _____   Funny papers _____

Others (please name):

2. Have you noticed your child having any reading problems? If so, please explain briefly.

3. What are some of your child's favorite books?

4. If you would like a conference to discuss your child's reading ability, please indicate which days and times (after school) would be most convenient.

Reading Benchmarks and Stages of Development

To be an effective kid watcher, a teacher must gain an understanding of the *end-of-year benchmark skills* and *stages of reading development* through which children grow. Knowing which of these skills students have and have not acquired will help you construct a classroom profile and plan whole-class, small-group, and individualized instruction. Figure 7.10 lays out benchmark skills for reading development through grade 3 and the typical development for students acquiring basic reading skills.

In the latter part of the 1990s, a major urban school district set out to identify what they called end-of-year **benchmark reading skills** for kindergarten through Grade 3 (Cooter, 2003). With the benefit of a major grant, they established a team composed of notable reading researchers, master teachers, and distinguished school administrators to review the latest reading research and develop a list of the reading skills that, if acquired by the end of Grade 3, would likely result in children reading fluently. Cooter and Cooter (1999) have adapted that list, adding the skills their own research indicates are essential for this range of students. They have also included reading skills required by most states as part of their accountability systems, thus giving this list a degree of national validity. Be sure to note that the use of grade-level indicators for their **reading milestones** (see Figure 7.10) is only an approximation because children develop at differing rates. We recommend that you carefully consider these skills as you attempt to assess young or otherwise emerging readers.

Comprehensive reading assessment begins with an understanding of these reading milestones. It is essential that teachers come to know these observable behaviors and abilities well in order to describe where students are in their development and to aid in planning future instruction fitted to the students' respective zones of proximal development. **Be sure to get a copy of your state's reading standards (benchmarks) for your grade level and use it to monitor the full range of readers you are likely to have in your classroom.** (Note: Your state standards are provided online on the Web page for your state department of education. Web addresses for each and every state standard document are located for your convenience in Appendix B of this book).

The end-of-the-year benchmark reading skills resulted from research started in a major urban school district.

Observations should be tied to the reading standards adopted by the school district.

Screening Checklists and Scales

Teachers often create their own screening checklists using the reading benchmarks for their grade level. As an example, Lamme and Hysmith (1991) developed a scale that can be used to identify key developmental behaviors in emergent readers. It describes 11 levels often seen in the elementary school and could be used in tandem with the much more comprehensive reading benchmarks previously discussed. Following is an adaptation of that scale:

Level 11:   The student can read fluently from books and other reading materials.

Level 10:   The student seeks out new sources of information. He or she volunteers to share information from books with other children.

Level 9:   The student has developed the ability to independently use context clues, sentence structure, structural analysis, and phonic analysis to read new passages.

Level 8:   The student reads unfamiliar stories haltingly (not fluently) but requires little adult assistance.

Level 7:   The student reads familiar stories fluently.

Level 6:   The student reads word by word. He or she recognizes words in a new context.

Level 5:   The student memorizes text and can pretend to "read" a story.

Level 4:   The student participates in reading by doing such things as supplying words that rhyme and predictable text.

Figure 7.10   Reading milestones for grades K–3

Kindergarten Literacy Milestones (English and Spanish)

Book and Print Awareness

K.BA.1   Knows parts of a book and their functions

K.BA.2   Follows print word by word when listening to familiar text read aloud

Phonemic Awareness

K. PA.1   Simple awareness that spoken words have individual sound parts

K. PA.2   Orally segmenting and blending simple compound words

K. PA.3   Orally segmenting and blending simple two-syllable words

K. PA.4   Orally segmenting and blending simple onsets and rimes

K. PA.5   Orally segmenting and blending sound by sound

K. PA.6   Oddity tasks and sound manipulation

K. PA.7   Produces a rhyming word when given a spoken word

Decoding and Word Recognition

K. D.1   Recognizes and names all uppercase and lowercase letters (an alphabetic principle component)

K. D.2   Knows that the sequence of written letters and the sequence of spoken sounds in a word are the same (an alphabetic principle component)

K. D.S.1   Applies letter sound knowledge of consonant-vowel patterns to produce syllables (Spanish only)

Spelling and Writing

K.S.1   Writes independently most uppercase and lowercase letters

K.S.2   Begins using phonemic awareness and letter knowledge to create simple "temporary" (invented) spellings

Oral Reading

K.OR.1   Recognizes some words by sight, including a few common "environmental print" words

Language Comprehension and Response to Text

K.C.1   Uses less new vocabulary and language in own speech

K.C.2   Distinguishes whether simple sentences do or don't make sense

K.C.3   Connects information and events in text to life experiences

K.C.4   Uses graphic organizers to comprehend text with guidance

K.C.5   Retells stories or parts of stories

K.C.6   Understands and follows oral directions

K.C.7   Demonstrates familiarity with a number of books and selections

K.C.8   Explains simple concepts from nonfiction text

First Grade Literacy Milestones (English and Spanish)

Decoding and Word Recognition

1.D.1   Can segment and blend simple compound words

1.D.2   Can segment and blend simple two syllable words

1.D.3   Can segment and blend a one-syllable word using its onset and rime

1.D.4   Decodes phonetically regular one-syllable words and nonsense words accurately

(continued)

From Cooter, R. B., Jr. & Cooter, K. S. (1999). *BLAST!: Balanced Literacy Assessment System and Training*. Memphis, TN: Unpublished workshop resources.

Figure 7.10 Reading milestones for grades K–3—*continued*

1.D.5	Uses context clues to help identify unknown words in print
1.D.6	Uses context clues plus beginning, medial, and ending sounds in words to decode unknown words in print
1.D.7	Decodes two-syllable words using knowledge of sounds, letters, and syllables including consonants, vowels, blends, and stress (Spanish only)

Spelling and Writing

1.D.1	Spells three- and four-letter short vowel words correctly (English only)
1.D.2	Uses phonics to spell simple one- and two-syllable words independently (temporary and correct spellings)
1.D.3	Uses basic punctuation (periods, question marks, capitalization)
1.D.4	Uses simple graphic organizers to plan writing with guidance
1.D.5	Produces a variety of composition types such as stories, descriptions, and journal entries
1.D.S.1	Recognizes words that use specific spelling patterns such as r/rr, y/ll, s/c/z, q/c/k, g/j, j/x, b/v, ch, h, i/y, gue, and gui (Spanish only)
1.D.S.2	Spells words with two syllables using dieresis marks, accents, r/rr, y/ll, s/c/z, q/c/k, g/j, j/x, b/v, ch, h, and i/y accurately (Spanish only)
1.D.S.3	Uses verb tenses appropriately and consistently (Spanish only)

Oral Reading

1.OR.1	Reads aloud with fluency texts on his/her independent reading level
1.OR.2	Comprehends any text that is on his/her independent reading level
1.OR.3	Uses phonic knowledge to sound out unknown words when reading text
1.OR.4	Recognizes common, irregularly spelled words by sight

Language Comprehension and Response to Text

1.C.1	Reads and comprehends fiction and nonfiction that is appropriate for the second half of grade one
1.C.2	Notices difficulties in understanding text (early metacognition skills)
1.C.3	Connects information and events in text to life experiences
1.C.4	Reads and understands simple written directions
1.C.5	Predicts and justifies what will happen next in stories
1.C.6	Discusses *how, why,* and *what* questions in sharing nonfiction text
1.C.7	Describes new information in his/her own words
1.C.8	Distinguishes whether simple sentences are incomplete or do not make sense
1.C.9	Expands sentences in response to *what, when, where,* and *how* questions
1.C.10	Uses new vocabulary and language in own speech and writing
1.C.11	Demonstrates familiarity with a number of genres including poetry, mysteries, humor, and everyday print sources such as newspapers, signs, phone books, notices, and labels
1.C.12	Summarizes the main points of a story

Reading Fluency and Rate (Minimum Expectations)

1.F.1	Frequent word-by-word reading
1.F.2	Some two- and three-word phrasing

Figure 7.10 *continued*

1.F.3	May reread for problem solving or to clarify (strategic reading)
1.F.4	Shows some awareness of syntax and punctuation
1.F.5	Forty (40) words per minute reading rate (minimum)

Second Grade Literacy Milestones (English and Spanish)

Decoding and Word Recognition

2.D.1	Decodes phonetically regular two-syllable words and nonsense words
2.D.S.1	Decodes words with three or more syllables using knowledge of sounds, letters, and syllables including consonants, vowels, blends, and stress (Spanish only)
2.D.S.2	Uses structural cues to recognize words such as compounds, base words, and inflections such as -mente, -ito, and -ando (Spanish only)

Spelling and Writing

2.SW.1	Spells previously studied words and spelling patterns correctly in own writing (application)
2.SW.2	Begins to use formal language patterns in place of oral language patterns in own writing
2.SW.3	Uses revision and editing processes to clarify and refine own writing with assistance
2.SW.4	Writes informative, well-structured reports with organizational help
2.SW.5	Attends to spelling, mechanics, and presentation for final products
2.SW.6	Produces a variety of types of compositions such as stories, reports, and correspondence
2.SW.7	Uses information from nonfiction text in independent writing
2.SW.S.1	Spells words with three or more syllables using silent letters, dieresis marks, accents, verbs, r/rr, y/ll, s/c/z, q/c/k, g/j, j/x, b/v, ch, h, and i/y accurately (Spanish only)

Oral Reading

2.OR.1	Reads aloud with fluency any text that is appropriate for the first half of grade two
2.OR.2	Comprehends any text that is appropriate for the first half of grade two
2.OR.3	Uses phonic knowledge to sound out words, including multisyllable words, when reading text
2.OR.4	Reads irregularly spelled words, diphthongs, special vowel spellings, and common word endings accurately

Language Comprehension and Response to Text

2.C.1	Reads and comprehends both fiction and nonfiction that is appropriate for the second half of grade two
2.C.2	Rereads sentences when meaning is not clear
2.C.3	Interprets information from diagrams, charts, and graphs
2.C.4	Recalls facts and details of text
2.C.5	Reads nonfiction materials for answers to specific questions
2.C.6	Develops literary awareness of character traits, point of view, setting, problem, solution, and outcome

(continued)

Figure 7.10 Reading milestones for grades K–3—*continued*

2.C.7	Connects and compares information across nonfiction selections
2.C.8	Poses possible answers to *how, why,* and *what-if* questions in interpreting nonfiction text
2.C.9	Explains and describes new concepts and information in own words
2.C.10	Identifies part of speech for concrete nouns, active verbs, adjectives, and adverbs
2.C.11	Uses new vocabulary and language in own speech and writing
2.C.12	Demonstrates familiarity with a number of read-aloud and independent reading selections, including nonfiction
2.C.13	Recognizes a variety of print resources and knows their contents, such as joke books, chapter books, dictionaries, atlases, weather reports, and *TV Guide*
2.C.14	Connects a variety of texts to literature and life experiences (language to literacy)
2.C.15	Summarizes a story, including the stated main idea

Reading Fluency and Rate (Minimum Skills)

2.F.1	Combination of word-by-word and fluent phrase reading
2.F.2	Some expressive phrasing
2.F.3	Shows attention to punctuation and syntax
2.F.4	Fifty (50) words per minute reading rate (minimum)

Third Grade Literacy Milestones (English and Spanish)

Decoding and Word Recognition

3.D.1	Uses context clues, phonic knowledge, and structural analysis to decode words

Spelling and Writing

3.SW.1	Spells previously studied words and spelling patterns correctly in own writing
3.SW.2	Uses the dictionary to check and correct spelling
3.SW.3	Uses all aspects of the writing process in compositions and reports with assistance, including

3.SW.3.1	Combines information from multiple sources in written reports
3.SW.3.2	Revises and edits written work independently on a level appropriate for first semester of third grade
3.SW.3.3	Produces a variety of written work (response to literature, reports, semantic maps)
3.SW.3.4	Uses graphic organizational tools with a variety of texts
3.SW.3.5	Incorporates elaborate descriptions and figurative language
3.SW.3.6	Uses a variety of formal sentence structures in own writing

3.SW.S.1	Writes proficiently using orthographic patterns and rules such as qu, use of n before v, m before b, m before p, and changing z to c when adding -es (Spanish only)

Figure 7.10 Reading milestones for grades K–3—*continued*

3.SW.S.2 Spells words with three or more syllables using silent letters, dieresis marks, accents, verbs, r/rr, y/ll, s/c/z, q/c/k, g/j, j/x, b/v, ch, h, and i/y accurately (Spanish only)

Oral Reading

3.OR.1 Reads aloud with fluency any text that is appropriate for the first half of grade three

3.OR.2 Comprehends any text that is appropriate for the first half of grade three

Language Comprehension and Response to Text

3.C.1 Reads and comprehends both fiction and nonfiction that is appropriate for grade three

3.C.2 Reads chapter books independently

3.C.3 Identifies specific words or phrases that are causing comprehension difficulties (metacognition)

3.C.4 Summarizes major points from fiction and nonfiction text

3.C.5 Can discuss similarities in characters and events across stories

3.C.6 Can discuss underlying theme or message when interpreting fiction

3.C.7 Distinguishes when interpreting nonfiction text between:

    3.C.7.1 Cause and effect

    3.C.7.2 Fact and opinion

    3.C.7.3 Main idea and supporting details

3.C.8 Uses information and reasoning to evaluate opinions

3.C.9 Infers word meaning from roots, prefixes, and suffixes that have been taught

3.C.10 Uses dictionary to determine meanings and usage of unknown words

3.C.11 Uses new vocabulary in own speech and writing

3.C.12 Uses basic grammar and parts of speech correctly in independent writing

3.C.13 Shows familiarity with a number of read-aloud and independent reading selections, including nonfiction

3.C.14 Uses multiple sources to locate information

    3.C.14.1 Tables of contents

    3.C.14.2 Indexes

    3.C.14.3 Internet search engines

3.C.15 Connects a variety of literary texts with life experiences

Reading Fluency

3.F.1 Very few word-by-word interruptions

3.F.2 Reads mostly in larger meaningful phrases

3.F.3 Reads with expression

3.F.4 Attends consistently to punctuation

3.F.5 Rereads to clarify or problem-solve

3.F.6 Sixty (60) words per minute reading rate (minimum)

Level 3:   The student talks about or describes pictures. He or she pretends to read (storytelling). He or she makes up words that go along with pictures.

Level 2:   The student watches pictures as an adult reads a story.

Level 1:   The student listens to a story but does not look at the pictures.

Many teachers find that checklists that include a *Likert scale* (a 5-point scale) can be useful in student portfolios because many reading behaviors become more fluent over time. One example developed by Diffily (1994) is shown in Figure 7.11.

Concepts About Print

Teachers in the primary grades must understand in some detail what children know about print concepts. The *Concepts About Print* (CAP) test was designed by Clay (1985) to help teachers establish priorities in reading instruction for emergent and early readers. Clay's test assesses some 24 basic print awareness elements, including

Figure 7.11   Diffily's classroom observation checklist

Student's Name _____ Date

Literacy Development Checklist

	Seldom				Often
Chooses books for personal enjoyment	1	2	3	4	5
Knows print/picture difference	1	2	3	4	5
Knows print is read from left to right	1	2	3	4	5
Asks to be read to	1	2	3	4	5
Asks that story be read again	1	2	3	4	5
Listens attentively during story time	1	2	3	4	5
Knows what a title is	1	2	3	4	5
Knows what an author is	1	2	3	4	5
Knows what an illustrator is	1	2	3	4	5
In retellings, repeats 2+ details	1	2	3	4	5
Tells beginning, middle, end	1	2	3	4	5
Can read logos	1	2	3	4	5
Uses text in functional ways	1	2	3	4	5
"Reads" familiar books to self/others	1	2	3	4	5
Can read personal words	1	2	3	4	5
Can read sight words from books	1	2	3	4	5
Willing to "write"	1	2	3	4	5
Willing to "read" personal story	1	2	3	4	5
Willing to dictate story to adult	1	2	3	4	5

Gratefully used by the authors with the permission of Deborah Diffily, Ph.D., and Alice Carlson Applied Learning Center, Ft. Worth, TX.

front of a book, print versus pictures, left-to-right progression, changes in word order, changes in letter order in words, meaning of a period, and location of a capital letter. The assessment is carried out using one of four available books called *Sand* (1985), *Stones* (1985), *No Shoes* (2000), and *Follow Me Moon* (2000). The procedure is for the teacher to read one of the books with the student and ask such questions as where to begin reading, which way to go, and where to go next (Fountas & Pinnell, 1996). Results of the CAP test can be especially helpful to kindergarten and first-grade teachers who want to establish an initial class profile of strengths and needs. A listing of the concepts about print assessed on the CAP test is shown in Figure 7.12

Assessing the "Big Five" Areas of Reading Development

Once you have taken an assessment "snap-shot" of your class, you will want to gather more detailed data for each student. In this section, we examine assessment methods that provide you with a "color movie" of each student's growth in reading. In most cases, these assessment strategies will be done in brief bursts of 5 to 10 minutes. You will repeat them throughout the year, so much so that they will become second nature.

Phonemic awareness and alphabet knowledge, phonics and word attack, vocabulary, comprehension, and fluency are what might be called the **big five areas of reading development.** We begin with the most basic forms that are useful in the early grades, then move quickly into strategies with much wider application.

Figure 7.12 Selected concepts about print surveyed adapted from the CAP test
(Clay, 1985)

Selected Print Concepts

Front of the book
Knows that print contains the author's message
Knows where to start reading
Knows which way to go when reading
Return sweep to the left
Word by word matching
First and last concept
Bottom of the picture
Left page before right
Notices one change in word order
Notices one change in letter order
Knows the meaning of the question mark (?)
Knows the meaning of the period (.)
Knows the meaning of the comma (,)
Knows the meaning of quotation marks (" ")
Can identify the first and last letter of a word
Can identify one letter and two letters
Can identify capital letters

Note: The learner is asked to identify each of the following within the context of a special book (e.g., *Sand* or *Stones*) developed for this purpose.

ASSESSING PHONEMIC AWARENESS AND ALPHABET KNOWLEDGE

The ability to perform phonemic awareness tasks develops from least difficult to more difficult tasks as listed here:

1. Rhyming
2. Hearing sounds in words (oddity and same-different judgment tasks)
3. Counting syllables and sounds
4. Isolating beginning, ending, and middle sounds in words
5. Substituting and deleting sounds in words and syllables
6. Blending syllables, onset and rimes, and sounds into words
7. Segmenting words into syllables, onset and rimes, and sounds
8. Representing sounds in language and words with symbols in spelling and writing

Because of the ways in which phonemic awareness and alphabetic principle develop, we present assessment tools helpful in assessing (a) phonemic awareness, (b) letter knowledge, and (c) knowledge of the alphabetic system. These ideas are drawn from our companion book for classroom teachers titled *Strategies for Reading Assessment and Instruction: Helping Every Child Succeed* (2nd ed.) (Reutzel & Cooter, 2003a).

Phonemic Awareness: Recognizing Rhyming Words

With this phonemic awareness activity, students are asked to recognize whether pairs of words rhyme. According to Adams (1990a, 1990b, 2001) and Adams, Foorman, Lundberg, and Beeler (1998), the ability to determine rhyme is the easiest of all phonemic awareness tasks.

To begin, you will need to create a list of 20 word pairs. At least 50% of the word pairs should rhyme. Figure 7.13 shows an example of what we mean.

Model the concept of rhyming by giving several examples and nonexamples. Explain that rhyming words end with the same sound(s). Then, using the word pairs shown in Figure 7.13, read aloud each pair of words, asking the child if they rhyme. Note their responses to each pair. According to Yopp (1988), kindergarten children usually achieve a mean score of 75% correct, or 15 out of the 20 target word pairs identified correctly. If students score poorly on this task, teachers should provide contextual reading and writing experiences to hear sounds in words with a particular emphasis on rhyming texts.

Phonemic Awareness: Oddity Task—Which Word Doesn't Belong?

Bradley and Bryant (1983) designed an oddity task to measure children's development of onset and rime awareness versus phonemic awareness. Oddity tasks require that students spot the "odd word out" of a list of spoken words. Typically, children listen to (or say from pictures) a group of spoken words, then select the word that has a different sound from the others. Oddity tasks can focus on rhyming words and beginning, ending, and middle sounds in words.

To begin this assessment, create a list of 10 word sets of three words each or a collection of 10 picture sets of three pictures each. The word set in Figure 7.14

Figure 7.13 Rhyming word pair task list

plate	dog
fat	cat
book	hook
desk	shelf
fish	swish
shoe	ball
tree	grass
flower	power
key	lock
pen	tape
swing	thing
sat	rat
box	clock
bark	smart
berry	hairy
cow	milk
brick	thick
malt	halt
wall	call
toy	love

Figure 7.14 Beginning consonant oddity task list

Soap	Six	Dog
Car	Man	Mop
Duck	Dog	Five
Pig	Pack	Fan
Fish	Fan	Leaf
Nest	Nut	Wheel
Cat	Cake	Nine
Sun	Tree	Tie
Clock	Bee	Bat
Sock	Feet	Fish

demonstrates a beginning consonant oddity task. The goal is for children to pick the odd word out from the list or picture collections with at least 70% accuracy.

Begin by seating the child across from you at a table. Place the list in your lap so that you can see the words. Using a puppet, demonstrate how the puppet listens and picks out the odd word. For example, say, "Kermit the Frog is going to listen to three words I will say." Next, say the three words—*pan, pig,* and *kite.* Then let the puppet figure, in this case Kermit the Frog, select which of the three words is the odd word out. Demonstrate this again with the words *coat, bus,* and *ball* if necessary.

Have a puppet figure pronounce the words in Figure 7.14 very slowly and clearly. Ask the child to tell the puppet which word is the odd word out. Make a record of how well the child does directly on a copy of the word list. This word list task can be modified to include oddity tasks related to rhyming words and ending and middle sounds as well.

Phonemic Awareness: Same-Different Word Pair Task

Treiman and Zukowski (1991) designed the same-different task to measure children's development of syllable, onset and rime, and phonemic awareness. Same-different tasks require that students say whether a pair of words (represented in pictures) share the same beginning, ending, or middle syllable or sounds. Typically, children listen to (or say from pictures) a pair of spoken words and then say if the word pair is the same or different. Same-different tasks can focus on rhyming words and beginning, ending, and middle syllables and sounds in words.

A list of 10 word pairs or a collection of 10 picture pairs is needed for the same-different task. The word set found in Figure 7.15 demonstrates a beginning syllable same-different task. Children should be able to respond if the word or picture pairs have the same syllable or sound with at least 50% accuracy.

Begin by seating the student across from you at a table. Place the list in your lap so that you can see the words. Using a puppet, demonstrate how the puppet listens and says whether the word pair is the same or different. For example, say, "Peter the bunny is going to listen to two words I will say or will look at two pictures I put on the table." Next, say the word pair—*partly* and *partition*. Then let the puppet figure, in this case Peter the Bunny, say whether the two words are the same or different. Demonstrate this again with the words *dandy* and *dislike* if necessary.

Phonemic Awareness: Syllable and Sound Counting Task

The counting task is a variation of the tapping task developed by Libermann, Shankweiler, Fischer, and Carter (1974). The counting task is designed to measure children's development of syllable and phonemic awareness. Counting tasks require that students count the number of syllables or sounds in a word or shown in a pic-

Figure 7.15 Beginning syllable same-different task list

Hammer	Hammock
Little	Local
Window	Winner
Single	Sickle
Maple	Motor
Donkey	Dinky
Camera	Camshaft
Twinkle	Twinkie
Belly	Balloon
Fabric	Furnish

ture. Typically, children listen to (or say from a picture) a word and then count the number of syllables or sounds. Counting tasks can focus on beginning, ending, and middle syllables and sounds of words.

A list of 10 word pairs or a collection of 10 picture pairs is needed for the counting task. The picture set found in Figure 7.16 demonstrates a sound counting task. Children should be able to accurately count the number of sounds or syllables within the words or pictures with at least 50% accuracy.

To begin, seat the child next to you at a table. Place the pictures in Figure 7.16 on the tabletop so that you and the child can see the words. Demonstrate how to count the sounds in samples A and B. For example, say, "I am looking at this picture (point)." Next, say the word aloud and count the sounds you hear with your fingers. Tell the child that the number of sounds in sample A is four: f-r-o-g. Demonstrate this again with the picture in sample B if necessary.

Have the child look at picture 1 in Figure 7.16 very carefully. Ask the child to say what the picture is and count the sounds with his or her fingers. Then ask him or her to tell you the number of sounds in the word. Make a record of how well the child does on a word list. This counting can be modified to include pictures related to ending and middle syllables and ending sounds as well.

Phonemic Awareness: Auditory Sound Blending Task

With this activity, students are asked to recognize words by blending the sounds in words that teachers stretch out into segmented units, such as m-an or sh-i-p (we call this "word rubber banding"). According to Griffith and Olson (1992), the ability to guess what the word is from its blended form demonstrates a slightly higher level of phonemic awareness than recognizing rhyming sounds.

You will need to prepare a list of 30 words divided into three sets of 10 each (see Figure 7.17):

Figure 7.16   Picture sound counting task

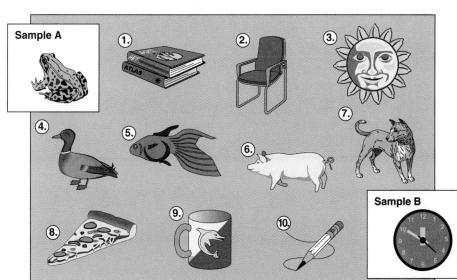

Figure 7.17   Word lists for blending

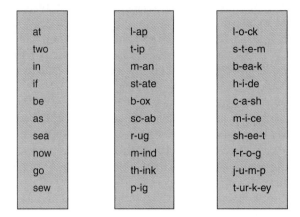

at	l-ap	l-o-ck
two	t-ip	s-t-e-m
in	m-an	b-ea-k
if	st-ate	h-i-de
be	b-ox	c-a-sh
as	sc-ab	m-i-ce
sea	r-ug	sh-ee-t
now	m-ind	f-r-o-g
go	th-ink	j-u-m-p
sew	p-ig	t-ur-k-ey

- The first 10 words should be two phoneme words.
- The second set of 10 words should be three or four phoneme words that are divided before the vowel demonstrating the onset and rime, such as c (onset)-ap (rime).
- The third set of 10 words should be three or four phoneme words that are segmented completely, such as ch-i-p.

Tell the child that you will be stretching words out like a rubber band, saying each sound. Model several of these stretched words for the child and tell him or her the word you have stretched. For example, stretch the word *s-i-t*. Then say the word— *sit*. Do this several times. Next, stretch a word and ask the child to tell you the word. Once this has been accomplished, tell the child you are going to play a game where you say a word stretched out and they are to answer the question *What am I saying?*

According to Yopp's (1988) research, kindergarten children achieve a mean score of 66% correct, or 20 out of the 30 target words identified correctly. If students score poorly on this task, teachers should provide reading and writing experiences that help children hear sounds in words. Creating invented spellings for writing new words and using word rubber banding to sound out new words found in trade books are just two examples.

Phonemic Awareness: Segmenting Sounds

In segmenting sounds, students are asked to listen to and isolate sounds in the beginning, middle, and ending positions in a word. A child's ability to isolate sounds in words is an excellent indication whether she can profit from decoding instruction.

Construct a list of 15 words consisting of three phonemes each. Target sounds in the beginning, middle, and end of the words like the one shown in Figure 7.18.

Model how phonemes can be pronounced by showing how *sit* starts with /s/, *hike* has the /i/ sound in the middle, and *look* ends with the /k/ sound. Next, tell the child you are going to play a quick game together. You will say a word, then you will ask him or her to tell you the sound he or she hears in a specific place in the word, such as beginning, middle, or end. For example, you may say, "*Slam*. Say the sound at the end of the word *slam*." The child responds correctly by articulating the sound /m/. Now, begin the list of words shown previously. Record each response.

Figure 7.18   Word list for segmenting sounds

dime
hu*sh*
f*i*ve
clock
c*u*t
fool
loop
rode
*h*ome
yar*d*
k*i*ss
get
raf*t*
bike
mug

According to Yopp's (1988) research study, kindergarten children achieve a mean score of 9% correct, or 1 or 2 correct responses out of 15 target words. If students score poorly on this task, teachers should provide reading and writing experiences focusing on hearing sounds in specific locations within words.

Alphabet Knowledge

Knowledge of the alphabet is essential in early reading instruction; it provides teachers and students with common language for discussing graphophonic relationships. Assessment of alphabet knowledge should occur in two contexts: identifying letters in isolation and letter production. Here are some simple assessment tasks that yield important insights.

Alphabet knowledge is a critical stage of literacy development following phonemic awareness.

Letter Knowledge: Alphabet Identification

This task is based on the work of Clay (1993a; 1993b) and determines whether readers can identify letters of the alphabet. Begin by reproducing the randomized alphabet letter display (shown in Figure 7.19) on a sheet of paper or chart paper for use in this exercise.

Invite the student to be seated next to you and explain that you would like to find out which letters of the alphabet he or she can name as you point to them on a chart. Begin pointing at the top of the alphabet letter display working line by line and left to right to the bottom of the display, keeping letters below your line of focus covered. Using a photocopy of the display, mark which of the letters were correctly named. Next, ask the child to point to the letter you named in the display. Record this information. Most children, even readers with special learning needs, will be able to identify at least 50% of the letters requested. However, students who have little familiarity with letters may perform poorly.

The National Research Centers provide many resources on assessment. Readers can link to their site from Chapter 7 on our Companion Website at www.prenhall.com/reutzel.

Figure 7.19   Alphabet letter display

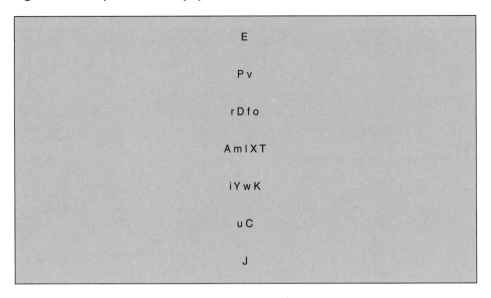

Letter Knowledge: Letter Production Task

This task is designed to determine whether students know and can write letters of the alphabet. Unlike simple letter identification, this task requires that students be able to produce letters from memory. Letter knowledge is an indication of how well students have sorted out sound/symbol processes but is not logically necessary for successful reading. It does, however, make learning to read easier (Venesky, 1975). Letter naming/production can be likened to a bridge that helps children cross the river of early reading and writing.

Create a list of 10 letters drawn randomly from the alphabet. Be sure to include at least three vowel letters in the selection, as shown in Figure 7.20.

Provide the child with a pencil and a blank piece of paper. Ask the student if he or she knows any letters. Next, ask him or her to write down any letters he or she may know and name them. Following this exercise, invite him or her to write the letters you name from the random letter list you created. Most first-grade students will score at least 70% on this task. However, students who have little familiarity with letters may perform poorly.

The Next Step in Reading Development: Phonics and Word Attack

Many students in your classroom already understand the rudiments of how letters and letter combinations can represent speech sounds and have learned some word attack

Figure 7.20   Random letter production task

1. b	2. m	3. e	4. f	5. t
6. l	7. p	8. o	9. s	10. h

strategies. Thus, we must survey this kind of reading knowledge to plan their instruction. This is the next area of assessment essentials we explore.

DECODING ASSESSMENT: PHONICS AND WORD ATTACK SKILLS

From the earliest days of formal reading instruction, the ability to decode words in print has been viewed as essential (Reutzel & Cooter, 2003a, 2003b). In 1915, for example, William S. Gray published the Standardized Oral Reading Paragraphs for grades 1 through 8, which focused on oral reading errors and reading speed exclusively. In the 1930s and 1940s, Durrell (1940) and Betts (1946) discussed at length the value of studying oral reading errors as a way to inform reading instruction. These and other writings began the development of assessment methods for analyzing oral reading errors.

Running Records

Clay (1972), in her manual called *The Early Detection of Reading Difficulties,* sought to formalize methodology for teachers conducting decoding assessments. Clay's **running records** for analyzing oral reading errors proved to be functional for many classroom teachers, and in the next section we describe in detail how running records are constructed and used to inform classroom teaching.

Running records are a preferred method for assessing oral reading.

Conducting Running Records

Marie Clay (1972, 1985, 1997), a New Zealand educator and former president of the International Reading Association, described the running record as an informal assessment procedure with high reliability (.90 on error only reliabilities) that informs teachers regarding students' decoding development. The procedure is not difficult but does require practice. Clay estimates that it takes about 2 hours of practice for teachers to become relatively proficient at running records. In essence, the teacher notes everything the student says or does while reading, including all the correct words read orally and all miscues (Wiener & Cohen, 1997). Clay recommends that three running records be obtained for each child on various levels of difficulty for initial reading assessment. Her criteria for oral reading evaluation are based on words correctly read aloud:

Independent level (easy to read)	95–100% correct
Instructional level (ideal for teaching)	90–94% correct
Frustration level (too difficult)	80–89% correct

Running records using Clay's method are taken without having to mark a prepared script and may be recorded on a sheet of paper; requiring about 10 minutes to transcribe. Guidelines for administration follow:

1. A sample from the book(s) to be used is needed that is 100 to 200 words in length. For early readers, the text may fall below 100 words. Allow the student to read the passage one or two times before you take the running record.
2. Sit along side the student while he or she reads so that both of you can see the page. It isn't really necessary to have your own photocopy of the text; a blank sheet of paper will do. Record all accurate reading by making check

Figure 7.21 Noting miscues in a running record

Reading Behavior	Notation	Explanation
Accurate Reading	√ √ √ √ √ √	*Notation:* A check is noted for each word pronounced correctly.
Self-Correction	attempt / word in text │ SC	The child corrects an error himself. This is not counted as a miscue. *Notation:* "SC" is the notation used for self-corrections.
Omission	—— / Word in text	A word or words are left out during the reading. *Notation:* A dash mark is written over a line above the word(s) from the text that has been omitted.
Insertion	Word inserted / ——	The child adds a word that is not in the text. *Notation:* The word inserted by the reader is placed above a line and a dash placed below it.
Student Appeal and Assistance	—— │ A / Word from text │	The child is "stuck" on a word he cannot call and asks (verbal or nonverbal) the teacher for help. *Notation:* "A" is written above a line for "assisted" and the problem word from the text is written below the line.
Repetition	R	Sometimes children will repeat words or phrases. These repetitions are not scored as an error but *are* recorded. *Notation:* Write an "R" after the word repeated and draw a line back to the point where the reader returned.
Substitution	Substituted word / Word from text	The child says a word that is different from the word in the text. *Notation:* The student's substitution word is written above a line under which the correct word from text is written.

234

Figure 7.21 *continued*

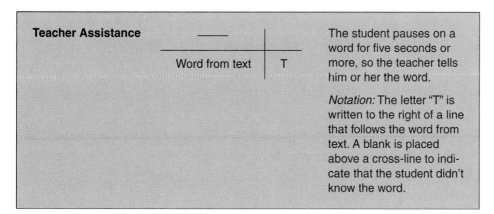

Teacher Assistance		
Word from text	T	The student pauses on a word for five seconds or more, so the teacher tells him or her the word.
		Notation: The letter "T" is written to the right of a line that follows the word from text. A blank is placed above a cross-line to indicate that the student didn't know the word.

marks on a sheet of blank paper for each word said correctly. Errors, or miscues, should be noted using the notations indicated in Figure 7.21. Figure 7.22 shows an example of a running record taken using a passage from the Flynt/Cooter Reading Inventory for the Classroom (Flynt & Cooter, 2004) using the marking system.

*Oral reading errors are known as **miscues.***

Understanding Miscues: MSV Analysis

Clay (1985) developed a way of interpreting miscues for use in her widely acclaimed Reading Recovery program, commonly referred to as **MSV analysis.** This way of thinking enables you to determine whether the student uses three primary **cueing strategies** when she encounters a new word and a miscue occurs: meaning cues (M), syntax cues (S), and visual cues (V). See the following, which is a summary of that work compiled by Flynt and Cooter (2004). We caution that the MSV process is much less reliable than error only analysis.

MSV analysis is used to determine if a student uses one of three cueing strategies when encountering a new word and a miscue occurs—meaning cues (M), syntax cues (S), or visual cues (V).

- *M = Semantic (Meaning—Does it make sense?).*   In reviewing each miscue, consider whether the student is using meaning cues in his her attempt to identify the word. Context clues, picture cues, and information from the passage are examples of meaning cues used by the reader.
- *S = Structure (Syntax—Does it sound right?).*   A rule system, or *grammar,* as with all languages, governs the English language. For example, English is essentially based on a "subject-verb" grammar system. *Syntax* is the application of this subject-verb grammar system in creating sentences. The goal in studying *syntax cues* as part of your miscue analysis is to try and determine the extent to which the student unconsciously uses rules of grammar in attempting to identify unknown words in print. For example, if a word in a passage causing a miscue for the reader is a verb, ask yourself whether the student's miscue was also a verb. Consistent use of the appropriate part of speech in miscues (e.g., a noun for a noun, a verb for a verb, or articles for articles) is an indication that the student has internalized the rule system of English grammar and is applying that knowledge in attacking unknown words.
- *V = Visual (Graphophonic—Does it look right?).*   Sometimes a miscue looks much like the correct word appearing in the text. The miscue may begin with

the same letter or letters, for example, saying the *top* for *toy* or *sit* for *seat*. Another possibility is the letters of the miscue may look very similar to the word appearing in text (e.g., *introduction* for *introspection*). Use of visual cues is essentially the student's ability (or inability) to apply phonics skills. The extent to which readers use visual cues is an important factor to consider when trying to better understand the skills employed by developing readers when attacking unknown words in print.

Applying MSV thinking is fairly simple once you get the hang of it. In Figure 7.23, we return to the miscues previously noted in Figure 7.22 and conduct an MSV analysis on each. Do you see why each interpretation was made?

An Alternative Running Records System

Flynt and Cooter (2004) developed a method of scoring running records that makes the process both time efficient and useful to classroom teachers. This system involves the use of what they call a "miscue grid" and can be extremely effective when used with text selections that are matched to student interests.

For best results, allow students at least some choice in the books to be read for running records.

In the following excerpt from the Flynt/Cooter Reading Inventory for the Classroom (Figure 7.24), you will notice how miscues can be noted on the left side of the grid over the text, then tallied after the student has finished reading in the appropriate columns to the right according to miscue type. This process makes the administration quicker and enables teachers to identify error patterns for each oral reading. The grid method can easily be adapted by teachers for use with excerpts from any literature sample.

Teachers should preselect passages on a range of reading levels or have students select the passage(s) to be read a day ahead of the actual reading so that the first 100 words can be transcribed onto the left-hand side of a blank grid patterned after the one shown in Figure 7.24. During the oral reading, tape-record the session so that the reading can later be reviewed for accuracy of transcription. Miscues should be noted in the left-hand column over the text facsimile using the symbols described earlier for miscues. After all miscues are noted, examine each miscue and make a final determination about its type (mispronunciation, substitution, insertion, and so on), then make a mark in the appropriate grid box on the right side of the form. Only one hash mark is made for each miscue. Once this process is completed, each column is tallied.

In Figure 7.24, you will note that the reader had two mispronunciations, two insertions, and so on. When the student has read several passages for the teacher over a period of weeks and months, it becomes easy to identify "error patterns"—types of miscues that happen regularly—and to plan appropriate instruction for small-group or individual instruction.

Finally, if you decide to use the grid system, be sure to conduct an MSV analysis on each miscue to better understand which cueing systems the reader is using.

VOCABULARY ASSESSMENT IN THE CLASSROOM

Decoding is an essential part of good reading ability, but it is not sufficient. If the reader can decode a word but does not know the word, then comprehension cannot occur. Thus, it is critical that we understand which words are known to students and,

Figure 7.22 Running records example

Student _____ Paco (Grade 2) _____	
Title: The Pig and the Snake	
One day Mr. Pig was walking to	✓ ✓ ✓ ✓ ✓ ✓ ✓
town. He saw a big hole in the	✓ ✓ $\frac{sam}{saw}$ | sc ✓ ✓ ✓ ✓ ✓
road. A big snake was in the	✓ ✓ $\frac{—}{big}$ ✓ ✓ ✓ ✓ ✓
hole. "Help me," said the snake,	✓ ✓ ✓ $\frac{out}{—}$ ✓ ✓ ✓
"and I will be your friend." "No, no,"	✓ ✓ ✓ ✓✓ $\frac{—}{friend}$ | A ✓ ✓
said Mr. Pig. "If I help you get	✓ ✓ ✓ ✓ ✓ ✓ ✓
out you will bite me. You're	✓ ✓ ✓ R ✓ ✓
a snake!" The snake cried and	✓ ✓ ✓ ✓ ✓ ✓
cried. So Mr. Pig pulled the	✓ ✓ ✓ ✓ $\frac{popped}{pulled}$
snake out of the hole.	✓ ✓ ✓ ✓ ✓
Then the snake said, "Now I am	✓ ✓ ✓ ✓ ✓ ✓ ✓
going to bite you, Mr. Pig."	✓ ✓ ✓ ✓ ✓ ✓
"How can you bite me after	✓ ✓ ✓ ✓ ✓ $\frac{—}{after}$ | T
I helped you out of the hole?"	✓ ✓ ✓ ✓ ✓ ✓ ✓
said Mr. Pig. The snake said,//	✓ ✓ ✓ ✓ ✓ ✓
"You knew I was a snake	✓ ✓ ✓ ✓ ✓ ✓
when you pulled me out!"	✓ ✓ ✓ ✓ ✓

From Flynt, E. S., & Cooter, R. B. (2001). *The Flynt/Cooter Reading Inventory for the Classroom,*
4/e. Upper Saddle River, NJ: Merrill/Prentice Hall. Used with permission of the authors.

Figure 7.23 Running record with MSV analysis

Student _____Paco_____ (Grade 2)

Title: **The Pig and the Snake**		E MSV	SC MSV
One day Mr. Pig was walking to	✓ ✓ ✓ ✓ ✓ ✓ ✓		
town. He saw a big hole in the	✓ ✓ sam/saw │ sc ✓ ✓ ✓ ✓ ✓		Ⓜ Ⓢ Ⓥ
road. A big snake was in the	✓ ✓ –/big ✓ ✓ ✓ ✓ ✓	M S V	
hole. "Help me," said the snake,	✓ ✓ ✓ out/– ✓ ✓ ✓	Ⓜ Ⓢ V	
"and I will be your friend." "No, no,"	✓ ✓ ✓ ✓✓ –│A/friend│ ✓ ✓	M S V	
said Mr. Pig. "If I help you get	✓ ✓ ✓ ✓ ✓ ✓ ✓ ✓		
out you will bite me. You're	✓ ✓ ✓ R ✓ ✓		Ⓜ Ⓢ Ⓥ
a snake!" The snake cried and	✓ ✓ ✓ ✓ ✓ ✓		
cried. So Mr. Pig pulled the	✓ ✓ ✓ ✓ popped/pulled	Ⓜ Ⓢ Ⓥ	
snake out of the hole.	✓ ✓ ✓ ✓ ✓		
Then the snake said, "Now I am	✓ ✓ ✓ ✓ ✓ ✓ ✓		
going to bite you, Mr. Pig."	✓ ✓ ✓ ✓ ✓ ✓		
"How can you bite me after	✓ ✓ ✓ ✓ ✓ –/after │ T	M S V	
I helped you out of the hole?"	✓ ✓ ✓ ✓ ✓ ✓ ✓		
said Mr. Pig. The snake said,//	✓ ✓ ✓ ✓ ✓ ✓		
"You knew I was a snake	✓ ✓ ✓ ✓ ✓ ✓		
when you pulled me out!"	✓ ✓ ✓ ✓ ✓		

From Flynt, E. S., & Cooter, R. B. (2001). *The Flynt/Cooter Reading Inventory for the Classroom, 4/e.* Upper Saddle River, NJ: Merrill/Prentice Hall. Used with permission of the authors.

Figure 7.24   Flynt/Cooter running records grid system

	Mispronounce	Substitute	Self-correct	Insertions	Teacher assist	Omissions	Other
Hot Shoes							
The guys at (the) I.B. Belcher					1		
Elementary School ~~loved~~ all the *lived (SC)*			1				
new sport shoes. Some ~~wore~~ the *wib*	1						
" Sky High" model by Nicky.							
Others who ^ couldn't ~~afford~~ Sky *really / buy*		1		1			
Highs would settle for ~~a lesser~~ *another*		1					
shoe. Some liked the "Street							
Smarts" by Concave, or (the)						1	
"Uptown-Downtown" ^ by Beebop. *s*				1			
The Belcher boys ~~get~~ to the point *go*		1					
with their shoes that they could							
~~identify~~ their friends just by *impea*	1						
looking at their ~~feet~~. But the boy *shoes (SC)*			1				
who was the ~~envy~~ of all the fifth *every*		1					
grade was Jamie Lee. He had a							
pair of "High Five Pump'em Ups"							
by Adeedee. The only thing Belcher							
boys loved as *ll* much as their							
shoes was basketball.							
TOTALS	2	4	2	2	0	2	0

conversely, which words are unknown so that we can teach them for optimal reading comprehension.

There are actually several different "vocabularies" housed in one's mind and usable for language transactions (Reutzel & Cooter, 2003). The largest of these is known as the **listening vocabulary.** These are words you are able to hear and understand but not necessarily use in your own speech. For example, when the famous Hale-Bopp comet visited our solar system in 1997, most children in the middle and upper elementary grades were quite capable of watching news telecasts about the comet and understanding most of what was reported. However, if you were to ask many of these same children to explain what they had just learned, many of the technical words and factual bits of information would not be included in their description. It's not that the children somehow forgot everything they had just learned; rather, they didn't "own" the words for speech purposes quite yet—they were able to only hear and understand the technical words.

Words that a student can hear, understand, and use in his or her speech are known as her **speaking vocabulary.** It is a subset of the listening vocabulary and, thus, is smaller. The gap between peoples' listening and speaking vocabularies is greatest in youth. The gap tends to narrow as adulthood approaches, though the two vocabularies are never equal. The next-largest vocabulary is the **reading vocabulary.** As you might guess, it is a subset of one's listening and speaking vocabularies and consists of words one can read and understand. The smallest vocabulary that one acquires is the **writing vocabulary,** or words that one can understand when listening, speaking, and reading and can reproduce when writing.

Listening and reading vocabularies can be grouped into a collective category known as the *receptive vocabulary* and writing and speaking vocabularies into a category known as the *expressive vocabulary* (Cooter & Flynt, 1996). These descriptors reflect the broader language functions of these vocabularies for the student as either *information receiver* or *spoken* or *written language producer.*

For a student to be able to read and understand a word, he or she must have first acquired it at the listening and speaking levels. Teachers, then, must somehow find out which words are already "owned" by their students as listening and speaking vocabulary and teach the unknown words that may be critical in their assigned reading. Without this kind of knowledge, adequate context for word identification will be missing and can threaten further reading development and, of course, damage comprehension.

A primary way of increasing vocabulary is through wide reading on a daily basis (Irwin, 1990; Johnson, 2001). This helps readers gain greater fluency and improves their ability to use context from the passage to interpret word meanings. Effective readers can maintain satisfactory comprehension when up to 15% of the words in a passage are unknown or new. On the other hand, research shows that English language learners (Johnson & Steele, 1996) and, we believe, others having inadequate vocabulary knowledge tend to be word-by-word readers and less able to tolerate unknown vocabulary. The teacher's role is to help these learners and typically developing readers learn the largest possible vocabularies.

In truth, most vocabulary assessment done by master teachers is through careful classroom observations of student reading behaviors. As teachers work with their pupils each day in needs-based group instruction, they discover high-utility words that seem to cause trouble for one or more students. Teachers can work these words into vocabulary instruction activities like those featured later in this chapter. But this is not to suggest that more cannot be done early in the school year to discover which words most of your students need to learn. Following are a few classroom-proven ideas to help with that process.

Oral Reading Assessment

Cassette recordings of oral reading can help teachers verify the accuracy of their fluency assessments.

Oral reading assessment is a method by which problem vocabulary words in print can be distinguished by the teacher in a quick and efficient manner. You will need photocopies (two copies each) of three or four passages for the student to read that you believe to be at the *instructional* or *frustration* reading level. The passages should be drawn from reading materials commonly used in your classroom curriculum. Ideally, the passages are sufficiently challenging so that students will have trouble with about 5% to 10% of the words. It will be necessary for you to do a quick word count to determine if the passages are appropriate once the student has read them. It is also essential that you have a range of passages, in terms of difficulty, to account for the vast differences between students' reading ability. (Note: If the student calls less than 10% of the words correctly, he or she may not be getting enough context from the passages for adequate comprehension.)

Give the student a copy of the first passage you want him or her to read and keep one for yourself. Ask the student to read the passage aloud. While he or she does, note any words that he or she either doesn't know or mispronounces. Repeat the procedure until the student has read all the passages. We recommend that you discontinue a passage if the student consistently has trouble with more than one or two words in any one sentence. After the student has finished, tally the number of miscalled words and determine if the passage is acceptable for analysis (no more than about 10% miscalled or unknown words). List any words that seem to be problematic for the student.

Repeat this procedure with all your students during the first week or so of the new school year and (a) create a master list of words that seem to be problematic and (b) determine the number or percentage of the class who seem to find each word difficult or unknown. Use the more frequent problem words as part of your vocabulary instruction program.

Vocabulary Flash Cards

A traditional way to do a quick assessment of a student's vocabulary knowledge is the flash card technique. High-frequency words (those appearing most in print) as well as other high-utility and specialized words for content instruction are printed individually on flash cards and shown to students for them to identify.

Create a list of high-frequency sight words or subject area words pertaining to your curriculum. We provide a copy of the Fry word list on page 69 in Chapter 3 in Figure 3.2. Copy each word, one word each, onto index cards using a bold marker. An alternative is to type the words into a classroom computer and print them in a large font size onto heavy paper stock. Then cut the words into a uniform flash card size. For recording purposes, you will also need a photocopy/master list of the words to record each student's responses.

"Flash" each card to the student one at a time and ask him or her to name the word. Allow about 5 seconds for the student to identify each word. Circle any unknown or mispronounced words on a copy of the master sheet you are using for that student (simply note the student's name at the top of the photocopy along with the date of testing). After you have shown the flash cards to all students, compile a master list of troublesome words for whole-class or small-group instruction.

COMPREHENSION ASSESSMENT

Comprehending the author's message is what reading is all about. Some students seem to easily grasp the meaning of texts, while others struggle (as with those who focus so much on decoding that meaning is lost). Questioning is one strategy used to examine students' reading comprehension.

Questioning

Perhaps the most fundamental method of assessing reading comprehension is to ask questions about the text following the student's reading. A popular and highly informative questioning format uses Bloom's taxonomy (Bloom, 1956; see also Anderson et al., 2000). In Figure 7.25, we offer a generic list of questions that may be

Figure 7.25 Bloom's taxonomy questions

LITERAL: LOW-LEVEL THINKING
(Should *ONLY* be used in about one out of four questions)

KNOWLEDGE—Ability to remember important information (recognizing, recalling)
Who, what, when, where, how?
Describe . . .

COMPREHENSION—Ability to understand instructional messages including oral, written, and graphic communications (interpret, example of, classifying, summarizing, comparing, explaining)
Retell _____ in your own words.
What is the main idea of _____ ?
Please paraphrase _____ . . .
How is _____ an example of _____ ?

INFERENTIAL LEVEL: HIGHER-ORDER THINKING
(Rely on this level for one-half of your questioning)

APPLICATION—Use of facts, rules, principles to carry out a procedure (executing, implementing, inferring)
How is _____ related to _____ ?
Why is _____ significant?
In which situations would _____ be appropriate?

ANALYSIS—Break information down into its component parts and decide how the parts relate to one another (differentiating, organizing, attributing)
What are the parts or features of _____ ?
Classify _____ according to _____ .
Outline/diagram/web _____ .
How does _____ compare/contrast with _____ ?
What evidence can you list for _____ ?

EVALUATIVE AND CREATIVE LEVELS: HIGHEST LEVELS OF THINKING
(Rely on this level for about one in four of your questions)

EVALUATION—Development of opinions, judgments, or decisions (checking, critiquing)
Do you agree _____ with the author's conclusions?
Judge between the _____ ideas presented and explain why one is better.
What is the most important _____ ? Why?
How would you prioritize _____ ?
What criteria would you use to assess _____ ?

CREATIVE—Reform ideas to develop a new concept or pattern (generating, planning, producing)
Explain why _____ happened.
Write an essay about _____ .
Build a diorama that shows _____ .

adapted for almost any reading passage. *Important: We recommend that you focus on higher-order questions almost exclusively* since to answer them requires the student to draw on lower level details to form a response (Flynt & Cooter, 1987).

Retelling

One of the best ways to find out if a student understands a passage he or she has read is through **retelling** (Benson & Cummins, 2000; Gambrell, Pfeiffer, & Wilson, 1985; Morrow, 1985). Retellings can be accomplished in many ways. First, the teacher may wish to use pictures from the story as a memory prompt. As the teacher flashes pictures sequentially from the book or story, the child retells the story from memory. A second option is *unaided recall,* or retelling without pictures or other prompts.

*A **retelling** record sheet can be constructed in such a way as to be useful in grading.*

We recommend a two-step process in which the teacher begins by having the student retell everything he or she can remember about the passage. If it is a narrative passage, the teacher can use a generic record sheet like the one shown in Figure 7.26 to record critical elements of the story grammar the student has recalled. After the student stops retelling the first time, the teacher asks, "What else can you remember?" Usually the student will recall more bits of information. The teacher continues to ask the child, "What else do you remember?" until he or she cannot remember anything more. Then the teacher refers to the story grammar record sheet for any categories (e.g., setting or characters) not addressed by the student and asks direct questions about the unaddressed areas. This is a form of *aided recall.*

Digging Deeper into Comprehension: Three Levels of Retelling

Benson and Cummins (2000), in their popular book *The Power of Retelling,* explained that students can demonstrate their comprehension on three increasingly sophisticated levels. The first level is *oral retelling,* which we have just discussed.

The second and deeper level of comprehension involves *written retelling using graphic organizers.* Here the student uses a graphic organizer to retell using words and phrases grouped in meaningful units. For example, teachers may teach students how to use a Venn diagram to compare and contrast two versions of a classic story such as *Jack and the Beanstalk.* In Figure 7.27, we present a comparison grid contrasting that very story with Richard Chase's (19xx) *Jack and the Bean Tree* as an example. In Figure 7.28, we also present several common graphic organizers that could be used for retelling assessment.

The third level and highest level of retelling is *written retellings in the form of compositions.* As with most learning, students require structure to achieve this retelling ability via teacher modeling, guided practice, and, ultimately, student demonstration of competence. Many teachers offer students a kind of structured overview for paragraph writing that helps students bridge from using the kind of graphic organizers shown in the previous section to the construction of compositions that make sense. In Figure 7.29, we share one used by K. S. Cooter (2003) with elementary and middle school students.

Assessing Knowledge of Expository Text Patterns

The key to effective expository (i.e., nonfiction) text instruction lies in the accurate identification of the types of content or expository texts that students are able to read

Figure 7.26   Story grammar retelling record sheet

STORY RETELLING CHECKLIST		
Name _____ Date _____		
Name of story _____		
	Unaided	**With Prompt**
Setting		
a. An introduction is included	_____	_____
b. Tells where story takes place	_____	_____
c. Tells when story takes place	_____	_____
Characters		
a. Tells about the main character/s	_____	_____
b. Other characters are mentioned	_____	_____
Problem or Goal		
a. Describes an event that causes a problem or a goal to be achieved	_____	_____
b. Tells how the main character/s respond to the challenge	_____	_____
Plot Episodes		
a. Tells one event that relates to the solution of the problem	_____	_____
b. Includes several events from the story that relate to the problem	_____	_____
Solution		
a. Tells how main problem is solved	_____	_____
b. Refers to other problems in story	_____	_____
c. Ends with a closing statement	_____	_____
Theme		
Conveys author's message/lesson	_____	_____
Sequence		
Story is presented in sequential order	_____	_____

effectively as well as the forms of expository writing that are difficult for them to comprehend. We have discovered that several rather common forms of reading assessment are easily adaptable to expository texts and can help teachers plan instruction. Offered in this section are some examples of each for your consideration.

Expository Text Frames

Expository text frames are useful in identifying types of expository text patterns that may be troublesome for students. Based on the "story frames" concept (Fowler, 1982; Nichols, 1980) expository text frames are completed by the student after reading an expository passage. Instruction can be focused much more precisely, based on student needs, as a result of this procedure.

Figure 7.27 A comparison grid of *Jack and the Beanstalk* with *Jack and the Bean Tree*

	Jack and the Beanstalk	*Jack and the Bean Tree*
Jack's goal(s)	To find treasure in the giant's world	To find treasure in the giant's world
Jack's mother's reaction to the beanstalk/beantree before he went up	Delighted	Thought Jack was lying when he told her about it
What Jack took from the giant	Hen (golden eggs), singing harp, bag of gold	Knife, gun, coverlet
Conclusion	Giant fell; Jack was rich	Giant fell; Jack was rich

Figure 7.28 Common graphic organizer patterns

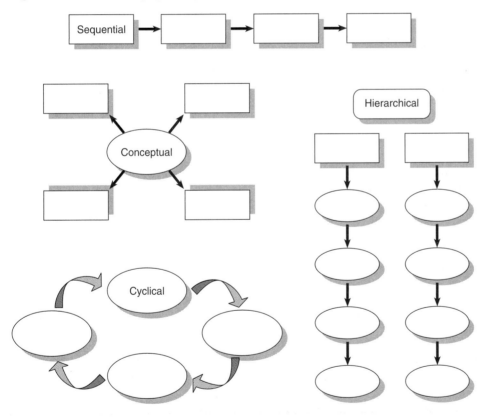

You will need a reading selection from the adopted textbook, a computer and word processing program, and means by which to copy the expository text frames for students. Abbreviated examples of expository text frames for each of the primary expository text patterns are shown in Figures 7.30 through 7.34.

Before asking students to read the selection, list the major vocabulary and concepts. Discuss what students already know about the topic and display it on the chalkboard or on chart paper. Next, have students read an expository selection similar to

Figure 7.29   Structure for written retellings

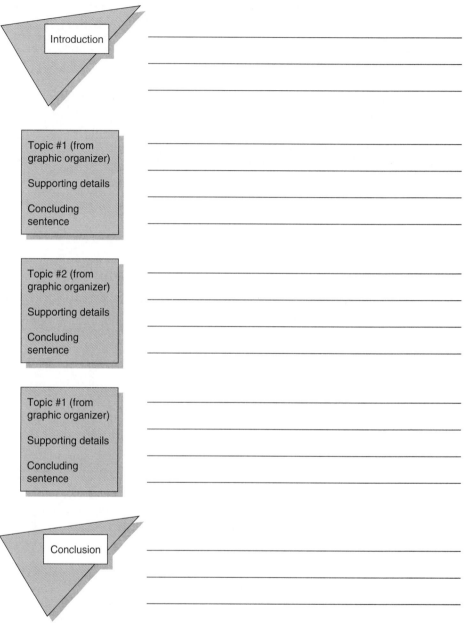

From Cooter, K. S. (2003). *Preparing middle school students for the TAKS in writing: A professional development seminar.* Used with permission.

the one you will ask them to read in class. Once the passage has been read, model the process for completing expository text frames using mock examples. Now have them read the actual selection for the unit of study. Finally, have students complete the expository text frame(s) you have prepared for this passage.

For students who have trouble with any of the frames, conduct a one-on-one reading conference to determine the thinking processes going on as the student completed the expository text frame.

Figure 7.30 Expository text frames: Description

Decimals are another way to write fractions when _____
_____
_____

Figure 7.31 Expository text frames: Collection

Water Habitats

Freshwater habitats are found in _____ , _____ , _____ , and rivers. Each freshwater habitat has special kinds of _____ and _____ that live there. Some plants and animals live in waters that are very _____ . Others live in waters that are _____ . Some plants and animals adapt to waters that flow _____ .

Figure 7.32 Expository text frames: Causation

America Enters the War

On Sunday, December 7, 1941, World War II came to the United States. The entry of the United States into World War II was triggered by _____ . Roosevelt said that it was a day that would "live in Infamy." *Infamy* (IN · fuh · mee) means remembered for being evil.

Figure 7.33 Expository text frames: Problem/solution

Agreement by Compromise

Events that led to the Civil War

For a while there were an equal number of Southern and Northern states. That meant that there were just as many senators in Congress from slave states as from free states. Neither had more votes in the Senate, so they usually reached agreement on new laws by compromise. One way that the balance of power was maintained in Congress was _____
_____ .

Figure 7.34 Expository text frames: Comparison

Segregation

Many people said that the segregation laws were unfair. But in 1896, the Supreme Court ruled segregation legal if _____
_____ . "Separate but equal" became the law in many parts of the country.

But separate was not equal. One of the most serious problems was education. Black parents felt _____ . Sometimes the segregated schools had teachers who were not _____ as teachers in the white schools. Textbooks were often _____ , if they had any books at all. But in many of the white schools the books were _____ . Without a good education, the blacks argued, their children would not be able to get good jobs as adults.

Cloze Passages

Cloze passages, from the word *closure,* are short passages (250 words) from expository books commonly used in the teacher's classroom that have certain words deleted (usually every fifth word) and replaced with a blank. Students are asked to read the cloze passages and fill in the missing words based on what they feel makes sense using context clues:

There exists an old Native American legend about an eagle who thought he was a chicken.

It ___ that a Hopi farmer _____ his only son decided to _____ to a nearby mountain to _____ an

eagle's nest. The _____ would take them all _____ so they brought along _____ rations and water

for the _____. The man and the boy _____ the enormous fields of _____ and beans into the _____.

Soon thereafter they were _____ the mountain and the climb _____ rigorous and hazardous.

They _____ looked back toward their _____ and at the panoramic _____ of the entire// valley . . .

Cloze tests cause students to use their background knowledge of a subject, their understanding of basic syntax (word-order relationships), and their word and sentence meaning (semantics) knowledge to guess what a missing or familiar word in print might be (Cooter & Flynt, 1996). If students are reading effectively and with adequate comprehension, they are usually able to accurately guess the missing words—or at least a word of the same part of speech. This helps the teacher know whether the student is able to use context clues when reading expository materials in the selected field of study and whether he or she has sufficient background knowledge and vocabulary to cope with the textbook being used.

Materials needed to complete a cloze test include the textbook, a computer and word processing program, and a means by which to copy the cloze passage for students. General instructions for the construction and scoring of cloze tests using content area texts are as follows:

1. *Choose a passage of about 250 words from the class textbook.* It is usually best to choose a passage at the beginning of a chapter or unit so that needed introductory information is included.
2. *Prepare the cloze passage, preferably using a computer word processing program.* The first sentence should be typed exactly as it is written in the original text. Thereafter, beginning with the second sentence, delete one of the first five words and replace it with a blank, then repeat this procedure every fifth word. The process is complete when you have 50 blanks in the cloze passage. After the 50th blank, finish typing the sentence in which the last blank occurred. Then type at least one more sentence intact (no deletions).

3. *Have students read the passage all the way through once without attempting to fill in any of the blanks.* Then have them reread the passage and fill in the blanks to the best of their ability.
4. *To score cloze passages, use the one-half/one-third formula.* Students who correctly complete one half (25 of 50) or more of the blanks are considered to be at the independent reading level, at least with the passage selected. Students who complete fewer than one third of the blanks correctly (17 of 50 blanks) will probably find the text frustrating or too difficult even with assistance. Those students falling somewhere between the one-third and one-half range will probably be able to succeed with the text if they receive some preparatory assistance from the teacher.

We encourage teachers working with students having reading problems to first assess the student's performance using cloze passages created from narrative texts as a baseline indicator of general reading ability. This will help you to find out how well the student normally performs at reading narrative books, which are the main focus of reading instruction in the elementary years. This approach also helps students practice the cloze procedure before being asked to take on the different—and perhaps more difficult—expository cloze passages.

Results from close testing inform the teacher as to whether the content of an expository text is likely to be at what is termed the independent level (easy to read), the instructional level (requiring some assistance from the teacher for student success), or the frustration level (far too difficult for the student).

Explain how cloze passages could be useful for both assessment and teaching sessions connected to context clue development.

Maze Passages

Maze passages (Guthrie, Seifert, Burnham, & Caplan, 1974) are a modification of cloze strategies that may be easily adapted to content classroom needs. Maze passages tend to be less frustrating to students than cloze passages because the students have three possible answers to choose from; thus, students tend to get a greater percentage of the items correct. The purpose of maze passages is otherwise identical to cloze. You will need the textbook, a computer and word processing program, and a means by which to create a maze passage for students:

There exists an old Native American legend about an eagle who thought he was a chicken.

It ____ a. happened / b. sharp / c. is   that a Hopi farmer ____ a. to / b. and / c. wheel   his only son decided

to ____ a. are / b. walk / c. Jim   to a nearby mountain to ____ a. bear / b. met / c. see   an eagle's nest. . .

In our adaptation of the maze, the criteria for the independent reading level is 85% or greater, the frustration level is 50% to 85%, and the instructional reading level is less than 50%. The procedure for constructing maze passages is identical to the construction of cloze passages, with the exception that, following each blank, three fill-in choices are included. One choice is a word that is the same part of speech as the missing word but that does not make sense, a second choice is usually one that does not make sense and that is a different part of speech from the missing word, and the third choice is, of course, the correct choice.

Content Area Reading Inventory

The Content Area Reading Inventory (CARI) (Farr, Tully, & Pritchard, 1989; Readence, Bean, & Baldwin, 1992) is an informal reading inventory assessing whether students have learned sufficient reading/study strategies to succeed with content materials. Constructing a CARI can be quite time consuming but is well worth the effort.

The CARI can be administered to groups of students and typically includes three major sections (Farr et al., 1989) that assess the following:

- Student knowledge of and ability to use common textbook components (i.e., table of contents, glossary, and index) and supplemental research aids (card catalog, reference books, and periodicals)
- Student knowledge of important vocabulary and skills, such as context clues
- Comprehension skills important to understanding expository texts

For the last two sections of the CARI assessment, students are asked to read a selection from the adopted text. Readence et al. (1992) suggest contents for developing a CARI.

Suggestions for Content in a CARI

Part I: Textual Reading/Study Aids

1. Internal aids
2. Table of contents
3. Index
4. Glossary
5. Chapter introduction/summaries
6. Information from pictures
7. Other aids included in the text
8. Supplemental research aids
9. Online "card catalog" searches
10. Periodicals
11. Encyclopedias
12. Other relevant resources that lead students to access additional information related to the content (e.g., online search engines like Google.com, video libraries, and online university periodicals)

Part II: Vocabulary Knowledge

1. Knowledge and recall of relevant vocabulary

    2. Use of context clues

Part III: Comprehension Skills and Strategies

    1. Text-explicit (literal) information

    2. Text-implicit (inferred) information

    3. Knowledge of text structures and related strategies

To develop a CARI, follow this process:

Step 1: Choose a passage of at least 3 to 4 pages from the textbook(s) to be used. The passage selected should represent the typical writing style of the author.

Step 2: Construct about 20 questions related to the text. Readence et al. (1992) recommend 8 to 10 questions for Part I, 4 to 6 questions for Part II, and 7 to 9 questions for Part III. We urge the use of questions based on writing patterns used in the sample selection; they should reflect the facts, concepts, and generalizations in the selection.

Step 3: Explain to students that the CARI is not used for grading purposes but is useful for planning teaching activities that will help them succeed. Be sure to walk students through the different sections of the CARI and to model appropriate responses.

Step 4: Administer Part I first, then Parts II and III on separate day(s). It may take several sessions to work through the CARI. We recommend devoting only about 20 minutes per day to administering parts of the CARI so that other class needs are not ignored during the assessment phase.

Readence et al. (1992) suggest the following criteria for assessing the CARI:

Percent Correct	Text Difficulty
86%–100%	Easy reading
64%–85%	Adequate for instruction
63% or below	Too difficult

From careful analysis of this assessment, teachers can plan special lessons to help students cope with difficult readings and internalize important information. Students can be grouped according to need for these lessons and practice strategies leading to success.

FLUENCY EVALUATION

Reading **fluency** is the ability of students to read at an appropriate speed and with proper phrasing. An informal assessment of fluency through teacher observations is not difficult, and more formal methods can sometimes consume a great deal of valuable classroom time. Two effective methods can streamline the process considerably.

Fluency includes the ability to read at an appropriate rate.

Multidimensional Fluency Scale

Zutell and Rasinski (1991) developed a Multidimensional Fluency Scale (MFS), which serves as a useful informal assessment of fluency. The MFS offers a practical measurement of students' oral reading fluency that provides clear and valid information.

Figure 7.35 Multidimensional Fluency Scale

Use the following scales to rate reader fluency on the dimensions of expression and volume, phrasing, smoothness, and pace.

A. Expression and Volume

1. Reads with little expression or enthusiasm in voice. Reads words as if simply to get them out. Little sense of trying to make text sound like natural language. Tends to read in a quiet voice.

2. Some expression. Begins to use voice to make text sound like natural language in some areas of the text, but not others. Focus remains largely on saying the words. Still reads in a voice that is quiet.

3. Sounds like natural language throughout the better part of the passage. Occasionally slips into expressionless reading. Voice volume is generally appropriate throughout the text.

4. Reads with good expression and enthusiasm throughout the text. Sounds like natural language. Reader is able to vary expression and volume to match his/her interpretation of the passage.

B. Phrasing

1. Monotonic with little sense of phrase boundaries, frequent word-by-word reading.

2. Frequent two and three word phrases giving the impression of choppy reading; improper stress and intonation that fails to mark ends of sentences and causes.

3. Mixture of run-ons, mid-sentence pauses for breath, and possibly some choppiness; reasonable stress/intonation.

4. Generally well-phrased, mostly in clause and sentence units, with adequate attention to expression.

C. Smoothness

1. Frequent extended pauses, hesitations, false starts, sound-outs, repetitions, and/or multiple attempts.

2. Several "rough spots" in text where extended pauses, hesitations, etc., are more frequent and disruptive.

3. Occasional breaks in smoothness caused by difficulties with specific words and/or structures.

4. Generally smooth reading with some breaks, but word and structure difficulties are resolved quickly, usually through self-correction.

D. Pace (during sections of minimal disruption)

1. Slow and laborious.

2. Moderately slow.

3. Uneven mixture of fast and slow reading.

4. Consistently conversational.

Sum the score for each of the four sections above here _____

Interpret the scores using the guide below.

Scores range from 4 to 16. Generally, scores below 8 indicate that fluency may be a concern. Scores of 8 or above indicate that the student is making good progress in fluency.

Adapted from Zutell & Rasinski, 1991

To administer an MFS, the teacher collects a student self-selected passage of 200 to 300 words, the MFS document (see Figure 7.35), and a cassette tape player/recorder with blank tape.

Reutzel and Cooter (2003) recommend that teachers practice giving this test by having students read a familiar passage (200–300 words) at least three times prior to using the MFS. It may be informative for teachers also to observe the difference in a student's fluency with a practiced, self-selected, familiar text and with an unpracticed, teacher-selected, unfamiliar text chosen at the child's approximate grade level.

Rubric for Fluency Evaluation

The Rubric for Fluency Evaluation (Fountas & Pinnell, 1996) is recommended as a formal assessment technique. A **rubric** is a tool for scoring student work; the concept is discussed in greater detail later in this chapter. Children are asked to read aloud a selection they have read twice before and can read with at least 90% accuracy. The oral reading should be taped for analysis purposes (this part could actually be done by students as a center activity or as an activity carried out by an adult volunteer). Listen to the tape and evaluate the oral reading using the Rubric for Fluency Evaluation shown in Figure 7.36 that we have adapted from Fountas and Pinnell (1996).

Rubrics are scoring guides that can make your evaluations more objective and consistent.

Figure 7.36 Rubric for fluency evaluation

1. **Nonfluent Reading**
   - Word-by-word reading.
   - Frequent pauses between words (poor phrasing).
   - Little recognition of syntax.
   - Little response to punctuation.
   - Some awkward word groupings.
2. **Beginning Fluency**
   - Frequent word-by-word reading.
   - Some two- and three-word phrasing.
   - May reread for problem solving or to clarify (strategic reading).
   - Shows some awareness of syntax and punctuation.
3. **Transitional Fluency**
   - Combination of word-by-word reading and fluent phrase reading.
   - Some expressive phrasing.
   - Shows attention to punctuation and syntax.
4. **Fluent Reading**
   - Fluent reading with very few word-by-word interruptions.
   - Reads mostly in larger meaningful phrases.
   - Reads with expression.
   - Attends consistently to punctuation.
   - Rereads as necessary to clarify or problem-solve.

Adapted from Fountas, I.C. and Pinnell, G. S. (1996). *Guided Reading: Good First Reading for All Children.* Portsmouth, NH: Heinemann.

COMMERCIAL SCREENING AND PROGRESS-MONITORING ASSESSMENTS

There are a number of commercial products on the market to help teachers survey their students. While they may be helpful, they can also be expensive. In this section, we present products that have been useful in our own classroom practices and meet with our general approval. We begin with the most valid of them all: informal reading inventories.

Informal Reading Inventories

Informal reading inventories typically have passages more like authentic books than most other commercial tests.

An **informal reading inventory** (IRI) is normally individually administered (though some can be given to groups of children) and often has graded word lists and story passages. Emmett A. Betts is generally considered to be the first developer of the IRI; however, several other individuals contributed to its development as far back as the early 1900s (Johns & Lunn, 1983).

The Teacher's Guide to Reading Tests (Cooter, 1990; Flippo, 2004) lists several advantages and unique features of IRIs that help explain why teachers continue to find them useful. One benefit is that IRIs provide for authentic assessments of the reading act; that is, an IRI more closely resembles real reading. Students are better able to "put it all together" by reading whole stories or passages. Another advantage of IRIs is that they usually provide a systematic procedure for studying student miscues or reading errors.

IRIs are rather unusual when compared to other commercial forms of reading assessment. First, because they are "informal," no norms, reliability data, or validity information are usually available. This is often seen as a disadvantage by some public school educators, especially when assessing students enrolled in federally funded remedial programs where reliability data are often required. Second, IRIs are unusual (in a positive way) because they provide a great deal of information that is helpful to teachers in making curricular decisions, especially teachers who place students into needs-based or guided reading groups (Fountas & Pinnell, 1996). IRIs provide an approximation of each child's ability in graded or "leveled" reading materials, such as basal readers and books used for guided reading.

IRIs tend to be somewhat different from each other. Beyond the usual graded word lists and reading passages, IRIs vary a great deal in the subtests offered (e.g., silent reading passages, phonics, interest inventories, concepts about print, phonemic awareness, auditory discrimination) and in the scoring criteria used to interpret reading miscues. Some argue (us included) that the best IRIs are those constructed by classroom teachers themselves using reading materials from their own classrooms. Several examples of IRIs now used in many school systems follow:

• *The Flynt/Cooter Reading Inventory for the Classroom, Fifth Edition* (Flynt & Cooter, 2004). The Flynt-Cooter Reading Inventory for the Classroom is a modern version of the traditional IRI concept. The authors incorporate current research on comprehension processes, running records, fluency, and miscue analysis into a more effective authentic reading assessment. They included such research-based procedures as unaided/aided recall and story grammar comprehension evaluation, high-interest selections, appropriate-length passages, both expository and narrative passages, and a time-efficient miscue grid system for quick analyses of running records.

- Developmental Reading Assessment (DRA) (Beaver, 2001). This is an informal reading inventory offering graded reading passages for students to read, rubrics for evaluating students' oral reading, and a handy box in which to store student portfolios.

- The English * Español Reading Inventory (Flynt & Cooter, 1999). This easy-to-use tool offers complete informal reading inventories for prekindergarten through grade 12 students in both Spanish and English. The Spanish passages were carefully developed and field tested with the aid of native Spanish-speaking teacher researchers from the United States, Mexico, and Central and South America to avoid problems with dialect differences and to maximize their usefulness in U.S. classrooms.

- Qualitative Reading Inventory—3 (Leslie & Caldwell, 2000). This IRI includes both narrative and expository passages and has pictures for each level passage and methods for assessing prior knowledge. This IRI also includes a text link to the Internet.

The English Espanol Reading Inventory incorporates recent assessment research and high-interest passages in both Spanish and English.*

Curriculum-Based Measurement

Curriculum-based measurement is a tool for measuring student skill development in the areas of reading fluency, spelling, math, and written language. CBM uses "probes" developed from each school district's curriculum; thus, it measures what the students are taught. For a wealth of information on CBM, search on the Internet using Google.com for "Curriculum-Based Measurement." One Internet site hosted by the University of Minnesota that offers a good overview of CBM can be found at http://education.umn.edu/research/ResearchWorks/CBM.htm.

Curriculum-based measurement looks at three different areas that pertain to reading:

- **Reading fluency** measures how many words a student correctly reads in 1 minute. In practice, three reading probes are given and the middle, or median, score is reported.
- The **spelling** measure presents 10 words (at first grade) or 17 words (second through fifth grades). Spelling lists are scored for words spelled correctly.
- For the **written expression** task, students are presented with a "story starter" and given 3 minutes to write a story. Student work is scored for total words written, words spelled correctly, and correct writing sequences.

CBM procedures are usually used to screen for students who may be at risk for reading difficulty and to monitor student progress and response to instructional interventions. Screenings are conducted three times each year in many school districts for all students: fall, winter, and spring. But if a student receives additional support in reading, CBM might be administered as much as several times weekly to evaluate the effects of the intervention. Similarly, CBM is often used for decision making when determining if a student should receive special education services.

GETTING ORGANIZED: PROFILING YOUR CLASS

The assessment ideas presented so far in this chapter provide the means for measuring the development of various reading skills, but that is only one part of the reading teacher's job. Organizing and analyzing the assessment data—first for each child

Profiling *is a way of charting the individual and group learning needs of students.*

individually and then for the entire class—are extremely important next steps in instructional planning. Charting the reading skills that students have learned and still need to acquire, both individually and as a class, is what we refer to as **profiling.**

Two Documents Needed for Profiling

Profiling documents teachers use should directly parallel the grade-level reading standards adopted by the school district. Teachers generally need two profiling documents: a *student profile* document to record individual strengths and needs in some detail and a *classroom profile* document to help organize the entire class's data for the formation of needs-based reading groups.

Cooter and Cooter (1999) developed a system that includes these two levels of profiling. Figure 7.37 is a portion of their student profiling document. A profiling system should be driven either by the state's reading standards or by the school district's scope and sequence skills list (these are usually provided in a curriculum guide to all teachers on assignment to a school).

Student Profiling Document

In Figure 7.37, you will note that each skill has a blank space to the left; this is for the teacher to note (a) the date he or she observed the student performing that skill and (b) the degree to which the student was able to execute the skill. For the latter, a 3-point

Figure 7.37   A partial student profiling instrument for third grade

---

Student Profile: THIRD GRADE LITERACY MILESTONES
Balanced Literacy Assessment System and Training
(BLAST™)

Student's Name _____

Teacher: Ms. K. M. Spencer

> **Instructions:** Record the date when each milestone skill was observed, and the degree of development
> (**E** = Emergent, **D** = Developing Skill, **P** = Proficient) in the blank to the left of each skill description.

Decoding and Word Recognition
_____   3.D.1   Uses context clues, phonic knowledge, and structural analysis to decode words

Spelling and Writing
_____   3.SW.1   Spells previously studied words and spelling patterns correctly in own writing
_____   3.SW.2   Uses the dictionary to check and correct spelling
_____   3.SW.3   Uses all aspects of the writing process in compositions and reports with assistance, including

                _____   3.SW.3.1   Combines information from multiple sources in written reports
                _____   3.SW.3.2   Revises and edits written work independently on a level appropriate for first
                              semester of third grade

Figure 7.37 *continued*

_____ 3.SW.3.3   Produces a variety of written work (response to literature, reports, semantic maps)

_____ 3.SW.3.4   Uses graphic organizational tools with a variety of texts

_____ 3.SW.3.5   Incorporates elaborate descriptions and figurative language

_____ 3.SW.3.6   Uses a variety of formal sentence structures in own writing

_____ 3.SW.S.1   Writes proficiently using orthographic patterns and rules such as qu, use of n before v, m before b, m before p, and changing z to c when adding -es (Spanish only)

_____ 3.SW.S.2   Spells words with three or more syllables using silent letters, dieresis marks, accents, verbs, r/rr, y/ll, s/c/z, q/c/k, g/j, j/x, b/v, ch, h, and i/y accurately (Spanish only)

Oral Reading

_____ 3.OR.1   Reads aloud with fluency any text that is appropriate for the first half of grade three

_____ 3.OR.2   Comprehends any text that is appropriate for the first half of grade three

Language Comprehension and Response to Text

_____ 3.C.1   Reads and comprehends both fiction and nonfiction that is appropriate for grade three

_____ 3.C.2   Reads chapter books independently

_____ 3.C.3   Identifies specific words or phrases that are causing comprehension difficulties (metacognition)

_____ 3.C.4   Summarizes major points from fiction and nonfiction text

_____ 3.C.5   Can discuss similarities in characters and events across stories

_____ 3.C.6   Can discuss underlying theme or message when interpreting fiction

_____ 3.C.7   Distinguishes between the following when interpreting nonfiction text:

    _____ 3.C.7.1   Cause and effect

    _____ 3.C.7.2   Fact and opinion

    _____ 3.C.7.3   Main idea and supporting details

_____ 3.C.8   Uses information and reasoning to evaluate opinions

_____ 3.C.9   Infers word meaning from roots, prefixes, and suffixes that have been taught

_____ 3.C.10   Uses dictionary to determine meanings and usage of unknown words

_____ 3.C.11   Uses new vocabulary in own speech and writing

_____ 3.C.12   Uses basic grammar and parts of speech correctly in independent writing

_____ 3.C.13   Shows familiarity with a number of read-aloud and independent reading selections, including nonfiction

_____ 3.C.14   Uses multiple sources to locate information:

    _____ 3.C.14.1   Tables of contents

    _____ 3.C.14.2   Indexes

    _____ 3.C.14.3   Internet search engines

_____ 3.C.15   Connects a variety of literary texts with life experiences

Reading Fluency

_____ 3.F.1   Very few word-by-word interruptions

_____ 3.F.2   Reads mostly in larger meaningful phrases

_____ 3.F.3   Reads with expression

_____ 3.F.4   Attends consistently to punctuation

_____ 3.F.5   Rereads to clarify or problem-solve

_____ 3.F.6   Sixty (60) words per minute reading rate (minimum)

rubric is provided: "E" for students who are just *emerging* with an awareness of the skill, "D" for students who are in the midst of *developing* competency in the skill, and "P" for students who have attained *proficiency* (i.e., mastery) of the skill. These designations are important because they help the teacher differentiate the needs of students in the class. The designations can also be useful for informing parents about how their child is developing as a reader. Note that in the example provided in Figure 7.38, the child has a number of skills at each level of development as well as some with no designation at all (this means that the child has not yet reached that developmental stage for the skill[s] even at an emergent level). The student profile document should probably be the first contribution a teacher makes to the student's reading portfolio folder.

Classroom Profiling Document

Necessarily accompanying the student profile is the classroom profile (*always* have both). This document lists the same reading standards as the student profile, only in abbreviated form. Figure 7.39 shows a partially completed classroom reading profile for third grade. Notice that each skill listed matches the same skills found in the student profile. Students' names are written in the blank spaces across the top, and the matching designations for how competent the student is with each skill (i.e., the codes "E," "D," or "P") are transcribed from their individual student profile forms.

   To demonstrate how individual student data can be collated into a class profile and help the teacher form reading groups based on needed skills, we provide an example in Figure 9.41. This example is for decoding and word recognition as well as spelling and writing skills assessment. It is easy to see in Figure 7.40 how the teacher can begin forming reading groups based on student needs. For instance, the teacher not only might form a group of students who need to develop the skill "revises and edits" but also might recognize that actually two groups are needed—one for those who are emerging in this ability (E-level students) and another for those who are a little further along or "developing" (D-level students).

OUTCOME ASSESSMENTS

Outcome assessments help us determine how effective our reading program and our teaching is in helping students attain grade level standards or benchmarks. These kinds of tests are usually given to whole groups of students at once, but may be given individually when necessary. The following two examples are used nationally and are considered to be the best examples in this emerging area of reading assessment.

DIBELS can effectively be used as an Outcome Assessment or for Progress-Monitoring.

Identify Rosa Maria's "emergent" reading skills from this example in Figure 7.38 on p. 259.

Dynamic Indicators of Basic Early Literacy Skills (DIBELS)

The Dynamic Indicators of Basic Early Literacy Skills (DIBELS) are a set of four standardized, individually administered measures of early literacy development. DIBELS was specifically designed to assess three of the "big five" ideas of early literacy development: phonological awareness, alphabetic principle, and oral reading fluency (measured as a corrected reading rate) with connected text. Another test not directly linked to these three ideas in early literacy but used as a risk indicator is the letter naming fluency (LNF) measure. These short, efficient, and highly predictive measures are designed to be 1-minute, timed indicators used to regularly monitor the development of prereading and early reading skills.

Figure 7.38 *Student profiling instrument (partial worksheet of third-grade example)*

Student Profile: THIRD GRADE LITERACY MILESTONES
Balanced Literacy Assessment System and Training
(BLAST™) (R. Cooter & K. S. Cooter, 1999)

Student's Name   *Rosa Maria*

Teacher: Ms. K. M. Spencer

Instructions: Record the date when each milestone skill was observed, and the degree of development (**E** = Emergent, **D** = Developing Skill, **P** = Proficient) in the blank to the left of each skill description.

Decoding and Word Recognition

11/5 D 3.D.1   Uses context clues, phonic knowledge, and structural analysis to decode words

Spelling and Writing

11/12 D 3.SW.1   Spells previously studied words and spelling patterns correctly in own writing

11/19 D 3.SW.2   Uses the dictionary to check and correct spelling

_____ 3.SW.3   Uses all aspects of the writing process in compositions and reports with assistance, including

    10/25 E 3.SW.3.1   Combines information from multiple sources in written reports

    10/18 E 3.SW.3.2   Revises and edits written work independently on a level appropriate for first semester of third grade

    9/3 D 3.SW.3.3   Produces a variety of written work (response to literature, reports, semantic maps)

    9/3 E 3.SW.3.4   Uses graphic organizational tools with a variety of texts

    9/3 E 3.SW.3.5   Incorporates elaborate descriptions and figurative language

    9/25 E 3.SW.3.6   Uses a variety of formal sentence structures in own writing

11/26 D 3.SW.S.1   Writes proficiently using orthographic patterns and rules such as qu, use of n before v, m before b, m before p, and changing z to c when adding -es (Spanish only)

9/14 P 3.SW.S.2   Spells words with three or more syllables using silent letters, dieresis marks, accents, verbs, r/rr, y/ll, s/c/z, q/c/k, g/j, j/x, b/v, ch, h, and i/y accurately (Spanish only)

Oral Reading

11/26 D 3.OR.1   Reads aloud with fluency any text that is appropriate for the first half of grade three

11/26 D 3.OR.2   Comprehends any text that is appropriate for the first half of grade three

Language Comprehension and Response to Text

9/1; 12/10 P/E 3.C.1   Reads and comprehends both fiction and nonfiction that is appropriate for grade three

10/3 P 3.C.2   Reads chapter books independently

12/2 E 3.C.3   Identifies specific words or phrases that are causing comprehension difficulties (metacognition)

12/2 D/E 3.C.4   Summarizes major points from fiction and nonfiction text

CLASSROOM PROFILE (BLAST™): THIRD GRADE LITERACY MILESTONES

Teacher: _____   Date/Grading Period Completed: _____

Instructions: Record the degree to which each milestone skill has been achieved by each student (**E** = Emergent, **D** = Developing Skill, **P** = Proficient) in each box corresponding to the student and skill in the grid.

Decoding and Word Recognition

3.D.1   Context clues, phonic knowledge, and structural analysis

Spelling and Writing

3.SW.1   Uses studied words and spelling patterns

3.SW.2   Uses the dictionary to check spelling

3.SW.3   Uses these aspects of the writing process:

    3.SW.3.1   Combines information/multiple sources

    3.SW.3.2   Revises and edits

    3.SW.3.3   Variety of written work

    3.SW.3.4   Graphic organizational tools

    3.SW.3.5   Descriptions and figurative language

    3.SW.3.6   Variety of formal sentence structures

3.SW.4.S.1   Orthographic patterns and rules (Spanish only)

3.SW.5.S.2   Spells words with three or more syllables using

    silent letters, dieresis marks, accents, verbs (Spanish only)

Oral Reading

3.OR.1   Reads aloud with fluency

Figure 7.39 Partial classroom profiling instrument

Reading Fluency

3.F.1	Very few word-by-word interruptions
3.F.2	Reads mostly in larger meaningful phrases
3.F.3	Reads with expression
3.F.4	Attends consistently to punctuation
3.F.5	Rereads to clarify or problem-solve
3.F.6	Reads sixty (60) words per minute (minimum)

Language Comprehension and Response to Text

3.C.1	Comprehends both fiction and nonfiction on level
3.C.2	Reads chapter books independently
3.C.3	Identifies problem words or phrases
3.C.4	Summarizes fiction and nonfiction text
3.C.5	Similarities: characters/events across stories
3.C.6	Theme or message: interpreting fiction
3.C.7	Nonfiction:
3.C.7.1	Cause/effect
3.C.7.2	Fact/opinion
3.C.7.3	Main idea/details
3.C.8	Evaluation: Uses information/reasoning
3.C.9	Word meaning from roots and affixes
3.C.10	Dictionary: Determine meanings/usage
3.C.11	Uses new vocabulary in own speech and writing
3.C.12	Writing: Basic grammar/parts of speech
3.C.13	Familiar w/read-aloud, indep. reading, nonfiction
3.C.14	Locates information using:
3.C.14.1	Tables of contents
3.C.14.2	Indexes
3.C.14.3	Internet search engines
3.C.15	Connects literary texts with life experiences

Figure 7.39 *continued*

CLASSROOM PROFILE (BLAST™): THIRD GRADE LITERACY MILESTONES

Teacher: K. Spencer   Date/Grading Period Completed: 12 – 14

> **Instructions:** Record the degree to which each milestone skill has been achieved by each student (**E** = Emergent, **D** = Developing Skill, **P** = Proficient) in each box corresponding to the student and skill in the grid.

Decoding and Word Recognition

	Dora	Paula	Ameenah	Jason	Rosa Maria	Harry	James	Dirk	Syoria	Alicia	Johnny	Anna
3.D.1 Context clues, phonic knowledge and structural analysis	P	P	P	D	D	P	P	D	D	D	P	P

Spelling and Writing

	Dora	Paula	Ameenah	Jason	Rosa Maria	Harry	James	Dirk	Syoria	Alicia	Johnny	Anna
3.SW.1 Uses studied words and spelling patterns	D	D	E	E	D	D	E	D	P	E	E	P
3.SW.2 Uses the dictionary to check spelling	D	D	D	D	D	D	P	D	D	E	E	P
3.SW.3 Uses these aspects of the writing process:												
3.SW.3.1 Combines information/multiple sources	E	E	E	E	E	E	E	E	E	E	E	E
3.SW.3.2 Revises and edits	D	E	D	E	E	E	E	D	D	E	E	P
3.SW.3.3 Variety of written work	E	D	P	E	D	P	E	D	E	E	E	P
3.SW.3.4 Graphic organizational tools	E	D	E	D	E	E	D	P	P	E	E	D
3.SW.3.5 Descriptions and figurative language	E	E	E	P	E	E	D	P	D	E	P	P
3.SW.3.6 Variety of formal sentence structures	D	D	D	D	E	E	D	D	E	D	D	P
3.SW.4.S.1 Orthographic patterns and rules (Spanish only)	D	P		D	D		D					
3.SW.5.S.2 Spells words with three or more syllables using silent letters, dieresis marks, accents, verbs (Spanish only)	P	P		P	P		D					

Figure 7.40 Selecting needs-based groups

Each of the four DIBELS measures— (a) initial sounds fluency (ISF), (b) phonemic segmentation fluency (PSF), (c) nonsense word fluency (NWF), and (d) oral reading fluency (ORF) and are particularly useful in aiding teachers in their early identification of students who are not progressing well when compared to district, state, and national performance standards. When used as described by the designers, results can be used to evaluate individual student development as well as provide grade-level feedback toward nationally validated instructional objectives. Let's take a look at the subtests.

- The Initial Sounds Fluency (ISF) measure assesses a child's ability to identify and produce the initial sound of a series of orally given words. The test begins when children are shown a page of four black-and-white pictures (available free on the Internet at http://dibels.uoregon.edu/index.php or in color through Sopris West Publishers at www.sopriswest.com). For example, on one page of the ISF measure, children look at four pictures of a mouse, flowers, pillow, envelops. The test administrator says:

    This is mouse, flowers, pillow, letters [point to each picture while saying its name]. "Mouse" [point to mouse] begins with the /m/ sound. Listen, /m/ mouse. Which one begins with the sounds /fl/?

- The Phonemic Segmentation Fluency (PSF) measure assesses a child's ability to produce individual sounds within a list of words. Children are instructed to listen to the examiner say a list of words and are then asked to tell the examiner the sounds they hear in the word. The test administrator says:

    I am going to say a word. After I say it, you tell me all the sound in the word. So, if I say, "Sam," you would say /s/ /a/ /m/. Let's try one. (one-second pause) Tell me the sounds in "mop."

- The Nonsense Word Fluency (NWF) measure assesses a child's knowledge of letter-sound correspondences (alphabetic principle) as well their ability to blend letters together to form unfamiliar "nonsense" words (e.g., *fik, lig,* and so on). For example, children are shown a listing of nonsense words such as *sim, lut, yiz, wan, zoc, ful, mik.* Children are asked to read each nonsense word in the list. The test administrator says:

    Look at this word [point to the first word]. It's a make-believe word. Watch me read the word: /s/ /i/ /m/ "sim" [point to each letter then run your finger fast beneath the whole word]. I can say the sounds of the letters, /s/ /i/ /m/ (point to each letter), or I can read the whole word "sim" [run your finger fast beneath the world word]. Your turn to read a make-believe word. Read this word the best you can. Make sure you say any sounds you know.

- The fourth and final DIBELS measure is Oral Reading Fluency (ORF). This measure assesses a child's ability to read connected text in grade-level materials. Children are provided a standardized, grade-level paragraph and asked to read it. They are timed for 1 minute. Children's fluency is assessed by using a correct-words-per-minute (cwpm) calculation that adjusts the total number of words read aloud by the number of errors. After handing a child a copy of the passage to be read, the examiner says:

    Please read this [point to the passage] out loud. If you get stuck, I will tell you the word so you can keep reading. When I say "stop," I may ask you to tell me about what you read, so do your best reading. Start here [point to the first word of the passage]. Begin.

Each student's comprehension of the ORF grade-level passage is also measured. A 1-minute oral retelling is requested immediately following the reading of the paragraph. Student oral retells are scored by counting the number of words used in the retell during a 1-minute recording period. *DIBELS developers do not claim that the ORF retelling process is either reliable or valid.*

- The Letter Naming Fluency (LNF) measure assesses a child's ability to identify a series of rows of upper- and lowercase block printed letters. Although letter identification isn't as important for reading as is an understanding of sounds, knowing letter names is predictive of reading success or failure and provides part of the equation for understanding the alphabetic principle. When a child is shown the rows of upper- and lowercase letters, the test administrator says:

Here are some letters [point]. Tell me the names of as many as you can. When I say "begin," start here [point to the first letter in upper left hand corner] and go across the page [point]. Point to each letter and tell me the name of that letter. Try to name each letter. If you come to a letter you don't know, I'll tell it to you. Put your finger on the first letter. Ready?

DIBELS measures have been used extensively in schools and with elementary-aged children. At the present, DIBELS developers claim that over 450,000 individual children's scores have been entered into the DIBELS database system. DIBELS developers have been careful to establish data indicating the relation between the four measures. This means that performance on one of the DIBELS measures is predictive of performance on the next appropriate DIBELS measure(s). For example, for the students finishing kindergarten and established on phonological awareness, 84% of them were established readers by the end of first grade. According to DIBELS developers, this means that the child is likely to succeed in being a reader in first grade if they have established phonemic awareness in kindergarten. Conversely, a student is likely to experience problems in reading if he or she finishes kindergarten with a score of 10 or less on PSF. Only 16% of those students were established readers at the end of first grade.

The DIBELS assessment battery was developed using U.S. federal grants and is available free to teachers and schools. Information is available over the Internet at http://dibels.uoregon.edu/index.php.

A DIBELS data and reporting service is available on the Internet for a fee of $1 per year per child tested. Using this Internet-based system, teachers can enter assessment data directly into the DIBELS database on the Web and receive a nearly instantaneous report as often as desired. More recently, DIBELS measures have become available in Spanish; however, such measures have not yet been validated or proven reliable among Spanish-speaking populations.

Texas Primary Reading Inventory

The TPRI can also be used as a Progress-Monitoring Assessment.

The Texas Primary Reading Inventory (TPRI) is an assessment tool that provides a picture of a student's reading progress in kindergarten and first and second grades. Originally developed to help teachers in Texas in measuring the state's "essential knowledge and skills" in reading, this instrument is suitable for outcome assessment as well as for screening and progress-monitoring assessment purposes. A quick screening section is designed to work together with a more detailed inventory section to help teachers identify strengths and problem areas as well as monitor student's progress.

TPRI covers all five of the "big ideas" in early reading development: phonemic awareness, phonics, fluency, vocabulary, and comprehension strategies. The TPRI also provides an *Interventions Activities Guide* directly linked to students' performance of each part of the TPRI.

The TPRI is administered individually by the classroom teacher. In the Screening Section of the TPRI, three assessment measures are provided: (a) graphophonemic knowledge, (b) phonemic awareness, and (c) word reading. In the Graphophonemic measure, students are assessed on their ability to recognize letters of the alphabet and their understanding of sound-to-symbol relationships. In the Phonemic Awareness measure, children are assessed on their ability to identify and manipulate individual sounds within spoken words so that "letters can be linked to sounds." In the Word Reading measure of the screening portion of the TPRI, students are asked to correctly recognize a list of high-frequency words.

In the Inventory Section of the TPRI, students are assessed across seven measures: (a) book and print knowledge, (b) phonemic awareness, (c) listening comprehension, (d) graphophonemic knowledge, (e) reading accuracy, (f) reading fluency, and (g) reading comprehension. The TPRI, unlike the DIBELS, addresses the important role of the "concepts about print" in the development of early reading.

The TRPI is based on longitudinal data on over 900 English-speaking students. More recently, the TPRI has also become available in Spanish and, like DIBELS, has yet to be shown to be a valid and reliable indicator of reading development in this population. For a more extensive review of the TPRI, we recommend that you consult the following Web site: www.tpri.org.

DIAGNOSTIC ASSESSMENTS

Diagnostic assessments are used to gather in-depth information about student's particular strengths and needs, typically for struggling readers. Diagnostic assessments probe deeper than other assessments and take extra time to conduct. An educational psychologist, certified diagnostician, or bilingual specialist is sometimes needed to administer certain tests because of time constraints or required special training. Students in special education or Title I programs for reading often require diagnostic testing.

Diagnosing Vocabulary Knowledge

When we notice students who seem to struggle with reading it is logical for teachers to want to know the extent to which their vocabulary has developed. There are three tests we recommend for assessing a students' word knowledge or "receptive vocabulary." One is intended for native English speakers, and the other two are for students who speak Spanish as their first language and are learning to speak and read in English.

- *Peabody Picture Vocabulary Test, Third Edition (PPVT-III) (Dunn & Dunn, 1997).* The PPVT-III is a quickly administered test (11–12 minutes) that indicates how strong a student's vocabulary knowledge is compared to other students of the same age nationally. Results can help the teacher better understand the needs of students in terms of formal and informal vocabulary instruction.

- *Test de Vocabulario en Imágenes Peabody (TVIP) (Dunn, Lugo, Padilla, & Dunn, 1986).*   This test is an adaptation of an early version of the previously described Peabody Picture Vocabulary Test for native Spanish speakers. It takes about 10 to 15 minutes to administer and measures Spanish vocabulary knowledge.
- *Woodcock-Muñoz Language Survey (WMLS), English and Spanish Forms (Woodcock & Muñoz-Sandoval, 1993).*   Teachers, particularly in urban centers, often have a large number of students who are learning English as a second language. The extent to which students have acquired a listening and speaking vocabulary in English is an important factor in reading instruction because reading (a) is a language skill and (b) depends on learners having a fairly strong English vocabulary. The WMLS is a widely respected instrument used throughout the United States and takes about 20 minutes to administer. It features two subtests: Oral Language and Reading/Writing.

Individual Diagnostic Reading Tests

Norm-referenced tests are helpful for making national and program comparisons.

Standards Note
Standard 10.2: The reading professional will be able to use able to use information from norm-referenced tests . . . and other indicators of student progress to inform learning. From the list of "tools" in this standard (see Appendix A), list two that you need to enhance or add and two you are satisfied with.

Individual diagnostic tests can be helpful in assessing new students for whom prior assessments or permanent records are not yet available.

Teachers sometimes feel it is necessary to assess an individual student's reading ability using norm-referenced measures. This often happens when new students move into a school district without their permanent records or when struggling readers are being considered for extra assistance programs, such as Title 1 or special education services provided in inclusive classrooms. Following is an example of a commonly used test:

The Woodcock Reading Mastery Tests—Revised (WRMT-R/NU) (Woodcock, Mather, & Barnes, 1987; Woodcock, 1997) is a battery of six individually administered subtests intended to measure reading abilities from kindergarten through adult levels. Subtests cover visual-auditory learning, letter identification, word identification, word attack, word comprehension, and passage comprehension. Its design reveals a skills perspective of reading, and divides the assessment into two sections according to age and ability levels: *readiness* and *reading achievement.* The WRMT-R/NU reports norm-referenced data for both of its forms as well as insights into remediation. Results may be calculated either manually or using the convenient scoring program developed for personal computers. This WRMT-R/NU is frequently used by teachers in special education and Chapter 1 reading programs.

Individually Administered Achievement Tests

It can be informative to know how well a student has developed over a wide range of academic subjects. Achievement tests are often given to whole groups of students at scheduled grade levels, but you may need this information right away to better understand a troubled reader's knowledge and abilities. Following is a description of our preferred wide-range achievement test that can be individually administered as a diagnostic tool.

Sometimes teachers require norm-referenced data to determine how a child is progressing compared to other children nationally, such as when teachers are working with a population of students who are performing at atypically high or low levels. That is, working with either struggling readers or gifted students over a long period of time may give teachers a distorted view of what "normal" achievement looks like. The Kaufman Test of Educational Achievement (K-TEA/NU) (Kaufman & Kaufman, 1997), available in both English and Spanish forms, can provide useful insights in these situations.

The K-TEA/NU is a norm-referenced test yielding information in the areas of reading, mathematics, and spelling. Intended for students in grades 1 to 12, the K-TEA/NU is available in a *brief form* for quick assessments (when only standardized data are needed) and a *comprehensive form* (provides both standardized data and insights into classroom remediation). Alternate forms are not available, but the authors suggest that the two versions may be used as pretest–posttest measures.

The K-TEA/NU is an individually administered achievement test.

Summary

In this chapter, we explored basic principles of classroom reading assessment, four principles or types of assessment that are consistent with *Reading First* legislation and scientifically based reading research (SBRR), and ways of profiling students according to their development of reading skills. Key strategies for measuring student growth in each of the "big five" areas of reading development were also presented. We saw that comprehensive reading assessment carefully analyzes overall student growth in the reading process and helps teachers plan effective instruction.

Comprehensive reading assessment procedures provide teachers with the clearest and most complete view of the learner. Many aspects of reading are studied using genuine reading situations whenever possible to reveal insights into the learner's zones of proximal development. Running records, home surveys, story retellings, fluency measures, affective surveys, and self assessment are just a few of the tools available in comprehensive reading assessment.

Current issues in reading assessment seem to be focusing on

- what is meant by "skill mastery,"
- the need for a variety of text forms and contexts in reading assessment,
- effective ways to use some of the leading published assessment tools such as DIBELS, informal reading inventories (IRI), the TPRI, and PPVT-III, and
- ways of reporting progress to families, school boards, and state officials.

Without doubt, the effective and consistent use of classroom assessments by teachers is critical to the success of all students.

Concept Applications

In the Classroom

1. As a review, develop a comparison grid or chart analyzing the differences and similarities between traditional and comprehensive assessment perspectives.
2. Develop a schedule for your classroom (name the grade level) that includes time for the daily assessment of at least four students. What will be the typical assessment "tools" you will probably use during this time period? (Name at least four.) Explain and justify why you have selected these particular tools.
3. Develop three evaluation checklist forms that could be used in your classroom or a grade level you specify for reading comprehension, word identification, and content reading strategies. Include a suggested rubric with a rationale for each item.

Check your understanding of chapter concepts by using the self-assessment for Chapter 7 on our Companion Website at www.prenhall.com/reutzel.

In the Field

Arrange through your college instructor or in your own classroom to work with an elementary-age student who is reportedly having difficulty in reading. The following two major assignments can be completed with your student.

Part 1: Complete the following informal assessment procedures:

- A running record and analysis of the miscues using a book chosen by the student
- A commercial informal reading inventory of your choice
- An oral retelling of a book read by the student
- Three classroom observations of the student in various settings, such as reading group, content area materials, and free reading
- An interest inventory that you have constructed or adapted from the one in this chapter

Part 2: After compiling and summarizing the preceding information, construct a reading profile of the student that includes the following:

- Approximate reading level (instructional)
- Reading skills that appear to be strengths for the child (use your state's standards for this)
- Reading skills that need to be developed

Recommended Readings and Assessment Instruments

Dunn, L., & Dunn, L. M. (1997). *Peabody Picture Vocabulary Test—Third Edition.* Circle Pines, MN: American Guidance Service.

Dunn, L., Lugo, D. E., Padilla, E. R., & Dunn, L. M. (1986). *Test de Vocabulario en Imágenes Peabody.* Circle Pines, MN: American Guidance Service.

Flippo, R. F. (2004). Texts and Tests: Teaching Study Skills Across Content Areas. Portsmouth, NH: Heinemann.

Flynt, E. S., & Cooter, R. B., Jr. (1999). *The Flynt/Cooter English * Español Reading Inventory.* Upper Saddle River, NJ: Merrill/Prentice Hall.

Flynt, E. S., & Cooter, R. B., Jr. (2004). *The Flynt/Cooter Reading Inventory for the Classroom* (5th ed.). Upper Saddle River, NJ: Merrill/Prentice Hall.

Reutzel, D. R., & Cooter, R. B. (2003b). *Strategies for reading assessment and instruction: Helping every child succeed* (2nd ed.). Upper Saddle River, NJ: Merrill/Prentice Hall.

Standards for the English Language Arts Sponsored by NCTE and IRA

The vision guiding these standards is that all students must have the opportunities and resources to develop the language skills they need to pursue life's goals and to participate fully as informed, productive members of society. These standards assume that literacy growth begins before children enter school as they experience and experiment with literacy activities—reading and writing and associating spoken words with their graphic representations. Recognizing this fact, these standards encourage the development of curriculum and instruction that make productive use of the emerging literacy abilities that children bring to school. Furthermore, the standards provide ample room for the innovation and creativity essential to teaching and learning. They are not prescriptions for particular curriculum or instruction. Although we present these standards as a list, we want to emphasize that they are not distinct and separable; they are, in fact, interrelated and should be considered as a whole.

1. Students read a wide range of print and nonprint texts to build an understanding of texts, of themselves, and of the cultures of the United States and the world; to acquire new information; to respond to the needs and demands of society and the workplace; and for personal fulfillment. Among these texts are fiction and nonfiction, classic and contemporary works.
2. Students read a wide range of literature from many periods in many genres to build an understanding of the many dimensions (e.g., philosophical, ethical, aesthetic) of human experience.
3. Students apply a wide range of strategies to comprehend, interpret, evaluate, and appreciate texts. They draw on their prior experience, their interactions with other readers and writers, their knowledge of word meaning and of other texts, their word identification strategies, and their understanding of textual features (e.g., sound-letter correspondence, sentence structure, context, graphics).
4. Students adjust their use of spoken, written, and visual language (e.g., conventions, style, vocabulary) to communicate effectively with a variety of audiences and for different purposes.
5. Students employ a wide range of strategies as they write and use different writing process elements appropriately to communicate with different audiences for a variety of purposes.
6. Students apply knowledge of language structure, language conventions (e.g., spelling and punctuation), media techniques, figurative language, and genre to create, critique, and discuss print and nonprint texts.

7. Students conduct research on issues and interests by generating ideas and questions and by posing problems. They gather, evaluate, and synthesize data from a variety of sources (e.g., print and nonprint texts, artifacts, people) to communicate their discoveries in ways that suit their purpose and audience.

8. Students use a variety of technological and information resources (e.g., libraries, databases, computer networks, video) to gather and synthesize information and to create and communicate knowledge.

9. Students develop an understanding of and respect for diversity in language use, patterns, and dialects across cultures, ethnic groups, geographic regions, and social roles.

10. Students whose first language is not English make use of their first language to develop competency in the English language arts and to develop understanding of content across the curriculum.

11. Students participate as knowledgeable, reflective, creative, and critical members of a variety of literacy communities.

12. Students use spoken, written, and visual language to accomplish their own purposes (e.g., for learning, enjoyment, persuasion, and the exchange of information).

Source: *Standards for the English Language Arts,* by the International Reading Association and the National Council of Teachers of English. Copyright 1996 by the International Reading Association and the National Council of Teachers of English. Reprinted with permission.

B Links to State Standards

Following are the Web site addresses for all 50 states' Department of Education offices, on which the state's literacy standards can be found. For a comprehensive listing of all 50 states' standards, see http://www.statestandards.com.

AL | Alabama—www.alsde.edu/html/home.asp

AK | Alaska—www.eed.state.ak.us/

AZ | Arizona—www.ade.state.az.us/

AR | Arkansas—arkedu.state.ar.us/

CA | California—goldmine.cde.ca.gov/

CO | Colorado—www.cde.state.co.us/index_home.htm

CT | Connecticut—www.state.ct.us/sde/

DE | Delaware—www.doe.state.de.us/

DC | District of Columbia—www.k12.dc.us/dcps/home.html

FL | Florida—www.fldoe.org/

GA | Georgia—www.doe.k12.ga.us/index.asp

HI | Hawaii—http://doe.k12.hi.us/

ID | Idaho—www.sde.state.id.us/Dept/

IL | Illinois—www.isbe.state.il.us/

IN | Indiana—www.doe.state.in.us/

IA | Iowa—www.state.ia.us/educate/

KS | Kansas—www.ksbe.state.ks.us/Welcome.html

KY | Kentucky—www.kde.state.ky.us/

LA | Louisiana—www.doe.state.la.us/lde/index.html

ME | Maine—www.state.me.us/education/homepage.htm

MD | Maryland—www.msde.state.md.us/

MA | Massachusetts—www.doe.mass.edu/

MI | Michigan—www.michigan.gov/mde

MN | Minnesota—http://children.state.mn.us/html/mde_home.htm

MS | Mississippi—www.mde.k12.ms.us/

MO | Missouri—http://services.dese.state.mo.us/

MT | Montana—**www.opi.state.mt.us/index.html**

NE | Nebraska—**www.nde.state.ne.us/**

NV | Nevada—**www.nde.state.nv.us/**

NH | New Hampshire—**www.ed.state.nh.us/**

NJ | New Jersey—**www.state.nj.us/education/**

NM | New Mexico—**hppt://sde.state.nm.us/**

NY | New York—**www.nysed.gov/**

NC | North Carolina—**www.dpi.state.nc.us/**

ND | North Dakota—**www.dpi.state.nd.us/index.shtm**

OH | Ohio—**www.ode.state.oh.us/**

OK | Oklahoma—**http://sde.state.ok.us/home/defaultie.html**

OR | Oregon—**www.ode.state.or.us/**

PA | Pennsylvania—**www.pde.state.pa.us/pde_internet/site/default.asp**

RI | Rhode Island—**www.ridoe.net/**

SC | South Carolina—**www.myscschools.com/**

SD | South Dakota—**www.state.sd.us/deca/**

TN | Tennessee—**www.state.tn.us/education/**

TX | Texas—**www.tea.state.tx.us/**

UT | Utah—**www.usoe.k12.ut.us/**

VA | Virginia—**www.pen.k12.va.us/**

VT | Vermont—**www.state.vt.us/educ/**

WA | Washington—**www.k12.wa.us/**

WV | West Virginia—**wvde.state.wv.us/**

WI | Wisconsin—**www.dpi.state.wi.us/**

WY | Wyoming—**www.k12.wy.us/index.htm**

References

Aardema, V. (1975). *Why mosquitoes buzz in people's ears.* New York: Scholastic.

Aaron, R. L., & Gillespie, C. (1990). Gates-MacGinitie Reading Tests, 3rd Ed. [Test review]. In R. B. Cooter, Jr. (Ed.), *The teacher's guide to reading tests.* Scottsdale, AZ: Gorsuch Scarisbrick.

Adams, M. J. (1990a). *Beginning to read: Thinking and learning about print.* Cambridge, MA: MIT Press.

Adams, M. J. (1990b). *Beginning to read: Thinking and learning about print (Summary).* Urbana-Champaign, IL: Center for the Study of Reading.

Adams, M. J. (1994). *Beginning to read: Thinking and learning about print.* Cambridge, MA: MIT Press.

Adams, M. J. (2001). Alphabetic anxiety and explicit, systematic phonics instruction: A cognitive science perspective. In S. B. Neuman & D. K. Dickinson (Eds.), *Handbook of early literacy research.* New York: Guildford Press.

Adams, M. J., Allington, R. L., Chaney, J. H., Goodman, Y. M., Kapinus, B. A., McGee, L. M., et al. (1991). Beginning to read: A critique by literacy professionals and a response by Marilyn Jager Adams. *The Reading Teacher, 44(6),* 370–395.

Adams, M. J., Foorman, B. R., Lundberg, I., & Beeler, T. (1998). *Phonemic awareness in young children: A classroom curriculum.* Baltimore: Paul H. Brookes.

Ahlberg, J., & Ahlberg, A. (1986). *The jolly postman or other people's letters.* Boston: Little, Brown.

Aldridge, J. T., & Rust, D. (1987). A beginning reading strategy. *Academic Therapy, 22(3),* 323–326.

Alexander, J. E. (Ed.). (1983). *Teaching reading* (2nd ed.). Boston: Little, Brown.

Alexander, J. E., & Filler, R. C. (1976). *Attitudes and reading.* Newark, DE: International Reading Association.

Alexander, J. E., & Heathington, B. S. (1988). *Assessing and correcting classroom reading problems.* Glenview, IL: Scott, Foresman.

Alexander, P. A., & Jetton, T. L. (2000). Learning from text: A multidimensional perspective. In M. L. Kamil, P. B. Mosenthal, P. D. Pearson, & R. Barr (Eds.), *Handbook of reading research* (Vol. 3, pp. 285–310). Mahwah, NJ: Erlbaum.

Allan, K. K. (1982). The development of young children's metalinguistic understanding of the word. *Journal of Educational Research, 76,* 89–93.

Allington, R. (1997, August/ September). Commentary: Overselling phonics. *Reading Today,* 15–16.

Allington, R. L. (1977). If they don't read much, how they ever gonna get good? *Journal of Reading, 21,* 57–61.

Allington, R. L. (1980). Teacher interruption behaviors during primary grade oral reading. *Journal of Educational Psychology, 72,* 371–377.

Allington, R. L. (1983a). Fluency: The neglected reading goal. *The Reading Teacher, 36(6),* 556–561.

Allington, R. L. (1983b). The reading instruction provided readers of differing reading ability. *Elementary School Journal, 83,* 255–265.

Allington, R. L. (1984). Oral reading. In R. Barr, M. L. Kamil, & P. Mosenthal (Eds.), *Handbook of Reading Research.* New York: Longman.

Allington, R. L. (1992). How to get information on several proven programs for accelerating the progress of low-achieving children. *The Reading Teacher, 46(3),* 246–248.

Allington, R. L. (1997, August–September). Overselling phonics. *Reading Today, 14,* 15.

Allington, R. L. (2001). *What really matters for struggling readers: Designing research-based programs.* New York: Addison-Wesley Longman.

Allington, R. L. (2002). *Big brother and the national reading curriculum: How ideology trumped evidence.* Portsmouth, NH: Heinemann.

Allington, R. L., & Cunningham, P. M. (1996). *Schools that work: Where all children read and write.* New York: HarperCollins.

Allington, R. L., & Woodside-Jiron, H. (1998). Thirty years of research in reading: When is a research summary not a research summary? In K. S. Goodman (Ed.), *In defense of good teaching: What teachers need to know about the "reading wars"* (pp. 143–158). York, ME: Stenhouse.

Altwerger, B., Edelsky, C., & Flores, B. M. (1987). Whole language: What's new? *The Reading Teacher, 41(2),* 144–154.

Altwerger, B., & Flores, B. (1989). Abandoning the basal: Some aspects of the change process. *Theory Into Practice, 28(4),* 288–294.

Alvermann, D. E. (1991). The discussion web: A graphic aid for learning across the curriculum. *The Reading Teacher, 45(2),* 92–99.

Alvermann, D. E., & Boothby, P. R. (1982). Text differences: Children's perceptions at the transition stage in reading. *The Reading Teacher, 36(3),* 298–302.

Alvermann, D. E., Dillon, D. R., & O'Brien, D. G. (1987). *Using* discussion to promote reading comprehension. Newark, DE: International Reading Association.

Alvermann, D. E., & Phelps, S. F. (1994). *Content reading and literacy.* Boston: Allyn & Bacon.

Alvermann, D. E., & Phelps, P. (2001). *Content reading and literacy: Succeeding in today's diverse classrooms* (3rd ed.). New York: Allyn & Bacon.

Alvermann, D. E., Smith, L. C., & Readence, J. E. (1985). Prior knowledge activation and the comprehension of compatible and incompatible text. *Reading Research Quarterly, 20*(4), 420–436.

Amarel, M., Bussis, A., & Chittenden, E. A. (1977). *An approach to the study of beginning reading: Longitudinal case studies.* Paper presented at the National Reading Conference, New Orleans, LA.

American Federation of Teachers. (1999). *Teaching reading is rocket science. What expert teachers of reading should know and be able to do.* Washington, DC: Author.

American people, The (Grade 6). (1982). New York: American.

Ancona, G. (1994). *The piñata maker: Piñatero.* San Diego: Harcourt Brace.

Andersen, H. C. (1965). *The ugly duckling* (R. P. Keigwin, Trans., & A. Adams, Illustrator). New York: Scribner.

Anderson, L., Evertson, C., & Brophy, J. (1979). An experimental study of effective teaching in first-grade reading groups. *Elementary School Journal, 79,* 193–222.

Anderson, R. C. (1970). Control of student mediating processes during verbal learning and instruction. *Review of Educational Research, 40,* 349–369.

Anderson, R. C., & Freebody, P. (1981). Vocabulary knowledge. In J. T. Guthrie (Ed.), *Comprehension and teaching: Research reviews*

(pp. 80–82). Newark, DE: International Reading Association.

Anderson, R. C., Hiebert, E. F., Scott, J. A., & Wilkinson, I. A. G. (1985). *Becoming a nation of readers: The report of the Commission on Reading.* Washington, DC: National Institute of Education.

Anderson, L. W., Krathwohl D. R., Airasian, P. W., Cruickshank, K. A., Mayer, R. E., Pintrich, P. R., et al. (2000). *A taxonomy for learning, teaching, and assessing: A revision of Bloom's taxonomy of educational objectives.* New York: Pearson Allyn & Bacon/Longman.

Anderson, R. C., Mason, J., & Shirey, L. (1984). The reading group: An experimental investigation of a labyrinth. *Reading Research Quarterly, 20*(1), 6–38.

Anderson, R. C., Osborn, J., & Tierney, R. J. (1984). *Learning to read in American schools.* Hillsdale, NJ: Erlbaum.

Anderson, R. C., & Pearson, P. D. (1984). A schema-theoretic view of basic processes in reading. In D. P. Pearson (Ed.), *Handbook of reading research* (pp. 255–291). New York: Longman.

Anderson, R. C., Reynolds, R. E., Schallert, D. L., & Goetz, E. T. (1977). Frameworks for comprehending discourse. *American Educational Research Journal, 14,* 367–382.

Anderson, R. C., Wilson, P. T., & Fielding, L. G. (1988). Growth in reading and how children spend their time outside of school. *Reading Research Quarterly, 23*(3), 285–303.

Anderson, T. H., & Armbruster, B. B. (1980). Studying. In P. D. Pearson (Ed.), *Handbook of reading research* (pp. 657–680). New York: Longman.

Anderson, V. (1991). *A teacher development project in transactional strategy instruction*

for teacher of severely reading disabled adolescents. Paper presented at the National Reading Conference annual meeting, Palm Springs, CA.

Anton, W. (1999). *Corn: From farm to table.* New York: Newbridge.

Apple Computer. (1984). *Macwrite* [Computer program]. Cupertino, CA: Author.

Applebee, A. N. (1979). *The child's concept of story: Ages two to seventeen.* Chicago: University of Chicago Press.

Applebee, A. N., Langer, J. A., & Mullis, I. V. S. (1988). *Who reads best.* Princeton, NJ: Educational Testing Service.

Appleby, E. (2001). *The three billy goats gruff: A Norwegian tale.* New York: Scholastic.

Armbruster, B., & Anderson, T. (1981). *Content area textbooks* (Reading Education Report No. 23). Urbana-Champaign: University of Illinois at Urbana-Champaign, Center for the Study of Reading.

Armbruster, B. B. (1984). The problem of "inconsiderate text." In G. G. Duffy, L. R. Roehler, & J. Mason (Eds.), *Comprehension instruction: Perspective and suggestions.* New York: Longman.

Armbruster, B. B., Lehr, F., & Osborn, J. (2001). *Put reading first: The research building blocks of teaching children to read.* Jessup, MD: National Institute for Literacy/ED.

Asbjornsen, P. C. (1973). *The three billy goats gruff* (Paul Galdone, Illustrator). New York: Seabury Press.

Asch, F. (1993). *Moondance.* New York: Scholastic.

Asheim, L., Baker, D. P., & Mathews, V. H. (1983). *Reading and successful living: The family school partnership.* Hamden, CT: Library Professional.

Asher, S. R. (1977). *Sex differences in reading achievement* (Reading Education Report No. 2). Urbana-Champaign: University of Illinois at Urbana-Champaign, Center for the Study of Reading.

Asher, S. R. (1980). Topic interest and children's reading comprehension. In R. J. Spiro, B. C. Bruce, & W. F. Brewer (Eds.), *Theoretical issues in reading comprehension* (pp. 525–534). Hillsdale, NJ: Erlbaum.

Ashton-Warner, S. (1963). *Teacher.* New York: Touchstone Press.

Atwell, N. (1987). *In the middle: Writing, reading, and learning with adolescents.* Portsmouth, NH: Heinemann.

Au, K. H. (1993). *Literacy instruction in multicultural settings.* Fort Worth, TX: Harcourt Brace.

Au, K. H. (1997). *Literacy instruction in multicultural settings.* Belmont, CA: Wadsworth.

Au, T. K., Depretto, M., & Song, Y. K. (1994). Input vs. constraints: Early word acquisition in Korean and English. *Journal of Memory and Language, 33,* 567–582.

Aukerman, R. (1981). *The basal reader approach to reading.* New York: Wiley.

Ausubel, D. P. (1959). Viewpoints from related disciplines: Human growth and development. *Teachers College Record, 60,* 245–254.

Avi. W. (1984). *The fighting ground.* Philadelphia: Lippincott.

Bacharach, N., & Alexander, P. (1986). Basal reader manuals: What do teachers think of them? *Reading Psychology, 3,* 163–172.

Bader, L. A. (1984). Instructional adjustments to vision problems. *The Reading Teacher, 37*(7), 566–569.

Baker, L., & Brown, A. L. (1984). Cognitive monitoring in reading. In J. Flood (Ed.), *Understanding reading comprehension* (pp. 21–44). Newark, DE: International Reading Association.

Baker, L., Dreher, M. J., & Guthrie, J. T. (2000). *Engaging young readers: Promoting*

achievement and motivation. New York: Guilford Press.

Baldwin, R. S., & Kaufman, R. K. (1979). A concurrent validity study of the Raygor readability estimate. *Journal of Reading, 23,* 148–153.

Bank Street writer [Computer program]. (1990). Jefferson City, MO: Scholastic Software.

Bantam. (1985). *Choose your own adventure.* New York: Bantam.

Barker, R. (1978). Stream of individual behavior. In R. Barker & Associates (Eds.), *Habitats, environments, and human behavior* (pp. 3–16). San Francisco: Jossey-Bass.

Barracca, D., & Barracca, S. (1990). *Taxi dog.* New York: Dial Books.

Barrentine, S. B. (1996). Engaging with reading through interactive read-alouds. *The Reading Teacher, 50*(1), 36–43.

Barrentine, S. J. (1999). *Reading assessment: Principles and practices for elementary teachers.* Newark, DE: International Reading Association.

Barrett, F. L. (1982). *A teacher's guide to shared reading.* Richmond Hill, Ontario, Canada: Scholastic-TAB.

Barrett, J. (1978). *Cloudy with a chance of meatballs* (R. Barrett, Illustrator). Hartford, CT: Atheneum.

Barrett, N. S. (1984). *Trucks* (Tony Bryan, Illustrator). London: F. Watts.

Barrett, N. S. (1989). *Spiders.* London: F. Watts.

Barrett, T. (1972). Taxonomy of reading comprehension. *Reading 360 monograph.* Boston: Ginn.

Barron, R. F. (1969). The use of vocabulary as an advance organizer. In H. L. Herber & P. L. Sanders (Eds.), *Research in reading in the content areas: First year report.* Syracuse, NY: Reading and Language Arts Center, Syracuse University.

Bartlett, B. J. (1978). *Top-level structure as an organizational strategy for recall of classroom*

text. Unpublished doctoral dissertation, Arizona State University, Tempe.

Barton, D., Miller, R., & Macken, M. A. (1980). Do children treat clusters as one unit or two? *Papers and Reports on Child Language Development, 18,* 137.

Basal reading texts. What's in them to comprehend? (1984). *The Reading Teacher,* 194–195.

Base, G. (1986). *Animalia.* New York: Harry N. Abrams.

Baskin, E. F. (2004). Change management concepts and models: Sponsorship, early adopters, and the development of urban teachers. In R. B. Cooter (Ed.), *Perspectives on rescuing urban literacy education* (pp. 25–40). Mahwah, NJ: Erlbaum.

Baum, L. F. (1972). *The Wizard of Oz.* World. New York.

Baumann, J. F. (1992). Basal reading programs and the deskilling of teachers: A critical examination of the argument. *Reading Research Quarterly, 27*(4), 390–398.

Baumann, J. F. (1993). Letters to the editor: Is it "You just don't understand," or am I simply confused? A response to Shannon. *Reading Research Quarterly, 28*(2), 86–87.

Baumann, J. F. (1996). Do basal readers deskill teachers: A national survey of educators' use and opinions of basals. *Elementary School Journal, 96*(5), 511–526.

Baumann, J. F., & Bergeron, B. S. (1993). Story map instruction using children's literature: Effects on first graders' comprehension of central narrative elements. *Journal of Reading Behavior, 25,* 407–437.

Baumann, J. F., Jones, L. A., & Siefert-Kessell, N. (1993). Using think alouds to enhance children's comprehension monitoring abilities. *The Reading Teacher, 47*(3), 184–193.

Baumann, J. F., & Stevenson, J. A. (1986). Teaching students to comprehend anaphoric relations. In J. W. Irwin (Ed.), *Understanding and teaching cohesion comprehension* (pp. 3–8). Newark, DE: International Reading Association.

Baylor, B. (1976). *Hawk, I'm your brother.* New York: Macmillan.

Bear, D. R., Inverizzi, M., Templeton, S., & Johnston, F. (2000). *Words their way: Word study for phonics, vocabulary, and spelling instruction.* Upper Saddle River, NJ: Merrill/Prentice Hall.

Bear, D. R., Templeton, S., Invernizzi, M., & Johnston, F. (1996). *Words their way: Word study for phonics, vocabulary, and spelling instruction.* Upper Saddle River, NJ: Merrill/Prentice Hall.

Beaver, J. (2001). *Developmental reading assessment.* Parsippany, NJ: Celebration Press.

Beck, I. L. (1986). Using research on reading. *Educational Leadership, 43*(7), 13–15.

Beck, I. L. (1997). Response to "Overselling phonics" [Letter to the editor]. *Reading Today*, 17.

Beck, I. L., Armbruster, B., Raphael, T., McKeown, M. G., Ringler, L., & Ogle, D. (1989). *Reading today and tomorrow: Treasures. Level 3.* New York: Holt, Rinehart and Winston.

Beck, I. L., & McKeown, M. G. (1981). Developing questions that promote comprehension: The story map. *Language Arts, 58,* 913–918.

Beck, I. L., & McKeown, M. G. (1985). *Educational Perspectives, 23,*(1), 11–15

Beck, I. L., & McKeown, M. G. (2001). Text talk: Capturing the benefits of read-aloud experiences for young children. *Reading Teacher, 55*(1), 10–20.

Beck, I. L., McKeown, M. G., Omanson, R. C., & Pople, M. T. (1984). Improving the comprehensibility of stories: The effects of revisions that improve coherence. *Reading Research Quarterly, 19,* 263–277.

Beck, I. L., Omanson, R. C., & McKeown, M. G. (1982). An instructional redesign of reading lessons: Effects on comprehension. *Reading Research Quarterly, 17,* 462–481.

Bennett, W. J. (2001, April 24). A cure for the illiteracy epidemic. *Wall Street Journal,* p. A24.

Benson, V. & Cummins, C. (2000). *The power of retelling.* New York: Wright Group/McGraw-Hill NY.

Berger, M. (1996). *Amazing water.* New York: Newbridge.

Berger, P. L. (1974). *Sociology: A biographical approach.* New York: Basic Books.

Berlak, H. (1992). The need for a new science of assessment. In H. Berlak et al., *Toward a new science of educational testing and assessment.* Albany: State University of New York Press.

Betts, E. A. (1946). *Foundation of reading instruction.* New York: American Book.

Bilingual writing center, The. (1992). Fremont, CA: The Learning Company. Aidenwood Tech Park, 493 Kaiser Drive, Fremont, CA 94555, (800) 852-2255

Bintz, W. P. (1991). Staying connected—Exploring new functions for assessment. *Contemporary Education, 62*(4), 307–312.

Birdshaw, D., Burns, S., Carlisle, J. F., Duke, N. K., Garcia, G. E., Hoffman, J. V., et al. (2001). *Teaching every child to read: Frequently asked questions.* Ann Arbor, MI: Center for the Improvement of Early Reading Achievement.

Bissex, G. L. (1980). *Gnys at wrk: A child learns to write and read.* Cambridge, MA: Harvard University Press.

Blachman, B. A. (1984). Relationship of rapid naming ability and language analysis skills to kindergarten and first-grade reading achievement. *Journal of Educational Psychology, 76,* 610–622.

Blachowicz, C. L. Z. (1977). Cloze activities for primary readers. *The Reading Teacher, 31*(3), 300–302.

Blachowicz, C. L. Z. (1986). Making connections: Alternatives to the vocabulary notebook. *Journal of Reading, 29*(7), 643–649.

Blackburn, L. (1997). *Whole music: A whole language approach to teaching music.* Westport, CT: Heinemann.

Blair, S. M., and Williams, K. A. (1999). *Balanced reading instruction: Achieving success with every child.* Newark, DE: International Reading Association.

Blanchard, J., & Rottenberg, C. J. (1990). Hypertext and hypermedia: Discovering and creating meaningful learning environments. *The Reading Teacher, 43*(9), 656–661.

Blanchard, J. S., Mason, G. E., & Daniel, D. (1987). *Computer applications in reading.* Newark, DE: International Reading Association.

Blanton, W. E., & Moorman, G. B. (1985). *Presentation of reading lessons. Technical Report No. 1.* Boone, NC: Center for Excellence on Teacher Education, Appalachian State University.

Blanton, W. E., Moorman, G. B., & Wood, K. D. (1986). A model of direct instruction applied to the basal skills lesson. *The Reading Teacher, 40,* 299–305.

Blecher, S., & Jaffee, K. (1998). *Weaving in the arts: Widening the learning circle.* Westport, CT: Heinemann.

Bleich, D. (1978). *Subjective criticism.* Baltimore: Johns Hopkins University Press.

Blevins, W. (1997). *Phonemic awareness activities for early reading success.* New York: Scholastic.

Blevins, W. (1998). *Phonics from A to Z.* New York: Scholastic.

Block, C. C. (1993). Strategy instruction in a literature-based program. *Elementary School Journal, 94,* 103–120.

Block, C. C., Gambrell, L. B., Hamilton, V., Hartman, D. K.,

Hasselbring, T. S., Klein, A., et al. (2000). *Scholastic literacy place.* New York: Scholastic.

Block, C. C., & Mangieri, J. (1996). *Reasons to read: Thinking strategies for life through literature* (Vols. 1–3). Menlo Park, CA: Addison.

Block, C. C., Oakar, M., & Hurt, N. (2002). The expertise of literacy teachers: A continuum from preschool to grade 5. *Reading Research Quarterly, 37*(2), 178–206.

Block, J. H. (1989). *Building effective mastery learning schools.* New York: Longman.

Blok, H., Oostdam, R., Otter, M. E., & Overmaat, M. (2002). Computer-assisted instruction in support of beginning reading instruction: A review. *Review of Educational Research, 72*(1), 101–130.

Bloom, A. (1987). *The closing of the American mind: How higher education has failed democracy and impoverished the souls of today's students.* New York: Simon & Schuster.

Bloom, B. (1956). *Taxonomy of educational objectives.* New York: David McKay.

Blum, I. (1995). Using audiotaped books to extend classroom literacy instruction into the homes of second-language learners. *Journal of Reading Behavior, 27*(4), 535–563.

Blume, J. (1972). *Tales of a fourth grade nothing.* New York: Dell.

Bohning, G. (1986). The McGuffey eclectic readers: 1836–1986. *The Reading Teacher, 40,* 263–269.

Bond, G. L., & Dykstra, R. (1967). The cooperative research program in first-grade reading instruction. *Reading Research Quarterly, 2,* 5–142.

Bonne, R. (1985). *I know an old lady.* New York: Scholastic.

Bonners, S. (1989). *Just in passing.* New York: Lothrop, Lee & Shepard.

Booth, J. (1985). *Impressions.* Toronto: Holt, Rinehart and Winston.

Bourgeois, P., & Clark, B. (1986). *Franklin in the dark.* New York: Scholastic.

Boyle, O. F., & Peregoy, S. F. (1990). Literacy scaffolds: Strategies for first- and second-language readers and writers. *The Reading Teacher, 44*(3), 194–200.

Brackett, G. (1989). *Super story tree.* Jefferson City, MO: Scholastic.

Bradley, L., & Bryant, P. E. (1983). Categorising sounds and learning to read: A causal connection. *Nature, 310,* 419–421.

Branley, F. (1983). *Saturn: The spectacular planet.* New York: HarperCollins.

Bransford, J. C., & Johnson, M. K. (1972). Contextual prerequisites for understanding: Some investigations of comprehension and recall. *Journal of Verbal Learning and Verbal Behavior, 11,* 717–726.

Bransford, J. D., & Franks, J. J. (1971). The abstraction of linguistic ideas. *Cognitive Psychology, 2,* 331–350.

Braun, C. (1969). Interest-loading and modality effects on textual response acquisition. *Reading Research Quarterly, 4,* 428–444.

Brennan, J. (1994, September 3). Been there done that: Three John Grisham stories, one John Grisham plot. *Fort Worth Star Telegram,* p. 1E.

Bridge, C. (1978). Predictable materials for beginning readers. *Language Arts, 55,* 593–597.

Bridge, C. A., Winograd, P. N., & Haley, D. (1983). Using predictable materials vs. preprimers to teach beginning sight words. *The Reading Teacher, 36,* 84–91.

Brigance, A. H. (1999). *Brigance® comprehensive inventory of basic skills—revised.* North Billerica, MA: Curriculum Associates.

Brimner, L. D. (1992). *A migrant family.* Minneapolis: Lerner.

Bromley, K. D. (1991). *Webbing with literature: Creating story maps with children's books.* Boston: Allyn & Bacon.

Bronfenbrenner, U. (1977). Toward an experimental ecology of human development. *American Psychologist, 32,* 513–531.

Bronfenbrenner, U., McClelland, P., Wethington, E., Moen, P., & Ceci, S. J. (1996). *The state of Americans.* New York: Free Press.

Brown, A. (1982). Learning how to learn from reading. In J. A. Langer & M. T. Smith-Burke (Eds.), *Reader meets author: Bridging the gap* (pp. 26–54). Newark, DE: International Reading Association.

Brown, A., & Smiley, S. S. (1978). The development of strategies for studying texts. *Child Development, 49,* 1076–1088.

Brown, D. J., Engin, A. W., & Wallbrown, F. J. (1979). Developmental changes in reading attitudes during the intermediate grades. *Journal of Experimental Education, 47,* 262–279.

Brown, K. J. (2000). What kind of text—For whom and when? Textual scaffolding for beginning readers. *The Reading Teacher, 53*(4), 292–307.

Brown, M. (1947). *Stone soup.* New York: Scribner.

Brown, R., Pressley, M., Van Meter, P., & Schuder, T. (1996). A quasi-experimental validation of transactional strategies instruction with low-achieving second grade readers. *Journal of Educational Psychology, 88,* 18–37.

Brown, T. (1986). *Hello, amigos.* New York: Holt, Rinehart and Winston.

Brozo, W. G., & Simpson, M. L. (1995). *Readers, teachers, learners: Expanding literacy in secondary schools.* Upper Saddle River, NJ: Merrill/Prentice Hall.

Bruner, J. (1986). *Actual minds, possible worlds.* Cambridge, MA: Harvard University Press.

Burke, C. (1987). Burke reading interview. In Y. Goodman, D. Watson, & C. Burke (Eds.), *Reading miscue inventory: Alternative procedures.* New York: Owen.

Burkhart, A. L. (2000). Breaking the parental barrier. In T. V. Rasinski, N. D. Padak, et al. (Eds.), *Motivating recreational reading and promoting home–school connections* (pp. 110–113). Newark, DE: International Reading Association.

Burnford, S. (1960). *The incredible journey.* Boston: Little, Brown.

Burns, M. (1987). *The I hate mathematics book* (Martha Hairston, Illustrator). Cambridge, MA: Cambridge University Press.

Burns, M. S., Griffin, P., & Snow, C. E. (1999). *Starting out right: A guide to promoting children's reading success.* Washington, DC: National Academy Press.

Burns, P. C., Roe, B. D., & Ross, E. P. (1992). *Teaching reading in today's elementary schools,* (5th ed.). Dallas: Houghton Mifflin.

Byars, B. (1970). *The summer of the swans.* New York: Viking.

Byars, B. (1981). *The Cybil war.* New York: Viking.

Byrne, B., & Fielding-Barnsley, R. (1989). Phonemic awareness and letter knowledge in the child's acquisition of the alphabetic principle. *Journal of Educational Psychology, 81,* 313–321.

Byrne, B., & Fielding-Barnsley, R. (1990). Acquiring the alphabetic principle: A case for teaching recognition of phoneme identity. *Journal of Educational Psychology, 82*(4), 805–812.

Byrne, B., Freebody, P., & Gates, A. (1992). Longitudinal data on the relations of word-reading strategies to comprehension, reading time, and phonemic awareness. *Reading Research Quarterly, 27*(2), 140–151.

Cafolla, R., Kauffman, D., & Knee, R. (1997). *World Wide Web for teachers: An interactive guide.* Boston: Allyn & Bacon.

California Department of Education. (1980). *Report on the special studies of selected ECE schools with increasing and decreasing reading scores.* Available from Publication Sales, California State Department of Education, P.O. Box 271, Sacramento, CA 95802.

California Reading Task Force. (1995). *Every child a reader: The report of the California Reading Task Force.* Sacramento: California Department of Education.

Calkins, L. (1994). *The art of teaching writing.* Portsmouth, CT: Heinemann.

Calkins, L. (2001). *The art of teaching reading.* New York: Addison-Wesley.

Calkins, L. M. (1980). When children want to punctuate: Basic skills belong in context. *Language Arts, 57,* 567–573.

Calkins, L. M., & Harwayne, S. (1987). *The writing workshop: A world of difference* [Video]. Portsmouth, NH: Heinemann.

Cambourne, B. (1988). *The whole story: Natural learning and the acquisition of literacy in the classroom.* New York: Ashton-Scholastic.

Cambourne, B., & Turbill, J. (1990). Assessment in whole-language classrooms: Theory into practice. *Elementary School Journal, 90*(3), 337–349.

Campbell, R. (1992). *Reading real books.* Philadelphia: Open University Press.

Canney, G., & Winograd, P. (1979). *Schemata for reading and reading comprehension performance* (Technical Report No. 120). Urbana-Champaign: University of Illinois at Urbana-Champaign, Center for the Study of Reading. (ERIC Document Reproduction Service)

Cantrell, S. C. (1999). Effective teaching and literacy learning: A look inside primary classrooms. *The Reading Teacher, 52*(4), 370–378.

Carbo, M. (1988). The evidence supporting reading styles: A response to Stahl. *Phi Delta Kappan, 70,* 323–327.

Carle, E. (1981). *The very hungry caterpillar.* New York: HarperCollins.

Carle, E. (1986). *The grouchy ladybug.* New York: HarperCollins.

Carr, E. (1985). The vocabulary overview guide: A metacognitive strategy to improve vocabulary comprehension and retention. *Journal of Reading, 28*(8), 684–689.

Carr, E., Dewitz, P., & Patberg, J. (1989). Using cloze for inference training with expository text. *The Reading Teacher, 43*(6), 380–385.

Carr, E., & Wixson, K. K. (1986). Guidelines for evaluating vocabulary instruction. *Journal of Reading, 29*(7), 588–589.

Carr, H. K. (1986). *Developing metacognitive skills: The key to success in reading and learning.* For the MERIT, Chapter 2 project, The School District of Philadelphia, H. K. Carr, MERIT supervisor. Philadelphia: School District of Philadelphia.

Carr, S., & Thompson, B. (1996). The effects of prior knowledge and schema activation strategies on the inferential reading comprehension of children with and without learning disabilities. *Learning Disabilities Quarterly, 19*(2), 48–61.

Carroll, J. B., Davies, P., & Richman, B. (1971). *Word frequency book.* Boston: Houghton Mifflin.

Carroll, L. (1872). *Through the looking glass.* New York: Macmillan.

Cassidy, J. (1981). Grey power in the reading program—A direction for the eighties. *The Reading Teacher, 35,* 287–291.

Cattell, J. M. (1885). Ueber die Zeit der Erkennung und Bennenung von Schriftzeichen, Bildern und Farben. *Philosophische Studien, 2,* 635–650.

Caverly, D. C., & Buswell, J. (1988). Computer assisted instruction that supports whole language instruction. *Colorado Communicator, 11*(3), 6–7.

Chall, J. S. (1967). *Learning to read: The great debate.* New York: McGraw-Hill.

Chall, J. S. (1979). The great debate: Ten years later, with a modest proposal for reading stages. In L. B. Resnick & P. A. Weaver, (Eds.), *Theory and practice of early reading* (pp. 29–55). Hillsdale, NJ: Erlbaum.

Chall, J. S. (1983). *Stages of reading development.* New York: McGraw-Hill.

Chall, J. S. (1998). My life in reading. In E. Sturtevant, J. Dugan, P. Linder, & W. Linek (Eds.), *Literacy and community, the twentieth yearbook of the College Reading Association, USA,* (pp. 12–24). Nashville, TN: College Reading Association.

Chapman, L. J., & Hoffman, M. (1977). *Developing fluent reading.* Milton Keynes, OK: Open University Press.

Chard, S. C. (1998). *The project approach: Making curriculum come alive,* (Book 1). New York: Scholastic Professional Books.

Chase, R. (1948). *Grandfather tales.* Boston: Houghton Mifflin.

Chase, R. (2003). *The Jack tales.* Boston: Houghton Mifflin.

Cheney, L. V. (1990). *Tyrannical machines.* Washington, DC: National Endowment for the Humanities.

Chisom, F. P. (1989). *Jump start: The federal role in adult literacy.* Southport, CT: Southport Institute for Policy Analysis.

Choi, S. N. (1991). *Year of impossible goodbyes.* Boston: Houghton Mifflin.

Chomsky, C. (1971). Write first, read later. *Childhood Education, 47,* 230–237.

Chomsky, N. (1974). *Aspects of the theory of syntax.* Cambridge, MA: MIT Press.

Chomsky, N. (1975). *The logical structure of linguistic theory.* Chicago: University of Chicago Press.

Chomsky, N. (1979). Human language and other semiotic systems. *Semiotica, 25,* 31–44.

Christopher, J. (1967). *The white mountains.* New York: Macmillan.

Clark, E. (1993). *The lexicon in acquisition.* Cambridge, UK: Cambridge University Press.

Clark, H. H., & Clark, E. V. (1977). *Psychology and language: An introduction to psycholinguistics.* New York: Harcourt Brace Jovanovich.

Clarke, M. A. (1989). Negotiating agendas: Preliminary considerations. *Language Arts, 66*(4), 370–380.

Clay, M. M. (1967). The reading behaviour of five year old children: A research report. *New Zealand Journal of Educational Studies, 2*(1), 11–31.

Clay, M. M. (1972). *Reading: The patterning of complex behaviour.* Exeter, NH: Heinemann.

Clay, M. M. (1975). *What did I write? Beginning writing behaviour.* Portsmouth, NH: Heinemann.

Clay, M. M. (1985). *The early detection of reading difficulties,* (3rd ed.). Portsmouth, NH: Heinemann.

Clay, M. M. (1985b). *Sand.* Portsmouth, NH: Heinemann.

Clay, M. M. (1985c). *Stones.* Portsmouth, NH: Heinemann.

Clay, M. M. (1987). *Writing begins at home: Preparing children for writing before they go to school.* Portsmouth, NH: Heinemann.

Clay, M. M. (1990a). The Reading Recovery Programme, 1984–88: Coverage, outcomes and Education Board district figures.

New Zealand Journal of Educational Studies, 25, 61–70.

Clay, M. M. (1990b). What is and what might be in evaluation (research currents). *Language Arts, 67*(3), 288–298.

Clay, M. M. (1993a). *An observation survey for early literacy achievement.* Portsmouth, NH: Heinemann.

Clay, M. M. (1993b). *Reading recovery: A guidebook for teachers in training.* Portsmouth, NH: Heinemann.

Clay, M. M. (1997). *Running records for classroom teachers.* Portsmouth, NH: Heinemann.

Clay, M. M. (1998). *By different paths to common outcomes.* York, ME: Stenhouse.

Clay, M. M. (2000a). *Follow me, moon.* Portsmouth, NH: Heinemann.

Clay, M. M. (2000b). *No shoes.* Portsmouth, NH: Heinemann.

Cleary, B. (1952). *Henry and Beezus.* New York: William Morrow.

Clifford, J. (1991). *The experience of reading: Louise Rosenblatt and reader-response theory.* Portsmouth, NH: Heinemann.

Cochrane, O., Cochrane, D., Scalena, D., & Buchanan, E. (1984). *Reading, writing and caring.* New York: Owen.

Cohen, M. (1980). *First grade takes a test.* New York: Dell Books.

Cole, B. (1983). *The trouble with mom.* New York: Coward-McCann.

Cole, J. (1986). *This is the place for me.* New York: Scholastic.

Cole, J. (1990). *The magic school bus lost in the solar system.* New York: Scholastic.

Cole, J., & Calmenson, S. (1990). *Miss Mary Mack.* New York: Morrow Junior Books.

Cole, J. E. (2003). What motivates students to read? Four literacy personalities. *The Reading Teacher, 56*(4), 326–336.

Cole, R. (1997). *The world of matter.* New York: Newbridge Educational.

Collier, J., & Collier, C. (1981). *Jump ship to freedom.* New York: Delacorte.

Collins, A., & Smith, E. (1980). *Teaching the process of reading comprehension* (Technical Report No. 182). Urbana-Champaign: University of Illinois at Urbana-Champaign, Center for the Study of Reading.

Collins, A. M., & Quillian, M. R. (1969). Retrieval time from semantic memory. *Journal of Verbal Learning and Verbal Behavior, 8,* 240–247.

Collins, C. (1988). Research windows. *The Computing Teacher, 15,* 15–16, 61.

Collins C. (1991). Reading instruction that increases thinking abilities. *Journal of Reading, 34,* 510–515.

Collins-Block, C., Gambrell, L. B., & Pressley, M. (2003). *Improving comprehension instruction: Advances in research, theory, and classroom practice.* San Francisco: Jossey-Bass.

Collins-Block, C., & Mangeri, J. (1996). *Reason to read: Thinking strategies for life through literature,* Palo Alto, CA: Addison-Wesley.

Collins-Block, C., Oaker, M., & Hurt, N. (2002). The expertise of literacy teachers: A continuum from preschool to grade 3. *Reading Research Quarterly, 37*(2), 178–206.

Collins-Block, C., & Pressley, M. (2002). *Comprehension instruction: Research-based best practices.* New York: Guilford Press.

Commeyras, M., & DeGroff, L. (1998). Literacy professionals' perspectives on professional development and pedagogy: A United States survey. *Reading Research Quarterly, 33*(4), 434–472.

Cone, M. (1964). *A promise is a promise.* Boston: Houghton Mifflin.

Cooter, K. S. (2003). *Preparing middle school students for the TAAS in writing.* Unpublished manuscript.

Cooter, K. S., & Cooter, R. B., Jr. (2004). Challenges to change: Implementing research-based reading instruction in urban schools. In R. B. Cooter (Ed.), *Perspectives on rescuing urban literacy education* (pp. 41–56). Mahwah, NJ: Erlbaum.

Cooter, K. S., & Cooter, R. B., Jr. (in press). One size doesn't fit all: Slow learners in the reading classroom. *The Reading Teacher.*

Cooter, R. B., Jr. (1988). Effects of Ritalin on reading. *Academic Therapy, 23,* 461–468.

Cooter, R. B., Jr. (Ed.). (1990). *The teacher's guide to reading tests.* Scottsdale, AZ: Gorsuch Scarisbrick.

Cooter, R. B., Jr. (1993). *Improving oral reading fluency through repeated readings using simultaneous recordings.* Unpublished manuscript, PDS Urban Schools Project, Texas Christian University, Fort Worth, TX.

Cooter, R. B., Jr. (1994). Assessing affective and conative factors in reading. *Reading Psychology, 15*(2), 77–90.

Cooter, R. B., Jr. (1998). *Balanced literacy instructional strands* (Reading Research Report No. 91). Dallas.

Cooter, R. B., Jr. (1999). *Realizing the dream: Meeting the literacy needs of Dallas children.* Unpublished manuscript.

Cooter, R. B., Jr. (2003a). Teacher "capacity-building" helps urban children succeed in reading. *The Reading Teacher, 57*(2), 198–205.

Cooter, R. B. (Ed.). (2003). *Perspectives on rescuing urban literacy education: Spies, saboteurs & saints.* Mahwah, NJ: Erlbaum.

Cooter, R. B., Jr., & Cooter, K. S. (1999). *BLAST!: Balanced Literacy Assessment System and Training.* Memphis, TN: Unpublished workshop resources.

Cooter, R. B., Jr., & Cooter, K. S. (2002). The Fluency Formula: A comprehensive model of instruction. *Creating Comprehensive Reading Programs.* Symposium series for Title I teachers and administrators, Wichita, KS.

Cooter, R. B., Jr., Diffily, D., Gist-Evans, D., & Sacken, M. A. (1994). *Literacy development milestones research project* (Report No. 94–100). Unpublished manuscript.

Cooter, R. B., Jr., & Flynt, E. S. (1989). Blending basal reader and whole language instruction. *Reading Horizons, 29*(4), 275–282.

Cooter, R. B., Jr., & Flynt, E. S. (1996). *Teaching reading in the content areas: Developing content literacy for all students.* Upper Saddle River, NJ: Merrill/Prentice Hall.

Cooter, R. B., Jr., & Griffith, R. (1989). Thematic units for middle school: An honorable seduction. *Journal of Reading, 32*(8), 676–681.

Cooter, R. B., Jr., Jacobson, J. J., & Cooter, K. S. (1998, December 5). *Technically simple and socially complex: Three school-based attempts to improve literacy achievement.* Paper presented at The National Reading Conference Annual Convention, Austin, TX.

Cooter, R. B., Jr., Joseph, D. G., & Flynt, E. S. (1987). Eliminating the literal pursuit in reading comprehension. *Journal of Clinical Reading, 2*(1), 9–11.

Cooter, R. B., Jr., Mills-House, E., Marrin, P., Mathews, B., & Campbell, S. (1999). Family and community involvement: The bedrock of reading success. *The Reading Teacher, 52*(8), 891–896.

Cooter, R. B., Mills-House, E., Marrin, P., Mathews, B. A., Campbell, S., & Baker, T. (1999). Family and community involvement: The bedrock of reading. *The Reading Teacher, 52*(8), 891–896.

Cooter, R. B., Jr., & Reutzel, D. R. (1987). Teaching reading skills for mastery. *Academic Therapy, 23*(2), 127–134.

Cooter, R. B., Jr., & Reutzel, D. R. (1990). *Yakity-yak: A reciprocal response procedure for improving reading comprehension.* Unpublished manuscript.

Cooter, R. B., Jr., Reutzel, D. R., & Cooter, K. S. (1998). *Sequence of development and instruction for phonemic awareness.* Unpublished paper.

Cornejo, R. (1972). *Spanish high frequency word list.* Austin, TX: Southwestern Educational Laboratory.

Corno, L., & Randi, J. (1997). Motivation, volition, and collaborative innovation in classroom literacy. In J. T. Guthrie & A. Wigfield (Eds.), *Reading engagement: Motivating readers through integrated instruction.* Newark, DE: International Reading Association.

Cousin, P. T., Weekly, T., & Gerard, J. (1993). The functional uses of language and literacy by students with severe language and learning problems. *Language Arts, 70*(7), 548–556.

Cowley, J. (1980). *Hairy bear.* San Diego: The Wright Group.

Cowley, J. (1982). *What a mess!* San Diego: The Wright Group.

Cox, C., & Zarillo, J. (1993). *Teaching reading with children's literature.* Upper Saddle River, NJ: Merrill/Prentice Hall.

Craft, H., & Krout, J. (1970). *The adventure of the American people.* Chicago: Rand McNally.

Crist, B. I. (1975). One capsule a week—A painless remedy for vocabulary ills. *Journal of Reading, 19*(2), 147–149.

Cronin, V., Farrell, D., & Delaney, M. (1999). Environmental print and word reading. *Journal of Research in Reading, 22*(3), 271–282.

CTB McGraw-Hill. (2000). *Fox in a box.* Monterey, CA: CTB McGraw-Hill.

Cudd, E. T., & Roberts, L. L. (1987). Using story frames to develop reading comprehension in a 1st grade classroom. *The Reading Teacher, 41*(1), 74–81.

Cudd, E. T., & Roberts, L. L. (1993). A scaffolding technique to develop sentence sense and vocabulary. *The Reading Teacher, 47*(4), 346–349.

Cunningham, A. E., & Stanovich, K. E. (1998). What reading does for the mind. *American Educator, 22,* 8–15.

Cunningham, P. (1980). Teaching were, with, what, and other "four-letter" words. *The Reading Teacher 34,* 160–163.

Cunningham, P. A., Hall, D. P., & Defee, M. (1998). Nonability-grouped, multi-level instruction: Eight years later. *The Reading Teacher, 51*(8), 652–664.

Cunningham, P. M. (1995). *Phonics they use: Words for reading and writing* (2nd ed.). New York: HarperCollins.

Cunningham, P. M. (2000). *Phonics they use: Words for reading and writing.* New York: Longman.

Cunningham, P. M., & Cunningham, J. (1992). Making words: Enhancing the invented spelling-decoding connection. *The Reading Teacher, 46*(2), 106–115.

Cunningham, P. M., Hall, D. P., & Sigmon, C. M. (2001). *The teacher's guide to the four-blocks: A multimethod, multilevel framework for grades 1–3.* Greensboro, NC: Carson Dellosa.

Dahl, R. (1961). *James and the giant peach: A children's story* (Nancy Ekholm Burkert, Illustrator). New York: Alfred A. Knopf.

Dahl, R. (1964). *Charlie and the chocolate factory.* New York: Alfred A. Knopf.

Dale, E. (1969). *Audiovisual methods in teaching* (3rd ed.). New York: Holt, Rinehart and Winston.

Dallin, L., & Dallin, L. (1980). *Heritage songster.* Dubuque, IA: Wm C Brown.

Dana, C. (1989). Strategy families for disabled readers. *Journal of Reading, 33*(1), 30–35.

Daniels, H. (2002). *Literature circles: Voice and choice in book clubs and reading groups* (2nd ed.). York, ME: Stenhouse.

Darling-Hammond, L. (1999). Educating teachers: The academy's greatest failure or its most important future? *Academe, 85*(1), 26–33.

Davis, D. (1990). *Listening for the crack of dawn.* Little Rock, AR: August House.

Day, K. C., & Day, H. D. (1979). Development of kindergarten children's understanding of concepts about print and oral language. In M. L. Damil & A. H. Moe (Eds.), *Twenty-eighth yearbook of the National Reading Conference* (pp. 19–22). Clemson, SC: National Reading Conference.

DeBruin-Parecki, A., & Krol-Sinclair, B. (2003). *Family literacy: From theory to practice.* Newark, DE: International Reading Association.

Dechant, E. V. (1970). *Improving the teaching of reading* (2nd ed.). Upper Saddle River, NJ: Prentice Hall.

DeFord, D., & Harste, J. C. (1982). Child language research and curriculum. *Language Arts, 59*(6), 590–601.

DeFord, D. E. (1985). Validating the construct of theoretical orientation in reading instruction. *Reading Research Quarterly, 20*(3), 351–367.

DeFord, D. E., Lyons, C. A., & Pinnell, G. S. (1991). *Bridges to literacy: Learning from Reading Recovery.* Portsmouth, NH: Heinemann.

DeGroff, L. (1990). Is there a place for computers in whole language classrooms? *The Reading Teacher, 43*(8), 568–572.

DeJong, M. (1953). *Hurry home, Candy.* New York: Harper.

Delacre, L. (1996). *Golden tales: Myths, legends and folktales from Latin America.* New York: Scholastic.

Delpit, L. D. (1988). The silenced dialogue: Power and pedagogy in educating other people's children. *Harvard Educational Review, 58*(3), 280–298.

Denson, K. (2001). *Final report. Reading and language arts grades K–6: 2000–01* (REIS01-147-2). Dallas: Dallas Independent School District, Division of Evaluation, Assessment, and Information Systems.

dePaola, T. (1978). *The popcorn book.* New York: Holiday House.

Department of Education. (1985). *Reading in junior classes. Wellington, New Zealand.* New York: Owen.

De Ridder, I. (2002). Visible or invisible links: Does the highlighting of hyperlinks affect incidental vocabulary learning, text comprehension, and the reading process? *Language Learning and Technology, 6*(1), 123–146.

D.E.S. (1975). *A language for life (The Bulloch Report).* London: Her Majesty's Stationery Office.

Developmental Learning Materials. (1985). *The writing adventure.* Allen, TX: Developmental Learning Materials.

Devillar, R. A., Faltis, C. J., & Cummins, J. P. (1994). *Cultural diversity in schools: From rhetoric to practice.* Albany State University of New York Press.

Dewey, J. (1913). *Interest and effort in education.* New York: Houghton Mifflin.

Dewey, J., & Bentley, A. F. (1949). *Knowing and the known.* Boston: Beacon Press.

Dewitz, P., & Carr, E. M. (1987). Teaching comprehension as a student directed process. In P. Dewitz (Chair), *Teaching reading comprehension, summarizing and writing in content area.* Symposium conducted at the National Reading Conference, Orlando, FL.

Dewitz, P., Stammer, J., & Jensen, J. (1980). *The development of linguistic awareness in young children from label reading to word recognition.* Paper presented at the annual meeting of the National Reading Conference, San Diego, CA.

Dickinson, D. K., & Tabors, P. O. (2001). *Beginning literacy with language.* Baltimore: Paul H. Brookes.

Dickson, S. V., Simmons, D. C., & Kameenui, E. J. (1998a). Text organization: Instructional and curricular basics and implications. In D. C. Simmons & E. J. Kameenui (Eds.), *What reading research tells us about children with diverse learning needs.* (pp. 279–302). Mahwah, NJ: Erlbaum.

Dickson, S. V., Simmons, D. C., & Kameenui, E. J. (1998b). Text organization: Research bases. In D. C. Simmons & E. J. Kameenui (Eds.), *What reading research tells us about children with diverse learning needs* (pp. 239–278). Mahwah, NJ: Erlbaum.

Dickson, S. V., Simmons, D. C., & Kameenui, E. J. (1998b). Text organization: Instructional and curricular basics and implications. In D. C. Simmons & E. J. Kameenui (Eds.), *What reading research tells us about children with diverse learning needs: Bases and basics.*

(pp. 279–294). Mahwah, NJ: L. Erlbaum.

Diffily, D. (1994, April). *Portfolio assessment in early literacy settings.* Paper presented at a professional development schools workshop at Texas Christian University, Fort Worth, TX.

Dillner, M. (1993–94). Using hypermedia to enhance content area instruction. *Journal of Reading, 37*(4), 260–270.

Dixon-Krauss, L. (1996). *Vygotsky in the classroom: Mediated literacy instruction and assessment.* New York: Longman.

Doctorow, M., Wittrock, M. C., & Marks, C. (1978). Generative processes in reading comprehension. *Journal of Educational Psychology, 70*(2), 109–118.

D'Odorico, L. (1984). Nonsegmental features in prelinguistic communications: An analysis of some types of infant cry and noncry vocalizations. *Journal of Child Language, 11,* 17–27.

Dole, J. A., Brown, K. J., & Trathen, W. (1996). The effects of strategy instruction on the comprehension performance of at-risk students. *Reading Research Quarterly, 31,* 62–88.

Dole, J. A., Osborn, J., & Lehr, F. (1990). *A guide to selecting basal reader programs.* Champaign, IL: Center for the Study of Reading.

Dole, J. A., Rogers, T., & Osborn, J. (1987). Improving the selection of basal reading programs: A report of the textbook adoption guidelines project. *Elementary School Journal, 87,* 282–298.

Donelson, K. L., & Nilsen, A. P. (1985). *Literature for today's young adults.* Boston: Scott, Foresman.

Dowd, C. A., & Sinatra, R. (1990). Computer programs and the learning of text structure. *Journal of Reading, 34*(2), 104–112.

Dowhower, S. (1987). Effects of repeated readings on second-grade transitional readers' fluency and comprehension. *Reading Research Quarterly, 22,* 389–406.

Dowhower, S. (1991). Speaking of prosody: Fluency's unattended bedfellow. *Theory Into Practice, 30*(3), 158–164.

Downing, J. (1977). How society creates reading disability. *Elementary School Journal, 77,* 274–279.

Downing, J. G. (1990). *A study of the relationship between literacy levels and instructional behaviors of incarcerated male felons.* Unpublished doctoral dissertation, Ball State University, Muncie, IN.

Downing, J., & Oliver, P. (1973). The child's concept of a word. *Reading Research Quarterly, 9,* 568–582.

Downing, J., & Thomson, D. (1977). Sex role stereotypes in learning to read. *Research in the Teaching of English, 11,* 149–155.

Downing, J. G. (1990). *A study of the relationship between literacy levels and institutional behaviors of incarcerated male felons.* Unpublished doctoral dissertation, Ball State University, Muncie, IN.

Doyle, C. (1988). Creative applications of computer assisted reading and writing instruction. *Journal of Reading, 32*(3), 236–239.

Dreher, M. J., & Gambrell, L. B. (1985). Teaching children to use a self-questioning strategy for studying expository prose. *Reading Improvement, 22,* 2–7.

Drew, D. (1989). *The life of the butterfly.* Crystal Lake, IL: Rigby.

Driscoll, M. P. (1994). *Psychology of learning for instruction.* Boston: Allyn & Bacon.

Drucker, P. F. (1998, August 24). The next information revolution. *Forbes ASAP,* 47–58.

Duffy, G. G., Roehler, L. R., & Putnam, J. (1987). Putting the teacher in control: Basal reading textbooks and instructional decision making. *Elementary School Journal, 87*(3), 357–366.

Duke, N. K. (2000a). For the rich it's richer: print experiences and environments offered to children in very low- and very high-socioeconomic status first-grade classrooms. *American Educational Research Journal, 37,* 441–478.

Duke, N. K. (2000b). 3.6 minutes per day: The scarcity of informational texts in first grade. *Reading Research Quarterly, 35*(2), 202–224.

Duke, N. K., Bennett-Armistead, S., & Roberts, E. M. (2002). Incorporating informational text in the primary grades 40–54. In C. M. Roller (Ed.), *Comprehensive reading instruction across the grade levels: A collection of papers from the 2001 reading research conference.* Newark, DE: International Reading Association.

Duke, N. K., & Purcell-Gates, V. (in press). Genres at home and at school: Bridging the new to the known. *The Reading Teacher.*

Dunn, L., & Dunn, L. M. (1997). *Peabody picture vocabulary test—third edition (PPVT-III).* Circle Pines, MN: American Guidance Service.

Dunn, L., Lugo, D. E., Padilla, E. R., & Dunn, L. M. (1986). *Test de Vocabulario en Imágenes Peabody (TVIP).* Circle Pines, MN: American Guidance Service.

Dunn, L. M., & Markwardt, F. C. (1970). *Peabody individual achievement test.* Circle Pines, MN: American Guidance Service.

Dunn, R. (1988). Teaching students through their perceptual strengths or preferences. *Journal of Reading, 31,* 304–309.

Dunn, S. (1987). *Butterscotch dreams.* Markham, Ontario, Canada: Pembroke.

Durkin, D. (1966). *Children who read early: Two longitudinal studies.* New York: Teachers College Press.

Durkin, D. (1974). A six year study of children who learned to read in

school at the age of four. *Reading Research Quarterly, 10,* 9–61.

Durkin, D. (1978). What classroom observations reveal about reading comprehension instruction. *Reading Research Quarterly, 14*(4), 482–533.

Durkin, D. (1981a). Reading comprehension in five basal reader series. *Reading Research Quarterly, 16*(4), 515–543.

Durkin, D. (1981b). What is the value of the new interest in reading comprehension? *Language Arts, 58,* 23–43.

Durkin, D. (1983). *Reading comprehension instruction: What the research says.* Presentation at the first Tarleton State University Reading Conference, Stephenville, TX.

Durkin, D. (1984). Is there a match between what elementary teachers do and what basal reader manuals recommend? *The Reading Teacher, 37,* 734–745.

Durkin, D. (1987). *Teaching young children to read* (4th ed.). New York: Allyn & Bacon.

Durkin, D. (1989). *Teaching them to read,* (5th ed.). New York: Allyn & Bacon.

Durrell, D. D. (1940). *Improvement of basic reading abilities.* New York: World Book.

Duthie, J. (1986). The web: A powerful tool for the teaching and evaluation of the expository essay. *The History and Social Science Teacher, 21,* 232–236.

Dyer, P. C. (1992). Reading Recovery: A cost-effectiveness and educational-outcomes analysis. *ERS Spectrum, 10,* 10–19.

Eastlund, J. (1980). Working with the language deficient child. *Music Educators Journal, 67*(3), 60–65.

Eckhoff, B. (1983). How reading affects children's writing. *Language Arts, 60*(5), 607–616.

Edelsky, C. (1988). Living in the author's world: Analyzing the author's craft. *The California Reader, 21,* 14–17.

Edelsky, C., Altwerger, B., & Flores, B. (1991). *Whole language: What's the difference?* Portsmouth, NH: Heinemann.

Eder, D. (1983). Ability grouping and student's academic self-concepts: A case study. *Elementary School Journal, 84,* 149–161.

Educational Testing Service. (1988). *Who reads best?* Princeton, NJ: Educational Testing Service.

Edwards, P. (1999). *A path to follow: Learning to listen to parents.* Portsmouth, NH: Heinemann.

Ehri, L. C. (1984). How orthography alters spoken language competencies in children. In J. Downing & R. Valtin (Eds.), *Language awareness and learning to read* (pp. 118–147). New York: Springer-Verlag.

Ehri, L. C., & Sweet, J. (1991). Fingerpoint-reading of memorized text: What enables beginners to process the print? *Reading Research Quarterly, 26,* 442–462.

Ehri, L. C., & Wilce, L. C. (1980). The influence of orthography on readers' conceptualization of the phonemic structure of words. *Applied Psycholinguistics, 1,* 371–385.

Ehri, L. C., & Wilce, L. C. (1985). Movement into reading: Is the first stage of printed word learning visual or phonetic? *Reading Research Quarterly, 20,* 163–179.

Ekwall, E. E., & Shanker, J. L. (1989). *Teaching reading in the elementary school,* (2nd ed.). Upper Saddle River, NJ: Merrill/Prentice Hall.

Elbow, P. (1994). Will the virtues of portfolios blind us to their potential dangers? In L. Black, D. Daiker, J. Sommers, & G. Stygall (Eds.), *New directions in portfolio assessment* (pp. 40–55). Portsmouth, NH: Boynton/Cook.

Eldredge, J. L. (1990). Increasing the performance of poor readers in the third grade with a group assisted strategy. *Journal of Educational Research, 84*(2), 69–77.

Eldredge, J. L., & Quinn, D. W. (1988). Increasing reading performance of low-achieving second graders with dyad reading groups. *Journal of Educational Research, 82,* 40–46.

Eldredge, J. L., Reutzel, D. R., & Hollingsworth, P. M. (1996). Comparing the effectiveness of two oral reading practices: Round-robin reading and the shared book experience. *Journal of Literacy Research, 28*(2), 201–225.

Ellis, A. K., & Fouts, J. T. (1993). *Research on educational innovations.* Princeton Junction, NJ: Eye on Education.

Ellison, C. (1989, January). PCs in the schools: An American tragedy. *PC/Computing,* 96–104.

Engelmann, S., & Bruner, E. C. (1995). *Reading mastery I: Presentation book C* (Rainbow Edition). Columbus, OH: Science Research Associates/Macmillan/McGraw-Hill.

Engelmann, S., & Bruner, E. C. (2002). *SRA reading mastery plus.* Columbus, OH: SRA-McGraw Hill.

Englert, C. S., & Tarrant, K. L. (1995). Creating collaborative cultures for educational change. *Remedial and Special Education, 16*(6), 325–336.

Ericson, L., & Juliebo, M. F. (1998). *The phonological awareness handbook for kindergarten and primary teachers.* Newark, DE: International Reading Association.

Ervin, J. (1982). *How to have a successful parents and reading program: A practical guide.* New York: Allyn & Bacon.

Esch, M. (1991, February 17). Whole language teaches reading. *The Daily Herald* (Provo, UT), p. D1.

Estes, T. H., & Vaughn, J. L. (1978). *Reading and learning in the content classroom.* Boston: Allyn & Bacon.

Fader, D. N. (1976). *The new hooked on books.* New York: Berkley.

Farr, R. (1991). *Portfolios: Assessment in the language arts.* (ERIC Document Reproduction Service No. ED334603). Urbana, IL.

Farr, R., & Tone, B. (1994). *Portfolio and performance assessment.* Fort Worth, TX: Harcourt Brace.

Farr, R., & Tulley, M. (1989). State level adoption of basal readers: Goals, processes, and recommendations. *Theory Into Practice, 28*(4), 248–253.

Farr, R., Tulley, M. A., & Powell, D. (1987). The evaluation and selection of basal readers. *Elementary School Journal, 87,* 267–281.

Farr, R., Tulley, M. A., & Pritchard, R. (1989). Assessment instruments and techniques used by the content area teacher. In D. Lapp, J. Flood, & N. Farnan (Eds.), *Content area reading and learning* (pp. 346–356). Englewood Cliffs, NJ: Prentice Hall.

Farrar, M. T. (1984). Asking better questions. *The Reading Teacher, 38,* 10–17.

Fawson, P. C., & Reutzel, D. R. (2000). But I only have a basal: Implementing guided reading in the early grades. *The Reading Teacher, 54*(1), 84–97.

Fay, L. (1965). Reading study skills: Math and science. In J. A. Figurel (Ed.), *Reading and inquiry.* Newark, DE: International Reading Association.

Felmlee, D., & Eder, D. (1983). Contextual effects in the classroom: The impact of ability groups on student attention. *Sociology of Education, 56,* 77–87.

Ferreiro, E., & Teberosky, A. (1982). *Literacy before schooling.* Portsmouth, NH: Heinemann.

Fielding, L., Kerr, N., & Rosier, P. (1998). *The 90% reading goal.* Kennewick, WA: National Reading Foundation.

Fields, M. V., & Spangler, K. L. (2000). *Let's begin reading right: A developmental approach to emergent literacy.* Upper Saddle River, NJ: Merrill.

Fillmore, C. J. (1968). The case for case. In E. Bach & R. T. Harms (Eds.), *Universals in Linguistic Theory,* (pp. 1–88). New York: Holt, Rinehart, and Winston.

Finchler, J. (2001). *Testing Miss Malarkey.* New York: Walker & Company.

Fisher-Nagel, H. (1987). *The life of a butterfly.* Minneapolis: Carolrhoda Books.

Fitzgerald, J. (1993). Literacy and students who are learning English as a second language. *The Reading Teacher, 46*(8), 638–647.

Fitzgerald, J. (1994). Crossing boundaries: What do second-language-learning theories say to reading and writing teachers of English-as-a-second-language learners? *Reading Horizons, 34*(4), 339–355.

Fitzgerald, J. (1995). English-as-a-second-language reading instruction in the United States: A research review. *Journal of Reading Behavior, 27*(2), 115–152.

Fitzgerald, J. (1999). What is this thing called "balance"? *The Reading Teacher, 53*(2), 100–115.

Fleischman, S. (1986). *The whipping boy.* Mahwah, NJ: Troll Associates.

Flesch, R. (1955). *Why Johnny can't read.* New York: HarperCollins.

Flesch, R. (1979, November 1). Why Johnny still can't read. *Family Circle, 26,* 43–46.

Flesch, R. (1981). *Why Johnny still can't read.* New York: HarperCollins.

Flippo, R. F. (2001). *Reading researchers in search of common ground.* Newark, DE: International Reading Association.

Flood, J., & Lapp, D. (1986). Types of texts: The match between what students read in basals and what they encounter in tests. *Reading Research Quarterly, 21,* 284–297.

Flynt, E. S., & Cooter, R. B. (1987). Literal comprehension: The cognitive caboose? *Kansas Journal of Reading, 3*(1), 8–12.

Flynt, E. S., & Cooter, R. B., Jr. (2001). *The Flynt/Cooter reading inventory for the classroom* (4th ed.). Upper Saddle River, NJ: Merrill/Prentice Hall.

Flynt, E. S., & Cooter, R. B, Jr. (1999). *The Flynt/Cooter English * Español reading inventory.* Upper Saddle River, NJ: Merrill/Prentice Hall.

Flynt, E. S., & Cooter, R. B., Jr. (2004). *The Flynt/Cooter reading inventory for the classroom,* (5th ed.). Upper Saddle River, NJ: Merrill/Prentice Hall.

Follett, R. (1985). The school textbook adoption process. *Book Research Quarterly, 1,* 19–23.

Foorman, B. R., et al. (1997). Early intervention for children with reading problems: Study designs and preliminary findings. *Learning Disabilities: A Multidisciplinary Journal, 8*(1), 63–71.

Foorman, B. R., Francis, D. J., Fletcher, J. M., Schatschneider, C., & Mehta, P. (1998). The role of instruction in learning to read: Preventing reading failure in at-risk children. *Journal of Educational Psychology, 90,* 37–55.

Forbes, E. (1943). *Johnny Tremain.* Boston: Houghton Mifflin.

Fosnot, C. T. (1996). *Constructivism: Theory, perspectives, and practice.* New York: Teachers College Press.

Fountas, I. C., & Pinnell, G. S. (1996). *Guided reading instruction: Good first teaching for all children.* Portsmouth, NH: Heinemann Educational Books.

Fountas, I. C., & Pinnell, G. S. (1999). *Matching books to readers: Using leveled books in reading, K–3.* Portsmouth, NH: Heinemann Educational Books.

Fountas, I. C., & Pinnell, G. S. (2001). *Guiding readers and writers: Grades 3–6. Teaching comprehension genre, and content literacy.* Portsmouth, NH: Heinemann.

Fowler, G. L. (1982). Developing comprehension skills in primary students through the use of story frames. *The Reading Teacher, 36*(2), 176–179.

Fox, B. J. (1996). *Strategies for word identification: Phonics from a new perspective.* Upper Saddle River, NJ: Merrill/ Prentice Hall.

Fox, B. J., & Hull, M. A. (2002). *Phonics for the teacher of reading* (8th ed.). Upper Saddle River, NJ: Prentice Hall.

Fox, P. (1973). *The slave dancer.* New York: Bradbury.

Fox, P. (1986). *The moonlight man.* New York: Bradbury.

Fractor, J. S., Woodruff, M. C., Martinez, M. G., & Teale, W. H. (1993). Let's not miss opportunities to promote voluntary reading: Classroom libraries in the elementary school. *The Reading Teacher, 46,* 476–484.

Fredericks, A. D., & Rasinski, T. V. (1990). Working with parents: Involving the uninvolved: How to. *The Reading Teacher, 43*(6), 424–425.

Freeman, D. E., & Freeman, Y. S. (1994). *Between worlds: Access to second language acquisition.* Portsmouth, NH: Heinemann.

Freeman, D. E., & Freeman, Y S. (2000). *Teaching reading in multilingual classrooms.* Portsmouth, NH: Heinemann.

Freeman, Y. S., & Freeman, D. E. (1992). *Whole language for second language learners.* Portsmouth, NH: Heinemann.

Freppon, P. A., & Dahl, K. L. (1998). Balanced instruction: Insights and considerations. *Reading Research Quarterly, 33*(2), 240–251.

Fry, E. (1977). Fry's readability graph: Clarifications, validity, and extension to level 17. *Journal of Reading, 21,* 242–252.

Fry, E. (1980). The new instant word list. *The Reading Teacher, 34,* 284–289.

Fry, E. B., Kress, J. E., & Fountoukidis, D. (2000). *The reading teacher's book of lists.* New York: Jossey-Bass.

Fry, E. B., Polk, J. K., & Fountoukidis, D. (1984). *The reading teacher's book of lists.* Upper Saddle River, NJ: Prentice Hall.

Gahn, S. M. (1989). A practical guide for teaching writing in the content areas. *Journal of Reading, 33,* 525–531.

Galindo, R., & Escamilla, K. (1995). A biographical perspective on Chicano educational success. *Urban Review, 27*(1), 1–25.

Galdone, Paul. *The little red hen* (L. McQueen, Illustrator). New York: Scholastic.

Gall, M. D., Ward, B. A., Berliner, D. C., Cahen, L. S., Crown, K. A., Elashoff, J. D., et al. (1975). *The effects of teacher use of questioning techniques on student achievement and attitude.* San Francisco: Far West Laboratory for Educational Research and Development.

Gallant, M. G. (1986). *More fun with Dick and Jane.* New York: Penguin Books.

Gallup, G. (1969). *The Gallup poll.* New York: American Institute of Public Opinion.

Gamberg, R., Kwak, W., Hutchings, M., & Altheim, J. (1988). *Learning and loving it: Theme studies in the classroom.* Portsmouth, NH: Heinemann.

Gambrell, L. B. (1985). Dialogue journals: Reading-writing instruction. *The Reading Teacher, 38*(6), 512–515.

Gambrell, L. B., & Almasi, J. F. (1996). *Lively discussions:*

Fostering engaged reading. Newark, DE: International Reading Association.

Gambrell, L. B., & Bales, R. J. (1986). Mental imagery and the comprehension-monitoring performance of fourth- and fifth-grade poor readers. *Reading Research Quarterly, 21*(4), 454–464.

Gambrell, L. B., & Marnak, B. A. (1997). Incentives and intrinsic motivation to read. In J. T. Guthrie & A. Wigfield (Eds.), *Reading engagement: Motivating readers through integrated instruction* (pp. 205–217). Newark, DE: International Reading Association.

Gambrell, L. B., Morrow, L. M., Neuman, S. B., & Pressley, M. (1999). *Best practices in literacy instruction.* New York: Guilford Press.

Gambrell, L. B., Pfeiffer, W., & Wilson, R. (1985). The effects of retelling upon reading comprehension and recall of text information. *Journal of Educational Research, 78,* 216–220.

Gambrell, L. B., Wilson, R. M., & Gnatt, W. N. (1981). Classroom observations of task-attending behaviors of good and poor readers. *Journal of Educational Research, 74,* 400–404.

Garcia, S. B., & Malkin, D. H. (1993). Toward defining programs and services for culturally and linguistically diverse learners in special education. *Teaching Exceptional Children,* Fall, 52–58.

Gardener, H. (1993). *Frames of mind: The theory of multiple intelligences.* New York: Basic Books.

Gardiner, J. R. (1980). *Stone fox.* New York: Scholastic.

Garza, C. L. (1990). *Cuadros de familia: Family pictures.* San Francisco: Children's Book Press.

Gates, A. I. (1921). An experimental and statistical study of reading and reading tests (in three parts). *Journal of Educational Psychology, 12,* 303–314, 378–391, 445–465.

Gates, A. I. (1937). The necessary mental age for beginning reading. *Elementary School Journal, 37,* 497–508.

Gates, A. I. (1961). Sex differences in reading ability. *Elementary School Journal, 61,* 431–434.

Gelman, R. G. (1976). *Why can't I fly?* New York: Scholastic.

Gelman, R. G. (1977). *More spaghetti, I say!* New York: Scholastic.

Gelman, R. G. (1985). *Cats and mice.* New York: Scholastic.

Gentry, R. (1987). *Spel . . . is a four-letter word.* Portsmouth, NH: Heinemann.

George, J. (1972). *Julie of the wolves.* New York: HarperCollins.

Gertson, R., Fuchs, L. S., Williams, J. P., & Baker, S. (2001). Teaching reading comprehension strategies to students with learning disabilities: A review of research. *Review of Educational Research, 71*(2), 279–320.

Gibson, E. J., & Levin, H. (1975). *The psychology of reading.* Cambridge, MA: MIT Press.

Gillet, J. W., & Temple, C. (1986). *Understanding reading problems: Assessment and instruction.* Boston: Little, Brown.

Gingerbread man, The. (1985). K. Schmidt, Illustrator. New York: Scholastic.

Giordano, G. (2001). *Twentieth-century reading education: Understanding practices of today in terms of patterns of the past.* New York: JAI Press.

Gipe, J. P. (1980). Use of a relevant context helps kids learn new word meanings. *The Reading Teacher, 33,* 398–402.

Gipe, J. P. (1987). *Corrective reading techniques for the classroom teacher.* Scottsdale, AZ: Gorsuch Scarisbrick.

Glatthorn, A. A. (1993). Outcome-based education: Reform and the curriculum process. *Journal of Curriculum and Supervision, 8*(4), 354–363.

Glazer, S. M. (1989). Oral language and literacy development. In D. S. Strickland & L. M. Morrow (Eds.), *Emerging literacy: Young children learn to read and write* (pp. 16–26). Newark, DE: International Reading Association.

Glazer, S. M., & Brown, C. S. (1993). *Portfolios and beyond: Collaborative assessment in reading and writing.* Norwood, MA: Christopher-Gordon.

Gleason, J. B. (1989). *The development of language* (2nd ed.). Upper Saddle River. NJ: Merrill/Prentice Hall.

Glowacki, D., Lanucha, C., & Pietrus, D. (2001). *Improving vocabulary acquisition through direct and indirect teaching.* Syracuse, NY: Educational Resources Information Center.

Goetz, E. T., Reynolds, R. E., Schallert, D. L., & Radin, D. I. (1983). Reading in perspective: What real cops and pretend burglars look for in a story. *Journal of Educational Psychology, 75*(4), 500–510.

Golden, J. M. (1992). The growth of story meaning. *Language Arts, 69*(1), 22–27.

Good, T. (1979). Teacher effectiveness in the elementary school. *Journal of Teacher Education, 30,* 52–64.

Goodman, K., Shannon, P., Freeman, Y., & Murphy, S. (1988). *Report card on basal readers.* Katona, NY: Owen.

Goodman, K., Smith, E. B., Meredith, R., & Goodman, Y. M. (1987). *Language and thinking in school: A whole-language curriculum.* Katona, NY: Owen.

Goodman, K. S. (1967). Reading: A psycholinguistic guessing game. *Journal of the Reading Specialist, 6,* 126–135.

Goodman, K. S. (1968). *Study of children's behavior while reading orally* (Final Report, Project No. S 425). Washington, DC: U.S. Department of Health, Education, and Welfare.

Goodman, K. S. (1976). Behind the eye: What happens in reading. In H. Singer & R. B. Ruddell (Eds.), *Theoretical models and processes of reading* (2nd ed., pp. 470–496). Newark, DE: International Reading Association.

Goodman, K. S. (1985). Unity in reading. In H. Singer & R. B. Ruddell (Eds.), *Theoretical models and processes of reading,* (3rd ed.). Newark, DE: International Reading Association.

Goodman, K. S. (1986). *What's whole in whole language?* Portsmouth, NH: Heinemann Educ. Book.

Goodman, K. S. (1987). Look what they've done to Judy Blume!: The "basalization" of children's literature. *The New Advocate, 1*(1), 29–41.

Goodman, K. S., & Goodman, Y. M. (1983). Reading and writing relationships: Pragmatic functions. *Language Arts, 60*(5), 590–599.

Goodman, Y. M. (1986). Children coming to know literacy. In W. H. Teale & E. Sulzby (Eds.), *Emergent literacy: Writing and reading* (pp. 1–14). Norwood, NJ: Ablex.

Goodman, Y. M., & Altwerger, B. (1981). *Print awareness in preschool children: A study of the development of literacy in preschool children.* Occasional paper, Program in Language and Literacy, University of Arizona Tucson.

Gordon, C. J., & Braun, C. (1983). Using story schema as an aid to reading and writing. *The Reading Teacher, 37*(2), 116–121.

Gordon, N. (Ed.). (1984). *Classroom experiences: The writing process in action.* Exeter, NH: Heinemann.

Goswami, U., & Bryant, P. (1990). *Phonological skills and learning to read.* East Sussex, UK: Erlbaum.

Goswami, U., & Mead, F. (1992). Onset and rime awareness and analogies in reading. *Reading Research Quarterly, 27*(2), 152–163.

Gough, P. B. (1972). One second of reading. In J. F. Kavanagh & I. G. Mattingly (Eds.), *Language by ear and by eye.* Cambridge, MA: MIT Press.

Gove, M. K. (1983). Clarifying teacher's beliefs about reading. *The Reading Teacher, 37*(3), 261–268.

Graesser, A., Golding, J. M., & Long, D. L. (1991). Narrative representation and compre-hension. In R. Barr, M. L. Kamil, P. Mosenthal, & P. D. Pearson (Eds.), *Handbook of reading research* (Vol. 2., pp. 171–205). New York: Longman.

Graves, D. H. (1983). *Writing: Teachers and children at work.* Portsmouth, NH: Heinemann.

Graves, M. F., & Slater, W. H. (1987). *Development of reading vocabularies in rural disadvan-taged students, intercity disad-vantaged students and middle class suburban students.* Paper presented at AERA conference, Washington, DC.

Greaney, V. (1994). World illiteracy. In F. Lehr & J. Osborn (Eds.), *Reading, language, and literacy: Instruction for the twenty-first century.* Hillsdale, NJ: Erlbaum.

Greene, F. P. (1970). *Paired reading.* Unpublished manuscript.

Greene, F. P. (1973). *OPIN.* Unpublished paper.

Greenwald, R., Hedges, L. V., & Laine, R. (1996). Interpreting research on school resources and student achievement: A rejoinder to Hanushek. *Review of*

Educational Research, 66, 411–416.

Griffith, P. L., & Olson, M. W. (1992). Phonemic awareness helps beginning readers break the code. *The Reading Teacher, 45,* 516–523.

Groff, P. J. (1984). Resolving the letter name controversy. *The Reading Teacher, 37*(4), 384–389.

Groom, W. (1986). *Forrest Gump.* New York: Pocket Books.

Gross, A. D. (1978). The relationship between sex differences and reading ability in an Israeli kibbutz system. In D. Feitelson (Ed.), *Cross-cultural perspectives on reading and reading research* (pp. 72–88). Newark, DE: International Reading Association.

Grossen, B. (1997). *30 years of research: What we know about how children learn to read.* Santa Cruz, CA: Center for the Future of Teaching and Learning.

Guilfoile, E. (1957). *Nobody listens to Andrew.* Cleveland: Modern Curriculum Press.

Gunderson, L. (1991). *ESL literacy instruction: A guidebook to theory and practice.* Upper Saddle River, NJ: Prentice Hall.

Guszak, F. J. (1967). Teacher questioning and reading. *The Reading Teacher, 21*(1), 227–234.

Guthrie, J. T. (1982). Effective teaching practices. *The Reading Teacher, 35*(7), 766–768.

Guthrie, J. T., & McCann, A. D. (1997). Characteristics of classrooms that promote motivations and strategies for learning. In J. T. Guthrie & A. Wigfield (Eds.), *Reading engagement: Motivating readers through integrated instruction.* Newark, DE: International Reading Association.

Guthrie, J. T., Seifert, M., Burnham, N. A., & Caplan, R. J. (1974). The maze technique to assess and monitor reading comprehension. *The Reading Teacher, 28*(2), 161–168.

Gwynne, F. (1970). *A chocolate moose for dinner.* New York: Windmill Books.

Gwynne, F. (1976). *The king who rained.* New York: Windmill Books.

Gwynne, F. (1999). *A chocolate moose for dinner.* New York: Aladdin Library.

Hagerty, P. (1992). *Reader's workshop: Real reading.* New York: Scholastic.

Haggard, M. R. (1986). The vocabulary self-collection strategy: Using student interest and world knowledge to enhance vocabulary growth. *Journal of Reading, 29*(7), 634–642.

Hagood, B. F. (1997). Reading and writing with help from story grammar. *Teaching Exceptional Children, 29*(4), 10–14.

Hall, M. A. (1978). *The language experience approach for teaching reading: A research perspective.* Newark, DE: International Reading Association.

Hall, M. A. (1981). *Teaching reading as a language experience* (3rd ed.). Upper Saddle River, NJ: Merrill/Prentice Hall.

Hall, N. (1987). *The emergence of literacy.* Portsmouth, NH: Heinemann.

Hall, R. (1984). *Sniglets.* Upper Saddle River, NJ: Merrill/Prentice Hall.

Haller, E. J., & Waterman, M. (1985). The criteria of reading group assignments. *The Reading Teacher, 38,* 772–781.

Halliday, M. A. K. (1975). *Learning how to mean: Explorations in the development of language.* London: Edward Arnold.

Hallinan, M. T., & Sorensen, A. B. (1985). Ability grouping and student friendships. *American Educational Research Journal, 22,* 485–499.

Hammill, D., & Larsen, S. C. (1974). The relationship of selected auditory perceptual skills and reading ability. *Journal of Learning Disabilities, 7,* 429–435.

Handel, R. D. (1999). The multiple meanings of family literacy. *Education of Urban Society, 32*(1), 127–144.

Hansen, J. (1981). The effects of inference training and practice on young children's reading comprehension. *Reading Research Quarterly, 16*(3), 391–417.

Hansen, J. (1987). *When writers read.* Portsmouth, NH: Heinemann.

Harkrader, M. A., & Moore, R. (1997). Literature preferences of fourth graders. *Reading Research and Instruction, 36*(4), 325–339.

Harp, B. (1988). When the principal asks: "Why are your kids singing during reading time?" *The Reading Teacher, 41*(4), 454–457.

Harp, B. (1989a). What do we do in the place of ability grouping? *The Reading Teacher, 42,* 534–535.

Harp, B. (1989b). When the principal asks: "Why don't you ask comprehension questions?" *The Reading Teacher, 42*(8), 638–639.

Harris, A. J., & Hodges, R. E. (Eds.). (1981). *A dictionary of reading and related terms.* Newark, DE: International Reading Association.

Harris, A. J., & Sipay, E. R. (1990). *How to increase reading ability* (9th ed.). New York: Longman.

Harris, T., Matteoni, L., Anderson, L., & Creekmore, M. (1975). *Keys to reading.* Oklahoma City: Economy.

Harris, T. L., & Hodges, R. E. (Eds.). (1995). *The literacy dictionary: The vocabulary of reading and writing.* Newark, DE: International Reading Association.

Harste, J. C., & Burke, C. L. (1977). A new hypothesis for reading teacher research: Both the teaching and learning of reading are theoretically based. In D. P. Pearson (Ed.),. *Reading: Theory, research, and practice* (pp. 32–40). Clemson, SC: National Reading Conference.

Harste, J. C., Short, K. G., & Burke, C. (1988). *Creating*

classrooms for authors: The reading writing connection. Portsmouth, NH: Heinemann.

Harste, J. C., Woodward, V. A., & Burke, C. L. (1984). Language stories and literacy lessons. Portsmouth, NH: Heinemann.

Harwayne, S. (1992). Lasting impressions. Portsmouth, NH: Heinemann.

Hasbrouck, J. E., & Tindal, G. (1992). Curriculum-based oral reading fluency for students in grades 2 through 5. Teaching Exceptional Children, 24(3), 41–44.

Hawking, S. W. (1988). A brief history of time: From the big bang to black holes. Toronto, Ontario, Canada: Bantam.

Heald-Taylor, G. (1989). The administrator's guide to whole language. Katona, NY: Owen.

Heald-Taylor, G. (1991). Whole language strategies for ESL students. San Diego: Dominie Press.

Heald-Taylor, G. (2001). The beginning reading handbook: Strategies for success. Portsmouth, NH: Heinemann.

Healy, J. M. (1990). Endangered minds: Why children don't think and what can be done about it. New York: Touchstone.

Heath. (no date). Quill [Computer program]. Lexington, MA: Heath.

Heathington, B. S. (1990). Test review: Concepts about print test. In R. B. Cooter, Jr. (Ed.), The teacher's guide to reading tests (pp. 110–114). Scottsdale, AZ: Gorsuch Scarisbrick.

Heckleman, R. G. (1966). Using the neurological impress remedial reading technique. Academic Therapy, 1, 235–239, 250.

Heckleman, R. G. (1969). A neurological impress method of remedial reading instruction. Academic Therapy, 4, 277–282.

Heide, F. P., & Gilliland, J. H. (1990). Day of Ahmed's secret. New York: Lothrop, Lee & Shepard Books.

Heilman, A. W., Blair, T. R., & Rupley, W. H. (2001). Principles and practices of teaching reading (10th ed.). Upper Saddle River, NJ: Merrill/Prentice Hall.

Henderson, J. (2001). Incidental vocabulary acquisition: Learning new vocabulary from reading silently and listening to stories read aloud. Syracuse, NY: Educational Resources Information Center.

Henk, W. A. (1983). Adapting the NIM to improve comprehension. Academic Therapy, 19, 97–101.

Henk, W. A., & Holmes, B. C. (1988). Effects of content-related attitude on the comprehension and retention of expository text. Reading Psychology, 9(3), 203–225.

Hennings, K. (1974). Drama reading, an on-going classroom activity at the elementary school level. Elementary English, 51, 48–51.

Henwood, C. (1988). Frogs (Barrie Watts, Photographer). London: NY: Franklin Watts.

Herber, H. L. (1978). Teaching reading in the content areas (2nd ed.). Upper Saddle River, NJ: Prentice Hall.

Heymsfeld, C. R. (1989, March). Filling the hole in whole language. Educational Leadership, 65–68.

Hiebert, E. (1978). Preschool children's understanding of written language. Child Development, 49, 1231–1241.

Hiebert, E. (1981). Developmental patterns and interrelationships of preschool children's print awareness. Reading Research Quarterly, 16, 236–260.

Hiebert E., & Ham, D. (1981). Young children and environmental print. Paper presented at the annual meeting of the National Reading Conference, Dallas, TX.

Hiebert, E. H. (1983). An examination of ability grouping for reading instruction. Reading Research Quarterly, 18, 231–255.

Hiebert, E. H. (1999). Text matters in learning to read. The Reading Teacher, 52(6), 552–566.

Hiebert, E. H., & Colt, J. (1989). Patterns of literature-based reading. The Reading Teacher, 43(1), 14–20.

Hiebert, E. H., & Martin, L. A. (2001). The texts of beginning reading instruction. In S. B. Neuman & D. K. Dickinson (Eds.), Handbook of early literacy. (pp. 361–376). New York: Guilford Press.

Hill, B., & Ruptic, C. (1994). Practical aspects of authentic assessment: Putting the pieces together. Norwood, MA: Christopher-Gordon.

Hill, S. (1990a). Raps and rhymes. Armadale, Victoria, Australia: Eleanor Curtain.

Hill, S. (1990b). Readers theatre: Performing the text. Armadale, Victoria, Australia: Eleanor Curtain.

Hirsch, E. D. (1987). Cultural literacy: What every American needs to know. Boston: Houghton Mifflin.

Hirschfelder, A. B., & Singer, B. R. (1992). Rising voices: Writing of young Native Americans. New York: Scribner's.

Hoffman, J. V. (1987). Rethinking the role of oral reading in basal instruction. Elementary School Journal, 87(3), 367–374.

Hoffman, J. V. (2001). WORDS (on words in leveled texts for beginning readers). Ann Arbor, MI: Center for the Improvement of Early Reading Achievement. Available at http://www.ciera.org/library/presos/2001/

Hoffman, J. V., McCarthey, S. J., Abbott, J., Christian, C., Corman, L., Curry, et al. (1994). So what's new in the new basals? A focus on first grade. Journal of Reading Behavior, 26(1), 47–73.

Hoffman, J. V., Roser, N., & Battle, J. (1993). Reading aloud in classrooms: From the modal to a "model." *The Reading Teacher, 46*(6), 496–503.

Hoffman, J. V., & Segel, K. W. (1982). *Oral reading instruction: A century of controversy.* (ERIC Document Reproduction Service) Urbana, IL.

Hoffman, M. (1991). *Amazing grace.* New York: Dial Books.

Holdaway, D. (1979). *The foundations of literacy.* Exeter, NH: Heinemann.

Holdaway, D. (1981). Shared book experience: Teaching reading using favorite books. *Theory Into Practice, 21,* 293–300.

Holdaway, D. (1984). *Stability and change in literacy learning.* Portsmouth, NH: Heinemann.

Hollingsworth, P. H. (1978). An experimental approach to the impress method of teaching reading. *The Reading Teacher, 31,* 624–626.

Hollingsworth, P. M., & Reutzel, D. R. (1988). Get a grip on comprehension. *Reading Horizons, 29*(1), 71–78.

Hollingsworth, P. M., & Reutzel, D. R. (1990). Prior knowledge, content-related attitude, reading comprehension: Testing Mathewson's affective model of reading. *Journal of Educational Research, 83*(4), 194–200.

Holmes, J. A. (1953). *The substrata-factor theory of reading.* Berkeley, CA: California Books.

Homan, S. P., Klesius, J. P., & Hite, C. (1993). Effects of repeated readings and non-repetitive strategies on students' fluency and comprehension. *Journal of Educational Research, 87*(2), 94–99.

Hook, P. E., and Jones, S. (2002). The importance of automaticity and fluency for efficient reading comprehension. *Perspectives, 28*(1), 9–14.

Hopkins, C. (1979). Using every-pupil response techniques in reading instruction. *The Reading Teacher, 33,* 173–175.

Hoskisson, K., & Tompkins, G. E. (1987). *Language arts: Content and teaching strategies.* Upper Saddle River, NJ: Merrill/Prentice Hall.

Houston, J. (1977). *Frozen fire.* New York: Atheneum.

Hoyt, L. (1999). *Revisit, reflect; retell: Strategies for improving reading comprehension.* Portsmouth, NH: Heinemann.

Huck, C. S., Helper, S., & Hickman, J. (1987). *Children's literature in the elementary school.* New York: Holt, Rinehart and Winston.

Huck, C. S., & Kuhn, D. Y. (1968). *Children's literature in the elementary school.* New York: Holt, Rinehart and Winston.

Hughes, T. O. (1975). *Sentence-combining: A means of increasing reading comprehension.* Kalamazoo: Western Michigan University, Department of English.

Hull, M. A. (1989). *Phonics for the teacher of reading.* Upper Saddle River, NJ: Merrill/Prentice Hall.

Hunt, L. C. (1970). Effect of self-selection, interest, and motivation upon independent, instructional, and frustrational levels. *Reading Teacher, 24,* 146–151.

Hunter, M. (1984). Knowing, teaching and supervising. In P. L. Hosford (Ed.), *Using what we know about teaching.* Alexandria, VA: Association for Supervision and Curriculum Development.

Hymes, D. (Ed.). (1964). *Language in culture and society.* New York: HarperCollins.

Invernizzi, M., Juel, C., & Rosemary, C. (1997). A community volunteer tutorial that works. *The Reading Teacher, 50*(4), 304–311.

Irwin, J. L. (1990). *Vocabulary knowledge: Guidelines for instruction. What research says to the teacher.* Washington, DC: National Education Association. (ERIC Document Reproduction Service No. ED319001)

Irwin, J. L. (2001). Assisting struggling readers in building vocabulary and background knowledge. *Voices from the Middle, 8*(4), 37–43.

Irwin, J. W. (1996). *Teaching reading comprehension processes* (2nd ed.). Englewood Cliffs, NJ: Prentice Hall.

Jachym, N. K., Allington, R. L., & Broikou, K. A. (1989). Estimating the cost of seatwork. *The Reading Teacher, 43,* 30–37.

Jacobs, H. H., & Borland, J. H. (1986). The interdisciplinary concept model: Theory and practice. *Gifted Child Quarterly, 30*(4), 159–163.

Jaffe, N. (1993). *The uninvited guest and other Jewish holiday tales.* New York: Scholastic.

Jenkins, R. (1990). *Whole language in Australia.* Scholastic Company workshop at Brigham Young University, Provo, UT.

Jobe, F. W. (1976). *Screening vision in schools.* Newark, DE: International Reading Association.

Johns, J. L. (1980). First graders' concepts about print. *Reading Research Quarterly, 15,* 529–549.

Johns, J. L. (1986). Students: Perceptions of reading: Thirty years of inquiry. In D. B. Yaden, Jr. & S. Templeton (Eds.), *Awareness and beginning literacy: Conceptualizing what it means to read and write* (pp. 31–40). Portsmouth, NH: Heinemann.

Johns, J. L., & Ellis, D. W. (1976). Reading: Children tell it like it is. *Reading World, 16,* 115–128.

Johns, J. L., & Johns, A. L. (1971). How do children in the elementary school view the reading process? *Michigan Reading Journal, 5,* 44–53.

Johns, J. L., & Lunn, M. K. (1983). The informal reading inventory: 1910–1980. *Reading World, 23*(1), 8–18.

Johnson, D. (1989). *Pressing problems in world literacy: The plight of the homeless.* Paper presented at the 23rd annual meeting of the Utah Council of the International Reading Association, Salt Lake City, UT.

Johnson, D., & Pearson, P. D. (1984). *Teaching reading vocabulary.* New York: Holt, Rinehart and Winston.

Johnson, D., & Steele, V. (1996). So many words, so little time: Helping college ESL learners acquire vocabulary strategies. *Journal of Adolescent and Adult Literacy, 39*(5), 348–357.

Johnson, D. D. (1973). Sex differences in reading across cultures. *Reading Research Quarterly, 9*(1), 67–86.

Johnson, D. D. (2001). *Vocabulary in the elementary and middle school.* Needham Heights, MA: Allyn & Bacon.

Johnson, D. D., & Baumann, J. F. (1984). Word identification. In P. D. Pearson (Ed.), *Handbook of reading research* (pp. 583–608). New York: Longman.

Johnson, D. D., & Pearson. P. D. (1975). Skills management systems: A critique. *The Reading Teacher, 28,* 757–764.

Johnson, D. D., & Pearson, P. D. (1984). *Teaching reading vocabulary.* New York: Holt, Rinehart and Winston.

Johnson, D. W. (1976). *Jack and the beanstalk* (D. William Johnson, Illustrator). Boston: Little, Brown.

Johnson, D. W., & Johnson, R. T. (1999). *Learning together and alone: Cooperative, competitive, and individualistic learning* (5th ed.). Boston: Allyn & Bacon.

Johnson, D. W., Maruyama, G., Johnson, R. T., Nelson, D., & Skon, L. (1981). Effects of cooperative, competitive and individualistic goal structures on achievement: A meta-analysis. *Psychological Bulletin, 89,* 47–62.

Johnson, T. D., & Louis, D. R. (1987). *Literacy through literature.* Portsmouth, NH: Heinemann.

Johnston, F. R. (1998). The reader, the text, and the task: Learning words in first grade. *The Reading Teacher, 51,* 666–676.

Jones, M. B., & Nessel, D. D. (1985). Enhancing the curriculum with experience stories. *The Reading Teacher, 39,* 18–23.

Jongsma, K. S. (1989). Questions and answers: Portfolio assessment. *The Reading Teacher, 43*(3), 264–265.

Jongsma, K. S. (1990). Questions and answers: Collaborative learning, *The Reading Teacher, 43*(4), 346–347.

Joseph, D. G., Flynt, E. S., & Cooter, R. B., Jr. (1987, March). *Diagnosis and correction of reading difficulties: A new model.* Paper presented at the National Association of School Psychologists annual convention, New Orleans, LA.

Juel, C. (1988). Learning to read and write: A longitudinal study of the fifty-four children from first through fourth grade. *Journal of Educational Psychology, 80*(4), 437–447.

Juel, C. (1991). Cross-age tutoring between student athletes and at-risk children. *Reading Teacher, 45*(3), 178–186.

Juel, C., Biancarosa, G., Coker, D., & Deffes, R. (2003). Walking with Rosie: A cautionary tale of early reading instruction. *Educational Leadership, 60*(7), 12 18.

Juster, N. (1961). *The phantom tollbooth.* New York: Random House.

Kagan, J. (1966). Reflection-impulsivity: The generality and dynamics of conceptual tempo. *Journal of Abnormal Psychology, 71,* 17–24.

Kang, H. W. (1994). Helping second language readers learn from content area text through collaboration and support. *The Journal of Reading, 37*(8), 646–652.

Karlsen, B., & Gardner, E. F. (1984). *Stanford diagnostic reading test* (3rd ed.). New York: Harcourt Brace.

Kaufman, A. S., & Kaufman, N. L. (1997). *Kaufman test of educational achievement— Normative update (K-TEA/NU).* Circle Pines, MN: AGS.

Kearsley, R. (1973). The newborn's response to auditory stimulation: A demonstration of orienting and defensive behavior. *Child Development, 44,* 582–590.

Keegan, M. (1991). *Pueblo boy: Growing up in two worlds.* New York: Cobblehill Books.

Keene, E. O., & Zimmerman, S. (1997). *Mosaic of thought.* Portsmouth, NH: Heinemann.

Keith, S. (1981). *Politics of textbook selection* (Research Report No. 81-AT). Stanford, CA: Stanford University School of Education, Institute for Research on School Finance and Governance.

Kemp, M. (1987). *Watching children read and write.* Portsmouth, NH: Heinemann.

Kessen, W., Levine, J., & Wendrich, K. (1979). The imitation of pitch in infants. *Infant Behavior and Development, 2,* 93–100.

Kiefer, Z., Levstik, L. S., & Pappas, C. C. (1998). *An integrated language perspective in the elementary school: An action approach* (3rd ed.). Boston: Addison-Wesley.

Killilea, M. (1954). *Karen.* New York: Dodd, Mead.

Kintsch, W. (1974). *The representation of meaning in memory.* Hillsdale, NJ: Erlbaum.

Kirsch, I. S., Jungeblut, A., Jenkins, L., & Kolstad, A. (1993). *Adult literacy in America: A first look at the results of the national adult literacy survey.* Washington, DC: National Center for Educational Statistics.

Kirshner, D., & Whitson, J. A. (1997). *Situated cognition: Social, semiotic, and psychological perspectives.* Mahwah, NJ: Erlbaum.

Klare, G. R. (1963). Assessing readability. *Reading Research Quarterly, 10,* 62–102.

Klenk, L., & Kibby, M. W. (2000). Remediating reading difficulties: Appraising the past, reconciling the present, constructing the future. In M. L. Kamil, P. B. Mosenthal, P. D., Pearson, & R. Barr (Eds.), *Handbook of reading research* (Vol. 3, pp. ___). Mahwah, NJ: Erlbaum.

Klobukowski, P. (2000). Parents, buddy journals, and teacher response. In T. V. Rasinski, N. D. Padak, et al. (Eds.), *Motivating recreational reading and promoting home-school connections* (pp. 51–52). Newark, DE: International Reading Association.

Knapp, M. S. (1991). *What is taught, and how, to the children of poverty: Interim report from a two-year investigation.* Menlo Park, CA: SRI.

Koskinen, P., Wilson, R., & Jensema, C. (1985). Closed-captioned television: A new tool for reading instruction. *Reading World, 24,* 1–7.

Koskinen, P. S., Blum, I. H., Bisson, S. A., Phillips, S. M., Creamer, T. S., & Baker, T. K. (1999). Shared reading, books, and audiotapes: Supporting diverse students in school and at home. *The Reading Teacher, 52*(5), 430–444.

Kownslar, A. O. (1977). *People and our world: A study of world history.* New York: Holt, Rinehart and Winston.

Kozol, J. (1985). *Illiterate America.* New York: New American Library.

Krashen, S. (1982). *Principles and practices in second language acquisition.* New York: Pergamon Press.

Krashen, S. (1992). *The power of reading.* Englewood, CO: Libraries Unlimited.

Krashen, S. (1993). *The power of reading: Insights from the research.* Englewood. CO: Libraries Unlimited.

Krashen, S., & Biber, D. (1988). *On course.* Sacramento, CA: CABE.

Krauss, R. (1945). *The carrot seed* (Crockett Johnson, Illustrator). New York: Scholastic.

Krulik, N. E. (1991). *My picture book of the planets.* New York: Scholastic.

Kuby, P., & Aldridge, J. (1997). Direct vs. indirect environmental print instruction and early reading ability in kindergarten children. *Reading Psychology 15*(1), 1–9.

Kuby, P., Aldridge, J., & Snyder, S. (1994). Developmental progression of environmental print recognition in kindergarten children. *Reading Psychology 18*(2), 91–104.

Kuby, P., Kirkland, L., & Aldridge, J. (1996). Learning about environmental print through picture books. *Early Childhood Education Journal, 24*(1), 33–36.

Kuchinskas, G., & Radencich, M. C. (1986). *The semantic mapper.* Gainesville, FL: Teacher Support Software.

Kuhn, M., & Stahl, S. (2000). *Fluency: A review of developmental and remedial reading practices* (CIERA Report No. 2-008. Ann Arbor: University of Michigan, Center for Improvement of Early Reading Achievement.

Kulik, C. C., & Kulik, J. A. (1982). Effects of ability grouping on secondary students: A meta-analysis of evaluation findings. *American Educational Research Journal, 19,* 415–428.

Labbo, L. D. (2001). Supporting children's comprehension of informational text through interactive read alouds. *Literacy and Nonfiction Series, 1*(2), 1–4.

LaBerge, D., & Samuels, S. J. (1974). Toward a theory of automatic information processing in reading. *Cognitive Psychology, 6,* 293–323.

LaBerge, D., & Samuels, S. J. (1985). Toward a theory of automatic information processing in reading. In H. Singer & R. B. Ruddell (Eds.), *Theoretical models and processes of reading* (pp. 689–718). Newark, DE: International Reading Association.

Lamme, L. L., & Hysmith, C. (1991). One school's adventure into portfolio assessment. *Language Arts, 68,* 629–640.

Lamoreaux, L., & Lee, D. M. (1943). *Learning to read through experience.* New York: Appleton-Century-Crofts.

Langer, J. (1981). From theory to practice: A prereading plan. *Journal of Reading, 25,* 152–156.

Langer, J. A. (1982). Facilitating text processing: The elaboration of prior knowledge. In J. A. Langer & M. Smith-Burke (Eds.), *Reader meets author: Bridging the gap* (pp. 149–162). Newark, DE: International Reading Association.

Langer, J. A. (1984). Examining background knowledge and text comprehension. *Reading Research Quarterly, 19,* 468–481.

Langer, J. A. (1985). Levels of questioning: An alternative view. *Reading Research Quarterly, 20*(5), 586–602.

Langer, P., Kalk, J. M., & Searls, D. T. (1984). Age of admission and trends in achievement: A comparison of blacks and Caucasians. *American Educational Research Journal, 21,* 61–78.

Larsen, N. (1994). *The publisher's chopping block: What happens to children's trade books when they are published in a basal reading series?* Unpublished master's projects, Brigham Young University, Provo, UT.

Lass, B., & Davis, B. (1985). *The remedial reading handbook.* Upper Saddle River, NJ: Prentice Hall.

Lathlaen, P. (1993). A meeting of minds: Teaching using biographies. *The Reading Teacher, 46*(6), 529–531.

Law, B., & Eckes, M. (1990). *The more than just surviving handbook: ESL for every classroom teacher.* Winnipeg, Manitoba, Canada: Peguis.

Leinhardt, G., Zigmond, N., & Cooley, W. (1981). Reading instruction and its effects. *American Educational Research Journal, 18,* 343–361.

Lemann, N. (1997, November). The reading wars. *The Atlantic Monthly, 280*(5), 128–134.

L'Engle, M. (1962). *A wrinkle in time.* New York: Dell.

Lenneberg, E. H. (1964). *New directions in the study of language.* Cambridge, MA: MIT Press.

Leslie, L., Caldwell, J. (2000). *Qualitative reading inventory—3* (3ʳᵈ ed.). Upper Saddle River, NJ: Pearson Allyn & Bacon. Levin, J.R., Johnson, D. D., Pittelman, S. D., Levin, K., Shriberg, L. K., Toms-Bronowski, S., et al. (1984). A comparison of semantic- and mnemonic-based vocabulary-learning strategies. *Reading Psychology, 5,* 1–15.

Levin, J. R., Levin, M. E., Glasman, L. D., & Nordwall, M. B. (1992). Mnemonic vocabulary instruction: Additional effectiveness evidence. *Contemporary Educational Psychology, 17,* 156–174.

Levine, S. S. (1976). *The effect of transformational sentence-combining exercises on the reading comprehension and written composition of third-grade children.* Unpublished doctoral dissertation, Hofstra University, New York.

Lewis, C. S. (1961). *The lion, the witch, and the wardrobe.* New York: Macmillan.

Liberman, I. Y., Shankweiler, D., Fischer, F. W., & Carter, B. (1974). Explicit syllable and phoneme segmentation in the young child. *Journal of Experimental Child Psychology, 18,* 201–212.

Liberman, I. Y., Shankweiler, D., Liberman, A., Fowler, C., & Fischer, F. (1977). Phonetic segmentation and decoding in the beginning reader. In A. S. Reber & D. L. Scarborough (Eds.), *Toward a psychology of reading* (pp. 207–225). Hillsdale, NJ: Erlbaum.

Lima, C., & Lima, J. (1993). *A to zoo: A subject access to children's picture books.* New York: Bowker.

Lindsay, P. H., & Norman, D. A. (1977). *Human information processing: An introduction to psychology.* New York: Academic Press.

Lipson, M. Y. (1983). The influence of religious affiliation on children's memory for text information. *Reading Research Quarterly, 18*(4), 448–457.

Lipson, M. Y. (1984). Some unexpected issues in prior knowledge and comprehension. *The Reading Teacher, 37*(8), 760–764.

Lisle, J. T. (1989). *Afternoon of the elves.* New York: Franklin Watts.

Littlejohn, C. (1988). *The lion and the mouse.* New York: Dial Books for Young Readers.

Livingston, N., & Birrell, J. R. (1994). Learning about cultural diversity through literature. *BYU Children's Book Review, 54*(5), 1–6.

Lobel, A. (1981). *On Market Street* (Pictures by Anita Lobel). New York: Scholastic.

Lobel, A. (1983). *Fables.* New York: Harper & Row.

Lock, S. (1980). *Hubert hunts his hum* (J. Newnham, Illustrator). Sydney, Australia: Ashton Scholastic.

Lomax, R. G., & McGee, L. M. (1987). Young children's concepts about print and reading: Toward a model of word reading acquisition. *Reading Research Quarterly, 22*(2), 237–256.

Loranger, A. L. (1997). Comprehension strategies instruction: Does it make a difference? *Reading Psychology, 18*(1), 31–68.

Loughlin, C. E., & Martin, M. D. (1987). *Supporting literacy: Developing effective learning environments.* New York: Columbia Teachers College Press.

Lowery, L. F., & Grafft, W. (1967). Paperback books and reading attitudes. *The Reading Teacher, 21*(7), 618–623.

Luria, A. R., & Yudovich, F. I. (1971). *Speech and the development of mental processes in the child.* London: Staples Press.

Lyman, F. (1988). Think-Pair-Share, Wait time two, and on . . . *Mid-Atlantic Association for Cooperation in Education Cooperative News, 2,* 1.

Lyon, G. R. (1997). Statement of G. Reid Lyon to the Committee on Education and the Workforce, U.S. House of Representatives (July 19, 1997). Washington, DC.

Lyon, G. R. (1998). Why reading is not a natural process. *Educational Leadership, 55*(6), 14–18.

Lyon, R. (1977). Auditory-perceptual training: The state of the art. *Journal of Learning Disabilities, 10,* 564–572.

Lyons, C. A., & Beaver, J. (1995). Reducing retention and learning disability placement through reading recovery: An educationally sound, cost-effective choice. In R. L. Allington & S. A. Walmsley (Eds.), *No quick fix: Rethinking literacy programs in America's elementary schools.* New York: Teachers College Press.

MacGinitie, W. H. (1969). Evaluating readiness for learning to read: A critical review and evaluation of research. *Reading Research Quarterly, 4,* 396–410.

MacGinitie, W. H., & MacGinitie, R. K. (1989). *Gates-MacGinitie reading tests* (3rd ed.). Chicago: Riverside.

Macmillan/McGraw-Hill. (1993). *Macmillan/McGraw-Hill*

reading/language: A new view. New York: Author.

Manarino-Leggett, P., & Salomon, P. A. (1989, April–May). *Cooperation vs. competition: Techniques for keeping your classroom alive but not endangered.* Paper presented at the 34th annual convention of the International Reading Association, New Orleans, LA.

Mandler, J. M., & Johnson, N. S. (1977). Remembrance of things parsed: Story structure and recall. *Cognitive Psychology, 9,* 111–151.

Manzo, A. V. (1969). The request procedure. *Journal of Reading, 13,* 123–126.

Manzo, A. V., & Manzo, U. C. (1990). *Content area reading: A heuristic approach.* Upper Saddle River, NJ: Merrill/Prentice Hall.

Manzo, A. V., Manzo, U. C., & Estes, T. (2000). *Content area literacy: Interactive teaching for active learning* (3rd ed.). San Francisco: Wiley.

Marchionini, G. (1988). Hypermedia and learning: Freedom and chaos. *Educational Technology, 28,* 8–12.

Martin, B. (1983). *Brown bear, brown bear, what do you see?* New York: Henry Holt.

Martin, B. (1990). *Brown bear, brown bear, what do you see?* New York: Henry Holt.

Martin, B. (1991). *Polar bear, polar bear, what do you hear?* New York: Henry Holt.

Martin, B., & Archaumbalt, J. (1987). *Knots on a counting rope.* New York: Holt, Rinehart and Winston.

Martin, J. H. (1987). *Writing to read* [Computer program]. Boca Raton, FL: IBM.

Martinez, M. (1993). Motivating dramatic story reenactments. *The Reading Teacher, 46*(8), 682–688.

Martinez, M., & Nash, M. F. (1990). Bookalogues: Talking about children's literature. *Language Arts, 67,* 576–580.

Martorella, P. H. (1985). *Elementary social studies.* Boston: Little, Brown.

Martorella, P. H. (2000). *Teaching social studies in middle and secondary schools.* Upper Saddle River, NJ: Prentice Hall.

Marzano, R. J. (1993–94). When two world views collide. *Educational Leadership, 51*(4), 6–11.

Marzollo, J., & Marzollo, C. (1982). *Jed's junior space patrol: A science fiction easy to read.* New York: Dial.

Mason, J. (1983). An examination of reading instruction in third and fourth grades. *The Reading Teacher, 36*(9), 906–913.

Mason, J. M. (1980). When do children begin to read: An exploration of four-year-old children's letter and word reading competencies. *Reading Research Quarterly, 15,* 203–227.

Masonheimer, P. E., Drum, P. A., & Ehri, L. C. (1984). Does environmental print identification lead children into word reading? *Journal of Reading Behavior, 16,* 257–271.

Math, I. (1981). *Wires and watts: Understanding and using electricity.* New York: Scribner's.

Mathes, P. G. (1997). Cooperative story mapping. *Remedial and Special Education, 18*(1), 20–27.

Mathes, P. G., Simmons, D. C., & Davis, B. I. (1992). Assisted reading techniques for developing reading fluency. *Reading Research and Instruction, 31*(4), 70–77.

Mathewson, G. C. (1985). Toward a comprehensive model of affect in the reading process. In H. Singer & R. B. Ruddell (Eds.), *Theoretical models and processes of reading* (3rd ed., pp. 841–856). Newark, DE: International Reading Association.

Mathewson, G. C. (1994). Model of attitude influence upon reading and learning to read. In H. Singer & R. B. Ruddell (Eds.), *Theoretical models and processes of reading* 4th Ed. (pp. 1131–1161). Newark, DE: International Reading Association.

Maxim, G. (1989). *The very young: Guiding children from infancy through the early years* (3rd ed.). Upper Saddle River, NJ: Merrill/Prentice Hall.

May, F. B., & Elliot, S. B. (1978). *To help children read: Mastery performance modules for teachers in training* (2nd ed.). Upper Saddle River, NJ: Merrill/Prentice Hall.

May, F. B., & Rizzardi, L. (2002). *Reading as communication* (6th ed.). Upper Saddle River, NJ: Merrill/Prentice Hall.

Mayer, M. (1976a). *Ah-choo.* New York: Dial Books.

Mayer, M. (1976b). *Hiccup.* New York: Dial Books.

McCallum, R. D. (1988). Don't throw the basals out with the bath water. *The Reading Teacher, 42,* 204–209.

McCarrier, A., Pinnell, G. S., & Fountas, I. C. (1999). *Interactive writing: How language and literacy come together, K–2.* Portsmouth, NH: Heinemann.

McCarthey, S. J., Hoffman, J. V., Christian, C., Corman, L., Elliott, B., Matherne, D., et al. (1994). Engaging the new basal readers. *Reading Research and Instruction, 33*(3), 233–256.

McCormick, C. E., & Mason, J. (1986). Intervention procedures for increasing preschool children's interest in and knowledge about reading. In W. H. Teale & E. Sulzby (Eds.), *Emergent literacy: Writing and reading* (pp. 90–115). Norwood, NJ: Ablex Publishing.

McCormick, S. (1995). *Instructing students who have literacy problems.* Upper Saddle River, NJ: Merrill/Prentice Hall.

McCracken, R. A., & McCracken, M. J. (1978).

Modeling is the key to sustained reading. *The Reading Teacher, 31,* 406–408.

McDermott, G. (1993). *Raven: Trickster tale from the Pacific Northwest.* San Diego: Harcourt Brace.

McGee, L. M., Lomax, R. G., & Head, M. H. (1988). Young children's written language knowledge: What environmental and functional print reading reveals. *Journal of Reading Behavior, 20*(2), 99–118.

McGee, L. M., Ratliff, J. L., Sinex, A., Head, M., & LaCroix, K. (1984). Influence of story schema and concept of story on children's story compositions. In J. A. Niles & L. A. Harris (Eds.), *Thirty-third yearbook of the National Reading Conference* (pp. 270–277). Rochester, NY: National Reading Conference.

McGee, L. M., & Richgels, D. J. (2000). *Literacy's beginnings: Supporting young readers and writers* (3rd ed.). Needham Heights, MA: Allyn & Bacon.

McGuire, F. N. (1984). How arts instruction affects reading and language: Theory and research. *The Reading Teacher, 37*(9), 835–839.

McInnes, J. (1983). *Networks.* Toronto, Ontario, Canada: Nelson of Canada.

McKee, D. (1990). *Elmer.* London: Red Fox.

McKeown, M. G., & Beck, I. L. (1988). Learning vocabulary: Different ways for different goals. *Remedial and Special Education, 9*(1), 42–52.

McKeown, M. G., Beck, I. L., & Worthy, M. J. (1993). Grappling with text ideas: Questioning the author. *The Reading Teacher, 46*(7), 560–565.

McKissack, P. C. (1986). *Flossie and the fox.* New York: Dial Books for Young Readers.

McKuen, R. (1990). Ten books on CD ROM. *MacWorld, 7*(12), 217–218.

McMahon, S. I., & Raphael, T. E. (1997). *The book club connection: Literacy learning and classroom talk.* New York: Teachers College Press.

McNeil, J. D. (1987). *Reading comprehension* (2nd ed.). Glenview, IL: Scott, Foresman.

McTighe, J., & Lyman, F. T. (1988). Cueing thinking in the classroom: The promise of theory-embedded tools. *Educational Leadership, 45*(7), 18–24.

Meade, E. L. (1973). The first R-A point of view. *Reading World, 12,* 169–180.

MECC. (1984). *Writing a narrative* [Computer program]. St. Paul, MN: Minnesota Educational Computing Consortium.

Medina, M., & Escamilla, K. (1994). Language acquisition and gender for limited-language-proficient Mexican Americans in a maintenance bilingual program. *Hispanic Journal of Behavioral Sciences, 16*(4), 422–437.

Menke, D. J., & Pressley, M. (1994). Elaborative interrogation: Using "why" questions to enhance learning from text. *Journal of Reading, 37*(8), 642–645.

Menyuk, P. (1988). *Language development knowledge and use.* Glenview, IL: Scott, Foresman/Little, Brown.

Merrill Mathematics (Grade 5). (1985). Upper Saddle River, NJ: Merrill/Prentice Hall.

Merrill Science (Grade 3). (1989). Upper Saddle River, NJ: Merrill/Prentice Hall.

Meyer, B., Brandt, D., & Bluth, G. (1980). Use of top-level structure in text for reading comprehension of ninth-grade students. *Reading Research Quarterly, 16,* 72–103.

Meyer, B. J. (1979). Organizational patterns in prose and their use in reading. In M. L. Kamil & A. J. Moe (Eds.), *Reading research: Studies and applications* (pp. 109–117).

Twenty-Eighth Yearbook of the National Reading Conference.

Meyer, B. J. F., & Freedle, R. O. (1984). Effects of discourse type on recall. *American Educational Research Journal, 21*(1), 121–143.

Mezynski, K. (1983). Issues concerning the acquisition of knowledge: Effects of vocabulary training on reading comprehension. *Review of Educational Research, 53*(2), 253–279.

Michaels, J. R. (2001). *Dancing with words: Helping students love language through authentic vocabulary instruction.* Urbana, IL: National Council of Teachers of English.

Miller, B. F., Rosenberg, E. B., & Stackowski, B. L. (1971). *Investigating your health.* Boston: Houghton Mifflin.

Mindplay. (1990). *Author! Author!* Danvers, MA: Methods and Solutions.

Moe, A. J., & Irwin, J. W. (1986). Cohesion, coherence, and comprehension. In J. W. Irwin (Ed.), *Understanding and teaching cohesion comprehension* (pp. 3–8). Newark, DE: International Reading Association.

Moffett, J. (1983). *Teaching the universe of discourse.* Boston: Houghton Mifflin.

Moffett, J., & Wagner, B. J. (1976). *Student-centered language arts and reading K–12. A handbook for teachers* (2nd ed.). Boston: Houghton Mifflin.

Monjo, F. N. (1970). *The drinking gourd.* New York: HarperCollins.

Mooney, M. E. (1990). *Reading to, with, and by children.* Katonah, NY: Owen.

Moore, M. A. (1991). Electronic dialoguing: An avenue to literacy. *The Reading Teacher, 45*(4), 280–286.

Morphett, M. V., & Washburne, C. (1931). When should children begin to read? *Elementary School Journal, 31,* 496–503.

Morris, D., Shaw, B., & Perney, J. (1990). Helping low readers in grades 2 and 3: An after-school volunteer tutoring program. *Elementary School Journal, 91,* 133–150.

Morrow, L. M. (1984). Reading stories to young children: Effects of story structure and traditional questioning strategies on comprehension. *Journal of Reading Behavior, 16,* 273–288.

Morrow, L. M. (1985). Retelling stories: A strategy for improving children's comprehension, concept of story structure and oral language complexity. *Elementary School Journal, 85,* 647–661.

Morrow, L. M. (1988a). Retelling as a diagnostic tool. In S. M. Glazer, L. W. Searfoss, & L. Gentile (Eds.), *Re-examining reading diagnosis: New trends and procedures in classrooms and clinics* (pp. 128–149). Newark, DE: International Reading Association.

Morrow, L. M. (1988b). Young children's responses to one-to-one story reading in school settings. *The Reading Teacher, 23*(1), 89–107.

Morrow, L. M. (1990). Preparing the classroom environment to promote literacy during play. *Early Childhood Education Research Quarterly, 5,* 537–554.

Morrow, L. M. (1993). *Literacy development in the early years: Helping children read and write* (2nd ed.). Boston: Allyn & Bacon.

Morrow, L. M. (1995). *Family literacy: Connections in schools and communities.* Newark, DE: International Reading Association.

Morrow, L. M. (2001). *Literacy development in the early years: Helping children read and write* (4th ed.). Needham Heights, MA: Allyn & Bacon.

Morrow, L. M. (2002). *The literacy center: Contexts for reading and writing* (2nd ed.). Portland, ME: Stenhouse.

Morrow, L. M., & Rand, M. K. (1991). Promoting literacy during play by designing early childhood classroom environments. *The Reading Teacher, 44*(6), 396–402.

Morrow, L. M., Tracey, D. H., Woo, D. G., & Pressley, M. (1999). Characteristics of exemplary first-grade literacy instruction. *The Reading Teacher, 52*(5), 462–476.

Mosenthal, P. B. (1989a). From random events to predictive reading models. *The Reading Teacher, 42*(7), 524–525.

Mosenthal, P. B. (1989b). The whole language approach: Teachers between a rock and a hard place. *The Reading Teacher, 42*(8), 628–629.

Mosenthal, J., Lipson, M., Mekkelsen, J., Russ, B., & Sortino, S. (2001). *Elementary schools where students succeed in reading.* Providence, RI: LAB at Brown.

Moss, B., & Newton, E. (2001). An examination of the information text genre in basal readers. *Reading Psychology, 23*(1), 1–13.

Moustafa, M. (1997). *Beyond traditional phonics: Research discoveries and reading instruction.* Portsmouth, NH: Heinemann.

Moustafa, M., & Maldonado-Colon, E. (1999). Whole-to-parts phonics instruction: Building on what children know to help them know more. *The Reading Teacher, 52*(5), 448–458.

Mullis, I. V. S., Campbell, J. R., & Farstrup, A. E. (Eds.). (1993). *NAEP 1992 reading report card for the nation and the states* (Report No. 23-ST06). Washington, DC: National Center for Education Statistics, U.S. Department of Education.

Munsch, R. (1980). *The paper bag princess.* Toronto, Ontario, Canada: Annick Press.

Muth, K. D. (1989). *Children's comprehension of text: Research into practice.* Newark, DE: International Reading Association.

Myers, W. D. (1975). *Fast Sam, Cool Clyde, and stuff.* New York: Puffin Books.

Nagy, W. (1988). *Teaching vocabulary to improve reading comprehension.* Unpublished manuscript.

Nagy, W. E., & Anderson, R. C. (1984). How many words are there in printed school English? *Reading Research Quarterly, 19*(3), 304–330.

Nagy, W. E., Anderson, R., & Herman, P. (1987). Learning word meanings from context during normal reading. *American Educational Research Journal, 24,* 237–270.

Nagy, W. E., Herman, P. A., & Anderson, R. C. (1985). Learning words from context. *Reading Research Quarterly, 20,* 233–253.

Naiden, N. (1976). Ratio of boys to girls among disabled readers. *The Reading Teacher, 29*(6), 439–442.

Namioka, L. (1992). *Yang the youngest and his terrible ear.* Boston: Little, Brown.

Nash, B., & Nash, G. (1980). *Pundles.* New York: Stone Song Press.

Naslund, J. C., & Samuel, J. S. (1992). Automatic access to word sounds and meaning in decoding written text. *Reading and Writing Quarterly, 8*(2), 135–156.

National Assessment of Educational Progress. (1990). *Learning to read in our nation's schools: Instruction and achievement in 1988 at grades 4, 8, and 12.* Princeton, NJ: Author.

National Assessment of Educational Progress. (1996). *Results from the NAEP 1994 reading assessment—at a glance.* Washington, DC: National Center for Educational Statistics.

National Assessment of Educational Progress. (2000). Washington,

DC: U. S. Department of Education.

National Association for the Education of Young Children. (1986). Position statement on developmentally appropriate practice in programs for 4- and 5-year-olds. *Young Children, 41*(6), 20–29.

National Center for Education Statistics. (1999). *NAEP 1998 reading report card: National and state highlights.* Washington, DC: National Center for Education Statistics.

National Commission on Teaching and America's Future. (1996). *What matters most: Teachers for America's future.* Woodbridge, VA: Author.

National Education Association. (2000). *Report of the National Education Association's Task Force on Reading 2000.* Washington, DC: Author.

National Institute of Child Health and Human Development. (2000). *Why children succeed or fail at reading: Research from NICHD's program in learning disabilities.* Retrieved from *http://www.nichd.nih.gov/ publications/pubs/readbro.htm*

National Institute of Child Health and Human Development. (2000). *Report of the National Reading Panel: Teaching Children to read.* Retrieved from http://www. nationalreadingpanel.org.

National Institute of Child Health and Human Development. (2000b). *Why children succeed or fail at reading.* Retrieved from http://www.nichd.gov/ publications/pubs/readbro.htm

National Reading Panel. (2000). *Report of the National Reading Panel: Teaching children to read* (NIH Publication No. 00-4769). Washington, DC: National Institute of Child Health and Human Development.

National Research Council. (1998). Preventing reading difficulties in young children. Washington, DC: U.S. Department of Education. Retrieved from *http://www.nap. edu/readingroom/enter2. cgi?030906418X.html*

Nelson, T. (1988, January). Managing immense storage. *Byte,* 225–238.

Neuman, S., & Koskinen, P. (1992). Captioned television as comprehensible input: Effects of incidental word learning from context for language minority students. *Reading Research Quarterly, 27*(3), 94–106.

Neuman, S., & Roskos, K. (1992). Literacy objects as cultural tools: Effects on children's literacy behaviors in play. *Reading Research Quarterly, 27*(3), 203–225.

Neuman, S. B. (1981). Effect of teaching auditory perceptual skill on reading achievement in first grade. *The Reading Teacher, 34,* 422–426.

Neuman, S. B. (1999). Books make a difference: A study of access to literacy. *Reading Research Quarterly, 34*(3), 2–31.

Neuman, S. B. (2001). The role of knowledge in early literacy. *Reading Research Quarterly, 36*(4), 468–475.

Neuman, S. B., & Celano, D. (2001). Access to print in low-income and middle-income communities: An ecological study of four neighborhoods. *Reading Research Quarterly, 36*(1), 8–27.

Neuman, S. B., & Roskos, K. (1990). Play, print, and purpose: Enriching play environments for literacy development. *The Reading Teacher, 44*(3), 214–221.

Neuman, S. B., & Roskos, K. (1993). *Language and literacy learning in the early years: An integrated approach.* New York: Harcourt Brace.

Neuman, S. B., & Roskos, K. (1997). Literacy knowledge in practice: Contexts of participation for young writers and readers. *Reading Research Quarterly, 32*(1), 10–33.

Newman, J. M. (1985a). Yes, that's an interesting idea, but. . . . In J. M. Newman (Ed.), *Whole language: Theory in use* (pp. 181–186). Portsmouth, NH: Heinemann.

Newman, J. M. (Ed.). (1985b). *Whole language: Theory in use.* Portsmouth, NH: Heinemann.

Newman, M. L. (1996). *The association of academic achievement, types of offenses, family, and other characteristics of males who have been adjudicated as juvenile delinquents.* Unpublished master's thesis, California State University, Long Beach, CA.

Nichols, J. (1980). Using paragraph frames to help remedial high school students with written assignments. *Journal of Reading, 24,* 228–231.

Nilsen, A. P., & Nilsen, D. L. F. (2002). Lessons in the teaching of vocabulary from September 11 and Harry Potter. *Journal of Adolescent and Adult Literacy, 46*(3), 254–260.

Nist, S. L., & Simpson, M. L. (1993). *Developing vocabulary concepts for college thinking.* Lexington, MA: Heath.

Nolan, E. A., & Berry, M. (1993). Learning to listen. *The Reading Teacher, 46*(7), 606–608.

Nordquist, V. M., & Twardosz, S. (1990). Preventing behavior problems in early childhood special education classrooms through environmental organization. *Education and Treatment of Children, 13*(4), 274–287.

Norton, D. E. (1998). *Through the eyes of a child: An introduction to children's literature* (5th ed.). Upper Saddle River, NJ: Merrill/Prentice Hall.

Norton, D. E., & Norton, S. (2003). *Through the eyes of a child: An introduction to children's literature* (6th ed.). Upper Saddle River, NJ: Merrill/Prentice Hall.

Novick, R. (2002). Learning to read the heart: Nurturing emotional literacy. *Young Children, 57*(3), 84–89.

Numeroff, L. J. (1985). *If you give a mouse a cookie.* New York: Scholastic.

Nurss, J. R., Hough, R. A., & Goodson, M. S. (1981). Prereading/language development in two day care centers. *Journal of Reading Behavior, 13,* 23–31.

Oakes, J. (1992). Can tracking research inform practice? *Educational Researcher, 21*(4), 12–21.

O'Bruba, W. S. (1987). Reading through the creative arts. *Reading Horizons, 27*(3), 170–177.

Ogle, D. M. (1986). K-W-L: A teaching model that develops active reading of expository text. *The Reading Teacher, 39*(6), 564–570.

Ohanian, S. (1984). Hot new item or same old stew? *Classroom Computer Learning, 5,* 30–31.

O'Huigin, S. (1988). *Scary poems for rotten kids.* New York: Firefly Books.

Olson, M. W., & Gee, T. C. (1988). Understanding narratives: A review of story grammar research. *Childhood Education, 64*(4), 302–306.

Olson, M. W., & Longnion, B. (1982). Pattern guides: A workable alternative for content teachers. *Journal of Reading, 25,* 736–741.

Opitz, M. F. (1992). The cooperative reading activity: An alternative to ability grouping. *The Reading Teacher, 45*(9), 736–738.

Opitz, M. F. (1998). *Flexible grouping in reading: Practical ways to help all students become better readers.* New York: Scholastic.

Opitz, M. F., & Ford, M. P. (2001). *Reaching readers: Flexible and innovative strategies for guided reading.* Portsmouth, NH: Heinemann.

Opitz, M. F., & Rasinski, T. V. (1998). *Good-bye round robin: 25 effective oral reading strategies.* Portsmouth, NH: Heinemann.

Orellana, M. F., & Hernandez, A. (1999). Talking the walk: Children reading urban environmental print. *The Reading Teacher, 52*(6), 612–619.

Osborn, J. (1984). The purposes, uses, and contents of workbooks and some guidelines for publishers. In R. C. Anderson, J. Osborn, & R. J. Tierney (Eds.), *Learning to read in American schools* (pp. 45–112). Hillsdale, NJ: Erlbaum.

Osborn, J. (1985). Workbooks: Counting, matching, and judging. In J. Osborn, P. T. Wilson, & R. C. Anderson (Eds.), *Reading education: Foundations for a literate America* (pp. 11–28). Lexington, MA: Lexington Books.

Otto, J. (1982). The new debate in reading. *The Reading Teacher, 36*(1), 14–18.

Palincsar, A. S., & Brown, A. L. (1984). Reciprocal teaching of comprehension-fostering and monitoring activities. *Cognition and Instruction, 1,* 117–175.

Palincsar, A. S., & Brown, A. L. (1985). Reciprocal teaching: A means to a meaningful end. In J. Osborn, P. T. Wilson, & R. C. Anderson (Eds.), *Reading education: Foundations for a Literate America* (pp. 299–310). Lexington, MA: Heath.

Pankake, M., & Pankake, J. (1988). *A Prairie Home Companion folk song book.* New York: Viking.

Pappas, C. C., Kiefer, B. Z., & Levstik, L. S. (1990). *An integrated language perspective in the elementary school.* New York: Longman.

Paradis, E., & Peterson, J. (1975). Readiness training implications from research. *The Reading Teacher, 28*(5), 445–448.

Paradis, E. E. (1974). The appropriateness of visual discrimination exercises in reading readiness materials. *Journal of Educational Research, 67,* 276–278.

Paradis, E. E. (1984). *Comprehension: Thematic units* [videotape]. Laramie: University of Wyoming.

Paris, S. G., Lipson, M. Y., & Wixson, K. K. (1983). Issues concerning the acquisition of knowledge: Effects of vocabulary training on reading comprehension. *Review of Educational Research, 53,* 293–316.

Parish, P. (1963). *Amelia Bedelia.* New York: HarperCollins.

Park, L. S. (2001). *A single shard.* New York: Clarion.

Parker, A., & Paradis, E. (1986). Attitude development toward reading in grades one through six. *Journal of Educational Research, 79*(5), 313–315.

Parkes, B. (1986a). *The enormous watermelon.* Crystal Lake, IL: Rigby.

Parkes, B. (1986b). *Who's in the shed?* Crystal Lake, IL: Rigby.

Parsons, L. (1990). *Response journals.* Portsmouth, NH: Heinemann.

Partnership for Reading (2001). *Put reading first: The research building blocks for teaching children to read.* Washington. DC: Author. Report available online at *www.nifl.gov/partnershipforreading*

Paterson, K. (1977). *Bridge to Terabithia.* New York: Thomas Y. Crowell.

Paulsen, G. (1987). *Hatchet.* New York: Simon & Schuster.

Payne, C. D., & Schulman, M. B. (1998). *Getting the most out of morning message and other shared writing lessons.* New York: Scholastic.

Payne, R. (1998). *A framework for understanding poverty.* Highlands, TX: RFT.

Pearson, P. D. (1974). The effects of grammatical complexity on children's comprehension, recall, and conception of certain semantic relations. *Reading Research Quarterly, 10*(2), 155–192.

Pearson, P. D. (1985). Changing the face of reading comprehension instruction. *The Reading Teacher, 38*(8), 724–738.

Pearson, P. D. (1989a). *Improving national reading assessment: The key to improved reading instruction.* Paper presented at the 1989 annual reading conference of the Utah Council of the International Reading Association, Salt Lake City, UT.

Pearson, P. D. (1989b). Reading the whole language movement. *Elementary School Journal, 90*(2), 231–242.

Pearson, P. D. (2000). *What sorts of programs and practices are supported by research? A reading from the radical middle.* Ann Arbor, MI: Center for the Improvement of Early Reading Instruction.

Pearson, P. D., & Duke, N. (2002). Comprehension instruction in the primary grades. In C. Collins-Block & M. Pressley (Eds.), *Comprehension instruction: Research-based best practices* (pp. 247–258). New York: Guildford Press.

Pearson, P. D., & Fielding, L. (1982). Listening comprehension. *Language Arts, 59*(6), 617–629.

Pearson, P. D., & Gallagher, M. C. (1983). The instruction of reading comprehension. *Contemporary Educational Psychology, 8*(3), 317–344.

Pearson, P. D., Hansen, J., & Gordon, C. (1979). The effect of background knowledge on children's comprehension of implicit and explicit information. *Journal of Reading Behavior, 11*(3), 201–209.

Pearson, P. D., & Johnson, D. D. (1978). *Teaching reading comprehension.* New York: Holt, Rinehart and Winston.

Peregoy, S. F., & Boyle, O. F. (2001). *Reading, writing, and learning in ESL.* New York: Longman.

Perez, S. A. (1983). Teaching writing from the inside: Teachers as writers. *Language Arts, 60*(7), 847–850.

Perfetti, C. A., & Lesgold, A. M. (1977). Discourse comprehension and sources of individual differences. In M. A. Just & P. A. Carpenter (Eds.), *Cognitive processes in comprehension* (pp. 141–184). Hillsdale, NJ: Erlbaum.

Perkins, J. H. (2001). Listen to their teachers' voices: Effective reading instruction for fourth grade African American students. *Reading Horizons, 41*(4), 239–255.

Perspectives on basal readers (Special issue). (1989). *Theory Into Practice, 28*(4).

Peterson, B. (1991). Selecting books for beginning readers. In D. E. DeFord, C. A. Lyons, & G. S. Pinnell (Eds.), *Bridges to literacy: Learning from reading recovery* (pp. 119–147). Portsmouth, NH: Heinemann.

Peterson, R., & Eeds, M. (1990). *Grand conversations: Literature groups in action.* New York: Scholastic.

Pfeffer, S. B. (1989). *Future forward.* New York: Holt.

Piaget, J. (1955). *The language and thought of the child.* New York: World.

Pikulski, J. J. (1985). Questions and answers. *The Reading Teacher, 39*(1), 127–128.

Pikulski, J. J., & Templeton, S. (1997). *The role of phonemic awareness in learning to read.* Boston: Houghton Mifflin.

Pinkney, A. D. (1993). *Alvin Ailey.* New York: Hyperion Books for Children.

Pinnell, G. S., Deford, D. E., & Lyons, C. A. (1994). Comparing instructional models for the literacy education of high-risk first

graders. *Reading Research Quarterly, 29*(1), 8–39.

Pinnell, G. S., & Fountas, I. C. (1997a). *A handbook for volunteers: Help America read.* Portsmouth, NH: Heinemann.

Pinnell, G. S., & Fountas, I. C. (1997b). *Help America read: Coordinator's guide.* Portsmouth, NH: Heinemann.

Pinnell, G. S., & Fountas, I. C. (1998). *Word matters.* Portsmouth, NH: Heinemann.

Pinnell, G. S., & Fountas, I. C. (2002). *Leveled books for readers grades 3–6: A companion volume to guiding readers and writers.* Portsmouth, NH: Heineman.

Pinnell, G. S., Fried, M. D., & Estice, R. M. (1990). Reading recovery: Learning how to make a difference. *The Reading Teacher, 43,* 282–295.

Pinnell, G. S., Lyons, C. A., DeFord, D. E., Bryk, A. S., & Seltzer, M. (1994). Comparing instructional models for the literacy education of high-risk first graders. *Reading Research Quarterly, 29*(1), 8–39.

Pino, E. (1978). *Schools are out of proportion to man.* Seminar on discipline, Utah State University, Logan, UT.

Pintrich, P. R., & DeGroot, E. V. (1990). Motivational and self-regulated learning components of classroom academic performance. *Journal of Educational Psychology, 82,* 33–40.

Piper, T. (1993). *Language for all our children.* New York: Merrill/Macmillan.

Plecki, M. (2000). Economic perspectives on investments in teacher quality. *Education Policy Analysis Archives, 8*(33). Retrieved from http://epaa.asu.edu/epaa/v8n33.html

Point/counterpoint. The value of basal readers. (1989, August–September). *Reading Today, 7,* 18.

Polacco, P. (2002). *When lightning comes in a jar*. New York: Philomel.

Pollack, P. (1982). *Keeping it secret*. New York: Putnam.

Potter, B. (1903). *The tale of Peter Rabbit*. New York: F. Warne.

Powell, D. A. (1986). *Retrospective case studies of individual and group decision making in district-level elementary reading textbook selection*. Unpublished doctoral dissertation, Indiana University, Bloomington, IN.

Pray, R. T. (1983). *A comparison of good and poor readers in an adult, incarcerated population*. Unpublished doctoral dissertation, Harvard University, Cambridge, MA.

Prelutsky, J. (1976). *Nightmares: Poems to trouble your sleep*. New York: Greenwillow Books.

Prelutsky, J. (1984). *A new kid on the block*. New York: Greenwillow Books.

Prelutsky, J. (1990). *Something big has been here*. New York: Greenwillow Books.

Prelutsky, J. (1991). *Poems for laughing out loud*. New York: Alfred A. Knopf.

Prelutsky, J. (1996). *A pizza the size of the sun*. New York: Greenwillow Books.

Pressley, M. (2000). What should comprehension instruction be the instruction of? In M. L. Kamil, P. B. Mosenthal, P. D. Pearson, & R. Barr (Eds.), *Handbook of Reading Research* (Vol. 3, pp. 545–562). Mahwah, NJ: Erlbaum.

Pressley, M. (2002a). Comprehension strategies instruction: A turn-of-the-century status report. In C. Collins-Block, & M. Pressley (Eds.) *Improving comprehension instruction: Advances in research, theory, and classroom practice* (pp. 11–27). New York: Guilford Press.

Pressley, M. (2002b). *Reading instruction that works: The case for balanced teaching* (2nd ed.). New York: Guilford Press.

Pressley, M., Allington, R. L., Wharton-McDonald, R., Collins-Block, C., and Morrow, L. M. (2001). *Learning to read: Lessons from exemplary first-grade classrooms*. New York: Guilford Press.

Prince, A. T., & Mancus, D. S. (1987). Enriching comprehension: A schema altered basal reading lesson. *Reading Research and Instruction, 27,* 45–53.

Proudfoot, G. (1992). Pssst! There is literacy at the laundromat. *English Quarterly, 24*(1), 10–11.

Provensen, A., & Provensen, M. (1983). *The glorious flight: Across the channel with Louis Bleriot*. New York: Viking Penguin.

Puckett, M. B., & Black, J. K. (1994). *Authentic assessment of the young child*. Upper Saddle River, NJ: Merrill/Prentice Hall.

Pulver, C. J. (1986). Teaching students to understand explicit and implicit connectives. In J. W. Irwin (Ed.), *Understanding and teaching cohesion comprehension* (pp. 3–8). Newark, DE: International Reading Association.

Radencich, M., Beers, P., & Schumm, J. S. (1995). *Handbook for the K–12 reading specialist*. Boston: Allyn & Bacon.

Ramirez, G., & Ramirez, J. L. (1994). *Multiethnic literature*. Albany, NY: Delmar.

RAND Reading Study Group. (2001). *Reading for understanding: Towards an R & D program in reading comprehension*. Washington, DC: Author/OERI/ U. S. Department of Education.

Raphael, T. E. (1982). Question-answering strategies for children. *The Reading Teacher, 36,* 186–191.

Raphael, T. E. (1986). Teaching question-answer relationships, revisited. *The Reading Teacher, 39*(6), 516–523.

Raphael, T. E., Pardo, L., Highfield, K., & McMahon, S. I. (1997). *Book club: A literature-based curriculum*. Littleton, MA: Small Planet Communications.

Raphael, T. E., & Pearson, P. D. (1982). *The effect of metacognitive awareness training on children's question answering behavior* (Technical Report. No. 238). Urbana-Champaign: University of Illinois at Urbana-Champaign, Center for the Study of Reading.

Rasinski, T. (1989). Fluency for everyone: Incorporating fluency instruction in the classroom. *The Reading Teacher, 42*(9), 690–693.

Rasinski, T. (1990b). Investigating measure of reading fluency. *Educational Research Quarterly, 14*(3), 37–44.

Rasinski, T. (1998, September). *Reading to learn: Vocabulary development strategies*. Paper presented at the Fall Session of the Dallas Reading Plan Grades 4–6 Professional Development Series, Dallas, TX.

Rasinski, T. (2000). Speed does matter. *The Reading Teacher, 54*(2), 146–151.

Rasinski, T., & Opitz, M. F. (1998). *Good-bye round robin: 25 effective oral reading strategies*. Portsmouth, NH: Heinemann.

Rasinski, T., & Padak, N. D. (1990). Multicultural learning through children's literature. *Language Arts, 69,* 14–20.

Rasinski, T., & Padak, N. (2004). *Effective reading strategies: Teaching children who find reading difficult*. Upper Saddle River, NJ: Merrill/Prentice Hall.

Rasinski, T. V. (1984). *Developing models of reading fluency*. (ERIC Document Reproduction Service No. ED269721) Urbana, IL.

Rasinski, T. V. (1990). Effects of repeated reading and listening-while-reading on reading fluency. *Journal of Educational Research, 83*(2), 147–150.

Rasinski, T. V. (1995). *Parents and teachers: Helping children learn* to read and write. New York: Harcourt Brace.

Rasinski, T. V. & Fredericks, A. D. (1988). Sharing literacy: Guiding principles and practices for parent involvement. *The Reading Teacher, 41,* 508–512.

Rasinski, T. V., & Fredericks, A. D. (1989). Working with parents: What do parents think about reading in the schools? *The Reading Teacher, 43*(3), 262–263.

Rasinski, T. V., and Padak, N. (1996). Five lessons to increase reading fluency. In L. R. Putnam (Ed.), *How to become a better reading teacher: Strategies for assessment and intervention.* Columbus, OH: Merrill/Prentice Hall.

Raven, J. (1992). A model of competence, motivation, and behavior, and a paradigm for assessment. In H. Berlak (Ed.), *Toward a new science of educational testing and assessment.* Albany: State University of New York Press.

Ravitch, D., & Finn, C. E., Jr. (1987). *What do our 17-year-olds know?* New York: HarperCollins.

Rawls, W. (1961). *Where the red fern grows.* New York: Doubleday.

Raygor, A. L. (1977). The Raygor readability estimate: A quick and easy way to determine difficulty. In P. D. Pearson (Ed.), *Reading: Theory, research and practice* (pp. 259–263). Clemson, SC: National Reading Conference.

Rayner, K., Foorman, B. R., Perfetti, C. A., Pesetsky, D., & Seidenberg, M. S. (2001). How psychological science informs the teaching of reading. *Psychological Science in the Public Interest 2*(2), 31–74.

Rayner, K., Foorman, B. R., Perfetti, C. A., Pesetsky, D., & Seidenberg, M. S. (2002, March). How should reading be taught? *Scientific American,* 85–91.

Read, C. (1971). Preschool children's knowledge of English phonology. *Harvard Educational Review, 41,* 1–34.

Read, S. J., & Rosson, M. B. (1982). Rewriting history: The biasing effects of attitudes on memory. *Social Cognition, 1,* 240–255.

Readence, J. E., Bean, T. W., & Baldwin, R. S. (1992). *Content area reading: An integrated approach (4*th *ed.).* Dubuque, IA: Kendall/Hunt.

Reid, J. F. (1966). Learning to think about reading. *Educational Research Quarterly, 9,* 56–62.

Reimer, B. L. (1983). Recipes for language experience stories. *The Reading Teacher, 36*(4), 396–401.

Reinking, D. (Ed.). (1987). *Computers and reading: Issues for theory and practice.* New York: Teachers College Press.

Reinking, D., & Rickman, S. S. (1990). The effects of computer-mediated texts on the vocabulary learning and comprehension of intermediate-grade readers. *Journal of Reading Behavior, 22*(4), 395–409.

Reutzel, D. R. (1985a). Reconciling schema theory and the basal reading lesson. *The Reading Teacher, 39,* 194–197.

Reutzel, D. R. (1985b). Story maps improve comprehension. *The Reading Teacher, 38*(4), 400–405.

Reutzel, D. R. (1991). Understanding and using basal readers effectively. In Bernard L. Hayes (Ed.), *Reading instruction and the effective teacher* (pp. 254–280). New York: Allyn & Bacon.

Reutzel, D. R. (1992). Breaking the letter a week tradition: Conveying the alphabetic principle to young children. *Childhood Education, 69*(1), 20–23.

Reutzel, D. R. (1995). Fingerpoint-reading and beyond: Learning about print strategies (LAPS). *Reading Horizons, 35*(4), 310–328.

Reutzel, D. R. (1996a). A balanced reading approach. In J. Baltas & S. Shafer (Eds.), *Scholastic guide to balanced reading: Grade 3–6* (pp. 7–11). New York: Scholastic.

Reutzel, D. R. (1996b). A balanced reading approach. In J. Baltas & S. Shafer (Eds.), *Scholastic guide to balanced reading: K-2.* New York: Scholastic.

Reutzel, D. R. (1999a). On balanced reading. *The Reading Teacher, 52*(4), 2–4.

Reutzel, D. R. (1999b). Organizing literacy instruction: Effective grouping strategies and organizational plans. In L. M Morrow, L. B. Gambrell, S. Neuman, & M. Pressley (Eds.), *Best practices for literacy instruction.* New York: Guilford Press.

Reutzel, D. R., Camperell, K., & Smith, J. A. (2002). Helping struggling readers make sense of reading. In C. Collins-Block, L. B. Gambrell, & M. Pressley (Eds.), *Improving comprehension instruction: Advances in research, theory, and classroom practice.* San Francisco: Jossey-Bass.

Reutzel, D. R., & Cooter, R. B., Jr. (1990). Whole language: Comparative effects on first-grade reading achievement. *Journal of Educational Research, 83,* 252–257.

Reutzel, D. R., & Cooter, R. B., Jr. (1991). Organizing for effective instruction: The reading workshop. *The Reading Teacher, 44*(8), 548–555.

Reutzel, D. R., & Cooter, R. B., Jr. (1999). *Balanced reading strategies and practices: Assessing and assisting readers with special needs.* Upper Saddle River, NJ: Merrill/Prentice Hall.

Reutzel, D. R., & Cooter, R. B. (2003b). *Strategies for reading assessment and instruction: Helping every child succeed* (2nd ed.). Upper Saddle River, NJ: Merrill/Prentice Hall.

Reutzel, D. R., & Cooter, R. B. (2003a). *Strategies for assessment and intervention.*

Upper Saddle River, NJ: Merrill/Prentice Hall.

Reutzel, D. R., & Cooter, R. B., Jr. (2004*). Teaching children to read: Putting the pieces together* (4th ed.). Upper Saddle River, NJ: Merrill/Prentice Hall.

Reutzel, D. R., & Daines, D. (1987a). The instructional cohesion of reading lessons in seven basal reading series. *Reading Psychology, 8,* 33–44.

Reutzel, D. R., & Daines, D. (1987b). The text-relatedness of seven basal reading series. *Reading Research and Instruction, 27,* 26–35.

Reutzel, D. R., & Fawson, P. C. (1989). Using a literature webbing strategy lesson with predictable books. *The Reading Teacher, 43*(3), 208–215.

Reutzel, D. R., & Fawson, P. C. (1990). Traveling tales: Connecting parents and children in writing. *The Reading Teacher, 44,* 222–227.

Reutzel, D. R., & Fawson, P. C. (1991). Literature webbing predictable books: A prediction strategy that helps below-average, first-grade readers. *Reading Research and Instruction, 30*(4), 20–30.

Reutzel, D. R., & Fawson, P. C. (1998). Global literacy connections: Stepping into the future. *Think, 8*(2), 32–34.

Reutzel, D. R., & Fawson, P. C. (2002). *Your classroom library— giving it more teaching power: Research-based strategies for developing better readers and writers.* New York: Scholastic Professional Books.

Reutzel, D. R., Fawson, P. C., Young, J. R., Morrison, T. G., & Wilcox, B. (2004). Reading environmental print: What is the role of concepts about print in discriminating young readers' responses. *Reading Psychology, 24*(2), 123–162.

Reutzel, D. R., & Gali, K. (1998). The art of children's book

selection: A labyrinth unexplored. *Reading Psychology, 19*(1), 3–50.

Reutzel, D. R., & Hollingsworth, P. M. (1988a). Highlighting key vocabulary: A generative-reciprocal procedure for teaching selected inference types. *Reading Research Quarterly, 23*(3), 358–378.

Reutzel, D. R., & Hollingsworth, P. M. (1988b). Whole language and the practitioner. *Academic Therapy, 23*(4), 405–416.

Reutzel, D. R., & Hollingsworth, P. M. (1991a). Investigating the development of topic-related attitude: Effect on children's reading and remembering text. *Journal of Educational Research, 84*(5), 334–344.

Reutzel, D. R., & Hollingsworth, P. M. (1991b). Reading comprehension skills: Testing the skills distinctiveness hypothesis. *Reading Research and Instruction, 30*(2), 32–46.

Reutzel, D. R., & Hollingsworth, P. M. (1991c). Reading time in school: Effect on fourth graders' performance on a criterion-referenced comprehension test. *Journal of Educational Research, 84*(3), 170–176.

Reutzel, D. R., & Hollingsworth, P. M. (1991d). Using literature webbing for books with predictable narrative: Improving young readers' predictions, comprehension, and story structure knowledge. *Reading Psychology, 12*(4), 319–333.

Reutzel, D. R., & Hollingsworth, P. M. (1993). Effects of fluency training on second grader's reading comprehension. *Journal of Educational Research, 86*(6), 325–331.

Reutzel, D. R., Hollingsworth, P. M., & Eldredge, J. L. (1994). Oral reading instruction: The impact on student reading development. *Reading Research Quarterly, 23*(1), 40–62.

Reutzel, D. R., & Larsen, N. S. (1995). Look what they've done

to real children's books in the new basal readers. *Language Arts, 72*(7), 495–507.

Reutzel, D. R., & Morgan, B. C. (1990). Effects of prior knowledge, explicitness, and clause order on children's comprehension of causal relationships. *Reading Psychology: An International Quarterly, 11,* 93–114.

Reutzel, D. R., Oda, L. K., & Moore, B. H. (1989). Developing print awareness: The effect of three instructional approaches on kindergartners: Print awareness, reading readiness, and word reading. *Journal of Reading Behavior, 21*(3), 197–217.

Reutzel, D. R., & Sabey, B. (1995). Teacher beliefs about reading and children's conceptions: Are there connections? *Reading Research and Instruction, 35*(4), 323–342.

Reutzel, D. R., & Wolfersberger, M. (1996). An environmental impact statement: Designing supportive literacy classrooms for young children. *Reading Horizons, 36*(3), 266–282.

Reznitskaya, A., & Anderson, R. C. (2002). The argument schema and learning to reason. In C. Collins-Block, L. B. Gambrell, & M. Pressley (Eds.) *Improving comprehension instruction: Advances in research, theory, and classroom practice* (pp. 319–334). San Francisco: Jossey-Bass.

Rhodes, L. K., & Dudley-Marling, C. (1988). *Readers and writers with a difference.* Portsmouth, NH: Heinemann.

Rhodes, L. K., & Shanklin, N. (1993). *Windows into literacy: Assessing learners K–8.* Portsmouth, NH: Heinemann.

Ribowsky, H. (1985). *The effects of a code emphasis approach and a whole language approach upon emergent literacy of kindergarten children* (Report No. CS-008-397). (ERIC Document Reproduction Service) Urbana, IL.

Rice, P. E. (1991). Novels in the news. *The Reading Teacher, 45*(2), 159–160.

Rich, E. S. (1964). *Hannah Elizabeth.* New York: HarperCollins.

Richards, M. (2000). Be a good detective: Solve the case of oral reading fluency. *The Reading Teacher, 53*(7), 534–539.

Richek, M. A. (1978). Readiness skills that predict initial word learning using 2 different methods of instruction. *Reading Research Quarterly, 13,* 200–222.

Richgels, D. J. (2001). Invented spelling, phonemic awareness, and reading and writing instruction, In S. B. Neuman & D. K. Dickinson, (Eds.), *Handbook of early literacy research (*pp. 142–155). New York: Guilford Press.

Richgels, D. J., & Wold, L. S. (1998). Literacy on the road: Backpacking partnerships between school and home. *The Reading Teacher, 52*(1), 18–29.

Riley, R. E. (1993). *Adult literacy in America.* Washington, DC: U. S. Department of Education.

Roberts, B. (1992). The evolution of the young child's concept of word as a unit of spoken and written language. *Reading Research Quarterly, 27*(2), 124–139.

Roberts, T. (1975). Skills of analysis and synthesis in the early stages of reading. *British Journal of Educational Psychology, 45,* 3–9.

Robinson, A. (2002). *American reading instruction* (Rev. ed.). Newark, DE: International Reading Association.

Robinson, B. (1972). *The best Christmas pageant ever.* New York: HarperCollins.

Robinson, F. (1946). *Effective study.* New York: Harper Brothers.

Robinson, H. M. (1972). Perceptual training—does it result in reading improvement? In R. C. Aukerman (Ed.), *Some persistent questions on beginning reading* (pp. 135–150). Newark,

DE: International Reading Association.

Rogg, L. J. (2001). *Early literacy instruction in kindergarten.* Newark, DE: International Reading Association.

Roller, C. M. (2002). *Comprehensive reading instruction across the grade levels: A collection of papers from the Reading Research 2001 Conference.* Newark, DE: International Reading Association.

Romero, G. G. (1983). *Print awareness of the preschool bilingual Spanish English speaking child.* Unpublished doctoral dissertation, University of Arizona, Tucson, AZ.

Rosenbaum, J. (1980). *Making inequality: The hidden curriculum of high school tracking.* New York: Wiley.

Rosenblatt, L. M. (1978). *The reader, the text, and the poem.* Carbondale: Southern Illinois University Press.

Rosenblatt, L. M. (1989). Writing and reading: The transactional theory. In J. M. Mason (Ed.), *Reading and writing connections.* Boston: Allyn & Bacon.

Rosenhouse, J., Feitelson, D., & Kita, B. (1997). Interactive reading aloud to Israeli first graders: Its contribution to literacy development. *Reading Research Quarterly, 32,* 168–183.

Rosenshine, B., & Meister, C. (1994). Reciprocal teaching: A review of nineteen experimental studies. *Review of Educational Research, 64,* 479–530.

Rosenshine, B. V. (1980). Skill hierarchies in reading comprehension. In R. J. Spiro, B. C. Bruce, & W. F. Brewer (Eds.), *Theoretical issues in reading comprehension* (pp. 535–554). Hillsdale, NJ: Erlbaum.

Roser, N. L., Hoffman, J. V., & Farest, C. (1990). Language,

literature, and at-risk children. *The Reading Teacher, 43*(8), 554–561.

Roskos, K., & Neuman, S. B. (2001). Environment and its influences for early literacy teaching and learning. In S. B. Neuman & D. K. Dickinson (Eds.), *Handbook of early literacy research* (pp. 281–294). New York: Guilford Press.

Routman, R. (1988). *Transitions: From literature to literacy.* Portsmouth, NH: Heinemann.

Routman, R. (1996). *Literacy at the crossroads: Crucial talk about reading, writing, and other teaching dilemmas.* Portsmouth, NH: Heinemann.

Routman, R. (2003). *Reading essentials: The specifics you need to know to teach reading well.* Portsmouth, NH: Heinemann.

Rowe, M. B. (1974). Wait-time and rewards as instructional variables, their influence on language, logic, and fate control: Part one—Wait time. *Journal of Research in Science Teaching, 11,* 81–94.

Rowling, J. K. (1998). *Harry Potter and the Sorcerer's stone.* New York: Scholastic.

Ruddell, R. (1974). *Reading-language instruction: Innovative practices.* Upper Saddle River, NJ: Prentice Hall.

Ruddell, R. B., & Ruddell, M. R. (1995). *Teaching children to read and write: Becoming an influential teacher.* Boston: Allyn & Bacon.

Ruddell, R. B., & Unrau, N. J. (1997). The role of responsive teaching in focusing reader intention and developing reader motivation. In J. T. Guthrie & A. Wigfield (Eds.), *Reading engagement: Motivating readers through integrated instruction.* Newark, DE: International Reading Association.

Rule, A. C. (2001). Alphabetizing with environmental print. *The*

Reading Teacher, 54(6), 558–562.

Rumelhart, D. E. (1975). Notes on a schema for stories. In D. G. Bobrow & A. Collins (Eds.), *Representation and understanding: Studies in cognitive science* (pp. 211–236). New York: Academic Press.

Rumelhart, D. E. (1980). Schemata: The building blocks of cognition. In R. J. Spiro (Ed.), *Theoretical issues in reading comprehension* (pp. 33–58). Hillsdale, NJ: Erlbaum.

Rumelhart, D. E. (1981). Schemata: The building blocks of cognition. In J. T. Guthrie, (Ed.), *Comprehension and teaching: Research reviews* (pp. 3–26). Newark, DE: International Reading Association.

Rumelhart, D. E. (1984). Understanding understanding. In J. Flood (Ed.), *Understanding reading comprehension* (pp. 1–20). Newark, DE: International Reading Association.

Rupley, W., & Blair, T. (1987). Assignment and supervision of reading seatwork: Looking in on 12 primary teachers. *The Reading Teacher, 40*(4), 391–393.

Rupley, W. H., & Blair, T. R. (1978). Teacher effectiveness in reading instruction. *The Reading Teacher, 31,* 970–973.

Ryder, R. J., & Graves, M. F. (1994). Vocabulary instruction presented prior to reading in two basal readers. *Elementary School Journal, 95,* 139–153.

Rye, J. (1982). *Cloze procedure and the teaching of reading.* Portsmouth, NH: Heinemann.

Sadoski, M., & Quast, Z. (1990). Reader response and long-term recall for journalistic text: The roles of imagery, affect, and importance. *Reading Research Quarterly, 24*(4), 256–272.

Sadow, M. W. (1982). The use of story grammar in the design of

questions. *The Reading Teacher, 35,* 518–523.

Samuels, S. J. (1967). Attentional process in reading: The effect of pictures on the acquisition of reading responses. *Journal of Educational Psychology, 58,* 337–342.

Samuels, S. J. (1970). Effects of pictures on learning to read, comprehension, and attitudes. *Review of Educational Research, 40,* 397–408.

Samuels, S. J. (1979). The method of repeated readings. *The Reading Teacher, 32*(4), 403–408.

Sandora, C., Beck, I. L., & McKeown, M. G. (1999). A comparison of two discussion strategies on students' comprehension and interpretation of complex literature. *Reading Psychology, 20*(3), 177–212.

Sanford, A. J., & Garrod, S. C. (1981). *Understanding written language.* New York: Wiley.

Santa, C. (1990). *Reporting on the Montana Teacher Change Project: Kallispell reading/ language initiative.* Salt Lake City: Utah Council of the International Reading Association.

Santa, C. M. (1997). School change and literacy engagement: Preparing teaching and learning environments. In J. T. Guthrie & A. Wigfield (Eds.), *Reading engagement: Motivating readers through integrated instruction.* (pp. 218–233). Newark, DE: International Reading Association.

Santa, C. M., & Heien, T. (1998). An assessment of Early Steps: A program for early interventions of reading problems. *Reading Research Quarterly, 34*(1), 54–79.

Savage, J. F. (1994). *Teaching reading using literature.* Madison, WI: Brown & Benchmark.

Schneider, W., & Shiffrin, R. M. (1977). Controlled and automatic human information processing: 1.

Detection, search, and attention, *Psychological Review, 84*(1), 1–66.

Scholastic. (1986). *Talking text* [Computer program]. Jefferson City, MO: Scholastic.

Scholastic. (1990). *Bank Street writer III* [Computer program]. Jefferson City, MO: Scholastic Software.

Scholastic. (1995). *Literary place program.* New York: Author.

Schreiber, A., & Tuchman, G. (1997). *Scholastic Phonics Readers. The Big Hit: Book 14.* New York: Scholastic.

Schunk, D. H., & Zimmerman, B. J. (1997). Developing self-efficacious readers and writers: The role of social and self-regulatory processes. In J. T. Guthrie and A. Wigfield (Eds.), *Reading engagement: Motivating readers through integrated instruction* (pp. 34–50). Newark, DE: International Reading Association.

Schwartz, D. M. (1985). *How much is a million?* Richard Hill, Ontario, Canada: Scholastic-TAB.

Schwartz, R. M., & Raphael, T. E. (1985). Concept of definition: A key to improving students' vocabulary. *The Reading Teacher, 39*(2), 198–205.

Scieszka, J. (1989). *The true story of the 3 little pigs: By A. Wolf.* New York: Viking Kestrel.

Searfoss, L. W. (1975). Radio reading. *The Reading Teacher, 29,* 295–296.

Searfoss, L. W., & Readence, J. E. (1989). *Helping children learn to read* (2nd ed.). Upper Saddle River, NJ: Prentice Hall.

Seefeldt, C., & Barbour, N. (1986). *Early childhood education: An introduction.* Upper Saddle River, NJ: Merrill/Prentice Hall.

Sendak, M. (1962). *Chicken soup with rice.* New York: Scholastic.

Sendak, M. (1963). *Where the wild things are.* New York: HarperCollins.

Senechal, M., & Cornell, E. H. (1993). Vocabulary acquisition through shared reading experiences. *Reading Research Quarterly, 28*(4), 361–373.

Seuss, D. (1954). *Horton hears a Who!* New York: Random House.

Shake, M. (1986). Teacher interruptions during oral reading instruction: Self-monitoring as an impetus for change in corrective feedback. *Remedial and Special Education, 7*(5), 18–24.

Shake, M. C., & Allington, R. L. (1985). Where do teacher's questions come from? *The Reading Teacher, 38*, 432–439.

Shanahan, T. (1984). Nature of the reading-writing relation: An exploratory multi-variate analysis. *Journal of Educational Psychology, 76*, 466–477.

Shanahan, T., & Barr, R. (1995). Reading Recovery: An independent evaluation of the effects of an early intervention for at-risk learners. *Reading Research Quarterly, 30*(40), 958–996.

Shanahan, T., & Lomax, R. G. (1986). An analysis and comparison of theoretical models of the reading-writing relationship. *Journal of Educational Psychology, 78*, 116–123.

Shanklin, N. L., & Rhodes, L. K. (1989). Comprehension instruction as sharing and extending. *The Reading Teacher, 43*(7), 496–500.

Shannon, P. (1983). The use of commercial reading materials in American elementary schools. *Reading Research Quarterly, 19*, 68–85.

Shannon, P. (1989a). Basal readers: Three perspectives. *Theory Into Practice, 28*(4), 235–239.

Shannon, P. (1989b). *Broken promises.* Granby, MA: Bergin & Garvey.

Shannon, P. (1992). *Becoming political: Readings and writings in the politics of literacy education.* Portsmouth, NH: Heinemann.

Shannon, P. (1993). Letters to the editor: Comments on Baumann.

Reading Research Quarterly, 28(2), 86.

Shannon, P., & Goodman, K. (1994). *Basal readers: A second look.* New York: Owen.

Sharmat, M. W. (1980). *Gila monsters meet you at the airport.* New York: Aladdin.

Shockley, B., Michalove, B., & Allen, J. (1995). *Engaging families.* Portsmouth, NH: Heinemann.

Short, K. G., Harste, J. C., & Burke, C. (1996). *Creating classrooms for authors and inquirers.* Portsmouth, NH: Heinemann.

Siegel, M. (1983). *Reading as signification.* Unpublished doctoral dissertation, Indiana University, Bloomington, IN.

Silvaroli, N. J. (1986). *Classroom reading inventory* (5th ed.). Dubuque, IA: Wm C Brown.

Silverstein, S. (1974). *Where the sidewalk ends.* New York: HarperCollins.

Silverstein, S. (1996). *Falling Up.* New York: HarperCollins.

Simmons, D. C., & Kameenui, E. J. (1998). *What reading research tells us about children with diverse learning needs: Bases and basics.* Mahwah, NJ: Erlbaum.

Sinatra, R. C., Stahl-Gemake, J., & Berg, W. (1984). Improving reading comprehension of disabled readers through semantic mapping. *The Reading Teacher, 38*(1), 22–29.

Singer, H. (1960). *Conceptual ability in the substrata-factor theory of reading.* Unpublished doctoral dissertation, University of California, Berkeley, CA.

Singer, H. (1978a). Active comprehension: From answering to asking questions. *The Reading Teacher, 31*, 901–908.

Singer, H. (1978b). Research in reading that should make a difference in classroom instruction. In S. Jay Samuels *What research has to say about*

reading instruction (pp. 57–71). Newark, DE: International Reading Association.

Singer, H., & Donlan, D. (1989). *Reading and learning from text* (2nd ed.). Hillsdale, NJ: Erlbaum.

Sippola, A. E. (1994). Holistic analysis of basal readers: An assessment tool. *Reading Horizons, 34*(3), 234–246.

Skaar, G. (1972). *What do the animals say?* New York: Scholastic.

Slaughter, H. B. (1988). Indirect and direct teaching in a whole language program. *The Reading Teacher, 42*(1), 30–35.

Slavin, R. E. (1987). Ability grouping and student achievement in elementary schools: A best-evidence synthesis. *Review of Educational Research, 57*(3), 293–336.

Slavin, R. E. (1988). Cooperative learning and student achievement. *Educational Leadership, 45*, 31–33.

Slavin, R. E. (1991). Are cooperative learning and "untracking" harmful to the gifted? *Education Leadership, 48*(6), 68–71.

Slavin, R. E. (1995). *Cooperative learning: Theory, research, and practice.* Needham Heights, MA: Allyn & Bacon.

Slavin, R. E., & Madden, N. (1995, April). *Effects of success for all on the achievement of English language learners.* Paper presented at the annual meeting of the American Educational Research Association, San Francisco, CA.

Slavin, R. E., Madden, N. A., Karweit, N. L., Livermon, B. J., & Dolan, L. (1990). Success for all: First-year outcomes of a comprehensive plan for reforming urban education. *American Educational Research Journal, 27*, 255–278.

Slavin, R. E., Madden, N. L., Dolan, L., & Wasik, B. A. (1996). *Every child, every school: Success for all.* Thousand Oaks, CA: Corwin.

Slavin, R. E., Madden, N. L., Karweit, N. L., Dolan, L., & Wasik, B. A. (1992). *Success for all: A relentless approach to prevention and early intervention in elementary schools.* Arlington, VA: Educational Research Services.

Slosson, R. L. (1971). *Slosson intelligence test.* East Aurora, NY: Slosson Educational Publications.

Sloyer, S. (1982). *Reader's theater: Story dramatization in the classroom.* Urbana, IL: National Council of Teachers of English.

Smith, D. E. P. (1967). *Learning to learn.* New York: Harcourt Brace.

Smith, E. B., Goodman, K. S., & Meredith, R. (1976). *Language and thinking in school* (2nd ed.). New York: Holt, Rinehart and Winston.

Smith, F. (1977). The uses of language. *Language Arts, 54*(6), 638–644.

Smith, F. (1983). *Essays into literacy.* Exeter, NH: Heinemann.

Smith, F. (1985). *Reading without nonsense* (2nd ed.). New York: Teachers College Press.

Smith, F. (1987). *Insult to intelligence.* New York: Arbor House.

Smith, F. (1988). *Understanding reading* (4th ed.). Hillsdale, NJ: Erlbaum.

Smith, K. A. (1989). *A checkup with the doctor.* New York: McDougal, Littell.

Smith, M. W., & Dickinson, D. K. (2002). *Early language and literacy classroom observation (ELLCO).* Baltimore: Paul H. Brookes.

Smith, N. B. (1986). *American reading instruction.* Newark, DE: International Reading Association.

Smith, R. K. (1981). *Jelly belly.* New York: Dell.

Smolkin, L. B., & Donovan, C. A. (2000). *The contexts of comprehension: Information book read alouds and comprehension acquisition.* (CIERA Report No. 2-009). Ann Arbor, MI: Center for the Improvement of Early Reading Achievement.

Smoot, R. C., & Price, J. (1975). *Chemistry, a modern course.* Upper Saddle River, NJ: Merrill/Prentice Hall.

Snow, C. (1999). *Preventing reading difficulties.* Keynote address at the Second Annual Commissioner's Reading Day, Austin, TX.

Snow, C. E., Burns, M. S., & Griffin, P. (1998). *Preventing reading difficulties in young children.* Washington, DC: National Academy Press.

Snow, C. E., Burns, M. S., & Griffin, P. (1998). *Preventing reading failure in young children.* Washington, DC: National Academy Press.

Snowball, D., & Bolton, F. (1999). *Spelling K–8: Planning and teaching.* York, ME: Stenhouse.

Soto, G. (1993). *Local news.* San Diego: Harcourt Brace.

Spache, G., & Spache, E. (1977). *Reading in the elementary school* (4th ed.). Boston: Allyn & Bacon.

Spady, W., & Marshall, K. J. (1991). Beyond traditional outcome-based education. *Educational Leadership, 48,* 67–72.

Spangler, K. L. (1983). Reading interests vs. reading preferences: Using the research. *The Reading Teacher, 36*(9), 876–878.

Speare, E. G. (1958). *The witch of Blackbird Pond.* New York: Dell.

Sperry, A. (1940). *Call it courage.* New York: Macmillan.

Spiegel, D. L. (1981). Six alternatives to the directed reading activity. *The Reading Teacher, 34,* 914–922.

Spiegel, D. L. (1999). The perspective of the balanced approach. In S. M. Blair-Larsen & K. A. Williams (Eds.), *The balanced reading program: Helping all students achieve success* (pp. 8–23). Newark, DE: International Reading Association.

Spier, P. (1977). *Noah's ark.* Garden City, NY: Doubleday.

Spinelli, J. (1991). Catching Maniac Magee. *The Reading Teacher, 45*(3), 174–176.

Spivak, M. (1973). Archetypal place. *Architectural Forum, 140,* 44–49.

Squire, J. R. (1983). Composing and comprehending: Two sides of the same basic process. *Language Arts, 60*(5), 581–589.

Squire, J. R. (1989). A reading program for all seasons. *Theory Into Practice, 28*(4), 254–257.

Stahl, S. A. (1986). Three principles of effective vocabulary instruction. *Journal of Reading, 29*(7), 662–668.

Stahl, S. A., & Fairbanks, M. M. (1986). The effects of vocabulary instruction: A model-based meta-analysis. *Review of Educational Research, 56*(1), 72–110.

Stahl, S. A., Hare, V. C., Sinatra, R., & Gregory, J. F. (1991). Defining the role of prior knowledge and vocabulary in reading comprehension: The retiring of number 41. *Journal of Reading Behavior, 23*(4), 487–507.

Stahl, S. A., & Jacobson, M. G. (1986). Vocabulary difficulty, prior knowledge, and text comprehension. *Journal of Reading Behavior, 18*(4), 309–319.

Stahl, S. A., & Kapinus, B. (2001). *Word power: What every educator needs to know about teaching vocabulary.* Washington, DC: National Education Association.

Stahl, S. A., & Miller, P. D. (1989). Whole language and language experience approaches for beginning reading: A quantitative research synthesis. *Review of Educational Research, 59,* 87–116.

Stahl, S. A., & Murray, B. A. (1993). Environmental print, phonemic awareness, letter recognition, and word recognition. In D. J. Leu & C. I. Kinzer (Eds.), *Examining central issues in literacy research, theory, and practice* (pp. 227–233). Chicago: National Reading Conference.

Standard for the English Language Arts. (1996). A project of the International Reading Association and National Council of Teachers of English. Newark, DE: International Reading Association.

Stanovich, K. (1980). Toward an interactive-compensatory model of individual differences in the development of reading fluency. *Reading Research Quarterly, 16*(1), 37–71.

Stauffer, R. G. (1969). *Directing reading maturity as a cognitive process.* New York: HarperCollins.

Stauffer, R. G. (1975). *Directing the reading-thinking process.* New York: HarperCollins.

Stayter, F. Z., & Allington, R. L. (1991). Fluency and the understanding of texts. *Theory Into Practice, 30*(3), 143–148.

Stedman, L. C., & Kaestle, C. E. (1987). Literacy and reading performance in the United States from 1880 to the present. *Reading Research Quarterly, 22,* 8–46.

Steele, W. O. (1958). *The perilous road.* Orlando, FL: Harcourt Brace.

Stein, M. (1993). *The beginning reading instruction study.* Syracuse, NY: Educational Resources Information Center.

Stein, N. L., & Glenn, C. G. (1979). An analysis of story comprehension in elementary school children. In R. O. Freedle (Ed.), *New directions in discourse processing* (pp. 53–120). Hillsdale, NJ: Erlbaum.

Steinbeck, J. (1937). *The red pony.* New York: Bantam Books.

Stenner, A. J. (1996). *Measuring reading comprehension with the Lexile framework.* Paper presented at the 4th North American Conference on Adolescent/Adult Literacy, Washington, DC.

Stenner, A. J., & Burdick, D. S. (1997). *The objective measurement of reading comprehension.* Durham, NC: MetaMetrics.

Steptoe, J. (1987). *Mufaro's beautiful daughters: An African tale.* New York: Lothrop, Lee, & Shepard Books.

Stern, D. N., & Wasserman, G. A. (1979). *Maternal language to infants.* Paper presented at a meeting of the Society for Research in Child Development. Ann Arbor, MI.

Stevens, R., & Rosenshine, B. (1981). Advances in research on teaching. *Exceptional Education Quarterly, 2,* 1–9.

Stevens, R. J., Madden, N. A., Slavin, R. E., & Farnish, A. (1987a). *Cooperative integrated reading and composition: A brief overview of the CIRC program.* Baltimore: Johns Hopkins University, Center for Research on Elementary and Middle Schools.

Stevens, R. J., Madden, N. A., Slavin, R. E., & Farnish, A. M. (1987b). Cooperative integrated reading and composition: Two field experiments. *Reading Research Quarterly, 22*(4), 433–454.

Stevens, R. J., & Slavin, R. E. (1995). Effects of a cooperative learning approach in reading and writing on academically handicapped and nonhandicapped students. *Elementary School Journal, 95*(3), 241–262.

Stolz, M. (1963). *Bully on Barkham Street.* New York: HarperCollins.

Stoodt, B. D. (1989). *Reading instruction.* New York: HarperCollins.

Strickland, D. S. (1998). *Teaching phonics today: A primer for educators.* Newark, DE: International Reading Association.

Strickland, D. S., Feeley, J. T., & Wepner, S. B. (1987). *Using computers in the teaching of reading.* New York: Teachers College Press.

Strickland, D., Snow, C., Griffin, P., Burns, M. S., & McNamara, P. (2002). *Preparing our teachers: Opportunities for better reading instruction.*

Washington, DC: Joseph Henry Press.

Sucher, F., & Allred, R. A. (1986). *Sucher-Allred group reading placement test.* Oklahoma City: Economy.

Sukhomlinsky, V. (1981). *To children I give my heart.* Moscow: Progress.

Sulzby, E. (1985). Children's emergent reading of favorite storybooks: A developmental study. *Reading Research Quarterly, 20*(4), 458–481.

Sulzby, E. (1991). Assessment of emergent literacy: Storybook reading. *The Reading Teacher, 44*(7), 498–500.

Sulzby, E., Hoffman, J., Niles, J., Shanahan, T., & Teale, W. (1989). *McGraw-Hill reading.* New York: McGraw-Hill.

Sunburst. (1987). *The puzzler.* Pleasantville, NY: Sunburst Communications.

Swafford, J. (1995). I wish all my groups were like this one: Facilitating peer interaction during group work. *Journal of Reading, 38*(8), 626–631.

Sweet, A. (1997). Teacher perceptions of student motivation and their relation to literacy learning. In J. T. Guthrie & A. Wigfield (Eds.), *Reading engagement: Motivating readers through integrated instruction.* (pp. 86–100) Newark, DE: International Reading Association.

Szymusiak, K., & Sibberson, F. (2001). *Beyond leveled books: Supporting transitional readers in grades 2–5.* York, ME: Stenhouse.

Taba, H. (1975). *Teacher's handbook for elementary social studies.* Reading, MA: Addison-Wesley.

Tarver, S. G., & Dawson, M. M. (1978). Modality preference and the teaching of reading: A review. *Journal of Learning Disabilities, 11*(1), 5–17.

Taxel, J. (1993). The politics of children's literature: Reflections on multiculturalism and Christopher Columbus. In

V. J. Harris (Ed.), *Teaching multicultural literature in grades K–8* (pp. 1–36). Norwood, MA: Christopher Gordon.

Taylor, B., Harris, L. A., & Pearson, P. D. (1988). *Reading difficulties: Instruction and assessment.* New York: Random House.

Taylor, B. M., Frye, B. J., & Gaetz, T. M. (1990). Reducing the number of reading skill activities in the elementary classroom. *Journal of Reading Behavior, 22*(2), 167–180.

Taylor, B. M., Graves, M. F., & Van den Broek, P. (2000). *Reading for meaning: Fostering comprehension in the middle grades.* New York: Teachers College Press.

Taylor, B. M., Pearson, P. D., Clark, K. F., & Walpole, S. (1999). *Beating the odds in teaching all children to read* (Report No. 2-006). Ann Arbor, MI: Center for the Improvement of Early Reading Achievement.

Taylor, B. M, Pearson, P. D., Clark, K. F., & Walpole, S. (2000). Effective schools and accomplished teachers: Lessons about primary grade reading instruction in low-income schools. *Elementary School Journal, 101,* 121–165.

Taylor, D. (1983). *Family literacy: Young children learning to read and write.* Portsmouth, NH: Heinemann.

Taylor, D., & Strickland, D. S. (1986). *Family storybook reading.* Portsmouth, NH: Heinemann.

Taylor, G. C. (1981). ERIC/RCS report: Music in language arts instruction. *Language Arts, 58,* 363–368.

Taylor, M. D. (1990). *Road to Memphis.* New York: Dial Books.

Taylor, N. E. (1986). Developing beginning literacy concepts: Content and context. In D. B. Yaden, Jr., & S. Templeton (Eds.), *Metalinguistic awareness and beginning literacy* (pp. 173–184). Portsmouth, NH: Heinemann.

Taylor, N. E., Blum, I. H., & Logsdon, M. (1986). The development of written language awareness: Environmental aspects and program characteristics. *Reading Research Quarterly, 21*(2), 132–149.

Taylor, W. L. (1953). Cloze procedure: A new tool for measuring readability. *Journalism Quarterly, 30,* 415–433.

Teale, W. H. (1987). Emergent literacy: Reading and writing development in early childhood. In J. E. Readence, R. S. Baldwin, J. P. Konopak, & H. Newton (Eds.), *Research in literacy: Merging perspectives* (pp. 45–74). Rochester, NY: National Reading Conference.

Teale, W. H., & Martinez, M. (1986a). Reading in a kindergarten classroom library. *The Reading Teacher, 41*(6), 568–73.

Teale, W. H., & Martinez, M. (1986b). *Teachers reading to their students: Differing styles, different effects?* ERIC Document Reproduction Service.

Teale, W. H., & Sulzby, E. (1986). *Emergent literacy: Writing and reading.* Norwood, NJ: Ablex.

Temple, C., & Gillet, J. (1996). *Language and literacy: A lively approach.* New York: HarperCollins.

Temple, C., Nathan, R., Burris, N., & Temple, F. (1993). *The beginnings of writing* (3rd ed.). Newton, MA: Allyn & Bacon.

Templeton, S. (1995). *Children's literacy: Contexts for meaningful learning.* Princeton, NJ: Houghton Mifflin.

Texas Education Agency. (2003–04). *Texas primary reading inventory* (TPRI). Austin, TX: Author. Available online, in both English and Spanish, at Reading Initiative at *http://www.tea.state.tx.us/reading.*

Thaler, M. (1989). *The teacher from the black lagoon.* New York: Scholastic.

Tharp, R. (1982). The effective instruction of comprehension: Results and description of the Kamehameha Early Education Program. *Reading Research Quarterly, 17*(4), 503–527.

Tharpe, R. G., & Gallimore, R. (1988). *Rousing minds to life.* Cambridge, MA: Cambridge University Press.

Thelen, J. N. (1984). *Improving reading in science.* Newark, DE: International Reading Association.

Thomas, D. G., & Readence, J. E. (1988). Effects of differential vocabulary instruction and lesson frameworks on the reading comprehension of primary children. *Reading Research and Instruction, 28,* 1–13.

Thompson, R. (1997). The philosophy of balanced reading instruction. *Journal of Balanced Reading Instruction, 4*(D1), 28–29.

Thorndike, R. L. (1973). *Reading comprehension education in fifteen countries: An empirical study.* New York: Wiley.

Thorndyke, P. N. (1977). Cognitive structure in comprehension and memory of narrative discourse. *Cognitive Psychology, 9*(1), 77–110.

Tierney, R. J. (1992). Setting a new agenda for assessment. *Learning, 21*(2), 61–64.

Tierney, R. J., Carter, M. A., & Desai, L. E. (1991). *Portfolio assessment in the reading-writing classroom.* Norwood, MA: Christopher-Gordon.

Tierney, R. J., & Cunningham, J. W. (1984). Research on teaching reading comprehension. In P. D. Pearson (Ed.), *Reading research handbook* (pp. 609–656). New York: Longman.

Tierney, R. J., & Pearson, P. D. (1983). Toward a composing model of reading. *Language Arts, 60*(5), 568–580.

Tierney, R. J., Readence, J. E., & Dishner, E. K. (1985). *Reading strategies and practices: A compendium* (2nd ed.). Boston: Allyn & Bacon.

Tomasello, M. (1996). Piagetian and Vygotskian approaches to language acquisition. *Human Development, 39,* 269–276.

Tompkins, G. E. (2000). *Teaching writing: Balancing process and product* (3rd ed.). Upper Saddle River, NJ: Merrill/Prentice Hall.

Tompkins, G. E. (2003). *Literacy for the 21st Century* (3rd ed.). Upper Saddle River, NJ: Merrill/Prentice Hall.

Tompkins, G. E., & Hoskisson, K. (1995). *Language arts: Content and teaching strategies,* 3rd ed. Upper Saddle River, NJ: Merrill/Prentice Hall.

Topping, K. (1989). Peer tutoring and paired reading: Combining two powerful techniques. *The Reading Teacher, 42,* 488–494.

Torgeson, J. K., Wagner, R. X., Rashotte, C. A., Alexander, A., & Conway, T. (1997). Prevention and remediation of severe reading disabilities: Keeping the end in mind. *Scientific Studies of Reading, 1*(3), 217–234.

Torrey, J. W. (1979). Reading that comes naturally. In G. Waller & G. E. MacKinnon (Eds.), *Reading research: Advance in theory and practice* (Vol. 1, pp. 115–144). New York: Academic Press.

Tovey, D. R., & Kerber, J. E. (Eds.) (1986). *Roles in literacy learning.* Newark, DE: International Reading Association.

Towers, J. M. (1992). Outcome-based education: Another educational bandwagon. *Educational Forum, 56*(3), 291–305.

Towle, (1993). *The real McCoy: The life of an African American inventor.* New York: Scholastic.

Town, S., & Holbrook, N. M. (1857). *Progressive primer.* Boston: Carter, Bazin & Company.

Trabasso, T. (1980). *On the making of inferences during reading and their assessment.* (Technical Report No. 157). Urbana-Champaign: University of Illinois, Center for the Study of Reading.

Treiman, R. (1985). Onsets and rimes as units of spoken syllables: Evidence from children. *Journal of Experimental Child Psychology, 39,* 161–181.

Trelease, J. (1995). *The new read-aloud handbook.* (4th ed.). New York: Penguin.

Tunnell, M. O., & Jacobs, J. S. (1989). Using "real" books: Research findings on literature based reading instruction. *The Reading Teacher, 42,* 470–477.

Tutolo, D. (1977). The study guide: Types, purpose and value. *Journal of Reading, 20,* 503–507.

U.S. Bureau of Labor. (1995). *Final report: Governor's Council on School-to-Work Transition.* Washington, DC: U.S. Department of Education.

U.S. Department of Education. (n.d.). Retrieved from http://www.ed.gov/nclb/landing.jhtml.

U.S. Department of Education. (1997). *President Clinton's America's Reading Challenge.* Washington, DC: U.S. Department of Education.

U.S. Department of Education. *National Assessment of Educational Progress: The nation's report card reading 2004.* Washington, DC: U.S. Department of Education, Office of Educational Research and Improvement.

United States and the other Americas, The (Grade 5). (1980). Upper Saddle River, NJ: Merrill/Prentice Hall.

United States: Its history and neighbors, The (Grade 5). (1985). San Diego: Harcourt Brace.

Unsworth, L. (1984). Meeting individual needs through flexible within-class grouping of pupils. *The Reading Teacher, 38*(3), 298–304.

Vacca, J. L., Vacca, R. T., & Gove, M. K. (1995). *Reading and learning to read* (3rd ed.). Boston: Little, Brown.

Vacca, R. T., & Vacca, J. L. (2001). *Content area reading: Literacy and learning across the curriculum* (7th ed.). New York: Allyn & Bacon.

Vacca, R. T., Vacca, J. L., Gove, M. K., Burkey, L. C., Lenhart, L. A., & McKeon, C. A. (2003). *Reading and learning to read* (5th ed.). Needham Heights, MA: Allyn & Bacon.

Valencia, S. (1990). A portfolio approach to classroom reading assessment: The whys, whats, and hows. *The Reading Teacher, 43*(4), 338–340.

Valencia, S. (1998). *Portfolios in action.* New York: HarperCollins.

Valencia, S., McGinley, W., & Pearson, P. D. (1990). *Assessing reading and writing: Building a more complete picture for middle school assessment* (Technical Report No. 500). Urbana, IL: Center for the Study of Reading.

Valencia, S., & Pearson, P. D. (1987). Reading assessment: Time for a change. *The Reading Teacher, 40*(8), 726–733.

Vallecorsa, A. L., & deBettencourt, L. U. (1997). Using a mapping procedure to teach reading and writing skills to middle grade students with learning disabilities. *Education and the Treatment of Children, 20*(2), 173–188.

Van Allsburg, C. (1985). *The polar express.* Boston: Houghton Mifflin.

Van Allsburg, C. (1987). *The Z was zapped.* Boston: Houghton Mifflin.

Van Manen, M. (1986). *The tone of teaching.* Markham, Ontario, Canada: Scholastic.

Varble, M. E. (1990). Analysis of writing samples of students taught by teachers using whole language and traditional approaches. *Journal of Educational Research, 83*(5), 245–251.

Veatch, J. (1968). *How to teach reading with children's books.* New York: Owen.

Veatch, J. (1978). *Reading in the elementary school* (2nd ed.). New York: Owen.

Veatch, J., & Cooter, R. B., Jr. (1986). The effect of teacher selection on reading achievement. *Language Arts, 63*(4), 364–368.

Venezky, R. L. (1975). The curious role of letter names in reading instruction. *Visible Language, 9*, 7–23.

Viorst, J. (1972). *Alexander and the terrible, horrible, no good, very bad day* (R. Cruz, Illustrator). New York: Atheneum.

Viorst, J. (1987). *Alexander and the terrible, horrible, no good, very bad day.* New York: Aladdin.

Voltz, D. L., & Demiano-Lantz, M. (1993, Summer). Developing ownership in learning. *Teaching Exceptional Children*, 18–22.

Vopat, J. (1994). *The parent project: A workshop approach to parent involvement.* York, ME: Stenhouse.

Vopat, J. (1998). *More than bake sales: The resource guide for family involvement in education.* York: ME: Stenhouse.

Vukelich, C. (1994). Effects of play interventions on young children's reading of environmental print. *Early Childhood Research Quarterly, 9*(2), 153–170.

Vygotsky, L. S. (1939). Thought and speech. *Psychiatry, 2*, 29–54.

Vygotsky, L. S. (1962). *Thought and language.* Cambridge, MA: MIT Press.

Vygotsky, L. S. (1978). *Mind in society.* Cambridge, MA: Harvard University Press.

Wade, S. E., & Moje, E. B. (2000). The role of text in classroom learning. In M. L. Kamil, P. B. Mosenthal, P. D. Pearson, & R. Barr (Eds.), *Handbook of Reading Research* (Vol. 3, pp. 609–627). Mahwah, NJ: Erlbaum.

Wagner, R., Torgesen, J., & Rashotte, C. (1999). *Comprehensive test of phonological processing (CTOPP).* Circle Pines, MN: American Guidance Service.

Walker, B. J. (2004). *Diagnostic teaching of reading: Techniques for instruction and assessment.* Upper Saddle River, NJ: Merrill/Prentice Hall.

Walker, J. E. (1991, May). *Affect in naturalistic assessment: Implementation and implications.* Paper presented at the 36th annual convention of the International Reading Association, Las Vegas, NV.

Wallach, L., Wallach, M. A., Dozier, M. G., & Kaplan, N. E. (1977). Poor children learning to read do not have trouble with auditory discrimination but do have trouble with phoneme recognition. *Journal of Educational Psychology, 69*, 36–39.

Walley, C. (1993). An invitation to reading fluency. *The Reading Teacher, 46*(6), 526–527.

Walters, K., & Gunderson, L. (1985). Effects of parent volunteers reading first language (L1) books to ESL students. *The Reading Teacher, 39*(1), 66–69.

Wang, M., Haertel, G., & Walberg, H. (1994, December). What helps students learn? *Educational Leadership*, 74–79.

Wasik, B. A. (1998). Using volunteers as reading tutors: Guidelines for successful practices. *The Reading Teacher, 51*(7), 562–573.

Watson, D., & Crowley, P. (1988). How can we implement a whole-language approach? In C. Weaver (Ed.), *Reading process and practice* (pp. 232–279). Portsmouth, NH: Heinemann.

Watson, R. (2001). Literacy and oral language: Implications for early literacy acquisition. In S. B. Neuman & D. K. Dickinson (Eds), *Handbook of early literacy research,* (pp. 43–53). New York: Guilford Press.

Watson, S. (1976). *No man's land.* New York: Greenwillow.

Weaver, C. (1988). *Reading process and practice: From socio-psycholinguistics to whole*

language. Portsmouth, NH: Heinemann.

Weaver, C. (1994). *Reading process and practice: From socio-psycholinguistics to whole language (2nd ed.).* Portsmouth, NH: Heinemann.

Weaver, C. (1998). *Reconsidering a balanced approach to reading.* Urbana, IL: National Council of Teachers of English.

Weaver, C., Chaston, J., & Peterson, S. (1993). *Theme exploration: A voyage of discovery.* Portsmouth, NH: Heinemann.

Webb, K., & Willoughby, N. (1993). An analytic rubric for scoring graphs. *The Texas School Teacher, 22*(3), 14–15.

Webb, M., & Schwartz, W. (1988, October). Children teaching children: A good way to learn. *PTA Today*, 16–17.

Weimans, E. (1981). *Which way courage?* New York: Atheneum.

Weinstein, R. S. (1976). Reading group membership in first grade: Teacher behaviors and pupil experience over time. *Journal of Educational Psychology, 68*, 103–116.

Weintraub, S., & Denny, T. P. (1965). What do beginning first graders say about reading? *Childhood Education, 41*, 326–327.

Wells, R. (1973). *Noisy Nora.* New York: Scholastic.

Wepner, S. B. (1985). Linking logos with print for beginning reading success. *The Reading Teacher, 38*(7), 633–639.

Wepner, S. B. (1990). Holistic computer applications in literature-based classrooms. *The Reading Teacher, 44*(1), 12–19.

Wepner, S. B. (1992). Technology and text sets. *The Reading Teacher, 46*(1), 68–71.

Wepner, S. B. (1993). Technology and thematic units: An elementary example on Japan. *The Reading Teacher, 46*(5), 442–445.

Wepner, S. B., & Feeley, J. T. (1993). *Moving forward with* literature: Basals, books, and beyond. Upper Saddle River, NJ: Merrill/Prentice Hall.

Wepner, S. B., Feeley, J. T., & Strickland, D. S. (1995). *The administration and supervision of reading programs* (2nd ed.). New York: Teacher's College Columbia Press.

Wessells, M. G. (1990). *Computer, self, and society.* Upper Saddle River, NJ: Prentice Hall.

Whaley, J. F. (1981). Readers' expectations for story structures. *Reading Research Quarterly, 17,* 90–114.

Wharton-McDonald, R., Pressley, M., Rankin, J., Mistretta, J., Yokoi, L., & Ettenberger, S. (1997). Effective primary-grades literacy instruction = balanced literacy instruction. *The Reading Teacher, 50*(6), 518–521.

Wheatley, E. A., Muller, D. H., & Miller, R. B. (1993). Computer-assisted vocabulary instruction. *Journal of Reading, 37*(2), 92–102.

Whitaker, B. T., Schwartz, E., & Vockell, E. (1989). *The computer in the reading curriculum.* New York: McGraw-Hill.

White, C. S. (1983). Learning style and reading instruction. *The Reading Teacher, 36,* 842–845.

White, E. B. (1952). *Charlotte's web.* New York: HarperCollins.

White, E. B. (1970). *The trumpet of the swan.* New York: HarperCollins.

Wiener, R. B., & Cohen, J. H. (1997). *Literacy portfolios: Using assessment to guide instruction.* Upper Saddle River, NJ: Merrill/Prentice Hall.

Wiesendanger, W. D. (1986). Durkin revisited. *Reading Horizons, 26,* 89–97.

Wigfield, A. (1997). Motivations, beliefs, and self-efficacy in literacy development. In J. T. Guthrie & A. Wigfield (Eds.), *Reading engagement: Motivating readers through integrated instruction.*

(pp. 14–33). Newark, DE: International Reading Association.

Wigfield, A. (1997b). Children's motivations for reading and reading engagement. In J. T. Guthrie & A. Wigfield (Eds.), *Reading engagement: Motivating reading through integrated instruction* (pp. 14–33). Newark, DE: International Reading Association.

Wigfield, A. (2000). Facilitating children's reading motivation. In L. Baker, M. J. Dreher, & J. T. Guthrie (Eds.), *Engaging young readers: Promoting achievement and motivation* (pp. 140–158). New York: Guilford Press.

Wigfield, A., & Guthrie, J. T. (1997). Relations of children's motivation for reading to the amount and breadth of their reading. *Journal of Educational Psychology, 89,* 420–432.

Wiggins, R. A. (1994). Large group lesson/small group follow-up: Flexible grouping in a basal reading program. *The Reading Teacher, 47*(6), 450–460.

Wilde, S. (1997). *What's a schwa sound anyway?* Portsmouth, NH: Heinemann.

Williams, J. P., Brown, L. G., Silverstein, A. K., & deCari, J. S. (1994). An instructional program in comprehension of narrative themes for adolescents with learning disabilities. *Learning Disability Quarterly, 17,* 205–221.

Willman, A. T. (2000). "Hello, Mrs. Willman, it's me!: Keep kids reading over the summer by using voice mail." In T. V. Rasinski, N. D. Padak, et al. (Eds.), *Motivating recreational reading and promoting home-school connections* (pp. 51–52). Newark, DE: International Reading Association.

Wilson, R. M., & Gambrell, L. B. (1988). *Reading comprehension in the elementary school.* Boston: Allyn & Bacon.

Wilson, R. M., Hall, M. A., Leu, D. J., & Kinzer, C. K. (2001). *Phonics, phonemic awareness, and word analysis for teachers: An interactive tutorial* (7th ed.). Upper Saddle River, NJ: Prentice Hall.

Winograd, P. (1989). Improving basal reading instruction: Beyond the carrot and the stick. *Theory Into Practice, 28*(4), 240–247.

Winograd, P. N. (1989). Introduction: Understanding reading instruction. In P. N. Winograd, K. K. Wixson, & M. Y. Lipson (Eds.). *Improving basal reader instruction* (pp. 1–20). New York: Teachers College Press.

Winograd, P. N., Paris, S., & Bridge, C. (1991). Improving the assessment of literacy. *The Reading Teacher, 45*(2), 108–116.

Winograd, P. N., Wixson, K. K., & Lipson, M. Y. (Eds.). (1989). *Improving basal reader instruction.* New York: Teachers College Press.

Wiseman, D. L. (1992). *Learning to read with literature.* Boston: Allyn & Bacon.

Wittrock, M. C. (1974). Learning as a generative process. *Educational Psychologist, 11,* 87–95.

Wixson, K. K., Peters, C. W., Weber, E. M., & Roeber, E. D. (1987). New directions in statewide reading assessment. *The Reading Teacher, 40*(8), 749–755.

Wong, H., & Wong, R. (1998). *The first days of school: How to be an effective teacher.* Mountain View, CA: Harry K. Wong.

Wong, J. W., & Au, K. H. (1985). The concept-text-application approach: Helping elementary students comprehend expository text. *The Reading Teacher, 38*(7), 612–618.

Wood, A. (1984). *The napping house* (Don Wood, Illustrator). San Diego: Harcourt Brace.

Wood, A. (1990). *Weird parents*. New York: Dial Books for Young Readers.

Wood, A., & Wood, D. (1988). *Elbert's bad word*. New York: Harcourt Brace Jovanovich.

Wood, E., Pressley, M., & Winne, P. H. (1990). Elaborative interrogation effects on children's learning of factual content. *Journal of Educational Psychology, 82,* 741–48.

Wood, K. D. (1983). A variation on an old theme: 4-way oral reading. *The Reading Teacher, 37*(1), 38–41.

Wood, K. D. (1987). Fostering cooperative learning in middle and secondary level classrooms. *Journal of Reading, 31,* 10–18.

Woodcock, R., Mather, N., & Barnes, E. K. (1987). *Woodcock reading mastery tests–revised.* Circle Pines, MN: American Guidance Service.

Woodcock, R. W. (1997). *Woodcock reading mastery tests–revised (WRMT–R).* Circle Pines, MN: American Guidance Service.

Woodcock, R. W., & Muñoz-Sandoval, A. F. (1993). *Woodcock-Muñoz language survey* (WMLS), English and Spanish forms. Chicago: Riverside.

Worby, D. Z. (1980). *An honorable seduction: Thematic studies in literature.* Arlington, VA: ERIC Document Reproduction Service

Worthy, J., Moorman, M., & Turner, M. (1999). What Johnny likes to read is hard to find in school. *Reading Research Quarterly, 34*(1), 12–27.

Yaden, D. B., Jr. (1982). A multivariate analysis of first graders' print awareness as related to reading achievement, intelligence, and gender (Doctoral dissertation, University of Oklahoma, 1982). *Dissertation Abstracts International, 43,* 1912A.

Yashima, T. (1983). *Crow boy.* New York: Viking.

Yellin, D., & Blake, M. E. (1994). *Integrating language arts: A holistic approach.* New York: HarperCollins.

Yep, L. (1989). *The rainbow people.* New York: HarperCollins.

Ylisto, I. P. (1967). An empirical investigation of early reading responses of young children (Doctoral dissertation, University of Michigan, 1967). *Dissertation Abstracts International, 28,* 2153A.

Yolen, J. (1976). *An invitation to a butterfly ball: A counting rhyme.* New York: Philomel.

Yolen, J. (1988). *The devil's arithmetic.* New York: Viking Kestrel.

Yopp, H. K. (1988). The validity and reliability of phonemic awareness tests. *Reading Research Quarterly, 23,* 159–177.

Yopp, H. K. (1992). Developing phonemic awareness in young children. *The Reading Teacher, 45*(9), 696–703.

Yopp, H. K., & Troyer, S. (1992). *Training phonemic awareness in young children.* Unpublished manuscript.

Yopp, R. H., & Yopp, H. K. (2000). *Literature-based reading activities* (3rd ed.). New York: Allyn & Bacon.

Young, E. (1989). *Lon Po Po.* New York: Philomel Books.

Young, T. A., & Vardell, S. (1993). Weaving readers theatre and nonfiction into the curriculum. *The Reading Teacher, 46,* 396–406.

Zahar, R., Cobb, T., & Sapda, N. (2001). Acquiring vocabulary through reading: Effects of frequency and contextual richness. *Canadian Modern Language Review, 57*(4), 541–572.

Zarillo, J. (1989). Teachers' interpretations of literature-based reading. *The Reading Teacher, 43*(1), 22–29.

Zemelman, S., Daniels, H., & Hyde, A. (1993). *Best practice: New standards for teaching and learning in America's schools.* Portsmouth, NH: Heinemann.

Zentall, S. S. (1993). Research on the educational implications of attention deficit hyperactivity disorder. *Exceptional Children, 60*(2), 143–153.

Zintz, M. V., & Maggart, Z. R. (1989). *The reading process: The teacher and the learner.* Dubuque, IA: Wm C Brown.

Zlatos, B. (1993). Outcomes-based outrage. *Executive Educator, 15*(9), 12–16.

Zutell, J., & Rasinski, T. (1991). Training teachers to attend to their students' oral reading fluency. *Theory Into Practice, 30*(3), 211–217.

Name Index

Subject Index